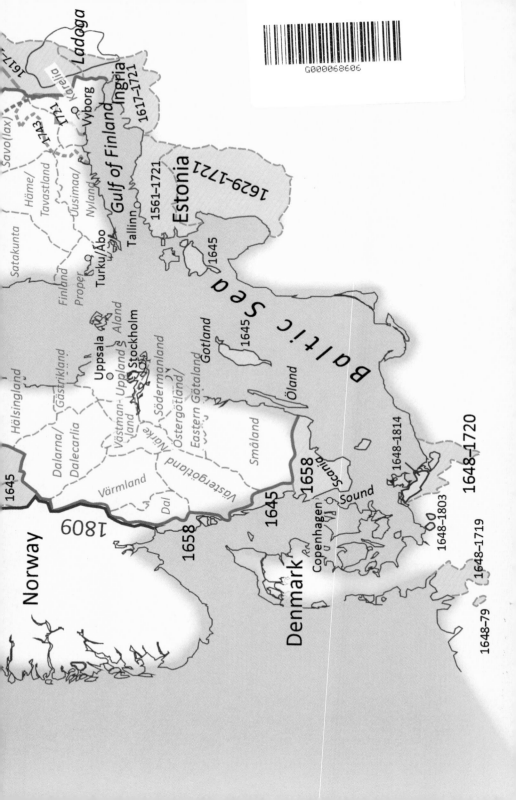

PHYSICAL AND CULTURAL SPACE
IN PRE-INDUSTRIAL EUROPE

Physical and Cultural Space in Pre-industrial Europe

Methodological Approaches to Spatiality

Edited by
Marko Lamberg, Marko Hakanen
and Janne Haikari

NORDIC ACADEMIC PRESS

Nordic Academic Press
P.O. Box 1206
SE-221 05 Lund
www.nordicacademicpress.com

© Nordic Academic Press and the Authors 2011
Linguistic proofreading: Liz Eastcott
Typesetting: Frederic Täckström, www.sbmolle.com
Cover: Jacob Wiberg
Cover image: Photo of the library at Skokloster castle, built in the 17th century.
Photo: Pål-Nils Nilsson
Printed by ScandBook AB, Falun 2011
ISBN: 978-91-85509-61-4

Contents

Acknowledgements

This volume largely stems from the research project 'Politics of Brothers, Neighbours and Friends – Political Culture and Strategies of Influence in Early Modern Sweden c. 1500–1700', funded by the Academy of Finland (2006–2008). From the outset, members of the research team were heavily influenced by the 'spatial turn', which had begun to make its presence felt within various disciplines, including the field of history. Consequently, it was relatively easy to find colleagues who shared this new or renewed interest in space. The book the reader now holds in his or her hands is the result of this fruitful interaction. The editors wish to thank all the contributors for their insightful chapters, as well as the patience and understanding they have shown during an editing process which lasted longer than expected. The preparation of this book also required linguistic and technical support, and warm thanks are addressed to all involved parties. Nordic Academic Press and its staff deserves acknowledgement for the smooth and pleasant cooperation. The Emil Aaltonen Foundation is also remembered with gratitude for its support in the production of this work. Finally, the editors would like to thank Professor Seppo Zetterberg for both his interest and his faith in this project.

Note on names
and administrative terms

Due to its regional emphasis, this book contains a considerable number of placenames that may sound exotic and unusual to readers who are unfamiliar with Finnish and Swedish geography. The feeling of exoticism and confusion over placenames is probably strengthened by the fact that many places in Finland have both a Finnish and a Swedish name – a reflection of age-old Swedish settlement in Finland. In some cases the variants are very similar, whereas in other cases it would be impossible to guess that the two very different names in fact refer to a single place: this holds true for, among others, the town of Hämeenlinna (Fi.) aka Tavastehus (Sw.). For the benefit of those unfamiliar with Finnish geography, a consistent approach has been adopted across all chapters: the first mention of a Finnish toponym has been accompanied by the Swedish variant in parentheses. In cases where an international variant also exists, this has been used consistently and both the Finnish and Swedish variants given in parentheses after the first occurrence: for example, Vyborg (Viipuri (Fi.); Viborg (Sw.)). However, the reader should also be aware that some Finnish placenames do not have a Swedish variant. Correspondingly, several places in Finland that have traditionally been inhabited by a Swedish-speaking population have only Swedish names – this is case especially in coastal areas and the archipelagos. Several maps (some of which are very detailed) have been included in order to help the reader to identify the locations referred to in the text. The maps and the indexes will provide assistance for the reader in any cases of confusion.

In a similar fashion, the authors and the editors have tried to help those who are unfamiliar with Finnish and Swedish terms to grasp the meaning of various administrative or judicial concepts and titles. Of course, not all medieval and early modern Swedish and Finnish terms can be easily translated into modern English through reference to concepts from the history of the English-speaking world. Such 'translations' are attempts to explain how an individual specific terms should be understood, and the reader should bear in mind that they do not necessarily imply full equivalence with standard English usage. For the sake of accuracy, the domestic (Nordic) forms of important concepts are also mentioned.

Moreover, there is considerable variation in the existing literature about how personal names should be written: since most official documents in Finland were written in Swedish before the late nineteenth century, nearly all the individuals found in the records bear Swedish names. Nowadays, many historians 'translate' such names into their Finnish equivalents, but not all do so. Of course, a man whose name was recorded as Erik Matsson may very well have lived his life as Erkki Matinpoika, but given the presence of Swedish speakers, we cannot always unequivocally determine an individual's first language. Irrespective of mother tongue, individuals could also use or be given unofficial name forms. Consequently, in this book personal names appear as they were recorded in the sources, although in some cases spellings have been slightly modernized. Internationally recognized (in practice Latin and English) forms of royal names have been used: for instance, Gustav Vasa (reigned 1523–1560) is referred to as King Gustavus I and his sons Erik, Johan and Karl appear as Eric XIV, John III and Charles IX.

Introduction

Mapping Physical and Cultural Space in Pre-industrial Europe

Marko Lamberg

Space in history

Stockholm is known for its picturesque Old Town, whose narrow streets and alleyways are often crowded with tourists. The heart of the Old Town remains, as it was in the Middle Ages, the Great Market Place and the tall brick houses that surround it. We know from old records that these elegant houses were once owned and in many cases occupied by wealthy townspeople. However, it seems that the southwestern corner of the square was a less attractive location and that well-to-do inhabitants avoided living in the adjacent houses. Why was this? The reason becomes apparent when we consider the name of the street that leads westwards from this corner: Kåkbrinken (Pillory Slope). In medieval and early modern times, the pillory stood in this corner of the Great Market Place. It is evident that the more respectable strata of the community did not want to be personally associated with such an environment, polluted as it was by shame, crime and the presence of the lower orders. Although a respectable burgher might buy a house next to the pillory, he would be more likely to rent it out than live in it himself.[1] This single corner of Stockholm thus provides us with one example of how space was used and perceived – both concretely and mentally – within an early modern society.

Over the past two decades, space has become a widely researched theme within the humanities. During the 1990s scholars from various disciplines began to show a growing interest in borders and boundaries, both as concrete entities and as abstractions. Although interest in borders and boundaries persists, the themes of publications and seminars since the turn of the century suggest that scholars are increasingly focusing on what lies in-between sites of demarcation: in other words, space.

One can claim that it has become fashionable to address and discuss space, for instance through analysis of how space is perceived and utilized. This 'spatial turn' can be seen as one of the most recent scholarly paradigm shifts.[2]

The concept of space has simultaneously undergone a deep process of theorization. Today, historians (like other humanists) operate with several spatial concepts such as space, place, area, environment, landscape, region, distance, proximity and mapping. Instead of being treated as a single entity, space is now seen as something multifaceted; consequently, we can speak of multiple spaces. The idea of multiple levels of space is reflected in the concept of 'place': there is agreement across several disciplines that this key concept should be defined as an aspect of space that has been given a special meaning in a specific cultural and temporal context.[3] The area close to the pillory in an early modern town could also no doubt be termed a 'place' according to this theorized meaning. But spaces do not need to be concrete, and not all spaces can be measured and defined numerically or by means of mathematical quantities. The Stockholm pillory example clearly demonstrates how a concrete space is also a social or mental space when it is connected to contemporary worldviews and values, in this case medieval and early modern conceptions of honour and dishonour. From the point of view of human culture, space (like any other aspect of human culture) is a social construction. The avoidance of the pillory site proves how the relationship towards space or a specific place is constructed in an interaction between the 'mental' dimension and the 'real' dimension of space: places are never merely concrete or imagined, since within the human mind concrete and imagined aspects of place interact and can even be intertwined.[4] In addition to the existence of the Stockholm pillory area in physical reality, people of the distant past ascribed their own culturally determined connotations to this particular space, the imagined character of the site. This imaginary or associative aspect of place, in turn, influenced (to some extent) how the physical space was perceived and utilized.

Correspondingly, places of fantasy, such as the settings of myths or folk tales, can reflect elements and contours of concrete physical places. Even ideas about the afterlife are not free from the spatial imagination. Both learned and popular medieval descriptions of hell, for example, are expressed through references to spatial features such as 'a waiting room', 'a narrow bridge' and 'the deepest gulf'. Likewise, although the lost souls have been separated from their physical bodies, they are nevertheless imagined as movable spatial beings upon whom eternal and renewed torments can be enacted.[5] As human beings, we live and act in physical space, and so it is natural that our perceptions of the world around us also affect the way we describe places we have never visited. In this sense, we can claim that human imagination always has some basis in reality. As Franco Moretti's mappings of nineteenth-century fiction indicate, it is possible to identify hidden and perhaps largely unconscious cultural structures through analysis of the use of real-life places as settings for fictional characters and action. One recurring pattern of the novels highlighted by Moretti was the ethnocentric worldview, one of the universalities of human culture.[6] This finding reflects the character of space as identity marker. Places have identities of their own and people usually have or develop an identity on the basis of the place where they are living – or they are at least expected to have an identity of their own by outsiders. Human identities are always interpretations of the boundaries between 'us' and 'others'. Simultaneously they are spatially determined.[7]

Due to the 'three-dimensionality' of human imagination the relationship between the spatial turn and the preceding important paradigm shift, the linguistic turn, should not be characterized as oppositional. Rather, the spatial turn can be viewed as a continuation and broadening of the insights of the linguistic turn. During the 1970s, humanists began to argue that language not only affects how we humans perceive the world around us but also constitutes and constructs our reality.[8] As we have already seen, perceptions and descriptions of space are connected to language. Maps, in turn, can be equated with language. According to the *Oxford Dictionary of the English Language*, a map is usually a 'drawing or other representation of the earth's surface or a part of it made on a flat surface, showing the distribution of physical or geographical features (and often also including socio-economic, political, agricultural, meteorological, etc., information), with each point in the representation corresponding to an actual geographical position according to a fixed scale or projection...'[9] A map is indeed a representation furnished with information. Thus, it functions in a similar way to human language, which in both its spoken and written forms is basically a symbolic code system whose purpose is to transmit information. Mind maps, with their visualization of cognitive processes, form a sort of a bridge between verbal communication and representations in maps and other illustrations.[10]

Human communication does not have to be objective and neutral; it can and usually does contain a message, a view or an expression of opinion. Maps not only reflect the world but also cast light upon the worldview of the map-drawer. Like words, maps are tools that facilitate the expression of reality within a specific cultural context. In the history of Western cartography, the creation and persistence of the projection devised by Flemish geographer Gerhardus Mercator (1512–1594) provides a well-known but remarkable example of how space can be presented in a way that simultaneously reflects and strengthens existing ideological patterns. All two-dimensional maps have to reconcile the reality of the Earth's curvature with the restrictions imposed by a flat surface. In the Mercator projection the southernmost and the northernmost latitudes are far longer than those at the equator. The result, given the positioning of the continents, is that Europe and the rest of the northern hemisphere appears to be larger than it is, while Africa, South America and Australia appear disproportionally small. Even today, most Western world maps seem to legitimize the leading economic, political and cultural role of Western civilization. 'Locally' accustomed variations of this ethnocentric worldview are also found: in US world maps, for example, the Americas usually occupy a central position (thus splitting Eurasia in half).[11]

Although the concept has enjoyed increased popularity over the past decade, space has been of interest to a number of scholars for much longer than this. Both Henri Lefebvre's *Production de l'espace* and Yi-Fu Tuan's *Topohilia* appeared in 1974 and three years later Yi-Fu Tuan published his *Space and Place*. Lefebvre was apparently influenced by the linguistic turn, and the same was true of Yi Fu-Tuan, at least to a certain extent. But within the fields of history, interest in space has even deeper roots. As Edward W. Soja points out, history and geography 'were almost inextricably connected' long before the ideas of Lefebvre and Yi-Fu Tuan began to inspire humanists.[12] Soja cites Herodotus as the earliest example of a pre-modern interdisciplinary scholar who addressed the concept of space. Indeed, in Antiquity, the Middle Ages and the early modern era it was customary to detail both history and geography within learned treatises about nations and realms. In addition, ethnographic details were also often included: early scholars were frequently interested in the habits and customs that prevailed in certain areas. A remarkable example of this holistic pre-scientific approach is offered by the Swedish scholar Olaus Magnus, who published not only the very detailed and beautifully illustrated map *Carta marina septentrionalis* (1537), but also a quantitative 'explicatio notarum' entitled *Historia de gentibus septentrionalibus* (1555).

The spatial aspect also persisted in more modern research which predated the spatial turn.[13] History essentially consists of stories about spaces. Traditional history writing was an interpretation of the past of a state and aimed to describe the development of its political and societal contours in spatial frameworks. Modern historians have also maintained their need for spatial descriptions – often combined with a variety of maps that depict a multitude of aspects of human culture. Historical school atlases with their versatile contents can be held as a classic example of mapping tradition within history. Although they are not objective reflections of the past cultures, these atlases (like the Mercator projection) reveal something about the historical context in which they came into being. The historical mapping tradition is connected with sociology and cultural geography in the field of social topography. Because it analyses the division of urban space between different social groups, social topography (which has long-standing roots in German research) can also be regarded as a form of structural mapping.

Ethnographers, in turn, have sought to clarify the geographic spread of different aspects of material culture. In ethnographic atlases, the distribution of different popular customs and beliefs has been presented in the form of maps. In a similar vein, linguists have identified linguistic patterns, including dialectal areas, connected to geographic frameworks.

Why do we still have to map?

Although earlier studies have cast light upon several aspects of human culture, the dynamics of the relationship between human beings and their surrounding physical space have usually been neglected: space has frequently been reduced to a mere static framework, and many maps tell us little, if anything, about how space actually affected the depicted phenomena. Despite standard dictionary definitions and everyday usage, it must be stressed that 'mapping' as a scholarly method is not synonymous with 'cartography' – although clearly historians can learn a lot from the past through map analysis and maps, too, can be utilized as sources for mapping. Mapping does not necessarily involve any concrete physical map: a historian who is undertaking mapping does not have to draw or analyse a visual map. Recognition of the spatial dimension within analysis is the defining characteristic of the mapping method. The spatial dimension can be expressed through non-pictorial means as well as through pictorial presentations. When we address the spatial structures of human culture, we are mapping irrespective of whether we use physical maps or not. Concrete visual maps function merely as tools of study, although naturally they make both the analysis and the presentation of the results more comprehensible for the scholar and his or her audience alike.

Mapping makes the scholar an active agent who considers the use of space and the cultural or societal impact of space in a specific context. When a historian adopts a mapping approach, the outcome is, or should be, a spatially orientated interpretation of a certain physical area – a place. Within present-day mapping there is particular interest in the ways in which space and human culture influence each other. But why should we once again deal with early modern space? Why should the current volume be devoted to mapping this space? Given all the existing theorizing approaches towards spaces, what new insights can be gleaned through the analysis of texts, maps, illustrations and even material remnants that are several hundred years old?

To put it succinctly: space mattered more then than it does nowadays. Of course, space is still significant (and will in all probability continue to be so), but in pre-modern and pre-industrial societies and communities, space was more segregated and hierarchical; the connotations attached to specific places could be very normative and even restrictive. Society was structured according to entirely undemocratic principles and state-formation and nation-building processes were in their infancy. Many everyday boundaries, especially those relating to 'others'[14] and mental and gendered taboos,[15] were more drastic and more sharply drawn than they are today. However, in other respects aspects of spatiality could be more flexible, blurred or a cause of dissonance: this was particularly true of the boundaries and relationships between different political and judicial unities. Within such unities, space affected the relationship between rulers and their subjects. Concrete physical space – experienced and measured in distances, areas, volumes and physical contours of the environment and nature – influenced the functions of societies in a far deeper way than has been case in later societies with advanced technology and faster means of communication.

Pre-industrial societies and communities could be far removed from each other. Naturally, all distances are relative: what was considered remote before the era of motorized travelling may appear proximate in our modern everyday experiences. Nowadays we spend only an hour or two in order to cover distances that previously necessitated a full day's travel.[16] Furthermore, factual distance was intertwined with social and mental distance: in early modern reality, ideas about otherness could result in even neighbouring villages being regarded as distant places.[17] The feeling of simultaneity, the consolidation of the calendar and the increasing spread of common information thanks to the invention of printing – all of which have been linked to the origins of national consciousness[18] – would not have been possible if societies had not managed to resolve their problems with distances and peripheries. Of course, this was a slow process and peripheral areas existed in later centuries, as they still do in the globalized world, at least from certain perspectives. Although peripheries persisted, development towards more unified spaces was clearly already underway in the early modern era.

In the course of the unifying processes in pre-industrial societies, the central power had to rely on written and oral information, gathered from across the realm or delivered from the ruler to local representatives. The administrative systems of early states had to take into account the distance between central government and local communities. Although a time-consuming process, map making was one way in which the central power could form an idea about space it controlled or at least should control. One solution was to try to not only control space but also utilize it as a tool of control. This could be achieved by erecting castles, churches and border stones or by sending representatives of the central power to local communities, at least temporarily. In spite of the distances involved, the influence of the central power could be felt at the local level. However, the control of space remained vague: in most cases, the real power that a ruler could wield decreased as distance from the centre increased.

Naturally, at the local level, there were also those who took advantage of the slow flow of information and the limits of central control. For some, unsatisfactorily controlled space offered freedom, a place of safety or a tool of resistance. Some early modern areas continued to remain beyond the control of local authorities, at least for some time. However, not only ordinary subjects of the Crown benefited from distance from the centre: energetic and unscrupulous officials were themselves able to occupy spaces of relative independence and thus build their own power networks. We know more about state formation and mental patterns in centres, less about processes and perceptions in peripheries. As interest in peripheral areas has developed relatively recently,[19] there is room for further analyses.

Presentation of the contents

This volume consists of case studies which describe how medieval and early modern societies conceived, controlled and utilized both physical and mental space. The book covers the period from the Middle

Ages to the present day, with a particular focus on the conditions in Western European culture between *c.* 1400 and *c.* 1800. The thirteen chapters provide concrete examples of how historians dealing with pre-modern societies collect data (some of which can be very fragmentary) when attempting to reconstruct spatial relationships in and over past environments. It is hoped that the relatively large number of authors has ensured the versatility of the contents. The roots of this book can be found in the research project 'Politics of Brothers, Neighbours and Friends – Political Culture and Strategies of Influence in Early Modern Sweden *c.* 1500–1700', funded by the Academy of Finland. The editors chose to solicit contributions from authors from various disciplines, in order to create a versatile textbook that could engage meaningfully with concepts of spatiality across the humanities.

The case studies are based on strong empirical evidence: various different kinds of sources have been consulted, thus allowing the text as a whole to cast light on pre-industrial societies from several perspectives. The variety of analysed source materials, applied theories and methodologies should ensure that this volume provides valuable resources for researchers, teachers and students with an interest in spatiality.

The following chapters have been divided into six major sub-themes, all of which are connected to spaces and spatiality. Of course, there is some overlap between the content of various chapters, and individual chapters may themselves treat their subjects from several viewpoints and premises.

In the opening chapter, Ismo Puhakka considers the ways in which cartography, topography and coeval religious and political structures were intertwined in the Reformation era. By focusing on the production of sixteenth-century atlases, Puhakka shows how, even though they were beginning to depict profane (non-ecclesiastic) spaces, cartographic and topographic representations continued to be deeply influenced by theological interpretations. However, one cannot trace any clearly Catholic, Lutheran, Calvinist or other narrowly defined religious tradition among atlas-makers. Rather, geographers borrowed various elements from each other, neglecting religious and cultural boundaries. Naturally, their 'excerpts' were influenced by their own mental and cultural backgrounds and surroundings.

Kimmo Katajala is also concerned with borders and maps. The borders of medieval and early modern states (pre-French Revolution) have often been viewed as indefinite frontier zones. Although this description seems well suited to theories about national state-building processes, it is less easy to maintain such a position when faced with archival sources from the sixteenth and seventeenth centuries: contrary to common beliefs among historians, the idea of the linear border already existed in the Middle Ages. Through analysis of a large collection of maps dating from the fifteenth century to 1800,[20] Katajala is able to outline and discuss the ideas and worldviews reflected in these medieval and early modern representations. Special attention is paid to the cartographic development of the early modern Swedish state, especially its eastern border and border zone (which lay in largely remote and scarcely populated forested areas, far away from Swedish political centres).

Although Jukka Korpela also considers borders and the same eastern geographic area discussed by Katajala, he focuses on the local level and provides analysis of movements in peripheral space. The vast forests of east Fennoscandia had originally been settled by semi-nomadic hunter–fisher populations. However, colonization movements by Sweden and Russia in the late medieval period saw the emergence of two competing realms within the region. Both administrations sought to extend their reach in order to secure resources and exert control: roads were built and there was a subsequent decline in the role played by the water routes used by the native population. Korpela considers how Europeanization and Christianization processes affected the division and conception of space and reach in the border forests.

Piia Einonen combines the concept of power with the spatial dimension of an individual officeholder's authority. In her chapter, we follow Johan Rosenhane, a seventeenth-century Swedish nobleman, on his journeys: first within the peripheral part of the Swedish realm (partially overlapping with the geographical foci of Katajala and Korpela) and then as a governor in a more central location. In practice, Rosenhane's political power was attached to a number of relatively remote towns. Moreover, the existing networks of local power elites in peripheral areas made it difficult for him, a royal official coming from 'outside', to exert any kind of control over his allocated region. Such a situation required the governor to travel extensively. Letters, gifts and even ritualistic welcomes and departures could also serve to diminish the impact of spatial distance and its consequences. For Johan Rosenhane the spatial dimensions of power were concrete and essential. It seems that distances were of great importance to him: he used to record the distance and duration of his journeys in his diary (a rare early modern source of its kind).

Ulla Koskinen remains in the same geographic and political periphery, but considers the transmission of information between the periphery and the centre. The analysis focuses on responses to the king's 1583 order that a fortress should be built on the river Neva (Sw. Nyen) in Ingria. At the same time, it is also a story of the everyday life, or struggle, of the noble officeholders who took care of administration at the edges of kingdom. Koskinen focuses on the process of executing the decisions and demands issued by the central power in the form of letters. The central concern addressed by Koskinen is whether local officeholders could take advantage of their distance from the centre, the slow speed of communication and the central power's lack of up-to-date knowledge of events on the ground.

Letters are also central in the next chapter, in which Christian Kühner maps the network of a politically active nobleman. Louis II de Bourbon, known as the Grand Condé, was a key figure in seventeenth-century France. His contacts stretched across the continent, even extending into the geographically peripheral kingdom of Sweden. By analysing the Grand Condé's correspondence, Kühner operates with European macro-space and considers the international and the spatial dimensions of the Grand Condé's network during his most politically active period (from the 1640s to the 1660s).

The importance of networks as a means of occupying and controlling space is examined in more depth by Marko Hakanen in his study of the space controlled by an influential family. This seventeenth-century family operated within an aristocratic fiefdom that covered a vast but sparsely populated area of northern Finland. Hakanen's analysis shows that although it was possible for one individual's sphere of influence to cover a very wide area, this was dependent upon the utilization of social networks. Such networks were based on family strategies: male family members would be appointed to various strategic offices within the state administration. Using data relating to the family and its networks, Hakanen maps out the area over which the head of the family was able to exert control, with the help of his eight children (who all held important local offices and acted as bailiffs, clergymen, rural police chiefs or jurisdictional district judges).

Networking and dawdling officeholders were not the only obstacles that obstructed the central power's aspirations to control local space. Janne Haikari implies that within local communities the power of the victorious military state – as seventeenth-century Swedish rule is usually depicted – was not always absolute. The great physical distances involved could also provide subjects of the Crown with opportunities to resist the local authorities. Haikari focuses on an adulterous affair that came to the attention of the courts in the mid-seventeenth century. Both suspects escaped and were never caught by the authorities. The scene of the crime is not the only place discussed. On the contrary, the limits imposed by the whole geography of the micro-space (including terrain and road network) provide us with a picture of the operational environments both of the local administration in this particular part of western Finland and of the individuals who succeeded in evading the law and its executors.

Power and local space are also addressed by Päivi Maaranen, who leads us to 'conquered peripheries'. The spatial representations of national or even transnational power were one way of extending such power into the local sphere. Many churches and castles built in the Middle Ages remained as monuments of power in the early modern era. Although some monuments are still standing today, certain landscapes have been lost: a number of churches, chapels and fortifications have disappeared, with few (if any) visible traces left behind. Fortunately, analysis of historical sources and archaeological evidence can provide us with glimpses of some lost landscapes. Maaranen is concerned with how landmarks of secular and religious power and their surroundings would have appeared at the beginning of the early modern period. Landscape analysis of southernmost Finland largely supports the idea that medieval landscapes were organized to some extent. Furthermore, buildings were not simply functional sites, in which necessary secular and religious tasks were performed, they were also built in order to impress others. This paves the way for interpretations of the ways in which members of society may have attempted to secure secular and religious power.

Kari Uotila and Isto Huvila continue with a similar theme but focus on the potential methodological innovations offered by new technology. The writers clarify the ways in which new technology can be used in archaeological research, specifically the modelling of pre-historic or historical sites and landscapes. Uotila and Huvila examine two sites in southwest Finland as case studies. Visualization is given considerable emphasis: it serves as both a tool for presenting results and a method by which collected data can be analysed. Despite the advantages of virtual archaeology, the authors also introduce a note of caution: modelled spaces must always be understood as interpretations and not as exact recreations.

Marko Lamberg, Minna Mäkinen and Merja Uotila lead us to everyday living spheres within early modern communities and societies. Their chapter focuses on the concept of the micro-level border, in the context of a village community. Combining historical and ethnological approaches, the writers explore the various forms of boundaries within the little village of Toivola (close to one of Finland's oldest highways but still relatively far removed from political and administrative centres). There are several ways to define the space of the village. At one level, the space could be defined by the geographical contours upon which judicial and administrative definitions were based. However, the more abstract aspects of boundaries are also considered: in other words, how 'concrete' or administrative boundaries have been involved in the construction of local conceptions of 'us' and 'others' and how those boundaries were nevertheless crossed.

Everyday space and culture is also considered by Vesa-Pekka Herva, Timo Ylimaunu, Titta Kallio-Seppä, Tiina Kuokkanen and Risto Nurmi, who focus their attention on eighteenth-century social topographies. Although one of the chapter's central topics is clearly the distribution of wealth, the need for privacy within an early modern space is also foregrounded. The authors chart the mention of curtains in probate inventories from the remote town of Tornio (Sw. Torneå) – curtains were gradually becoming a more common feature of the material culture of early modern elites. By mapping the distribution of curtains in urban homes, the authors are able to draw conclusions about the need to distinguish and mark the boundaries between private and public spaces.

The question of distribution of wealth is also considered in the final chapter. Here, Ilkka Nummela examines and maps variations in levels of wealth and the geographical concentration of wealth in late sixteenth-century Finland. The Reformation and the growing degree of centralism in administration and jurisdiction – all trends that had been initiated by the king – had changed the economic patterns of Finnish society in many ways. One outcome was a decline in the number of farms owned by peasants. However, because conditions and forms of agriculture varied across Finland, different kinds of premises and solutions were employed in order to react to the specific changes faced. Nummela's analysis of tax lists from 1571 highlights this variance.

This volume places considerable emphasis on peripheries: contacts with and from peripheries, as well as everyday patterns within peripheral areas. Of course, periphery and centre are relative concepts: for most western Europeans early modern Sweden appeared to occupy a geographical periphery, but within Swedish space there were internal conceptions of centre and periphery that could vary according to context. Similarly, seventeenth-century Sweden has often been seen as a prime example of an early modern military state, in which everyday culture was impregnated by religious fundamentalism and the lives of the subjects strictly controlled by the authorities. However, several of the chapters in this volume challenge this picture.

Although most case studies deal with Sweden and especially its eastern peripheries, the interested reader should find that the methods and findings presented in different chapters can be generalized and utilized as tools of comparison within a wider European context. Broadly speaking, our case studies deal with three different categories of spatial processes: how space was depicted and sensed; how space was occupied, divided, controlled and crossed; and how space could be used as a tool of independence and resistance within the early modern world. There are certainly more sub-themes, which the reader is now at leisure to explore.

Notes

1 Lamberg 2000, p. 147.
2 The spatial turn is discussed, for instance, in Warf & Arias (eds.) 2009 and Kingston 2010. See also the thematic issues of *Scandia* (2008:2) and *Historiallinen Aikakauskirja* (2010:1), both devoted to the spatial turn within the history discipline.
3 Yi-Fu Tuan 1977; Massey 2005, p. 138–142, 183–184; Knuuttila, Laaksonen & Piela (eds.) 2006.
4 Lefebvre 1991, pp. 6–7, 11–14 and Chapter 2; Soja 1996, Chapter 2.
5 Dinzelbacher 1999; Ankarloo 2003.
6 Moretti 1998. For an adaptation of Moretti's method in Nordic context, see Lamberg 2009. For other analyses of the relationship between space and cultural variety, see e.g. Gordon & Klein (eds.) 2001, esp. Part II; Sanford 2002, Chapter 1 and Clarke 2006, esp. Chapter 3.
7 Paasi 1986; Knuuttila & Paasi 1995; Soja 1996, pp. 87–88; Allen 1999; Lord Smail 2000; Tilley 2006; Knuuttila, Laaksonen & Piela (eds.) 2006; Jones & Olwig (eds.) 2007.
8 Clark 2004.
9 *Oxford Dictionary of the English Language*: 'map': I.1.a.
10 Buzan 1996.
11 Massey 1995; King 1996, p. 37; Brotton 1997, pp. 166–169. Maps as reflections of ethnocentrism or hegemonic aspirations are also discussed in Yi-Fu Tuan 1974, Chapter 4; Black 2000 and Anderson 2006, pp. 170–178.
12 Soja 1996, p. 167. See also François, P., Syrjämaa T. & Terho, H. 2008, p. xi.
13 See, for example, Robinson & Petchenik 1976, Chapter 5 ('The Conception of Space').
14 Snell 2003; Lamberg 2007.
15 Romano 1989; Stark 1998; Eilola 2004; Coster & Spicer 2005; Spicer & Hamilton (eds.) 2005; Raguin & Stanbury (eds.) 2005; Pohl 2006; Flather 2007; Cohen 2008.
16 Kühnel (ed.) 1992; Retsö 2007; Betteridge (ed.) 2007.

17 Snell 2003. Cf., though, Dyer (ed.) 2007. See also the chapter written by Marko Lamberg, Minna Mäkinen and Merja Uotila in this volume.
18 Anderson 2006, Chapter 3.
19 Regarding earlier approaches towards peripheries, especially in Nordic context, see Heikkinen 1988; Harrison 1995; Harrison 1998; Häyrynen & Landgren (eds.) 1997; Simonson 1999; Johansson (ed.) 2002; Lamberg 2003; Matikainen 2004; Stenqvist Millde 2007.
20 The Norderskiöld Collection in the National Library of Finland, Helsinki.

Bibliography

Allen, R. L. 1999. 'The Socio-Spatial Making and Marking of "Us". Toward a Critical Postmodern Spatial Theory of Difference and Community.' *Social Identities*, Vol. 5 (3), pp. 249–277.

Anderson, B. 2006. *Imagined Communities. Reflections on the Origin and Spread of Nationalism.* New edition. Verso, London & New York.

Ankarloo, B. 2003. *Helvetet. Döden och de eviga straffen i Västerlandets kristna tradition.* Historiska Media, Lund.

Betteridge, T. (ed.) 2007. *Borders and Travellers in Early Modern Europe.* Ashgate, Aldershot.

Black, J. 2000. *Maps and Politics.* University of Chicago Press, Chicago.

Brotton, J. 1998. *Trading Territories. Mapping the Early Modern World.* Reaktion Books, London.

Buzan, T. 1996. *The Mind Map Book. How to Use Radiant Thinking to Maximize Your Brain's Untapped Potential.* Penguin Books, Harmondsworth (Middlesex).

Clark, E. A. 2004. *History, Theory, Text. Historians and the Linguistic Turn.* Harvard University Press, Cambridge (Mass.).

Clarke, C. A. M. 2006. *Literary Landscapes and the Idea of England, 700–1400.* D. S. Brewer, Cambridge.

Cohen, E. S. 2008. 'To Pray, To Work, To Hear, To Speak. Women in Roman Streets c. 1600.' In Laitinen, R. & Cohen, T. V. (eds.) *Cultural History of Early Modern European Streets.* Brill, Leiden, pp. 95–118.

Coster, W. & Spicer, A. *(eds.)* 2005. *Sacred Space in Early Modern Europe.* Cambridge University Press, Cambridge.

Dinzelbacher, P. 1999. *Die letzten Dinge. Himmel, Hölle, Fegefeuer im Mittelalter.* Herder, Freiburg im Breisgau.

Dyer, C. (ed.) 2007. *The Self-Contained Village? The Social History of Rural Communities, 1250–1900.* University of Hertfordshire Press, Hatfield.

Eilola, J. 2004. 'Rajojen noituus ja taikuus.' In Katajala-Peltomaa, S. & Toivo, R. M. (eds.) *Paholainen, noituus ja magia – kristinuskon kääntöpuoli. Pahuuden kuvasto vanhassa maailmassa.* Finnish Literature Society, Helsinki, pp. 136–186.

Flather, A. 2007. *Gender and Space in Early Modern England.* Boydell Press Woodbridge.

François, P., Syrjämaa, T. & Terho, H. 2008. 'Introduction'. In François, P., Syrjämaa, T. & Terho, H. (eds.) *Power and Culture. New Perspectives on Spatiality in European History.* Pisa University Press, Pisa, pp. xi–xvi.

Gordon, A. & Klein, B. (eds.) 2001. *Literature, Mapping, and the Politics of Space in Early Modern Britain.* University of Cambridge Press, Cambridge.

Harrison, D. 1995. *Medieval Space. The Extent of Microspatial Knowledge in Western Europe during the Middle Ages.* University of Lund, Lund.

Harrison, D. 1998, *Skapelsens geografi. Föreställningar om rymd och rum i medeltidens Europa.* Ordfront, Stockholm.

Heikkinen, A. 1988. *Kirveskansan elämää. Ihmiskohtaloita Kuhmon erämaissa 1800-luvun alussa.* WSOY, Helsinki.

Historiallinen Aikakauskirja, Vol. 108 (1), 2010.

Häyrynen, M. & Landgren, L. F. (eds.) 1997. *The dividing line. Borders and national peripheries.* Helsinki, RI Publications.

Johansson, E. (ed.) 1992. *Periferins landskap. Historiska spar och nutida blickfält i svensk glesbygd.* Nordic Academic Press, Lund.

Jones, M. & Olwig, K. R. (eds.) 2007. *Nordic Landscapes. Region and Belonging on the Northern Edge of Europe.* University of Minnesota Press, Minneapolis & London.

King, G. 1996. *Mapping Reality. An Exploration of Cultural Cartographies.* Macmillan, Basingstoke & London.

Lefebvre, H. 1991. *The Production of Space.* Blackwell, Malden (Mass.), Oxford & Carlton (Australia).

Kingston, R. 2010. 'Mind over Matter? History and the Spatial Turn.' *Cultural & Social History. The Journal of the Social History Society*, Vol. 7, Issue 1, pp. 111–121.

Knuuttila, S. & Paasi, A. 1995. 'Tila, kulttuuri ja mentaliteetti. Maantieteen ja antropologian yhteyksiä etsimässä.' In Katajala, K. (ed.) *Manaajista maalaisaateliin. Tulkintoja toisesta historian, antropologian ja maantieteen välimaastossa.* Finnish Literature Society, Helsinki, pp. 28–94.

Knuuttila, S., Laaksonen, P. & Piela, U. (eds.) 2006. *Paikka. Eletty, kuviteltu, kerrottu. Kalevalaseuran vuosikirja*, Vol. 85. Finnish Literature Society, Helsinki.

Kühnel, H. (ed.) 1992. *Kommunikation und Alltag. Spätmittelalter und früher Neuzeit.* Verlag der Österreichischen Akademie der Wissenschaften, Vienna.

Lamberg, M. 2001. *Dannemännen i stadens råd. Rådmanskretsen i nordiska köpstäder under senmedeltiden.* Stockholmia förlag, Stockholm.

Lamberg, M. 2003. '1300-luvun suomalaisten tietoympäristöt.' In Ahonen, K. et al. (eds.) *Toivon historia. Toivo Nygårdille omistettu juhlakirja.* Department of History and Ethnology, Jyväskylä, pp. 261–271.

Lamberg, M. 2007. 'Ethnic Imagery and Social Boundaries in Early Modern Urban Communities. The Case of the Finnish Immigrants in Swedish Towns, c. 1450–1650.' In Lamberg, M. (ed.) *Shaping Ethnic Identities. Ethnic Minorities in Northern and East Central European States and Communities, c. 1450–2000.* East-West Books Helsinki, Helsinki, pp. 200–240.

Lamberg. M. 2009. 'Att kartera "Jöns Buddes bok". Tolkningar av det senmedeltida europeiska makrorummet i birgittinsk klosterlitteratur.' *Folkmålsstudier*, Vol. 48, pp. 67–92.

Lord Smail, D. 2000. *Imaginary Cartographies. Possession and Identity in Late Medieval Marseille.* Cornell University Press, Ithaca.

Massey, D. 1995. 'Imagining the World.' In Allen, J. & Massey, D. (eds.) *Geographical Worlds.* The Open University & Oxford University Press, Oxford.

Massey, D. 2005. *For Space.* Sage Publications, London.

Matikainen, O. 2004. *Verenperijät. Väkivalta ja yhteisön murros itäisessä Suomessa 1500–1600-luvuilla.* Finnish Literature Society, Helsinki.

Moretti, F. 1998. *Atlas of the European Novel 1800–1900*. Verso, London & New York.
Oxford Dictionary of the English language. <http://dictionary.oed.com/>.
Paasi, A. 1986. 'The Institutionalization of Regions. A Theoretical Framework for Understanding the Emergence of Regions and the Constitution of Regional Identity', *Fennia*, vol. 164 (1), pp. 105–146.
Pohl, N. 2006. *Women, Space And Utopia 1600–1800*. Ashgate, Aldershot.
Raguin, V. C. & Stanbury, S. (eds.) 2005. *Women's Space. Patronage, Place, and Gender in the Medieval Church*. State University of New York Press, New York.
Retsö, D. 2007. *Människans mobilitet och naturens motsträvighet. Studier kring frågan om reshastighet under medeltiden*. University of Stockholm, Stockholm.
Robinson, A. H. & Petchenik, B. B. 1976. *The Nature of Maps. Essays toward Understanding Maps and Mapping*. The University of Chicago Press, Chicago & London.
Romano, D. 1989. 'Gender and the Urban Geography of Renaissance Venice.' *Journal of Social History*, Vol. 23 (2), pp. 339–353.
Sanford, R. L. 2002. *Maps and Memory in Early Modern England. A Sense of Place*. Palgrave, Basingstoke.
Scandia, Vol. 74 (2), 2008.
Simonson, Ö. 1999. *Den lokala scenen. Torstuna härad som lokalsamhälle under 1600-talet*. Uppsala University, Uppsala.
Snell, K. D. M. 2003. 'The culture of local xenophobia', *Social History*, Vol. 28 (1), pp. 1–30.
Soja, E. 1996. *Thirdspace. Journeys to Los Angeles and Other Real-and-Imagined Places*. Blackwell, Malden (Mass.).
Spicer, A. & Hamilton, S. (eds.) 2005. *Defining the Holy. Sacred Space in Medieval and Early Modern Europe*. Ashgate, Aldershot.
Stark[-Arola], Laura 1998. *Magic, Body and Social Order. The Construction of Gender Through Women's Private Rituals in Traditional Finland*. Finnish Literature Society, Helsinki.
Stenqvist Millde, Y. 2007. *Vägar inom räckhåll. Spåren efter resande i det förindustriella bondesamhället*. University of Stockholm, Stockholm.
Tilley, C. 2006. 'Introduction. Identity, Place, Landscape and Heritage.' *Journal of Material Culture*, Vol. 11 (1–2), pp. 7–32.
Tuan, Y.-F. 1974. *Topophilia. A Study of Environmental Perception, Attitudes, and Values*. Prentice-Hall, Englewood Cliffs.
Tuan, Y.-F. 1977. *Space and Place. The Perspective of Experience*. University of Minnesota Press, Minneapolis.
Warf, B. & Arias, S. (eds.) 2009. *The Spatial Turn. Interdisciplinary Perspectives*. Routledge, London & New York.

PART I

EARLY MODERN MAPPING DECODED

CHAPTER I

Theology and Map Publishing

Ismo Puhakka

And in this corruption of nature, however, God has given such a good judgment on man, there is nothing in this universe, so well hidden or distant, that this sovereign spirit had not attacked and enforced to be seen till the core.[1]

> Antoine du Pinet, *Plantz, povrtraitz et descriptions de plvsieurs villes et forteresses, tant de l'evrope, Asie, que des Indes, & Terres neuues* (Lyon, 1564).

Introduction

Antoine du Pinet, a pastor and editor of one the first French atlases, praised Man's privileged ability with the noble disciplines of cosmography and chorography to allow the Cosmos to be seen. In this essay, I will draw some very tentative initial outlines of an interesting, but only narrowly researched, phenomenon of mid-sixteenth-century map publishing. The primary question raised here is: why during a certain period, broadly from the 1530s to the 1570s, did many of those (few) authors editing atlases in France seem to have links to some sort of Protestantism? Was there something within Protestant thought that supported map production? I am perfectly aware that 'Protestant thought' is not a monolith and that there were significant differences between different forms of Protestantism. However, this relative variety inside something we call Protestantism should not be used as a pretext to avoid considering new perspectives to aid our understanding of the history of cartography. Because an impressionistic view can sometimes illuminate better the contours and ideas of its subject than can a minutely detailed work, I hope that you, dear reader, will go through this humble draft with an open mind, taking the several obscure expressions and concepts contained within as 'bricks to knock the door with': when the door opens, the 'brick' can be thrown away.

The following pages are arranged in a somewhat head-to-toe manner. I will begin with theoretical considerations and then move on to the more solid landscape of a real case. Thus, in the first section I will take a broader look at the transformations which took place in sixteenth-century cartography and tentatively discuss what kind of role religion may have played in this process. The next section discusses the ideas of the two foremost Protestant theologians, Philip Melanchthon and John Calvin. Melanchthon and Calvin represent two different branches of Protestant theology: Lutheran and Calvinist. However, irrespective of the differences between them, in broader theological currents they both seem to have shared an interest in geography. In the final section we shall examine some of the early French atlases and their authors, and consider whether there were links between emerging atlas production in sixteenth-century France and the confessional backgrounds of atlas makers.

Novelties and continuities in sixteenth-century cartography

The map, a world seen as a picture, is a central feature of the modern age.[2] During the sixteenth and seventeenth centuries a profound intellectual and social change gave maps the central role they enjoy today and transformed the standards that guide map making. Is it possible that this transformation was connected, in one way or another, with the coeval Protestant Reformation, which simultaneously systematized and realized a number of the revolutionary ideas which developed during the late medieval period?[3] For some reason, the interaction between the Reformation and cartography has not attracted a great deal of attention. Perhaps the Reformation, understood solely as a *religious* movement (in the narrow modern sense of the word), is considered to be far removed from scientific debates, the area with which maps have usually been associated. The distance between the spheres of science and religion observed today is, in part, a consequence of the strong division between the sacral and the mundane in early modern Protestant theology. It is also here that the most important relationship between Protestantism and cartography lies: the impact of Protestant theology and social values on the practices and methods of cartography, and more generally its influence on science as a whole.

Cartographic revolution of the sixteenth century

The American historian David Buisseret was the first to refer to the unforeseen growth in the consumption and production of maps in the sixteenth century as a 'cartographical revolution'. In *The Map Makers' Quest*, he asked 'why there were so few maps in Europe in 1400, and so many by 1650.'[4] His idea of a cartographical revolution seems quite plausible, given Robert Karrow's research. According to Karrow, in the heartlands of Europe, there was 1 map for every 720 individuals in 1500 and 1 for every 4 in 1600.[5] In light of these figures there seems to be justification for the assertion that it was during the sixteenth century that maps gained the central role that they still enjoy in western culture today. Over the course of the sixteenth century, as Robert Karrow aptly summarized, 'What had been, in the Middle Ages, a marginal genre unlikely to have been known or used by any but a handful of scholars, became something common, something an average European from almost any walk of life might recognize and use. This change was so marked that it seems no exaggeration to call it a revolution.'[6]

There are several indications that the cartographical revolution was not only a quantitative change, but also a qualitative one. In his article 'Cartography and the Renaissance: Continuity and Change',[7] David Woodward has analysed these transformations and continuities, the most pertinent of which are discussed below. Following Woodward, carto-graphical changes broadly included liberation from medieval and classical authorities, the shift from the use of Latin to the use of the vernacular and the centrality of printing rather than the production of manuscripts. Some changes in the structure and graphical expression of maps were also evident: favouring of geometric-, perspective- or coordinate-based structuring; the change of focus from aural to visual and from closed to open sign-systems; and the cessation of temporally co-synchronous representations.[8] However, many things known in medieval times also continued to exist in the Renaissance. Textual descriptions as a form of spatial representation persisted, as did oblique and elevated topographi-cal views. There were also no great changes to the Mediterranean sea charts, or Portolans. The final (and from the viewpoint of this study, the most interesting) continuity was the continued sacred function of maps.

According to David Woodward, '[t]here was no clean break from the sacred mappamundi to the secular world map that can be pinpointed to a single time and place.'[9] Woodward is willing to consider the pos-sibility that 'the usual dichotomy between religious maps as belonging to the Middle Ages and secular ones as belonging to the Renaissance' might be misleading. Woodward raises two factors that illustrate the continued presence of religion in sixteenth-century cartography. First, religious themes continued to dominate map production:

> In the sixteenth century, the most popular country portrayed on maps was arguably the Holy Land. Certainly more maps were made of it during the century than of France, Spain, or Portugal. Almost as many maps of the Holy Land were made as world maps or maps of the African continent.[10]

Secondly, pilgrim maps were an important part of map production. For instance, in the city of Rome map sellers and printers were located in a quarter of the city (the Parione) that was strategically located to best profit from the pilgrims' presence.[11]

The centrality of religion within the maps, and society in general, during the sixteenth century may not come as a surprise to those familiar with Renaissance culture. Europeans, Protestants and Catholics alike, considered themselves destined to travel from this life to eternity. In order to avoid anachronistic thinking, this should also be kept in mind when the cartographical change is studied.

Another important continuity worthy of examination is the case of the Portolan or medieval sea charts. As David Woodward and many others have noted, Portolan charts pose a real challenge to the progressive model of cartographical development between the Middle Ages and the Renaissance.[12] As Tony Campbell has pointed out, with reference to the earliest extant copies dating from a little before 1300, Portolan maps provided an amazingly accurate outline of the Mediterranean.[13] The earliest Portolans both predated the Ptolemaic maps and surpassed them in extent of information and accuracy. Campbell argues that Portolans were far removed from contemporary mappamundi, in which cartographic content was largely shaped by a theological message.[14] However, the cartographic revolution did not affect Portolan charts: their alignment changed by some ten degrees during the sixteenth century, and their positional accuracy changed little over the course of the following three centuries.[15]

I think that the persistence of Portolan maps provides an objection to the claim that the cartographical revolution arose from technological and scientific advancement. This links to another continuity identified by David Woodward: the persistence of medieval written itineraries, which 'continued to be a robust tool for way finding' and 'were by no means replaced by their graphic equivalents.' In quantitative terms, the cartographic revolution refers to the growth of *printed* maps. In a number of cases these maps seem to serve purposes other than the technical needs of navigation, planning or way finding.

How, then, should we consider the cartographical revolution, given the fact that the sacral or religious function of maps persisted? Perhaps if there was a rupture, a qualitative change in sixteenth-century cartography, it was not so much in the production of knowledge but rather in its selection and arrangement. The existence of very accurate Portolan maps proves that medieval world maps could have been more accurate and *realistic*, if this had been their purpose. At the same time, cartographic novelties, which were largely *stylistic* transformations in the representation of the world, were not necessarily developed to provide better tools. Literal itineraries and Portolans continued to serve these functional needs. In summary, it seems more likely that the roots of the qualitative cartographic revolution can be found in a change in the religious interpretation of the world and from its visible consequences: the emerging consumption of a particular type of image.

If we now return to the changes that took place in sixteenth-century cartography, as presented by David Woodward, we can see that they seem to be, in the main, related to the arrangement of geographical knowledge, not to its creation. To recap, Woodward's areas of change included geometric-, perspective- and coordinate-based structuring (which I would like to call 'visual algorithms', since they provide mathematical methods of representing natural features); the shift from aural to visual description; and the cessation of co-synchronous images (that is, maps which represent past, present and future events on the same surface). However, I believe that the qualitative cartographic revolution was the result of a paradigm that favours these visual features above others. To simplify a great deal, we could for instance tentatively sketch out two major 'paradigms' and account for the visual changes by the idea of a paradigm shift. I call these the *as-above, so-below paradigm* and the *providence paradigm*. The latter, at least during the first half of the sixteenth century, can be attributed to the Protestant Reformation. To illuminate these messy expressions a little we should briefly examine the theology of John Calvin and Philip Melanchthon.

The Protestant revision of God, sight and nature

Given the limitations of this study it is not, unfortunately, possible to analyse Protestant theology and the differences between its two main branches in any great detail. However, a general overview of the subject is required. Broadly, the transformations which took place in early modern epistemology, causality and metaphysics were consequences of a very radical, essential division between the divine and the mundane. Protestant thinkers, strongly influenced by Augustinian thought, emphasized the difference between the absolute and infinite God and the fallen, mortal and sinful Man. From an anthropological perspective this led to a pessimistic view of Man's epistemological abilities. As a descendant of the fallen Adam, Man was considered degraded and incapable or, even worse, unworthy of knowing the divine.[16]

Scholars have noted that this degradation of Man had a twofold effect on culture and learning. The absolute distance between Man and God meant, especially in the Calvinist context, total *Entzauberung* (complete elimination) of *divine signs* from the everyday world. Consequently, Catholic rituals, images of saints and miracles were considered superstitious and were abandoned. Denis Crouzet has called this change, which reached its culmination in the theology of Calvin, a *véritable révolution du signe*. Medieval thinking in which an image could have a Theophanic function (the ability to rejoin the something of this world with the otherworldly) was rejected:

> The scandal for Calvin, in the cult of images, was that the signifier flew over the signified: that the representation seized the represented by enclosing it in itself. The visible took hold over the invisible and the finite absorbed the infinite.[17]

In a cultural *sens* this took the Protestant world to a situation described by Crouzet as a 'temps humain envahi par l'immédiateté, dénudé de tout interstice d'imaginaire symbolique dans le rapport de l'homme à Dieu et à la connaissance.'[18] This revolution of sign was, indeed, quite radical: it refuted a long dominant and very sophisticated view that had brought together the philosophy of antiquity and the Christian worldview. A quote from Pico della Mirandola's (1463–1494) platonic exegesis of world might be illustrative:

> Everything which is in the totality of worlds is also in each of them and none of them contains anything which is not to be found in

each of the others [... ...] whatever exists in the inferior world will also be found in the superior world, but in more elevated form; and whatever exists on the higher plane can also be seen down below but in somewhat degenerated and, so to say, adulterated shape [... ...] In our world we have fire as an element, in the celestial world the corresponding entity is the sun, in the supracelestial world the seraphic fire of the Intellect. But consider their difference: The elemental fire burns, the celestial fire gives life, the supracelestial loves.[19]

An argument of this kind would not have been accepted in Wittenberg or in Geneva. From this perspective, postlapsarian Man could not possess knowledge of whatever the relationship between the subcelestial and supracelestial worlds might have been. This, of course, did not mean that in the Protestant context the divine, God, could not be investigated from the natural sphere – quite the opposite, as Calvin wrote in the *Institutes of the Christian Religion*: 'His essence indeed is incomprehensible, so that his Majesty is not to be perceived by the human senses: but on all his works he hath inscribed his glory.'[20] Although the analogy was denied and the reading of the two books (the book of nature and the book of Scripture) were to be understood literally, nature as a scene of God's works could still be examined.

The discarding of the symbolic and the denial of analogy were thus one side of the consequences of Protestant anthropology, which emphasized the absolute degradation of Man's epistemic abilities. Another and certainly equally severe mutation was its challenge to the 'Aristotelian-scholastic dominance of human learning and foundations of knowledge', as Peter Harrison has plausibly argued.[21] The canon of Aristotelian natural philosophy, the authority of the Church fathers and the whole classical curriculum was brought into doubt. These authors, too, were themselves fallen men, and their words and ideas could be wrong. Thus, the basis of the knowledge and learning could no longer depend on the interpretations of canonized authors. The gaze was now turned to 'bare readings' of the Bible and nature.

The absolute and irreconcilable division between the mundane and the divine also had an impact on thinking surrounding causality and God's providential care of nature. In late medieval Aristotelian metaphysics, the creatures of Creation were believed to aim at their proper ends, according to the essences of their species.[22] For instance, according to their respective essential natures, the aim of a tree was to grow and the aim of Man was to acquire knowledge. Causality was thus understood in a twofold manner: God, the creator of beings and their proper ends, was understood as the primary cause, and the natural activities of beings were understood as secondary causes. As Reijo Työrinoja has clearly documented, this was largely denied in Protestant thinking:

> For Calvin the divine power is everywhere immediately present in nature and nothing is based in an ultimate ontological sense on secondary causes. There is no autonomous activity and finality in nature that is not sustained by divine sovereign power. Physical reality is an instrument of God by which he acts as he wills and which he directs according to his own aims.[23]

This change in causal conception was not without consequences: whereas in the Aristotelian scholastic tradition the focus of research could be on a single creature and all created things were understood to have their proper teleological ends, Protestant thought (particularly Calvinism) emphasized the causality of nature as a whole. Broadly, the focus shifted from the particular to the general. This change in thinking surrounding causality also affected the way in which nature was viewed. Whereas a late medieval Thomist 'scientist' who observed a single creature would have perceived it as aiming towards its own teleological end, the Calvinist 'scientist' would have seen it as fulfilling divine providence. For Calvin, in theoretical respects, no single creature could be a cause of its actions. The cause of all activity was God:

> [God] is the Creator of all things [but] also their perpetual governor and preserver; and that not by a certain universal motion, actuating the whole machine of the world, and all its respective parts, but by a particular providence sustaining, nourishing, and providing for every thing which he has made.[24]

Because every creature, every motion and all parts of nature were understood as God's acts, nature as a whole became a massive demonstration of God's providence. Although in many respects, Calvin took a much more radical position than the Lutheran Melanchthon (whose theology still slightly resembled Aristotelian thought), one can still speak of a common providential tendency shared by the two most prominent Protestant theologians. In some areas their opinions even seem to echo one another. For both Calvin and Melanchthon everything in nature was a reminder of divine providence, as Calvin wrote in the *Institutes*:

Nothing is more natural than the succession of spring to winter, of summer to spring, and of autumn to summer. But there is so great diversity and inequality discovered in this series, that it is obvious that every year, month, and day, is governed by a new and particular providence of God.[25]

Therefore, knowledge of nature was not simply an opportunity to understand God's works: it was almost a duty. It is small wonder that Melanchthon so severely exhorted his pupils to study astronomy and geography:

Who is so hard-hearted and so without feeling that he does not sometimes, looking at the sky and beholding the most beautiful stars in it, marvel at these varied alternations which are produced by their motions, or desire to know their traces, so to speak their motions, that is, the fixed computation shown by divine providence. [... ...] those who disdain these related lights do not contemplate the work of nature, and for that reason they deserve to have their eyes plucked out, since they do not want to use them for the purpose for which they are chiefly made – especially since that knowledge puts us in mind of God and of our immortality.[26]

The contemplation of nature, according to these Protestant theologians, provided an indirect way to contemplate God through his works. Nature was no longer understood as a symbolic or allegoric representation of the world above, but rather as a mechanism, which worked according to laws set by God, the heavenly architect. Thus, the science of astronomy and geography, rather than nature *per se*, was elevated. Melanchthon expressed this in his reference to Man's *telos* to know:

I would say how much pleasantness and sweetness there is to that science, if I could expound it in words. But these things need to be known by experience. For each one the activity most appropriate to his nature is the most agreeable one, such as swimming for fish or singing for the nightingale; so men are necessarily affected by great pleasure when they contemplate the entire nature of things, when they find proportions of numbers and magnitudes when they perceive the harmony and agreement of the heavenly and inferior bodies and when they see that everything is made by a fixed law, in order to remind us of the Architect.[27]

Calvin was no less clear:

> Of his wonderful wisdom, both heaven and earth contain innumerable proofs; not only those more abstruse things, which are the subjects of astronomy, medicine, and the whole science of physics, but those things which force themselves on the view of the most illiterate of mankind, so that they cannot open their eyes without being constrained to witness them. Adepts, indeed, in those liberal arts, or persons just initiated into them, are thereby enabled to proceed much further in investigating the secrets of Divine Wisdom. Yet ignorance of those sciences prevents no man from such a survey of the workmanship of God, as is more than sufficient to excite his admiration of the Divine Architect. In disquisitions concerning the motions of the stars, in fixing their situations, measuring their distances, and distinguishing their peculiar properties, there is need of skill, exactness, and industry; and the providence of God being more clearly revealed by these discoveries, the mind ought to rise to a sublimer elevation for the contemplation of his glory.[28]

According to Melanchthon and Calvin, the divine architect's works were evident in nature for all to see. Divine providence was so immediate and so visible that every man could understand it. Still, with the aid of natural science (in the form of astronomy and geography) an educated Christian could even better contemplate divine glory and perceive 'the mind of God'. Because postlapsarian Man had completely lost his connection with God, symbolic and allegoric readings of the divine were ultimately removed from him. Depending on His will, Man could be saved only through God's salvation. Natural science, however, still offered a legitimate way of contemplating the divine and providing instruction about how God's power and wisdom appeared.

Protestants did not invent maps or geography, but Protestant theology gave them an unforeseen prestige and role. In his *Preface to On the Sphere* (1531), Melanchthon expressed his gratitude to those men who introduce the noble arts to beginners:

> [T]he greatest due to the most excellent and learned men who wrote introductory works for us of the most beautiful disciplines, that is, of astronomy and cosmography.[29]

Melanchthon's target was what he called 'ignorant theology'. As a humanist and a professor of classical languages, he could of course appreciate the benefits of grammar and dialectic, but these arts of the medieval curriculum were, in his view, insufficient basis for religious education:

> Church has need of many arts. For in order to judge and to explain correctly and distinctly complicated and obscure things, it is not sufficient to know the common precepts of grammar and dialectic, but varied knowledge is needed.[30]

Thus he emphasized broad learning and the Church's need for 'liberal education': 'not only knowledge of grammar, but also of the skill of many other arts and of philosophy.'[31] In an oration delivered in 1536 (in Wittenberg, where he was dean of the faculty of arts), Melanchthon praised the importance of astronomy and geography: 'the science that teaches the laws of the movements of the heavens, and indicates the sizes, spaces, distances and boundaries of the regions'. Although he admits that in the University of Wittenberg 'these divine arts' were not 'disparaged', he nevertheless felt it was his duty to encourage the young to study astronomy and geography, since they were practised 'more sluggishly' than should have been the case.[32]

In a pragmatic manner, Melanchthon outlined the benefits that astronomy and geography could provide to theologians: navigation, administration and calendar calculations. However, maps seem to have had a concrete sacral meaning for Melanchthon, as is evident from his sermon 'On astronomy and geography' (1536), in which he preached about the benefits of geographical maps or 'paintings':

> Every day in our prayers, we need to contemplate the land where the Son of God dwelt and was made a sacrifice, and we need to think of the place where the heavenly voice first sounded. [... ...] Since the prayers of the mind need to dwell in these places every day, what sloth not to think where in all lands they are! Even the uneducated wish to see these paintings.'[33]

Maps of biblical places thus had special value in religious practice: they were used for contemplation and prayer. It is interesting that Melanchthon added that 'even the uneducated wish to see these paintings'. As we consider how the Reformed churches gradually began to discard a whole tranche of popular religious imagery (in the form of saints, angels and demons), it is easy to understand how these geographical maps, which could provide at least some instruction for the illiterate, must have held special value. For Calvin, science was gift from God, a great blessing that not only could, but should, be used:

> Now, if it has pleased the Lord that we should be assisted in physics, logic, mathematics, and other arts and sciences, by the labour and ministry of the impious [pagan philosophers], let us make use of them; lest, if we neglect to use the blessing therein freely offered to us by God, we suffer the just punishment of our negligence.[34]

Besides the important role given to geography and astronomy, we should also bear in mind the quite evident demand for legitimate images that resulted from the denial of religious images. This must have been a serious problem, particularly in the Calvinist context, in which iconoclasm soon gave way to a profound iconophobia. Geographical maps could pass even the most puritan norms, as Patrick Collinson suggests in his study of the English iconoclasm of the second Reformation:

> The real extent of practical Iconophobia in Jacobean England is unexplored and for the most part unexplorable. If the inventory of the household maintained at York by Henry Hastings third earl of Huntingdon means what it says, the earl had no pictures on the walls whatsoever: only maps, non-representational floral hangings, a table of the Ten Commandments in a frame and 'one table in frame contayninge the cause and damnation'.[35]

Geographical maps were an accepted way of creating images, and their didactic value for the illiterate population did not escape either Calvin's or Melanchthon's notice. 'Even the uneducated wish to see these paintings',[36] Melanchthon said of maps in his oration on astronomy and geography. In this light, the introduction of maps into Protestant bibles (especially those printed in Calvinist Geneva) seems less coincidental. The wider view of the relationship between Protestantism and maps still remains to be explored further here.

Now, it is time to provide a tentative summary of the relationship between Protestant theological thought and sixteenth-century cartography. As I proposed earlier, the stylistic change in cartography can be interpreted as a competition between the *as-above, so-below paradigm* and the *providence paradigm*. The basic values behind these two paradigms were the same: the aim of knowing God. In the *as-above, so-below paradigm*, divine transcendental ideas were also present on earth. Regardless of the differences between Aristotelian and Platonic thought, late medieval ontology allowed both that the divine could be present in the mundane and that Man could, under favourable circumstances, grasp some knowledge of the divine. Moreover, medieval causality by and large considered that individual beings could be causally responsible units, and thus knowledge of the qualities and aims of individual beings could be an acceptable way of creating a coherent worldview. The ontology that allowed the champions of the *as-above, so-below paradigm* to presume that divinity was present here on earth thus provided a legitimate method of knowing God – through the interpretation of the divine message of each being in the light of Scripture. For supporters of the *as-above, so-below paradigm*, the world was an encrypted symbol, whose referent was God. Thus symbolic art, frescoes, murals, icons and mappamundis, all of which decrypted the symbolic language of the world, were acceptable ways of interpreting the divine. Of course, we have to admit that maps as a form of expression would not have served the agenda of the *as-above, so-below paradigm* particularly well. It is therefore little wonder that, as David N. Livingstone notes, mapping did not flourish considerably before the Renaissance:

> In pre-Reformation Germany the cognitive content of geography, judging by the standard of Vincenticus's *Speculum Naturae*, was a conventional Catholic synthesis of biblical cosmogony and Aristotelianism. Its emphasis was on interpreting the creation; but it amounted to little more than classical geography squeezed into a biblical mould.[37]

I think that the power of this paradigm is not in its inclusion – what could be done with it – but in its exclusion – that is, what is denied. If we think now of the *providence paradigm*, it is clear that it could greatly benefit from the pre-existing forms in cartographical production. Its significance lies in how it modified these forms, what it excluded and the central place it gave to cartography within the changing worldview. The aim of the *providence paradigm* was also knowledge of God. Nonetheless, the denial of the *as-above-so-below* principle erased the divine from the world. Immanence and transcendence were absolutely separated, resulting in major secularization. Symbolic references to connections between the mundane and the divine were banned. Consequently, within the *providence paradigm* only testimonies of immanent reality were permissible. These transformations accord with the qualitative changes of cartography during the sixteenth century. Maps could no longer be co-synchronous: they were only supposed to depict immanent reality. Symbolic language was banned, because no creature could symbolize the divine. At the same time, nature was seen as an immediate proof of God's providence. Nevertheless, this providence was not to be grasped through symbolic readings. Providence was evident through objectification, using methods independent of observers' cognitive abilities (such as mathematization and visual algorithms). Sebastian Münster's *Cosmographia* was the first scientific work to adhere completely to this paradigm. Its topographical city maps do not contain obvious symbols; instead, they provide an illusion of the representation of immanent reality. Co-synchronous components were removed from the maps of *Cosmographia*, and the author was eager to inform his readers about the methods and mathematical or technical devices that had been used to gather the information contained in the book.

The Protestants behind atlas production

Some interesting features emerge when we examine the history of French cartography, especially the period when the first atlases or compendiums (books that assembled maps and topographical views) began to emerge. The first point of interest is the extent to which the production of such books was an international business rather than an enterprise that was tightly controlled by the French. For instance, the very first book classified as an atlas in Mireille Pastoureau's constitutive catalogue of French Atlases (Bernhard von Breidenbach's, *Des Sainctes Peregrinations de Iherusalem*) was printed in Lyon in 1488 by two Germans (Michel Topié and Jacques Heremberck) and its city views have been attributed to a native of Utrecht (Erhard Reuwich).[38] When it comes to the Latin editions of Ptolemy's *Geography* (published in Strasbourg in 1513, 1520 and 1522), which Pastoureau likewise has included in her catalogue, it is by no means clear that these works should be considered to be French at all. Even though the city of Strasbourg in the north-eastern corner of Alsace certainly was in French territory, the printers and authors of these books came from surrounding areas in Germany.[39] The 1525 edition of Ptolemy's *Geography* was also prepared by non-French authors – three men from Nüremberg.[40] Although the 1535 and 1540 editions of *Geography* were printed by two Lyonnais brothers, Melchior and Gaspard Trechsel, the work's textual descriptions were written by a Spaniard called Michel Servet.

Table 1. French atlases before 1575, after Mireille Pastoureau (1984). Unorthodox i.e. 'protestantizing' or 'Anabaptist' authors have been emphasized.

1488	B. von Breidenbach, Des Sainctes Pérégrinations de Ihérusalem
	B. von Breidenbach, le Saint Voiage et pèlerinage de la cité saincte de Hiérusalem
1513	C. Ptolémée, Géographie
1517	B. von Breidenbach, la Grant Voyage de Ihérusalem
1520	C. Ptolémée, Géographie
1522	B. von Breidenbach, le Grant Voyage de Ihérusalem
1522	Ptolemy's Geography
1525	Ptolemy's Geography
1535	Michel Servet, Ptolemy's Geography
1541	Michel Servet, Ptolemy's Geography
1552	G. Guéroult, Premier Livre des figures et pourtraitz des villes.
1553	G. Guéroult, Épitomé de la corographie d'Europe
1556	G. Guéroult, Épitomé de la corographie d'Europe
1564	A. du Pinet, Plantz, pourtraitz et descriptions de plusieurs villes
1575	Sebastian Münster & F. de Belleforest, Cosmographie universelle

Foreign domination within French publishing was not confined to atlases: it also characterized sixteenth-century French map publishing as a whole. France entered the European map market relatively late, and in the sixteenth century the country lacked both cartographic skills and publishing facilities.[41] However, during the first half of the century, the city of Lyon stands out from among the many dispersed centres of publication. Lyon was a politically, economically and culturally remarkable city (Picture 1). Its favourable position in the eastern corner of the kingdom benefited the city's economy and created an international atmosphere. Lyon was a remarkable commercial centre: its fairs attracted merchants from neighbouring countries, and its flourishing financial sector was largely dominated by German and Italian bankers. Foreign influences were also reflected in Lyonnais map publishing. In particular, the early publications were, according to Catherine Hoffman, strongly influenced by German models. Foreign influences and the importance of Lyon are connected to the third essential character of sixteenth-century French map publishing: Protestantism.

If we take the published atlases as landmarks which incorporate some of the broader currents in map publishing, the Protestant influence in

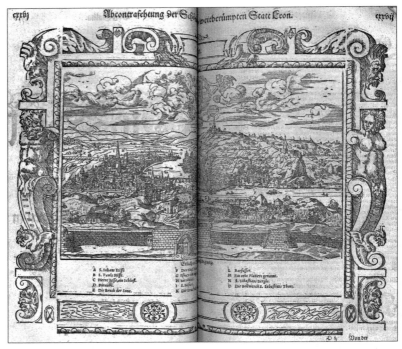

Picture 1. 'Abcontrafehtung der Schönen und weitberuempten Statt Leon.' In Münster, Sebastian, *Cosmographey – gemeine Beschreibung alle mittnächtigen Länder* (Basel, 1577), Fredrikson Map Collections, University of Jyväskylä, Finland. This intaglio portrait of the city of Lyon was used in Guillaume Gueroult's *Épitomé de la corographie* (1553) without the grotesque framing that was added later when the view was reprinted in Antoine du Pinet's *Plantz, povrtraitz et descriptions* (1564). Mireille Pastoureau (1984) has attributed the origin of these intaglio copies back to the woodcuts of Münster's *Cosmographia*. It is an interesting detail, that here in this 1577 version of Münster's *Cosmographia* the Lyonnese copperplate has been used again – this time with German texts – instead of the original woodcuts. Thus the copy has proven to be as good as the original. Photograph by Ismo Puhakka and Heikki Rantatupa.

sixteenth-century France is not merely conspicuous: there were certain links between these authors which suggest a more profound affair. As discussed above, one could question whether the Latin publications of Ptolemy's *Geography*, printed by foreigners at the outskirts of kingdom, were in fact French at all. A somewhat analogous judgment can also be made of Breidenbach's *Peregrinations*. It is true that these 'Pilgrim

44

stories' included relatively accurate views, which certainly provided topographical details of the places described, but it is arguable whether their intention was understood as cartographic (that is, chorographic). Rather, it seems that these views were a continuation of the medieval genre of moralized geography, in which frequently conventionalized and idealized city views served better as symbols than as accurate descriptions of geographical realities.[42] In this light, the first *scientific* atlas of France was the 1535 edition of Ptolemy's *Geography,* edited by Michel Servet, a controversial Protestant thinker.[43] After the two editions of Servet's version of *Geography,* the next five atlases published in France were all edited and printed in Lyon by Protestants. However, this group of Protestant authors was very limited: Michel Servet, Guillaume Guéroult and our pastor, Antoine du Pinet.

Michel Servet, the son of a notary, was born in Villa-nova in Aragon in 1509. He was educated in the liberal arts and classical languages by the Dominicans. He showed talent in his studies, and in 1526 he was sent to Toulouse to study Law. In 1528, at the age of nineteen he was appointed private secretary to Juan de Quintana (the confessor of Charles the Fifth and a professor at the University of Paris). Servet's profession soon took him to Italy and Germany, but the death of Quintana in 1529 left him to his own resources.[44]

Servet had been in contact with several prominent reformists. In 1530 he paid a visit to Johannes Oecolampadius in Basel, where he remained for six months, earning his living by correcting prints. In 1531 Servet met Martin Bucer and Wolfgang Fabricius Köpfel Capito in Strasbourg. During this time his Protestant confession strengthened, and later that year he published his controversial book *De trinitatis erroribus* ('The errors concerning the trinity'), which was followed by *Dialogorum de Trinitate libri duo* ('Dialogues on the Trinity in two volumes') in 1532 and *De Justitia Regni Christi* ('The Justice of rule of Christ') in 1534. In these texts he criticized the theology of the trinity and expressed his own view of the singularity of God. Servet argued that neither the Holy Spirit nor Jesus were separate divine beings. According to Servet, the divine *Logos* was incarnated in Jesus, a mortal man, and thus it was not Jesus that was eternal but the *Logos* that had manifested in him.

Servet's view was soon condemned by Lutherans and Roman Catholics alike. Soon after the publication of De *Trinitatis erroribus* on 5 August 1531, Johannes Oecolampadius sent a letter to Martin Bucer, in which he informed Bucer of the heretical views of their recent guest and uttered his intention to warn Luther of this great danger:

I beseech you in particular to keep a watchful eye over it, and to make an apology for our church at least, in your Confutation inscribed to the Emperor. We know not how that beast came to creep among us. He wrest all the passages of the Scripture to prove that the Son is not coeternal and consubstantial with the Father, and that the man Christ is the Son of God.[45]

Servet's views also attracted the attention of the Inquisition, and Servet was soon forced to escape from his sejour in Strasbourg to Paris, where he hid under a false name. There are some indications that Servet might have met Calvin during his time in Paris, and at the very least it seems clear that they tried to arrange a meeting.[46]

In 1535, however, Michel Servet reappeared in Lyon, where, according to several sources, he worked as a corrector and translator for two printer-publisher brothers, Melchior and Gaspard Treschel. The Treschels had bought the carvings of Ptolemy's *Geography* from Johannes Grüningen, who had printed his edition of *Geography* some ten years earlier. The new text that Servet composed for his work was based upon this earlier edition.[47] Servet included a somewhat controversial note on the map of Palestine, in which he declared that experience of merchants and pilgrims showed that this land was uncultivated, sterile and lacked any sweetness. This, of course, went against the testimony of Moses, who had described Palestine as the land of milk and honey. Later, during Servet's trial in Geneva this passage was cited as one of his heresies. He was subsequently condemned and executed. The death of Michel Servet in 1553 and the two French atlases discussed below are connected in a somewhat surprising manner.

The next two atlases to appear, *Premier livre des figures et pourtraitz des villes* (1552) and *Épitomé de la corograhie d'Europe* (1553), were the result of the collaboration of two men: humanist and emblemist Guillaume Guéroult (1507–1564) and printer-publisher Balthazar Arnoullet (1517–1556).[48] Guéroult had married Arnoullet's sister and worked for the publisher as a poet and corrector of prints. The connection between these two men and Michel Servet is quite interesting. Favouring Protestantism, Guéroult had left his birthplace in Normandy and travelled to Geneva.[49] In Geneva, however, he had joined the native Genevan party (led by Amy Perrin), which opposed Calvin and the authority of his consistory. As a result, he was soon forced to leave the city and emigrated to Lyon somewhere between 1548 and 1549.[50] It was probably during this time that Guéroult first came into contact with Michel Servet. In 1551

Guéroult and Arnoullet secretly printed Michel Servet's most important work, *Christianismi Restitutio*, in which Servet summarized many of his revolutionary ideas about theology and science.[51] (His discussion of the pulmonary circulation system of blood, for example, was ahead of its time and was not widely disseminated before William Harvey's famous dissections in 1616.) No matter how close Servet's views on the divine guidance of nature were to those held by Melanchthon and Calvin, his religious views were unsustainable in many respects. In *Restitutio* Servet criticized both Calvin's and Melanchthon's views on the trinity. He also attacked the Holy Roman Church, insulting the Pope, whom he regarded as the Antichrist.[52] The *Restitutio* was soon to prove costly for all those involved in its publication (Servet, Guéroult and Arnoullet).

However, we should first return to the atlases prepared by Guéroult and Arnoullet. In 1550 Arnoullet received a privilege from the king to publish *Description de l'Europe* (as a two-part volume).[53] In 1552 a trial version of the book was released. *Premier livre des figures et pourtraitz des villes* was a modest work both in length and in its print run. *Premier livre* consisted of seven views of cities, of which five were taken from Sebastian Münster's *Cosmographia*. During the following year, 1553, the second version was published as *Épitomé de la corographie d'Europe*. *Épitomé* contained maps of Europe and France and nineteen city views (all of which, save two, had their origins in Münster's *Cosmographia*).[54] Although *Épitomé* was supposed to be a two-volume publication, the second part was never published.

We cannot be sure whether or not, after the publication of Michel Servet's *Restitutio*, Calvin (who had received letters from Servet) made the Inquisition aware of the presence of these heretics in Lyon. Nevertheless, Arnouillet and Servet were both brought before the Inquisition in 1553, as William Drummond describes:

> Servetus had not the same good fortune. He was pursued, from the commencement of the process, with determined hostility. Arnoullet, the printer, was summoned to attend his examination, but being absent, his brother-in-law, Gueroult, corrector of press, was ordered to appear, but him no criminating information could be gathered. [... ...] the 4th of April a grand meeting was held at the castle of Roussillon, and after mature consultation, it was concluded that M. de Villaneuva, physician and B. Arnoullet should let custody, and detained as prisoners, to answer on their sincerity to the charges that should be brought against them.[55]

The inquisition condemned Servet to be burned, but he escaped (although the exact circumstances remain obscure). Soon after this, Servet and Guéroult were arrested in Geneva by the Calvinists.[56] After a short period of imprisonment Guéroult was released, and he escaped to the lands of the duke of Savoy. Servet did not fare so well: he was condemned to death by the Genevan consistory and was burned along with his heretical books. Balthazar Arnoullet died in 1556 and so the second part of *Épitomé* never materialized.

The editor of the next atlas to be published, Antoine du Pinet, was also a Protestant with a connection to Calvin (although his relationship with Calvin was slightly less fraught than that 'enjoyed' by Servet and Guéroult). According to Madeleine Lazard, Antoine du Pinet had been a friend of Calvin since their youth. They had both studied under the direction of Andre d'Alciat and Melchior Wolmar. The latter taught them Greek and Latin and converted them to Lutheranism. In 1536 Calvin appointed Du Pinet as pastor of Villa-la-Grand in Chablais.[57] Du Pinet also worked as Calvin's assistant, correcting his works and translating his texts from Latin into French during Calvin's period of exile in Strasbourg (1538–1540). During this time, he also helped Calvin to stay in contact with his printer, Jean Gerard.[58] However, in 1548, there was a rupture in the relationship between Du Pinet and Calvin in 1548. Madeleine Lazard has argued that the critique of the Calvinist regime by the inhabitants of Franc-Comtois persuaded Du Pinet to turn against his reformist friend. Irana Backus has brought to light letters written by Calvin, in which he triumphantly announces that he has crushed his opponents and forced Du Pinet to leave Geneva.[59] Whatever prompted his departure, Antoine du Pinet did leave Geneva and settle in Lyon in 1548.

Du Pinet was a productive humanist and translator. However, he was not opposed to plagiarism, when it served his purposes. He was also a fervent opponent of the Roman Catholic Church and published several propagandistic against the papal chair. The intellectual character of these works was not always very original, as Irena Backus has highlighted in her study of Du Pinet's *Apocalyptic exegesis*.[60] However, Du Pinet's character was probably better suited to the study of the humanities and science than to theological concerns. He translated Pliny's *World History* into French and edited one of the first herbal manuals *Historia Plantarum*. However, it is his book of topographical city views, *Plantz, pourtraitz et descriptions de plusieurs villes et forteresses*, that is of most interest to this study.

Although he was certainly their contemporary, we do not know whether or not Antoine du Pinet ever had any personal contact with Guéroult,

Servet or Arnoullet. Du Pinet left Geneva during the same year as Gué-roult, and they lived in the same areas in Geneva and Lyon for about ten years. However, we can trace an indisputable literary connection between Du Pinet and Guéroult: *Plantz, pourtraitz et descriptions* is, for the most part, an extended copy of Guillaume Guéroult's *Épitomé*. Du Pinet and his printer-publisher, Ian D'Ogerolles, reproduced not only all nineteen views that had already appeared in Guéroult's work, but also his textual descriptions. It is intriguing that the source for additional views was, once again, Münster's *Cosmographia*. At least thirty-one of the forty-two maps and views in Du Pinet's works originated directly or indirectly in the *Cosmographia*.

Münster's *Cosmographia* was an extremely influential work. In addition to the replication of its maps in Guéroult's and Du Pinet's works, *Cosmographia* was itself reissued five times in Basel (in 1552, 1556, 1560, 1565 and 1568) by Heinrich Petri, Münster's own publisher.[61] (In this context we should also remember the later 1575 Parisian edition of *Cosmographia*, edited by François Belleforest.) Why do I tend to view Münster's *Cosmographia* as paradigmatic, rather than claim that Guéroult and Du Pinet had simply plagiarized Münster? Because in their maps and views they followed the same visual standards as Münster. All the images in their books were faithful descriptions of *immanent* reality, without symbolization or co-synchronous elements. If there had been no paradigm, why would these printers not have added other kinds of maps and views? This 'paradigm' should not be understood simply as a set of shared theoretical commitments. Both Du Pinet and Münster explicitly explained their methodological principles, and these principles were the same. However, the core of the paradigm does not lie in these principles, but in the exemplary. The exemplary consists of successfully resolved puzzles. These examples also show what kinds of puzzles are admissible.[62] If we now turn to the atlases themselves, it is apparent that Münster's work has provided Guéroult and Du Pinet with a particular exemplary – in visual style, the graphic arrangement of the geographical information in these views, and in the style of textual descriptions. Münster's visual taxonomies, style and layout, have been reproduced faithfully within the covers of Guéroult's and Du Pinet's atlases. However, the influence or paradigmatic nature of *Cosmographia* still requires more detailed analysis.

The role of Protestantism in this process raises many further questions. It seems possible that Protestantism provided a social network that was able to move knowledge and paradigms from one city to another.

Basel, Strasbourg, Lyon and Geneva were meeting places for those who were critical of the dominant Roman Catholic ideas, and perhaps more importantly, they were also notable printing centres. Within this local network, the ideas of Ptolemy and, particularly, Sebastian Münster found favourable ground in which to grow and flourish. The gatekeepers of the worldview (that is, those who were able to define social values), great theologians such as Melanchthon, Calvin and Servet, were particularly positive towards mapping and natural science. However, within this space there were competing attitudes, which (armed with books and fire) were engaged in a struggle to define an exclusive worldview. At this stage of the research it is unclear to what extent Lutheran, Calvinist and Servetist attitudes towards mapping, geography and science differed. Broadly speaking, all three Protestant leaders adopted a largely positive stance towards mapping. However, those values that created a certain 'paradigm' or a worldview were tied to a social group and thus to its power to defend its particular worldview, using violent means if necessary. Servet's fate provides an illustrative example: without the necessary political power, Servet's attempt to oppose Calvinist and Catholic thinking led to his death.

A tentative conclusion and further signposts

Although a decisive conclusion about the interaction between Protestantism and cartography is still elusive, this study has hopefully been able to indicate that certain themes in Protestant thought generally favoured a scientific and cartographical interpretation of the world (rather than biblical frescoes or other forms of symbolic representations). This study has also discussed some of the ways in which religious background had an impact upon cartographical publications. Thus far, however, I have only been able to study only a very narrow group of map publishers and editors. These observations of cartographical practice, combined with findings on the theological plane, are encouraging.

It seems probable that Lyon's power as a cartographical centre waned as a result of the persecution that took place during the religious wars and the more sharply divided religious borders of the late 1560s and the 1570s. After this time, cartography did not regain its central position in France until the 1660s.[63] Interestingly the French map market (during the period between the flourishing of Lyon and the era of independent French cartography) was dominated by Flemish immigrant cartographers, who established themselves in Paris from the 1570s and who, perhaps not surprisingly, were largely Protestant.[64] The cartographical achievements of Catholic cartographers, such as the Jesuits, from the late 1580s onwards do not, in my view, weaken this hypothesis. The post-Tridentine Roman Catholic Church adopted many theological ideas relating to science, seeing and sacral images that had first been voiced by Melanchthon or Calvin. Gabriele Paleotti's treatise on sacred and profane images, *Discorso intorno alle imagini sacre e profane* (Bologna, 1582), analysed by Francesca Fiorani, provides a useful illustration of this transition in post-Tridentine Catholic thought:

> [Paleotti's] main theoretical assumption, based on the power of the images, was that images have the capacity, as he said, 'to delight, instruct, and move' the beholder. These three different functions of sacred images corresponded to three different levels of knowledge: sensual, rational, and spiritual. [... ...] But Paleotti's treatise contained, in addition, original ideas in relation to scientific illustrations, including maps. According to Paleotti, some profane images could function as sacred images, that is they could ultimately contribute to metaphysical contemplation. Paleotti dedicated to these special profane images an entire chapter entitled, 'Of profane images representing such images as wars, landscapes, buildings, animals, trees, plants and similar,' clarifying that these useful images were: 'geographical maps, [maps illustrating the] navigation to the Indies, descriptions of the sky and the stars, drawings of cities and countries, assaults of fortresses, [etc.]'.[65]

Paleotti's treatise was a decent compromise between classical Aristotelian aesthetics and the new Protestant-driven tendency to picture the profane world. These changes in theological thought soon enabled grandiose map murals to declare papal grandeur on the sacred walls of the Vatican. Broadly speaking from the beginning of seventeenth century onwards maps were adopted across Europe as the necessary and proper means by which nature should be described. Thus the stage was set for the great cartographical centuries that followed.

One more area for further examination should be raised here. Svetlana Alpers's detailed analysis has left us in no doubt as to the cartographical character of Dutch oil painting. However, the reasons behind dramatic differences in style between, for example, Dutch art and contemporaneous Italian art are less clear. It seems to me that, in her eminent and classic study, Alpers may have erred by excluding the Calvinist influence from her discussion of possible causes. One wonders why more than ninety per cent of the illustrations in Alpers's book date from the post-Reformation era, given that she argues that this pictorial phenomenon, which flourished in a Protestant state, really predated the Reformation. Her claim that 'the very centrality and trust to images seems to go against the most basic Calvinist tenet – trust in Word' seems to require further examination. Could one not also argue that when Calvinism outlawed the right of images to express the divine symbolically, the natural world still remained to be depicted? Thus one could argue that, with the intention of proving that their paintings were not meant for adoration or idolatry, Dutch painters aimed to create a descriptive surface, which would be nothing more than a faithful mirror or a map charting the divine providence of the natural world. Furthermore, although she highlights the resemblances between Dutch art and the thought of Francis Bacon and Constantijn Huygens, Alpers does not seem to recognize parallel similarities between Bacon or Huygens and Calvin, even though they are sometimes quite explicit. Huygens cited by Alpers:

> Nothing can compel us to honour more fully the infinite wisdom and power of God the Creator unless, satiated with the wonders of nature that up till now have been obvious to everyone – for usually our astonishment cools as we grow familiar with nature through frequent contact – we are led into this second treasure-house of nature, and in the most minute and disdained of creatures meet with the same careful labour of the Great Architect, everywhere an equally indescribable majesty.[66]

Calvin in *Institutions of Christian Religion*:

> Of his wonderful wisdom, both heaven and earth contain innumerable proofs; not only those more abstruse things, which are the subjects of astronomy, medicine, and the whole science of physics, but those things which force themselves on the view of the most illiterate of mankind, so that they cannot open their eyes without being constrained to witness them. Adepts, indeed, in those liberal arts, or persons just initiated into them, are thereby enabled to proceed much further in investigating the secrets of Divine Wisdom. Yet ignorance of those sciences prevents no man from such a survey of the workmanship of God, as is more than sufficient to excite his admiration of the Divine Architect. In disquisitions concerning the motions of the stars, in

fixing their situations, measuring their distances, and distinguishing their peculiar properties, there is need of skill, exactness, and industry; and the providence of God being more clearly revealed by these discoveries, the mind ought to rise to a sublimer elevation for the contemplation of his glory.[67]

Thus to conclude this still somewhat meandering and tentative attempt to illuminate probable links between Protestantism and cartography, one is forced to mention that in light of this passage it might be incorrect to argue that Calvinists turned their backs on images or seeing. Something quite the opposite seems more probable: Calvinist theology, even more clearly than Protestant theology in general, introduced new standards for images. In sixteenth-century parlance, these standards were proposed vis-à-vis the ability of images to express the divine. Having denied the ability of symbolic art to express the divine, the gaze now turned to nature and its description. If we look at the consequences of this shift in the Netherlands, where they are present in their most undiluted form, one cannot avoid the idea that the Reformation turned the world into a map.

Notes

1 'Et toutesfois en ceste corruption de nature, Dieu a laissé un iugement si bon à l'homme, pour le fait de cest Vniuers, qu'il n'y a chose, pour cachee ou eloignee qu'elle fut, que cest esprit tant soubelin n'ayt attaqué & enforcé voire iusques à la moëlle.'

2 A profound philosophical analysis of the world seen as a picture is presented in Martin Heidegger's essay *Die Zeit des Weltbildes: Gesamtausgabe*, I. Abteilung, Band 5, Frankfurt Am Main, Vittorio Klostermann, 1977, pp. 89–90.

3 Counter Reformation or Catholic Reformation adaptations of maps for theological purposes is beyond the scope of this study. However, it seems that similar voices which seemed to encourage the use of maps among Protestant theologians also came to be heard in the post Tridentine church (exemplified, for instance, by the Vatican's great map murals painted in the late 1570s.)

4 Buisseret 2003, p. xi.

5 Karrow 2007, p. 621.

6 Idem.

7 Woodward 2007, pp. 3–24.

8 Co-synchronous images incorporate elements from different temporal periods, that is, elements which did not necessarily exist co-synchronously, i.e. concurrently in reality. For instance, an ideal type of Rome in the Renaissance could represent lost monuments of antiquity and new buildings together in one plan or a map. These kinds of images could be explained in different narratives which followed different temporal synchrony. See for instance Besse & Dubourg Glatiny 2009.

9 Ibid, 10. It seems to me that Woodward is not familiar with how the conceptions

of images and the sacred differed in Protestant and Catholic theology. In Protestant theology in general, even more forcefully than in Calvinist thought, an image, as a product of a fallen Man, cannot have an immediate sacred function. The profane cannot grasp the divine. Although not *sacred*, Protestant maps could still have a *religious* function: depictions of nature could indirectly demonstrate God's divine providence in play.

10 Idem.
11 Idem.
12 Ibid, p. 8.
13 Campbell 1987, p. 371.
14 Ibid, p. 372.
15 Woodward 2007, p. 9.
16 Harrison 2005.
17 Crouzet 1995, p. 293: 'Le scandale, pour Calvin, tient dans le fait que, dans le culte de l'image, le signifié déborde sur le signifiant, ou que le représentant tend à s'emparer du représenté en l'enfermant en lui. Le visible prend possession de l'invisible, le fini absorbe l'infini.'
18 Idem.
19 Pico della Mirandola, *Heptaplus id est de Dei creatoris opere* (1489), quoted in E.H. Gombrich's *Symbolic Images*, London, Phaidon, 1972, p. 153.
20 John Calvin, *Institutes of Christian Religion* (1559), Book I, Chapter V, Translated by John Allen, Philadelphia, Presbyterian Board of Publication, 1844, p. 56.
21 Harrison 2005.
22 Työrinoja 2002.
23 Idem, 57.
24 John Calvin, *Institutes of Christian Religion* (1559), Book II, Chapter II, p. 183.
25 Idem.
26 Philip Melanchthon, 'Preface on the Sphere' (1531) in Philip Melanchthon, *Orations on Philosophy and Education*, Edited by Sachiko Kusukawa, Cambridge, Cambridge University Press, 1999, p. 106.
27 Philip Melanchthon, 'On astronomy and geography' (1559), in Philip Melanchthon, *Orations on Philosophy and Education*, Edited by Sachiko Kusukawa, Cambridge, Cambridge University Press, 1999, p. 118.
28 John Calvin, *Institutes of Christian Religion* (1559), Book I, Chapter V, pp. 56–57.
29 Philip Melanchthon, 'Preface on the Sphere', in Philip Melanchthon, *Orations on Philosophy and Education*, Edited by Sachiko Kusukawa, Cambridge, Cambridge University Press, 1999, p. 105.
30 Philip Melanchthon, 'On Philosophy' (1536), in Philip Melanchthon, *Orations on Philosophy and Education*, Edited by Sachiko Kusukawa, Cambridge, Cambridge University Press, 1999, p. 128.
31 Ibid., 126.
32 Philip Melanchthon, 'On astronomy and geography', in Philip Melanchthon, *Orations on Philosophy and Education*, Edited by Sachiko Kusukawa, Cambridge, Cambridge University Press, 1999, pp. 113–114.
33 Ibid., pp. 116–117.
34 John Calvin, *Institutes of Christian Religion* (1559), Book II, Chapter XVI, p. 248.
35 Collinson 2004, p. 348.
36 Melanchthon, 'On astronomy and geography', in Philip Melanchthon, *Orations on*

Philosophy and Education, Edited by Sachiko Kusukawa, Cambridge, Cambridge University Press, 1999, p. 117.

37 Livingstone 1992, p. 83.
38 Pastoureau 1984, pp. 85–87.
39 Ibid., pp. 371–377.
40 Ibid., p. 378.
41 Hofmann 2007, p. 1569.
42 Schultz 1978, pp. 425–474.
43 Pastoureau 1984, p. 380.
44 Drummond 1848.
45 Oecolampadius's letter to Bucer, dated 5 August 1531, in Drummond 1848, p. 12.
46 Beza 1836.
47 Pastoureau 1984, p. 380.
48 Ibid, p. 225.
49 Idem.
50 Balmas 1962.
51 Idem. See also Bainton 1936, p. 143.
52 Michel Servet, *Christianismi restitution,* Vienne en Dauphiné, B. Arnollat, 1553.
53 'Il est permis à Balthazar Arnoullet maistre Imprimeur de la Ville de Lyon, d'imprimer ou faire imprimer exposer & mettre en vente, la *Description de toute l'Europe*; dont le present liure intitulé, *l'Épitome du premier & second liure de la Corographie d'Europe,* depend.' Guillaume Guéroult, *Épitomé de la corographie d'Europe illustré des pourtraitz des villes plus renommées d'icelle,* Lyon, Arnoullet, 1553.
54 Guéroult, *Épitomé de la corographie d'Europe.* Also Pastoureau 1984, p. 225.
55 Drummond 1848, pp. 56–57.
56 Pastoureau refers to Gueroult and Arnoullet, Drummond to all three men.
57 Lazard 2003, p. 157
58 Ibid, p. 158.
59 Backus 2000, p. 38.
60 Ibid, p. 59.
61 McLean 2007, p. 346.
62 Kuhn 1970.
63 Petto 2007.
64 Hofmann 2007, p. 1576.
65 Fiorani 2005, pp. 152–153.
66 Constantijn Huygens quoted in Alpers 1983, p. 9.
67 Calvin, *Institutes of Christian Religion,* pp. 56–57.

Bibliography
Primary sources

Belleforest, François 1575. *La Cosmographie Vniverselle de tovt le monde.* Michel Sonnius, Paris.

Calvin, John 1844. *Institutes of Christian religion* (1536). Translated by J. Allen. Presbyterian Board of Publication, Philadelphia.

Guéroult, Guillaume 1553. *Épitomé de la corographie d'Europe illustré des pourtraitz des villes plus renommées d'icelle.* Arnoullet, Lyon.

Melanchthon, Philipp 1999. *Orations on Philosophy and Education.* Edited by S. Kasu-kawa. Cambridge University Press, Cambridge.

Servet, Michel 1553. *Christianismi restitutio. Totius ecclesiae apostolicae est ad sua limina vocatio, in integrum restituta cognitione Dei, fidei Christi, justificationis nostrae regenerationis baptismi et coenae Domini manducationis, restituto denique nobis regno coelesti, Babylonis impiae captivitate soluta, et Antichristo cum suis penitus destructo...,* B. Arnollat, Vienne en Dauphiné.

Pinet, Antoine du 1564. *Plantz, povrtraitz et descriptions de plvsieurs villes et forteresses, tant de l'Evrope, Asie & Afrique, que des Indes, & terres neuues.* Ian D'Ogerolles, Lyon.

Literature

Alpers, S. 1983. *The Art of Describing. Dutch Art in the Seventeenth Century.* John Murray, London.

Andrews, M. 1999. *Landscape and Western Art.* Oxford University Press, Oxford.

Backus, I. 2000. *Reformation Readings of the Apocalypse. Geneva, Zurich, and Wittenberg.* Oxford University Press, Oxford.

Bainton, R. H. 1936. 'Servetus and the Genevan Libertines.' *Church History*, Vol. 5 (2), pp. 141–149.

Balmas, E. 1963. *Montaigne a Padova e altri studi sulla letteratura francese del cinque-cento.* Liviana, Padova.

Besse, J.-M. & Dubourg Glatiny, P. 2009. 'Cartographier Rome au XVIe siècle (1544–1599), décrire et reconstituer.' In Romano, A (ed.) *Rome et la science moderne entre Renaissance et Lumières.* Ecole française de Rome, Rome, pp. 369–413.

Buisserett, D. 2003. *The Mapmakers' Quest. Depicting New Worlds in Renaissance Europe.* Oxford University Press, Oxford.

Campbell, T. 1987. 'Portolan Charts from the Late Thirteenth Century to 1500.' In Harley, J. B. (ed.) *The History of Cartography,* Vol. 1: *Cartography in Prehistoric, Ancient, and Medieval Europe and the Mediterranean.* The University of Chicago Press, Chicago, pp. 371–463.

Crouzet, D. 1995. *La Genèse de la Réforme Française 1520–1560.* Sedes, Paris.

Dillenberger, J. 1999. *Images and Relics. Theological Perceptions and Visual Images in Sixteenth-Century Europe.* Oxford University Press, Oxford.

Drummond, W. 1848. *Michael Servetus, the Spanish Physician, Who for the Alleged Crime of Herest, Was Entrapped, Imprisoned, and Burned by John Calvin the Reformer in the City of Geneva, October 27, 1553.* John Chapman, London.

Fiorani, F. 2005. *The Marvel of Maps. Art, Cartography and Politics in Renaissance Italy.* Yale University Press, New Haven.

Gombrich, E. H. 1972. *Symbolic Images.* Phaidon, London.

Harley, J. B. 1987. 'Preface.' In Harley, J. B. (ed.) *The History of Cartography,* Vol. 1: *Cartography in Prehistoric, Ancient, and Medieval Europe and the Mediterranean.* The University of Chicago Press, Chicago, pp. xv–xxi.

Harrison, P. 2005. *The Fall of Man and the Foundations of Science.* Cambridge University Press, Cambridge.

Heidegger, M. 1977. *Die Zeit des Weltbildes. Gesamtausgabe,* I. Abteilung, Band 5. Vittorio Klostermann, Frankfurt Am Main.

Hofmann, C. 2007. 'Publishing and the Map Trade in France, 1470–1670.' In Woodward, D. (ed.) *The History of Cartography*, Vol. 3: *Cartography in the European Renaissance*. The University of Chicago Press, Chicago, pp. 1575–1576.

Karrow, R. 2007. 'Centres of Map Publishing in Europe, 1472–1600.' In Woodward, D. (ed.) *The History of Cartography*, Vol. 3: *Cartography in the European Renaissance*. The University of Chicago Press, Chicago, pp. 611–621.

Kuhn, T. S 1970. *The Structure of Scientific Revolutions*. University of Chicago Press, Chicago.

Lazard, M. 2003. 'Antoine du Pinet, sieur de noroy, et la taxe de la boutique du pape.' *Revue d'histoire et de philosophie religieuses*, Vol. 83 (2), pp. 157–169.

Livingstone, D. N. 1992. *The Geographical Tradition. Episodes in the History of a Contested Enterprise*. Blackwell, Malden.

McLean, M. 2007. *The Cosmographia of Sebastian Münster. Describing the World in the Reformation*. Ashgate, Aldershot.

Merleau-Ponty, M. 1964. *L'oeil et l'esprit*. Gallimard, Paris.

Nietzsche, F. 1973. *Die Fröhliche Wissenshaft. Kritische Gesamtausgabe*, Abteilung 5, Band 2. Walter de Gruyter, Berlin.

Pastoureau, M. 1984. *Les Atlas Français XVIe–XVIIe siècles. Répertoire bibliographique et étude*. Bibliothèque nationale, Paris.

Petto, C. M. 2007. *When France Was King of Cartography. The Patronage and Production of Maps in Early Modern France*. Lexington Books, Lanham.

Schultz, J. 1978. 'Jacopo Barbari's View of Venice: Map Making, City Views, and Moralized Geography Before the Year 1500'. *The Art Bulletin*, Vol. 60 (3), pp. 425–474.

Turnbull, D. 2000. *Masons, Tricksters and Cartographers. Comparative Studies in the Sociology of Scientific and Indigenous Knowledge*. Routledge, London.

Työrinoja, R. 2002. 'God, Causality, and Nature. Some Problems of Causality in Medieval Theology.' in Martikainen, E. (ed.) *Infinity, Causality and Determinism. Cosmological Enterprises and their Preconditions*. Peter Lang, Frankfurt am Main, pp. 45–60.

Woodward, D. 2007. 'Cartography and the Renaissance: Continuity and Change'. In Woodward, D. (ed.) *The History of Cartography*, Vol. 3: *Cartography in the European Renaissance*. The University of Chicago Press, Chicago, pp. 3–24.

CHAPTER 2

Maps, Borders
and State-building

Kimmo Katajala

Introduction

Modern maps are created for many practical purposes. Maps help you to get from one place to another; they can be descriptions of the landscape that can allow one to manage in the wilderness, for example. Maps can also define ownership of land or the borders between the territories of parishes, communes, provinces and, finally, states. These borders are usually indicated by lines drawn on the map. Political maps which define the territories of states are probably the most familiar example of such linear borders. However, maps have not always been like this. Maps no longer serve some of their earlier purposes: the function of maps and mapping in society has changed over the centuries. The presentation of maps has also developed and changed fundamentally.

Do changes in maps reflect a different way of understanding one's living environment and its borders? During recent decades there has been a vibrant discussion among historians and social scientists about the early modern state-building process. This discussion is usually characterized as antagonism between the 'primordialists', who argue that territorial states with well-defined borders are an age-old phenomenon, and the 'modernists', who claim that the territorial state developed slowly during the early modern period and that the sovereign territorial state, with its well-defined and guarded linear borders, is a phenomenon that emerged with the nineteenth-century nation states. According to the 'modernists', medieval and early modern borders (that is, pre-eighteenth-century borders) were permeable and often zone-like frontiers.[1]

This discussion is in some ways connected to the history of cartography. If the territorial state (with linear and exact borders) had existed in classical antiquity, or at least during the Middle Ages, it is possible that these borders would be somehow present in maps of the period. On the other hand, if exact linear borders only existed from the late eighteenth century onwards and were preceded by permeable zone-like borders, how would such borders have been depicted in contemporary maps?

The history of mapping is usually presented as a development of drawing and measurement techniques; sometimes the connection between art and map drawing is discussed. Only quite recently have scholars paid attention to the connection between the development of administration and mapmaking.[2] The connection between state-building processes, the concept of borders and their relationship to how maps were drawn, is not often specifically addressed.[3]

The aim of this chapter is to look at early modern European maps and consider how and why borders are depicted in particular ways. The border between Sweden (Finland) and Russia is examined more closely as a case study. The Swedish and Russian states are often presented as age-old constructions that date back to the tenth century. The border between these two realms was a contentious issue from medieval times up until the beginning of the nineteenth century, when the territory of Finland was annexed to Russia. There is also quite extensive literature about the nature of this early border, a subject that has sometimes even provoked vigorous disputes.[4] Because of this, the northern border offers opportunities to compare the 'experiences' offered by old European maps.

The presupposition is that the concept of the border has not remained the same throughout history. The nature of the borders of medieval realms was different from those of eighteenth-century states. Therefore, descriptions of these maps are connected to discussions about the development of the territorial state and its borders. Here, by examining old maps and the ways in which borders are represented, I try to establish how the political border was understood at different times, bearing in mind discussions between 'primordialists' and 'modernists' about the nature of the early modern state.

The Nordenskiöld Collection (NC) in the National Library of Finland (Helsinki University Library) has provided the primary source material for my research. The collection consists of over 24,000 maps drawn before 1800 – the oldest of these maps dates from the fifteenth century. The Nordenskiöld Collection is one of the most remarkable collections of old European maps in the world. In this chapter the European maps in the collection drawn between 1478 and 1700 are examined, with special attention paid to border issues.[5] The cartographic material relating to the Swedish (Finnish)–Russian early modern border was found in the National Archives of Sweden (SRA) and from Uppsala University Library in Sweden. In addition, maps found in cartographic literature have been referred to in my analysis and interpretation.

From mappamundi to the maps of Ptolemy

Maps, in some form, are perhaps almost as old as the intellectual life of humankind. The ancient cultures of China and the Far East as well as the Hellenic culture all used maps for various purposes. Accounts of the history of cartography often mention Herodotus' description (from the fifth century BC) of the map of Aristagoras, prince of Miletus. Although we only have literal descriptions of what these ancient maps were like, we do know that the people and places of the known world were depicted in them. Moreover, we know that the Greeks and the Romans indicated the shapes of coasts of islands (such as Sardinia) or the outlines of a territory (in this case the Libyan territory) with a line.[6] This is not, of course, the equivalent of a more modern borderline. However, it does show us that enclosing a territory within a line was a familiar feature within cartographical depictions in Antiquity.

Many of the skills and knowledge of antiquity were lost and forgotten during the Middle Ages. This was also the case for maps and mapmaking. In every case, the medieval maps that have survived are maps without borders. Medieval maps can be roughly divided into three categories: mappamundi, portolan charts and local maps.

The mappamundi have drawn the most attention from scholars interested in medieval maps, perhaps because they seem so obscure from a modern perspective. In fact the mappamundi were not maps in the modern sense: rather, they were presentations of the known Christian world with the holy town of Jerusalem at their centres. The aim of those who made the mappamundi was not to present places that one could travel to, nor was it to show where and how territories of political units were located. Their aim was to map those people living in the Christian world and those who would soon be Christianized; the latter group was depicted on the edges of the world and the map. These maps were drawn to glorify God rather than to fulfil any practical purpose.[7]

The invention of the mariner's compass had a significant impact upon mapmaking. Portolan charts, which came into use in the thirteenth century, were a kind of predecessor of modern sea charts. In these maps the coastline – usually of the Mediterranean or the Black Sea – and ports are marked in a very precise manner. Instead of longitudes and latitudes, the portolan charts have 'degree roses'. Each 'rose' provides the centre for thirty-two degree lines, which criss-cross the map. The earliest surviving portolan chart, the Pisano map (c. 1290), charts the Mediterranean coasts and was drawn using two degree roses (with sixteen degree lines), one rose having its centre on the western side of Sardinia and the other in the Hellenic archipelago. It was possible to navigate from one place to another using a compass with these degree roses. However, portolan charts were not useful when attempting to estimate the location of a ship on the open seas. In portolan charts, inland areas have usually been left blank: there are no towns, geographical landforms or borders of political units, realms or states. Portolan charts were in use from at least the latter half of the thirteenth century until the seventeenth century.[8]

In the Middle Ages there were also some astonishingly well-drawn local maps, particularly of the British Isles. The most famous of these are probably Matthew Paris's map (dating from around the 1250s) and the Gough Map (around the 1360s). They provide a great deal of information about places, rivers and, in the case of the Gough Map, roads. However, no borders of counties are visible on either map. The only thing resembling a border on these maps is Hadrian's Wall, which divides Scotland from the other parts of the British mainland. On both maps it is depicted as an image of a wall rather than as an abstract line. We do not know exactly why these maps were drawn; however, it seems possible that they might have been used as tools of taxation or for military purposes.[9]

Claudius Ptolemy, a Greek geographer who lived in Alexandria during the first half of the second century AD, devised a way of drawing maps using a system of coordinates. He provided instructions for mapmaking in his major work *Geography*: each place, river, mountain or similar feature was given coordinates, nowadays called longitudes and latitudes, which in turn defined its position on the map. Ptolemy recorded coordinates for approximately 8,000 places.[10] However, the system of coordinates was forgotten for centuries. Medieval maps were drawn without latitudes and longitudes, or any other coordinates, until the works of Ptolemy were rediscovered at the beginning of the fifteenth century.[11] The significance of his work was soon understood, and during the fifteenth century maps bearing Ptolemy's name and system of coordinates were produced. Mistakes were corrected and new areas were mapped according to Ptolemy's instructions. These new maps were called '*Tabulae Novae*' or '*Tabulae Modernae*'. The development of printing techniques made it possible to produce printed series of Ptolemy's maps. The first such edition was printed in Bologna in 1477, followed rapidly by a second, printed in Rome the next year.[12] The adoption of the works of Ptolemy during the fifteenth century brought mapmaking to a level at which drawing borders with a degree of accuracy was technologically and ideologically possible. The aforementioned discussion between the 'primordialists' and 'modernists' was at its most fervent in the 1980s and so, as a result, medieval and late medieval borders became a popular topic of research in the 1990s. The question of linear or zone-like borders is not usually studied as keenly among those who research the early modern period. However, a fundamental question relating to our main topic, borders in early modern maps, is whether there were sharp linear borders between early modern states and realms or whether these areas were still zone-like permeable frontiers. Therefore, before looking at the maps of Ptolemy and other early modern maps from the late fifteenth and early sixteenth centuries, we must consider recent literature on medieval and late medieval borders. Only by these means can we possibly interpret the depiction of borders in early modern maps.

Similarities between ancient and late medieval borders

It is said that Rome was an ever-expanding empire without ends. Undoubtedly constructions such as rows of castles, citadels – and Hadrian's Wall in Britain – were built in frontier territories. These are often viewed as the borderline of the Roman Empire. However, ideologically, the areas behind Hadrian's Wall and the rows of citadels were just waiting to be conquered and annexed by Rome. Thus, the study of antiquity and the medieval period seems to suggest that the formation of borders has its origins in local communities rather than at the state level. The first borders were established between the yards, estates, clans, villages or other communal societies, parishes and counties. Although the Roman Empire itself was without fixed outer borders, inside the Empire estates, latifundia and provinces had well defined boundaries, often marked in the terrain by marker-stones or other suitable objects. In the British Isles these boundaries from the Roman period have formed the basis of many local borders, including those between certain parishes.[13]

Della Hooke and Michael Reed, who have studied borders in England during the Anglo-Saxon period (449–1066), argue that the borders between estates, villages and parishes were already well defined. However, they usually followed natural formations such as rivers, ditches, hedges or roads. Sometimes, when a border had to cross a moor or some other area without any suitable linear natural formations, it would be viewed as a straight line. However, this straight 'line' between two border-markers could, for example, pass through the middle of a densely populated village. In reality this was not the case and such a village would belong in its entirety to a single jurisdictional territory. Therefore, the medieval straight 'borderline' must be understood as an abstraction rather than a real dividing line on the ground. Local people were well aware of the borders of their estates, villages and communities. Often these local borders also formed the borders of the medieval kingdoms. Kings and knights were not aware of their territory in any great detail; they were more interested in their subjects as taxpayers and as a labour force. The borders of the kingdom were known only through local practices.[14]

The changing borders of the medieval Carolingian Empire (c. the ninth century) were located in the middle of Europe. Although the Franks and the Saxons both built up systems of castles and forts, there was no frontier line between these two chains of fortresses. However, the rivers Elbe, Hesse and Saale formed the basis of the frontiers of the expanding Carolingian Empire. Castles were built in strategic locations along these rivers and the lands between them. This system was very similar to that of the Roman frontier.[15] As Walter Pohl argues, 'Frontiers, so it seems, were not a matter of states, but of carefully surveyed agricultural property – not the business of Empires, but of *agrimensores*.'[16] Later, after the Carolingian Empire was divided in three according to the Treaty of Verdun (843), the rivers Scheldt, Meuse, Saône and Rhône formed the main section of the border between the kingdom that was later called France and the Holy Roman Empire. Political control was based upon fortresses but, although borders were fortified with castles, Daniel Power argues that the fixed lines of demarcation did not match this type of political control.[17]

The Frankish ruler of the borderland (*markgraf*) soon extended his power across the Elbe. By the eleventh century it was clear that the Elbe no longer formed the actual border between the Frankish Kingdom and the Holy Roman Empire. When Adam of Bremen (born before 1045 and died c.1081–1085) described the existing border of the Hamburg bishopric, the dominant natural formations mentioned were, again, rivers and streams, although he also referred to forests and individual objects such as stones and trees. According to Matthias Hardt, this border was not yet a strict and coherent line, but rather consisted of linear rivers, zone-like forests and sporadic orienting points such as stones and trees.

It was not until the thirteenth century that the bishopric began to extend the linear borderline to the forests and vegetation.[18] However, there is no proof that the medieval central powers had been interested in creating such lines. Giles Constable writes that 'frontiers and boundaries tended to be less clearly defined as the size of the unit increased. Few kingdoms had fixed borders'.[19] Medieval kings ruled over people rather than a precisely defined territory. In densely settled areas the local borders of estates, villages and dukedoms were increasingly well defined and began to be marked on the ground. The ecclesiastical borders of parishes and bishoprics followed the rule: borders of smaller units were more clearly defined; however they still enclosed people rather than territory.[20]

The border between the present-day Estonian territory and Russia is one of the oldest boundaries in Europe that has not undergone significant changes. In medieval times, it was the border between the Teutonic Order and the Tartu bishopric on one side and the 'city-states' of Novgorod and Pskov on the other. The first references to this border can be found in written sources from the early thirteenth century. The border between the Estonian territories of the Teutonic order and Novgorod ran from the Baltic Sea near the town of Narva and followed the river Narva to Lake Peipsi. The border between the Tartu bishopric and the Pskovian lands began at Lake Lämmijärv (the sound that connects Lake Peipsi and Lake Pskov) and continued along the rivers Võhandu, Mäda (a tributary of the Võhandu) and Piusa to Vastseliina, where a castle was built in the middle of the fourteenth century. According to Anti Selart, although at first sight this river and lake-based medieval border seems very clearly defined and fixed, in fact it was not. During the fifteenth century, settlers close to the border rivers had land-use and fishing rights, although now disputed, on both sides of the rivers. The division of disputed islands located in the rivers and lakes and agreements about settlers' rights did not take place any earlier than the fifteenth century. Some parts of the border between the rivers that crossed the lands and vast forests were still the subject of dispute in the seventeenth century. As Selart argues, although the border largely followed rivers, it was not a sharp linear division; however it can be 'considered as a slowly narrowing intermediate passage (*Grenzsaum*)'.[21]

Claes Tollin's study of border issues in southern parts of Sweden during the Viking Age (*c.* 800–1025) confirms that these patterns were also found in the European north. The borders between medieval local societies, villages and clans were denoted by several border-markers on the ground. The principles governing how the farms and areas of local communities should be distinguished from each other were defined in Swedish provincial laws, recorded in the twelfth and thirteenth centuries. According to these laws lakes, hills, mountains, stones and trees were acceptable border-markers. Lakes and rivers were the best markers because of their permanence; trees were least suitable for the purpose. According to Tollin, the borders between such markers were understood to be a straight line (Sw. *synrätt*, literally eyeshot).[22]

In conclusion, recent literature on medieval borders seems to be unanimous in its view that 'linear' natural formations – rivers, streams and mountain chains – formed the basis of medieval border formation. These were supplemented by zone-like borders such as forests, lakes and moors and 'point-shaped' border-markers including gorges, fords, stones, tree stumps and trees. The border between these points of orientation was understood to be an abstract line. However, this 'line' was not marked in the terrain or vegetation, nor was it understood to be literally 'straight'. Moreover, the first references to the idea of linear borderlines, which were extended to the forest or areas of vegetation, begin to emerge in local sources at the end of the medieval period. This is what we can expect to find in our primary source materials: the earliest maps of Ptolemy from the late fifteenth century and the European maps of the early sixteenth century.

The abstract border emerges in the maps of Ptolemy

The question of how borders and boundaries were represented in early modern maps is closely linked to general developments in map drawing. The relationship between the described object and the sign in the map changed significantly during the sixteenth century. Medieval maps usually depict a town, a mountain, a forest or other objects as a mimic image. There was, therefore, no need to explain the content of the markings on a map: a town looked like a town; a mountain was presented as a picture of a mountain. However, in some special cases, medieval maps would use abstract signs, whose connection to the object they represented was not based upon basic physical resemblance. In portolan charts, for example, small crosses were used to depict rocks. However, there was no need to provide an explanation for this abstract sign because everyone who used portolan charts already understood its meaning: they had been trained to read these early sea charts. It was a closed system of communication, obscure to the world outside. According to David Woodward, a system of abstract signs began to emerge in maps printed for a public audience during the first half of the sixteenth century. In these maps signs were explained using legends and slowly the system of signs became more coherent across all maps.[23]

David Buisseret looks at changes in map drawing from the perspective of art history. There was an immense change in both art and mapmaking between 1400 and 1500. Late medieval painters from the Netherlands and Italian Renaissance artists paid great attention to perspective and the realistic depiction of their subjects. Neo-Platonism, which found favour during the fifteenth and sixteenth centuries, presented a mathematical explanation for the presence of God and all that He had created. At the same time, the landscape became an important feature of the period's art. Artists began to use mathematical methods to create realistic pictures. For example, in 1525 Albrecht Dürer published his guide *Instruction in Mensuration with Compass and Triangle*, in which he outlined how to prepare exact and reliable topographical drawings.[24] This greatly influenced all visual presentations, in particular map drawing; many of those who are now known as famous Renaissance painters and artists also served as mapmakers to kings and princes.

The Nordenskiöld Collection contains the first editions of the printed atlases of Ptolemy (the first edition printed in Bologna in 1477 and the second, printed in Rome in 1478). An examination of the maps in these atlases clearly shows that natural formations were used as borders. On the map of the Frankish territory (later known as France), for example, the Rhine forms the border with the German areas to the east, and the Pyrenees form the southern border with the Iberian Peninsula (Map 3 see colour plate section 1, p. 1). A light handmade colouration on the map emphasizes the river's and the mountain chain's functions as borders. However, we do not know when this colouration was applied. It may well have been a later addition: there is no such colouration in the second edition published only a year later. Towns on these maps are marked by abstract dots, not by mimic images. Similarly, dotted lines represent rivers, but mountains and mountain chains are depicted as mimic images of mountains.[25]

Although in these maps from the 1470s the Frankish territory is presented as a single unit, the state of France did not yet exist. The English had been defeated in the Hundred Years War (1337–1453) about twenty-five years earlier, and the formation of the French kingdom was still in its infancy. The Frankish territory was a patchwork of rather independent provinces and dukedoms. Anjou, Provence, Maine and Burgundy were brought under the control of the French king in the 1480s; the northern parts of France and Bretagne in the 1490s; the dukedoms in the central parts of France in the 1520s; and the southernmost parts of France near the Pyrenees as late as the end of the sixteenth century. It would, therefore, have been quite inadequate or perhaps unthinkable to draw strong and abstract borderlines between the realms.

The atlas of Ptolemy from 1507 seems to be somewhat different. Looking at the map of the Iberian Peninsula, we can see quite strong, coloured borderlines between Granada, Hispania (Castile), Aragon, Catalonia, Navarre and Portugal. Even if we consider the colouration to be a later addition, we can, nevertheless, see some thin borderlines, unconnected to any natural formations, which indicate the limits of Granada and Portugal.[26] As is well known, the alliance of the kingdoms of Castile and Aragon was established by the marriage of Isabel and Ferdinand in the 1470s. The kingdom of Granada was taken from the Moors in 1498 and the kingdom of Navarre remained relatively independent until 1512. Portugal was a separate kingdom until the seventeenth century. The map of central Europe is somewhat similar to that of the Iberian Peninsula. Thick, coloured borders separate the territory of 'Germania' from the rest of the area depicted on the map. In addition the territory of Transylvania is enclosed by red borders. However, in this map all of the borders follow natural formations (drawn on the map): mostly rivers but also mountains and forests. There are no printed borderlines on the map, only coloured shading. In contrast, a map of the German territory ('Magna Germania') in the same atlas shows thin printed borderlines in places where the border crosses narrow tracts of land between two natural borders (such as rivers or mountain chains).[27] In these maps we can see the first traces of geographical maps that depict the territory of realms whose borders do not follow natural formations.[28]

The atlas of Ptolemy printed in 1513 also contains historical maps (*Tavola Antica*). The aim of these maps was to present the age-old unity of particular territories. They can be seen as part of the ideological 'territorialization' process of early states.[29] The depiction of borders in these historical maps differs from that in the 'modern' maps (*Tabula Moderna*). The borders of larger entities such as realms are still presented as natural formations. For example, although the territory of France is surrounded by the borders of the Rhine, the Mediterranean and the Pyrenees as is the case in 'modern' maps, the borders of local historical counties (real or imagined) form a network of abstract dotted lines (Map 4 see colour plate section 1, pp. 2–3). This clearly shows that the idea of describing a border as an abstract line already existed for mapmakers and the ruling elite, if not for others. The historical Ptolemy map of Italy from 1561 follows the same pattern: straight borderlines separate the territories of the ancient duchies and cities from each other.[30]

The lines in these sixteenth-century Ptolemy maps do not, however, show how borders were geographically situated in the terrain: they show the approximate location of each historical territorial unit. In maps of the 'modern' world in the same atlases, the traditional way of depicting borders of realms as natural formations dominates.[31] The Ptolemy map from 1561 ('Evrope' V) combines these two ways of depicting borders. The border between Italy and German areas ('Germania Magna Pars') is shown as a strong line of rivers and mountain chains. However, the borders between the duchies are drawn not only along rivers, but also using dotted lines drawn upon the mimic images of mountain chains.[32]

Techniques to measure land and the ability to use the results of such measurements in mapping were not yet sufficiently developed to allow the creation of maps with geographically measured and defined borders. This development took place during the sixteenth century (as will be discussed later). Maps before this time were still quite abstract schemes of the order of regions rather than strict descriptions of geographical reality.

Maps for the public: pictorial depiction of borders in maps

Overall the Ptolemy maps described above represent a quite modern and abstract type of mapmaking. The majority of the maps from the first half of the sixteenth century follow another tradition. In the Nordenskiöld collection we can find two well-known examples: Johan Stumpff's atlas (1548) and the *Carta Marina* (1539) by Olaus Magnus. When compared with modern maps, which have north at the top of the map, the map of Europe in Stumpff's atlas appears to be upside down: Italy is on the upper edge of the map; Denmark is at the bottom. On the map Spain ('Hispania') is separated from France ('Gallia Francia') by the Pyrenees, and the Rhine and the Alps separate France from Germany ('Germania'). The Alps and the river Po separate Italy ('Italia') from the rest of Europe.[33]

The Holy Roman Empire, often seen as a predecessor of Germany, had its own emperor, general law codifications and stipulations. However, in reality the German area was still a patchwork of largely autonomously ruled duchies and kingdoms with their own currencies, taxation and customs. The 'jigsaw puzzle' nature of the territory can be clearly seen in Stumpff's map of the German territory ('Germania/Teutschland'). The duchies are separated from each other by rivers or sometimes forests. A

circle of forests surrounds the territory of Bohemia ('Behem'). The duchies are marked not only with names, but also with the armorial bearings
of their ruling families. The legend in the upper right corner of the map
indicates that the mapmaker has not followed the traditional method of
depicting the German territory as limited by the Rhine and the Danube.
According to Stumpff, the German culture and language, and therefore
the German nation, reach far beyond these rivers and to the highest points
of the Alps (Map 5 see colour plate section 1, pp. 2–3).[34]

However, there are no abstract borderlines or other symbols on these
maps; all phenomena (including rivers, forests, mountains and towns) are
depicted as mimic images. In the map of Europe the seas are filled with
monstrous curled octopuses, sea snakes and other peculiarities. This way of
drawing maps was not due to primitiveness in mapmaking or the inability
of the mapmaker to think in abstract terms. Stumpff's atlas was meant to
be sold to a wider audience rather than used by the state bureaucracy or
other specialists. This concrete form of depiction ensured that everybody,
including those who had received no training, could understand and read
the maps. This tradition of map drawing was highly decorative and pictures
were specifically designed to appeal to potential customers.

The *Carta Marina*, printed in Venice in 1539 (a little earlier than
Stumpff's atlas), follows the same pattern. As one of the first maps of
Scandinavia,[35] it was based on descriptions of the Northern Kingdoms
by the Swedish bishop Olaus Magnus. King Gustavus I (r. 1521–1560),
introduced the Reformation to Sweden and decreed that the Lutheran
confession was the only acceptable religion in the kingdom. Olaus Magnus
(along with many other members of the higher clergy) resisted the Reformation and was therefore expelled from the realm. The remainder of his
life was largely spent in Rome, where he wrote an extended description of
the history of and life in the Northern countries (published in 1555). The
Carta Marina was a kind of forerunner of his great literary achievement.

The *Carta Marina* covers the territory of Scandinavia: Iceland and
the kingdoms of Denmark, Norway and Sweden (including present-day
Finland). The northern shores of the Baltic Sea (present-day Estonia and
Latvia) are also depicted. An examination of the Baltic area clearly shows
that forests form the borders in this region. Trees in linear formations
separate the territories of 'Moscovie', 'Rvssia Alba', 'Livonia Aqvilonaris',
'Livonia Avstralis', 'Rvsia Regalis Nigra' and 'Litvanie Pars' from each
other. In Lithuania the Polish king, Sigismundus ('Rex Polonie Magnvs
Dux Litvanie'), sits on his throne flanked by his coat of arms. Other kings
and princes (for example the unnamed 'Magnvs Princeps Moscovitar',

who sits near the town of Novgorod) are depicted in a similar way. The king of Denmark ('Dania') and his coat of arms are found in Jutland and the Swedish king Gustavus I, the political opponent of Olaus Magnus, sits in the middle of his realm next to a shield emblazoned with the Swedish symbol of three crowns. It is noteworthy that the southern part of the Swedish peninsula, 'Gothia', has its own king, even though the territory was actually under Danish rule. The bishopric of Uppsala also boasts a coat of arms and a text informing us that this is the bishopric of the author, Olaus Magnus.[36]

Inside the territory of Sweden, we can see rows of trees that separate the counties from each other; this is also the case in the eastern half of the Swedish realm, Finland. A mountain chain separates Sweden from the Kingdom of Norway, as it does in reality. In southern Sweden, we see a line of dots heading south-east, but the meaning of these marks cannot be clearly discerned from the map itself. However, it is obvious that this dotted line does not represent the border between the Swedish Kingdom and the province (Sw. *landskap*) of Scania ('Gothia'). This border is shown as a river flowing from Lake Vänern to the Baltic Sea and west from the lake with a series of marks, possibly depicting poles or stones, and then with a row of trees.

The border with the Grand Duchy of Moscow ('Moscovie') in the province of Karelia (Fi. Karjala, Sw. Karelen) in eastern Finland is particularly interesting. The border, indicated by a double row of trees, starts at the bottom of the Gulf of Finland and runs northwards to the mysterious Lake Albus ('Lacus Albvs'). At both ends of this row of trees are coat of arms emblazoned with the Swedish three crowns. Lake Albus (which seems to be an amalgamation of Lake Onega and the long western bay of the White Sea) forms a great part of the border between Karelia and the Grand Duchy. The border is marked in the middle of the lake by another coat of arms. The rest of the border from the northernmost corner of the lake to the Arctic Ocean is shown as a series of mountains, again marked with the familiar Swedish escutcheon.

The two examples – chosen from a large selection of early sixteenth-century maps held in the Nordenskiöld Collection – clearly show that the concept of the border was still closely connected to natural formations. Most often borders are depicted as rows of trees (indicating a forest) or as rivers. Forests were largely zone-like borders; borders could be indicated by stones and marks in trees or tree stumps, but it would be inaccurate to claim that these were sharp linear borders which defined exact territories. Although to us rivers seem to be clearly defined linear borders, in reality (as the example from the Estonian eastern border has shown) they could be zone-like borders, in which rights to exploit natural resources could extend across the river and the border.

A clear testimony of the vague terms in which territories were conceptualized in the northern kingdoms can be seen in the depiction of the border between Sweden and Moscow in the *Carta Marina*. Although it is clearly marked upon the map, the border between these realms was, in reality, situated hundreds of kilometres to the west of Lake Onega and the White Sea. Throughout almost the whole of the sixteenth century, the border was contested by both realms. Only local people knew where their landed properties and rights ended, and even these rights were also sometimes contested. The *Carta Marina* brings us to our case study of the border between Sweden and Russia. However, before we can further explore these border issues in the European North, we must briefly examine changes within European societies and realms, and the role that cartography played in the state-building process.

Cartography as a tool of state-building in Renaissance Europe

Cartography was a subject of great interest to European rulers during the latter part of the fifteenth century. Explorations by Portuguese and Spaniards (to the south along the African coast, to the new continent in the west and, finally, around Cape Horn to the Pacific Ocean and the Far East) had made the mapping 'the topic of the day'. New sea-routes, new territories and new conquests had to be mapped, not only to provide information for the conquerors and their rulers, but also to advertise one's possessions to other rulers. As Steve Harley puts it: 'Maps were also inscriptions of power [...] they acted in constructing the world they intended to represent.'[37] The new worlds were conquered, divided, disputed and also mapped. In 1494 Pope Alexander VI divided the non-Christian world between the Spaniards and Portuguese by drawing a north–south demarcation line 370 leagues west of the islands of Cape Verde. Lands to the east belonged to the Portuguese; those to the west went to Castile (Spain).[38] This demarcation was one early indication of how the concept of territory gained a new importance for European rulers at the beginning of the sixteenth century.

During the sixteenth century maps began to serve a wide range of political and economic needs in society. Maps met the growing bureaucracy's need for depictions of town planning, legal boundary issues, commercial navigation, military strategies and rural land management. The use of maps for administrative purposes was propagandized in the works of Niccolò Machiavelli in Italy, Baldassare Castiglione in Spain and Sir Thomas Elyot in Britain in the 1520s and the 1530s. During this time of change, units of length and weight were standardized in order to meet the needs of the rapidly expanding commercial world. Mathematical methods to measure land developed alongside, and perhaps in close connection with, the growth of interest in mapmaking and defining territories. For example, in 1533 Gemma Frisius outlined the technique of triangulation to fix place positions. Everything became more precise in the sixteenth century (at least in comparison with the Middle Ages).[39] Fundamental changes in mapmaking and the depiction of borders in maps took place during the sixteenth century.

These changes were not sudden; nor did they occur simultaneously everywhere across Europe. In sixteenth-century England, for example, maps were not commonly drawn at a local level or in order to address border issues. Borders were usually still described in the medieval manner: lists of border places, border-markers or neighbouring landowners. However, maps designed for administrative purposes became more common in England from the 1520s onwards.[40] The first and only 'state' that used maps for administrative purposes in the fifteenth century was Venice. Maps were used to clarify ambassadorial dispatches, for defence and fortress designs, to resolve disputes in court cases and also to define borders. The Venetian border commissioners' map (from 1538) of the border between the Venetian and German ('Tedeschi') territories clearly shows that river systems formed the basis of the border, divisions and the depiction of the borders on the maps. In other parts of Italy, maps were not generally used in administrative tasks before the last quarter of the sixteenth century.[41]

It is evident that many sixteenth-century European rulers were fascinated by maps. Charles V (Habsburg emperor of Spain and territories in the Netherlands) was extremely interested in mapping. Charles allowed the royal cosmographer, Alonso de Santa Cruz, to teach him geography and cosmography; the emperor found it not only amusing, but also very useful in governing his expanding realm. In 1551 Santa Cruz reported to the king that he had completed his map of Spain, which included all cities, towns and villages, mountains, and rivers, along with all of the boundaries of the various Spanish kingdoms.[42] Although we do not know how the boundaries in Cruz's map were drawn, it is evident that territories were now important not only for the mapmaker, but also for his ruler. Several maps of the Iberian Peninsula and Spain ('Hispania') were produced in the 1550s. The borders of Spain were depicted by a line in the Escorial Atlas (*c.* late 1570s).[43]

Charles VIII of France (r. 1483–1498) gave an order to furnish the French army with a map of the passages across the Alps to Italy. The maps were used in sixteenth-century France for military purposes and for planning the construction of town walls in a new artillery-resistant style. It was not until 1560 that the then ruler of France, Catherine de Medici, commissioned her royal geographer to draw up a general map of France, accompanied by maps of each individual province. However, only a small fraction of this task was ever completed. Catherine got her map of France in 1568, but it came from another source: the calligrapher and typographer Pierre Hamon.[44] In Hamon's map of France, the Pyrenees and the Rhine form the basis of the borders of the realm. However, some kind of fortified line connects the sources of the Rhine and the Elbe. The territorialization of France was underway.

Many other emperors of European realms were also interested in maps and began to use them as tools of administration. During the reign of Henry VIII of England (1491–1547), Sir Thomas Elyot wrote about the utility of cartography in administrative and military matters. Henry VIII was not deaf to Elyot's views, and during his reign mapping was developed and used for military purposes in particular. A number of rulers – François I (1494–1547) of France; Cosimo I de Medici (1519–1574) of Florence; the king of Denmark and Norway, Christian II (1481–1559); and Manuel I (1469–1521) of Portugal – all used cartography in order to better govern their territories. Most had their own 'royal' cosmographer or geographer. The existence of such posts was clearly connected to the emergence of the concept of territorial sovereignty. The first half of the sixteenth century is the period in which the idea of the state as a precisely defined and delimited geopolitical unit broke through in Europe. Mapmakers played a vital role in the articulation of the territories of the early modern states.[45]

The state-building process, like other historical processes, was neither simple nor coherent. The Habsburg emperors of Austria and the Holy Roman Empire – in particular Maximilian I (1459–1519) and his grandson Charles V (1500–1558) – were interested in cartography and maps. Charles V, as king of Spain, already had possessions in the Netherlands and Burgundy when he succeeded his grandfather to the throne of the Holy Roman Empire. As emperor his possessions reached from Austria and German lands to southern Italy, Sicily and Sardinia. Clearly his dominions did not form a territorial state and, therefore, the depiction of his position on maps of European lands was somewhat complex. The maps Charles V produced of his possessions in Central Europe stressed a particular territory, dukedom and so on; the possibility or existence of a larger unit was ignored in these maps. The split nature of the possessions meant that Charles V pursued a highly personalized and locally conducted form of national politics, which is evident in the maps.[46]

With the emergence of territorial states in the sixteenth century (or perhaps we should call them 'territorial realms' because of the strong connection between the territory and the person of the ruler), concepts of nationality in some forms were presented in, and even produced by, Renaissance maps. As we saw in Stumpff's map of 'Germania/Teutschland', some kind of consciousness of being German was evident in the map itself, particularly in the map's legend. This process of conscious construction of 'Englishness', 'Frenchness' and even 'Swedishness' was present in sixteenth-century Europe. It would be going too far to say that these realms were 'national states', but coherence was created within the realms through the writing of mythical histories, the creation of ceremonies and, as a part of this process, the drawing of maps depicting states. These maps of European territorial states begin to emerge in cartography during the latter part of the sixteenth century. However, such maps were often more a reflection of a ruler's ambitions than an accurate geographical description of his territory.[47]

In summary, the state-building process took significant steps towards the creation of territorial states during the sixteenth century. Realms and kingdoms were now understood as territories with borders. Maps of dukedoms, kingdoms and territorial realms (where such existed) were drawn. Borders were depicted on these maps first as mimic pictures of natural formations, as they existed in nature, and from the middle of the sixteenth century onwards as thin, dotted abstract lines. The development of methods to measure and survey land, and to fix and define the positions of places, led to the possibility of more accurate maps. Initially such methods were used at a local level for practical purposes, but soon these mapmaking skills were employed at a realm level, often in order to serve the ideological and propagandistic needs of European rulers.

The emergence of the linear border in maps of Scandiavia

Scandinavian cartography has its roots in the earliest maps of Ptolemy. The Danish cleric Claudius Clavus (1388–?) became familiar with cartography when visiting Rome in 1423 and 1424. Clavus produced an early map of Scandinavia: the first depiction of this territory, which was added to Ptolemy's *Geographica* in 1427 as a new map (*Tabula Modernae*).[48] Clavus included Iceland, the northern parts of the British Isles and the Danish and Scandinavian peninsulas in his map. The Scandinavian Peninsula is divided into three by almost straight lines, which indicate the borders between the three kingdoms: 'Suetia Regio', 'Norwegica Regio' and 'Danonum Regio'. The use of the Latin concept *regio* clearly seems to refer to the territorial aspect of the concept of kingdom. However, the three kingdoms of Scandinavia formed the Scandinavian Union in the fifteenth century. The Union was based upon an agreement that the king who resided in Denmark held the Crowns of all three kingdoms. The 1420s were a period of extreme political turbulence within the union. There were severe riots and uprisings against King Eric of Pomerania and his bailiffs in Sweden and Norway, and the personal union was close to total collapse.[49] Perhaps, therefore, the Danish mapmaker Clavus used the concept of 'region' instead of the concept of 'kingdom' primarily because of the specific circumstances of the 1420s.

Be that as it may, the map indicates clear territorial distinctions between the three Scandinavian kingdoms. The borderline drawn between the kingdoms of Norway and Sweden is strengthened by colouration that presumably indicates the Scandinavian mountain chain. The line separating Sweden from the provinces of 'Halandh' (Halland) and 'Scannigh' (Scania; Sw. and Da. Skåne) in the Danish kingdom is, however, also bolstered by a wide band of green colouration, presumably a forest. Here, we again have an example of a mixture of traditions of border representation: the use of a pictorial depiction and a line as a symbol. The borderlines in the map are very schematic and thus the depiction of the regions is more diagrammatic than geographic.[50]

At the right-hand edge of the map we find 'Findlandi' and above this 'Findhlappu'. Although these names are located next to Sweden and relatively close to Stockholm, they clearly refer to the Finnish territory. 'Findlandi' is separated from the east, which is left unnamed and outside the map, with two rivers reaching the interior from the Arctic Ocean (seemingly the White Sea) and from the Baltic Sea (the Gulf of Finland and Gulf of Bothnia are not shown). Presumably, in these rivers we have the first depiction of the border between the Russian (up to 1478, Novgorodian) and Finnish (Swedish) territories.

In the later fifteenth-century Ptolemy maps of Scandinavia, the borders between the three Scandinavian kingdoms and territories are shown as a network of mountain chains, not as borderlines.[51] The Bavarian-born

Jacob Ziegler (1470/71–1549) published his map of Scandinavia (Schondia) in 1532. There are several versions of Ziegler's map. The version published in Ulla Ehrensvärd's book on Scandinavian cartography (2006) seems to include drawn lines as borders of some territories. However, when these lines are studied alongside other versions, such as the Ziegler map published as part of William R. Mead's article on Scandinavian Renaissance cartography (2007), it becomes evident that these 'borders' are actually rivers. However, in the latter map, the border between the Swedish kingdom and 'Gothia' (Denmark) is drawn as a line, as is the border that separates Lapland (Lapponia; Fi. Lappi, Sw. Lappland) and the counties of Norrbotten ('Northbotenia') and Ostrobothnia (Fi. Pohjanmaa, Sw. Österbotten) from Sweden proper ('Svecia'). The line between Ostrobothnia and Finland (Finlandia) is drawn as a mountain chain.[52] In geographical terms there are no mountains in this area: the area is an upland formation, a watershed called 'Maanselkä' (literally, the backbone of the land). The border between the Swedish and Muscovite realms is not shown on these maps.

Chronologically, the next map to depict the Scandinavian territory and the borderland between Sweden and Russia was the aforementioned *Carta Marina* (Olaus Magnus) from 1539. The border on this map is fully pictorial and is comprised of natural formations such as forests and lakes and also of coats of arms that symbolized the limits of the Swedish king's power. However, the information given in the *Carta Marina* about the early sixteenth-century Swedish eastern border is quite vague and even partially false. King Gustavus was a typical Renaissance ruler in terms of his attitude towards the use of pictures and maps in administration. Although not a patron of the fine arts, Gustavus I did have several artists or painters in his service who were expected to plan fortifications, town centres and so on, rather than simply paint portraits.[53] The king himself even drew a sketch (*skamplun*), a kind of map, to explain to his warlords how an ambush should be put into practice. In 1555 and 1556 Jacob Larsson Teit, a secretary to Gustavus I, travelled around Finland collecting information about the area (particularly the borderlands) for the king. Teit attached some sketches of a number of areas to his report. The most famous of these sketches is Teit's map of the Karelian Isthmus around the town of Vyborg (Sw. Viborg, Fi. Viipuri) and the border with Russia.[54]

This hand-drawn sketch by Teit contains a great deal of information. However, we are primarily concerned with the way in which the border is depicted in this rather primitive map. The upper edge of the map heads to the east, to Russia. The border heading from the south to the north begins at the Gulf of Finland at the right-hand side of the map and follows the river Siestar into a marsh. A legend advises us that the marsh is the source of the rivers Saija and Siestar. At the other side of the marsh, the border follows the course of the Saija, a tributary of the Vuoksi. The border turns to follow the river Vuoksi until it reaches two border-stones on the bank of the river, located on the left-hand edge of the sketch. At the uttermost edge of the sketch we can see part of a lake that clearly indicates the continuation of the border. No borderline is marked on Teit's map: there are only two rivers (linear natural forma-tions), a lake and a marsh (zone-like border-markers) and two stones (dot-like border-markers). Of course, Teit was not a trained mapmaker and therefore his sketch is necessarily quite primitive. Important features such as rivers, churches, towns and castles are presented in pictorial form. The sketch seems to provide evidence that, in the minds of the people of Karelia and Finland, borders were still medieval in character and strongly connected to natural formations.

A map by Corneliz Anthoniz (c.1499–c.1557), from the same period as Teit's sketch, depicts the boundaries between the Danish and Swed-ish territories using a colour-strengthened line drawn upon a chain of mountains. This map, the *Caerte van Oostland*, was published for the first time in 1543, but only one copy of the third edition from c.1558 has survived.[55] This map shows us that professional mapmakers had started to adopt an abstract line as a common symbol of a border. How-ever, the common people and the Swedish administration, at the local level at least, perceived the border in a medieval manner: borders were understood to be connected to natural formations in reality and in maps.

The famous map of Northern Europe (1570) by Abraham Ortelius is very interesting in this respect.[56] The original print is uncoloured, although the versions found in books on cartography usually have borders marked by different colours.[57] This colouration was added by hand at a later date. In the original print, Sweden is separated from Norway and Denmark by a chain of mountains, Lake Vänern and the river flowing to the Sound (Sw. Öresund). The river Neva, Lake Ladoga, river Svir, Lake Onega and an imagined river flowing from Lake Onega to the White Sea form the eastern border of the Swedish realm. In reality in the north there are rivers which flow into Lake Onega and the White Sea that almost reach each other at their sources. However, the Swedish territory extended this far only in the daydreams of the Swedish kings. The atlas of Ortelius (1570) shows that, although linear borders could

77

already be seen in maps of southern Europe (for example, maps of the Iberian Peninsula), the borders in the north were still tightly entwined with natural formations, both in reality and in cartographic presentations.

The route across the Arctic Ocean to the Russian harbours was discovered in the 1550s. This soon led to competition between the English, Dutch, Danes, Norwegians and Swedes over trade routes and harbours. The region above the Arctic Circle was of great interest to traders and rulers alike. These areas were soon mapped; sea-routes were clearly marked, but the lands closest to these northern territories were also depicted. The trader Simon von Salingen, who sailed in these waters several times during the 1560s, was probably the first person to map the area. The map produced by von Salingen after his journeys depicted the whole of Scandinavia. However, his main focus was on the coasts of the Arctic Ocean and the Kola Peninsula.[58] Because of this, the forms of Sweden, Norway and especially Finland seem somewhat strange. The Finnish territory and the settlement close to the White Sea coast are separated from each other by a long chain of mountains similar to that which separates the territories of Sweden and Norway. Mountains clearly serve as borders in von Salingen's map.

The borderline appears in maps of the Swedish–Russian border

We now come to our case study: the development of the medieval and early modern Swedish–Russian border and its cartographical depiction. A brief outline of the history of the border is necessary here. The first known agreement on this border was the Peace Treaty of Nöteborg in 1323.[59] In fact this document – which has survived only as several slightly differing copies – was a letter by Yury, prince of Novgorod. In his letter, 'as a gesture of good will', Yury gave three large parishes in Karelia to Magnus, king of Sweden. In the medieval tradition a written list of names of border places was included as an appendix to the letter. The border was quite well defined in its southern sections: it followed rivers, and marshes, stones, lakes and ponds were used as border-markers. In the interior Finnish forests, the border to the north-west was defined by just a few widely interspersed placenames.[60]

In its southern section the first Swedish-Russian border was similar to the Estonian medieval eastern border described above. Although the border seems at first sight to be an almost modern and well-defined dividing line, Yury's letter sets out a number of conditions. Russian peasants were to retain their rights to many good fishing places and ponds (where beavers could be found) on the Swedish side. The Finnish peasants, who had been made Swedish subjects, enjoyed similar rights on the other side of the border. In the sparsely populated areas of the interior hardly anyone knew the exact course of the ill-defined border through the wilderness or forest.

Significantly the terms of the Nöteborg 'agreement' on the border was a matter of dispute for the Swedish and Russian realms from at least the start of the sixteenth century and remained a source of discord for the whole century. This clearly shows that territory and borders became an issue of importance for the rulers in the northern forest lands in the Renaissance period, just as it was for rulers on the Continent. The Grand Duchy of Muscovy began to define its territory and limits, as did the Swedish kingdom. The clash between the two powers over the ill-defined border was unavoidable. Quarrels over the border continued throughout the sixteenth century; in fact a war in the middle of the century had its origins in border issues. The conclusion of the Peace Pact of Teusina in 1595 ended the '25 Years War' that had begun in 1570. The peace treaty set out details of a new border dividing the lands between the Swedish and Muscovite realms. At the same time, there was a sudden change in the depiction of the border in maps of the northern territory.

According to the 1595 treaty, the southernmost border of the two realms would follow the route outlined in 1323; the number of named border places increased, but the route remained unchanged. At the river Vuoksi the border now took a new course northwards along the long system of narrow lakes that extended from Lake Saima (Fi. Saimaa, Sw. Saimen), thus halving eastern Finland. Thus far the new border continued to follow natural formations. At this point commissaries of both parties jointly marked out the border. The border-markers – adorned with three Swedish crowns and a cross symbolizing Muscovite power – were hammered onto stones, cliffs and, sometimes, trees. An exact description of the new border was written and accepted by both parties. During their examination of the boundaries, the Swedish commissaries drew several maps of the proposed, disputed and defined border routes.[61] These maps provide us with an interesting insight into how the border was understood during the commissaries' examination.

The border maps drawn by the Swedish commissaries can be divided into two main categories (Map 6 and 7 see colour plate section 1, p. 4). First, there are several versions of sketchy drawings of border-markers connected to each other by two lines, with a 'corridor' between them.

In these 'corridors' we can sometimes see written legends that detail the route of the border through the terrain. Some of these sketches show proposed and disputed routes. The second category is pictorial maps that resemble long paintings of the final border. The border is depicted as a row of different natural formations: rivers, marshes, stones, lakes, ponds etc. The Swedish commissaries' maps show that they were able to draw almost abstract sketches of the border accompanied by written legends explaining its exact course. However, the final border map was still a very concrete depiction of the terrain through which the border passed. One should remember that these maps were not documents drawn up together by the two realms: their function was to concretize the possible and agreed courses of the border for the Swedish government. The official document on the border route was, in the medieval manner, a descriptive border letter signed by representatives of both parties. However, the northernmost section of this border in northern Finland and Lapland was not examined, nor was it marked in the terrain.

Astonishingly, the first maps in Europe to present the Swedish–Russian border as a line appear at almost the same time as the new border was defined in the Peace Pact of Teusina. Competition for dominance of the northern route via the Arctic Ocean to Russian markets had a great impact upon the mapping of the northern territory. Jan Huyegn van Linschoten (1563–1611) drew a map of this northern route; he had clearly based his own work on that of Simon von Salingen. In van Linschoten's map, published in 1596, the divisions between the territories of Finnmarckia, Lappia and Sweden (the latter is not mentioned by name on the map) are indicated by dotted lines.[62] Similar borders can be found in the sea-map drawn by Theodore de Bry and Gerrit de Veer from 1598–1599. In de Bry and de Veer's map a double-dotted line separates 'Oost-Finlant' from 'Moscovia'.[63] The Nordenskiöld Collection holds the chart-book of the 'lands of the whole world' published by Barent Langenes in 1599. The border between the Swedish and Russian realms (as well as those between the Swedish, Norwegian and Danish territories) is again shown as a dotted line.[64] The map also uses another abstract symbol: fortified towns are represented on the map by a picture of a castle and on it there is a circle with a dot at its centre (Map 8 see colour plate section 1, p. 5).

Do we have, in these maps, a modern linear border between two territorial states? For several reasons, this seems doubtful. First, the maps are generally quite rough in their depictions of land territories. The seas and coasts of the Arctic Ocean and the White Sea are detailed; only a rough description of territorial division was required further inland. Second, although the Swedish and Russian commissaries defined and marked the new border on the ground, there was no mathematical measurement of the border they established. The border was described in a literal way with reference to natural formations only; similarly, maps of the border were drawn in a very concrete way. Third, on the maps the border is shown to extend to the Arctic Ocean, even though in its most northerly section the border was never defined and marked on the ground. It would still be some time before the Swedish–Russian border would be depicted on a map as an exact line that corresponded to the course of the border on the ground.

An exact border in Swedish maps

After the death of Gustavus I in 1560, Sweden experienced a rather politically turbulent period. His son and successor, Eric XIV (r. 1560–1568), was mentally unstable and became entangled in wars in the Baltic and against the Danes. In 1568 Eric was supplanted by his younger brother John (r. 1568–1592) However, the '25 Years War' against Russia (1570–1595) raged throughout most of his reign. John III had great visions of conquering vast territories in the east and thus had neither the interest nor the means to define and map the actual eastern border of his realm. John was succeeded by his son Sigismund, the king of Poland and a Catholic. However, Duke Charles, Sigismund's uncle and Lutheran pretender to the Swedish throne, managed to topple Sigismund in 1598. At first Charles ruled as a regent but was later crowned Charles IX (r. 1604–1611). It was during the reign of Charles IX that mapping began to reflect the exact shape of the Swedish realm.

Charles IX was keenly interested in opportunities to trade in Lapland and the Arctic Ocean. He put a great deal of effort into competing against the Danes, Norwegians, Dutch, English and Russians for rights in these areas. The definition of the northern borders became an important issue. Two expeditions of experts trained in European universities were sent to Lapland (the first in 1600–1601 and the second between 1601 and 1605) to survey, measure and mark the borders of the realm. Land surveys in the north continued until 1610. The results of these examinations were forwarded to the cartographer Andreas Bureus, who, in accordance with the king's orders, prepared a map of Lapland (Lapponia) in 1611.[65]

Bureus' map of Lapland was the first map of these northern areas in which the border was indicated by a (dotted) line and the geographical detail was so exact that it could be considered equivalent to the course of the border on the ground. The dotted borderline separates the Norwegian province of Jemtland (Sw. Jämtland) from Sweden and then follows the Scandinavian mountain chain (the line bisects a picture of a row of mountains). In the north, the dotted line heads first to the north-east and then, in the northernmost corner of the land, it turns south. The border clearly follows the literal description of the border laid out in the Peace Pact of Teusina. Near the Varangerfjord the border line separates the realms of Sweden, Norway and Muscovy ('Moscovitico parent Imperio') from each other.

However, there are some problems in equating this line with the border between the realms on the ground. First, this was how Charles IX, as king of Sweden, wanted to see the borderline and his realm. The Danish king, in particular, refused to accept the legality of the division of the northern areas. Second, the exact border between Sweden and Norway in the northern mountain areas was not precisely marked in the terrain before the eighteenth century. Third, again, the border established in 1595 between the Swedish and Muscovite realms was never defined on the ground in the northernmost section. So, although it is the best representation of the territory of its time, the map of Lapponia in fact depicts the borders as they should have been according to the investigations, peace treaties and Swedish hopes.

King Charles IX was well aware that knowledge of the kingdom's territory and its depiction were necessary for practical and propagandistic purposes. Therefore, by 1603 he had already ordered Andreas Bureus to prepare a map of the northern areas (*Tabulam Cosmographicum Regnorum Septentrionalium*) in which the territory of the Swedish Realm would be depicted. It took Bureus twenty-three years to fulfil the king's request. Before the map was completed, a great deal had happened both to Bureus and to the borders of the Swedish kingdom. A combination of politics, military expeditions and conquest resulted in the annexation of the Russian provinces of Käkisalmi (Sw. Kexholm) and Ingria (Fi. Inkeri, Sw. Ingermanland) to the Swedish realm in the Peace Treaty of Stolbov in 1617. The Swedish border was pushed several hundred kilometres to the east. Again, the border – which had been agreed upon in principle during the peace negotiations in Stolbov – was examined on the ground by both Swedish and Russian commissaries.

The royal cartographer Anders Bureus served as a secretary of the Swedish high commission that defined the course of the new Swedish–Russian border. Therefore, he was in an ideal position to survey, measure and record details of the borderlands and the course of the border through the Karelian wilderness. He also had the opportunity to familiarize himself with the north-eastern parts of the Muscovy Realm. This work in the eastern forests lasted until 1621. The map of the northern areas, ordered by Charles IX in 1603, was published in 1626 under the title *Orbis Arctoi nova et Accurata Delineatio*.[66] The map is usually known by its shortened name *Orbis Arctoi*. The border between the realms and the waters and villages in the borderland are marked upon the map quite precisely. There were many difficulties in defining the border on the ground, and this can also be seen in the map. A short section of the border in the north is shown as a chain of hills, without a dotted line. Then, a short dotted line heads north from Iivaara – a designated border placenamed in the treaty – but no border is marked in Lapland (Map 9 see colour plate section 1, p. 6).

This map reflects the reality of the time: the commissaries were never able to define the exact borders in Lapland. The borderline between the Swedish and Russian realms was examined, opened and marked on the ground between 1618 and 1621, and this border was drawn as a line on the map published in 1626 (Map 10 see colour plate section 1, p. 7). When this border was re-examined and marked out by the Swedish commissaries in the 1650s, a new map of the border was drawn. A thick red line with accurately positioned border-markers divides the two realms on this map.[67] Territoriality had finally arrived in these northern forests.

Conclusion

Developments in mapmaking are often connected to developments in mathematics, measurement and land-surveying techniques, exploration to new lands and progress in the arts. Only quite recently has the connection between the beginning of the state-building process and cartography been examined. The interest of rulers in maps and the increase in the number of maps in the first half and middle of the sixteenth century occurred concurrently. Interestingly, printing developed during the same period, a phenomenon that Benedict Anderson has argued was a crucial part of the state-building process.[68] Maps depicting the territory and terrain of the realms and nations (either real or imagined) appeared alongside books and leaflets that propagated the unity of the nation, its territory and terrain, and the role of the prince leading his nation. These maps were initially created for rulers and administrators, who would use them for practical purposes and to propagate their power both inside and outside the realm. Atlases intended for a wider audience were produced from the 1550s onwards. Our example from Stumpff's atlas clearly shows how territories and nations were described and even conceptually created by these maps. The territorial state (or should we say territorial realm), printing and cartography developed hand in hand, each having an impact upon the others. However, the prime mover was perhaps the territorialization process of the realms.

Now it is time to return to the division between 'primordialists', who seek out 'holy' state borders from ancient times, and 'modernists', who deny the existence of sharp linear borders between the sovereign territorial states before the modern era and the growth of nation states in the nineteenth century. Anthony D. Smith has argued that there is a mediating paradigm called 'perennialism' (particularly appealing to historians) in which although the nation-state is viewed as quite a recent phenomenon, nations (or at least many of them) have always existed.

This debate is only of partial relevance for our discussion of state borders and their depictions in maps. However, as we have seen, most of the major European states – or territorial realms as I suggest we should call them – took on their approximate shape during the sixteenth century. The ideological creation of the nation and its unity developed simultaneously, and maps were one part of this process. 'Nations' began to become aware of themselves as territorial units. This can be clearly seen in our example from Stumpff's atlas: although the state called Germany (or Prussia) was not 'born' earlier than the nineteenth century, the concept of a German territory and nation clearly existed and was already being propagated in the sixteenth century.

The borders of different medieval territories, bishoprics, dukedoms, kingdoms, realms and, finally, states were defined in written lists of placenames and border-markers. Borders were closely connected to natural formations: linear rivers, streams and ditches; zone-like lakes, forests, marshes and moors; points in the forms of stones, trees and tree stumps; and frequently chains of mountains and hills. This kind of border was seldom depicted as a line: it would usually be indicated by images of the natural formations that made up the border. Changes in the presentation of maps began in the middle of the sixteenth century. The final quarter of the century saw thin lines appearing between the various realms on maps of Europe. In addition, maps of territorial realms became more common. The Habsburg 'realm', having split possessions in most parts of the European continent, was presented not as a territorial unit in a single map but as several separate territories in separate maps. This clearly shows that although the Emperor of the Holy Roman Empire was the centre of the realm, territorialization at a local level (in dukedoms and kingdoms) was still a dominant factor in mapping.

As we have seen, territorialization and borders were part of a strong process of change during the sixteenth century. However, it would be going too far to argue that the 'modernists' were totally wrong in their thesis that linear and exact borders were phenomena that only emerged with the nineteenth-century nation-states. The borders of the late sixteenth century, although now often defined and marked on the ground, were still very far from the well-guarded borderlines of the modern era. Borders were still quite permeable: they seldom presented any kind of obstacle to those passing over them. Moreover, we must also bear in mind the discussion of the conglomerate nature of seventeenth-century European states.[69] The territorialization of states and nations was just in its infancy in the sixteenth century.

Notes

1 On the discussion of 'primordialists' and 'modernists' see Gustafsson 2002 and the literature mentioned in the article. For recent addresses to the question see Davies 2003; Reynolds 2003. pp. 550–555.

2 See for example Buisseret (ed.) 1992; Kagan & Schmidt 2007, pp. 661–679.

3 The article Biggs 1999 discusses mainly same questions as in this text, but without reference to any collection of primary sources. See also Iwańczak 2006.

4 On this discussion of the medieval border between the Swedish and Russian realms see Katajala 2006, pp. 92–93.

5 The Norderskiöld catalogues of the collection in the Finnish National Library (Helsinki University Library) have been published as *The A. E. Nordenskiöld Collection in the Helsinki University Library. Annotated catalogue of maps made up to 1800*. Eds. Ann-Mari Mickwitz & Leena Miekkavaara. Vols. 1 & 2, Almqvist & Wiksell International (1979). The catalogue system of the collection has been followed in the notes and the numbering of maps.

6 On Hellenic and Roman maps see Wilford 2002, pp. 57–60; Buisseret 2003, pp. 10–15.

7 On mappamundi see, for example, Järvinen 1998, pp. 12–15.

8 Järvinen 1998, pp. 21–23; Buisseret 2003, p. 5–7 (in fact, Buisseret claims that it is not known how sailors navigated using portolan charts). Regarding the Pisano map 1270, see Wigal 2006, p. 15.

9 Buisseret 2003, p. 4; the information in the Gough Map is analysed thoroughly in Lilley & Lloyd 2009.

10 On Ptolemy and his work see Wilford 2002, pp. 29–39; Buisseret 2003, pp. 14–16.

11 Roger Bacon, a thirteenth-century scholar, developed a system of longitudes and latitudes and even drew a map following his own system; however, his writings on this topic were soon forgotten and had no significant influence on medieval map drawing. See Woodward & Howe 1997, pp. 199–221; Woodward 1990, pp. 109–122.

12 Buisseret 2003, pp. 16–17.

13 On Roman land-surveying see e.g. Cuomo 2000; Arce 2001, pp. 5–9; Goetz 2001, pp. 74–82. On Roman and medieval borders in England, see Hooke 1998, pp. 62–80.

14 Reed 1984; Hooke 1998, pp. 62; Katajala 2006, pp. 95–96.

15 Hardt 2000, pp. 41–45; Hardt 2001, pp. 219–232.

16 Pohl 2001, pp. 247. Here, Pohl means a fixed borderline when he refers to a 'frontier'. On the messy use of the concepts of border, boundary and frontier in literature, see in short Katajala 2006, p. 86, note 1.

17 Power 1999, pp. 105–127.

18 Hardt 2000, pp. 46–56.

19 Constable 2006, p. 9.

20 Constable 2006, pp. 10–11.

21 Selart 1997, pp. 27–41.

22 Tollin 1999, especially, pp. 55–56; Katajala 2006, p. 94. In fact, Tollin's aim is to prove the conception of zone-like medieval borders to be false. However, he fails to draw a distinction between local borders and the borders of realms and kingdoms.

23 Woodward 2007, p. 18. However, Catherine Delano-Smith challenges the view presented by David Woodward and argues that the medieval maps used both pictorial and abstract signs. During the Renaissance a greater range of features began to be shown in the maps in more stylized form. Delano-Smith 1985, pp. 9–29.

24 Buisseret 2003, pp. 35–37.

25 NC 196:3 Ptolemaus, Claudius [1477]: [Cosmographia] Tabula Tercia; NC 197:5. Ptolemaus, Claudius 1478: Claudii Ptolemei Alexandrini Philosophi Cosmographia. Qvarta Europe Tabula.

26 NC 202:6 Ptolemaeus, Claudus 1507: In Hoc Operare haec Continetur Geographica Cl. Ptholemaei. Tabula Moderna Hispanie.

27 NC 202:10 Ptolemaeus, Claudus 1507: In Hoc Operare haec Continetur Geographica Cl. Ptholemaei. Tabula Moderna Polonie, Vngarie, Boemie, Germanie, Russie, Lithuanie; NC 202:xx Ptolemaeus, Claudus 1507: In Hoc Operare haec Continetur Geographica Cl. Ptholemaei. [Germania].

28 Matthew Paris prepared a map of the Anglo-Saxon Kingdoms of Britain in the thirteenth century. However, the presentation of this map is diagrammatic, not geographic, although Paris states that the map gives the locations of the kingdoms in relation to each other. The map and the analysis see Morse 2007, pp. 39–40.

29 See, for example, Serchuck 2006. Cf. Benedict Anderson presents a comparable process of establishing historical maps as a part of state-building in Siam in the nineteenth century. Anderson 2007, p. 170–178.

30 NC 205:4. Ptolemaues Claudius 1513: Claudii Ptolemei vivi Alexandrini Mathematice discipline Philosopi doctissimi Geographica. Tercia Evrope Tabula; NC 216:xx. Ptolemaeus, Claudius 1561: La Geografia di Claudio Tolometo Alessandrino. 7 d' Evropa, sesta tavola antica. La Sesta Tauola d'Europa contiente l'Italia tutta,.. Tabula Evropae VI. (Italy).

31 See, for example, NC 216:8. Ptolemaeus, Claudius 1561: La Geografia di Claudio Tolometo Alessandrino. 4. d' Evropa, Terza Tavola Antica. In Qvesta terza Tauola d'Europa si contiene la Gallia in quattro Prouincie… Tabula Evropae III (France).

32 NC 216:13. Ptolemaeus, Claudius 1561: La Geografia di Claudio Tolometo Alessandrino. 6'd Evropa, Qvinta Tavola Antica. La Quinta Tavola d'Europa contiene

la Retia, la Vindelcia, Norico, et le due Pannonie, con tutta l'Illria, et le isole, che le son vicine. Evropae Tabvla V (Italy).

33　NC 289:1. Stumpff, Johan 1548: Gemeiner loblicher Eydgnoschafft Stetten/ Landern und Völkeren.... Europa/ die erst Tafel des Ersten buchs.

34　NC 289:11. Stumpff, Johan 1548: Gemeiner loblicher Eydgnoschafft Stetten/ Landern und Völkeren... Germania Teutschland / die ander Landtafel des anderen buchs. The map's legend reads: "In dieser tafel Germanie haben wir nie gefolget der beschribung der Alten, die Germania allein zwischen dem Rhyn und Dunaw einschliessen, sondern wil mehr gesehen auf unserer zeyt sitten, art und sprach, darben wir Teutsche Nation befindend, weit ober die Dunaw hinaufz, bifz in die Öbersten Alpspitzen, defzglenchen ober den Rhyn, biz an die Schelde sich erstrecken."

35　On the first descriptions of Scandinavia in maps and on the origins of the Carta Marina see, for example, Ehrensvärd 2006a, pp.19–79. (Ehrensvärd's book has also been published in English, see Ehrensvärd 2006b.) See also Mead 2007, p. 1787 and p. 1789.

36　The Nordenskiöld Collection holds a copperplate engraving version of the *Carta Marina* made by Antonio Lafreri in 1572, NC 130:1 Lafreri, Antonio 1570: Geografia Tavole Moderne de Geografia de la Maggiore Parte del Mondo de Diversi Avtori. [Carta Marina]. One copy of the original wood engraving from 1539 is held in the Library of the Uppsala University, Sweden. For an illustration see, for example, Ehrensvärd 2006a, pp. 62–63. Both woodcut and copperplate versions are referred to and compared in that text.

37　Woodward 2007, p. 19, citation of Harley according to Woodward.

38　Kagan & Schmidt 2007, p. 663.

39　On the change see Woodward 2007, pp. 11–17.

40　On medieval border descriptions see Morse 2007, p. 38; Woodward 2007, p. 9–10. On English medieval and early modern maps, see Barber 1992, pp. 26–40.

41　Marino 1992, pp. 5–7 (The map of 1538 can be found on p. 7.)

42　Kagan & Schmidt 2007, p. 661.

43　These maps of Spain (Hispaina) from the 1550s were drawn by Vincenzo Palentino (1550), Thomas Geminus (1555), Pirro Ligorio (1559) and Vincenzo Lucini (1559). In addition, in the 1560 maps by Paolo Forlani and Domenico Zenoi on Spain were published. Parker 1992, pp. 126–134.

44　Buisseret 1992, pp. 101–107.

45　Kagan & Schmidt 2007, p. 662. In Poland, for example, several maps for military purposes were made in the sixteenth century but, as we can see, the regions were presented without borders. See Mikoś 1989.

46　Vann 1992, pp. 156–158.

47　Kagan & Schmidt 2007, pp. 669–677. James Akerman (1995) underlines that the princes and rulers of the sixteenth century were conscious of their territories but the absence of boundaries in printed maps of those times expresses well how the concept of sovereignty was different from ours.

48　Mead 2007, pp. 1782–1784 (The map by Clavus can be found on p. 1784.) See also Ehrensvärd 2006, pp. 38–40. (The map by Clavus can be found on pp. 38–39.)

49　On these uprisings of the 1420s in Sweden and Norway see Katajala 2004.

50　Cf. the diagrammatic map of English Kingdoms made by Matthew Paris in the thirteenth century (Morse 2007, p. 40).

51　See, for example, the maps of the north from Ptolemy's *Geography*, c. 1481 and c.

1490 in Mead 2007, p. 1785, fig. 60.4 and fig. 60.5 as well as the map by Nicolaus Germanus from 1486 in Ehrensvärd 2006a, pp. 40–41. See also the maps of Hieronymus Münzer (1493) in Ehrensvärd 2006a, pp. 42–43.

52 Regarding the maps, see Ehrensvärd 2006a, pp. 48–49 and Mead 2007, p. 1786.

53 See, for example, Ahlberg 2005, p. 259.

54 This sketch of Karelia and the border by Jacob Teit (Teitti) (c. 1555) has most recently been published in Mead 2007, p. 1783.

55 See Ehrensvärd 2006a, pp. 82–83. Ehrensvärd (2006a, p. 86) supposes that the third edition published in Venice (in 1558) was printed according to the original wooden plates of Anthoniz from 1543. This seems improbable: the town of Helsinki, founded by King Gustavus in 1550, can be seen in the upper right corner of the maps.

56 NC 163:45 Ortelius, Abraham 1570: Theatrum Orbis Terrarum. Septentrionalivm Regionvm Descrip.

57 See, for example, Ehrensvärd 2006a, pp. 94–95, who uses a coloured print from 1598.

58 Published in Ehrensvärd 2006a, p. 119.

59 Nöteborg is the Swedish name of the citadel the Russians founded on an island at the mouth of the Neva river in Lake Ladoga. (In Russian it was called Oreshek and in Finnish, Pähkinäsaari.) Peter the Great renamed the castle Schlüsselburg at the beginning of the eighteenth century and it continues to be largely known by this name.

60 The Peace Treaty of Nöteborg in 1323 has been the subject of many heated debates about the route of the border. For a brief description of this discussion see Katajala 2006, pp. 88–93, 99–105.

61 Gränsk., Sv (F) – R komm. 1595–1596, nr 1–8. SRA.

62 For Lindscoten's map see Ehrensvärd 2006a, pp. 120–121. A dotted line separates the territories of 'Finlant' and 'Russia' in Cornelis Doedtsz's map of Northern Europe from the year 1592. However, the '25 Years War' was still raging in these borderlands and the border was not yet agreed and the form of Finland in the Dodetsz map is based on Salingen's map and is therefore rather obscure. Therefore, the dotted line as a border is in this map more an imagined division of the realms than a border dividing territories in the map. See Enckell 1951, pp. 57.

63 De Bry and de Veer's map has been published in Ehrensvärd 2006a, pp. 122–123.

64 NC 131:61, Langenes, Barendt 1599: Chart-Thresoor Inhoudende dee tafelen des gantsche Werelts Landen. Amsterdam 1599, p. 285: Noordt Caep.

65 On Bureus, see Ehrensvärd 2006a, pp. 130–132. For the map 'Lapponia', see Ehrensvärd 2006a, pp. 130–131.

66 On Bureus'works as secretary of commissaries, see Ehrensvärd 2006a, p. 152. For the map Orbis Arctoi see Ehrensvärd 2006a, pp. 155–154.

67 Gränsk., Sv (F) – R komm. 1652–1653, nr 1 (parts 1–5). SRA.

68 Anderson 2006, pp. 37–46.

69 On the discussion in Scandinavia of seventeenth-century conglomerate states, see Gustafsson 1998, pp. 189–213.

Bibliography
Archival sources

The Finnish National Library (Helsinki University Library)
The Norderskiöld Collection (NC)

The National Archives of Sweden (Riksarkivet), Stockholm (SRA)
Maps made by the Swedish border commissaries in 1595 and 1652–1653.

Literature

Ahlberg, N. 2005. *Stadsgrundningar och planförändringar. Svensk stadsplanering 1521–1721.* Swedish University of Agricultural Sciences, Uppsala.

Akerman, J. R. 1995. 'The Structuring of Political Territory in Early Printed Atlases.' *Imago Mundi*, Vol. 47, pp. 138–154.

Anderson, B. 2006. *Imagined Communities. Reflections on the Origin and Spread of Nationalism.* New edition. Verso, London & New York.

Arce, J. 2001. 'Frontiers of the Late Roman Empire. Perceptions and Realities.' In Pohl, W. & Reimitz, H. (eds.) *The Transformation of Frontiers from Late Antiquity to the Carolingians.* Brill, Leiden, pp. 5–14.

Barber, P. 1992. 'England I: Pageantry, Defense and Government: Maps at Court to 1550.' In Buisseret, D. (ed.) *Monarchs, Ministers and Maps. The Emergence of Cartography as a Tool of Government in Early Modern Europe.* The University of Chicago Press, Chicago & London, pp. 26–40.

Biggs, M. 1999. 'Putting the State on the Map. Cartography, Territory, and European State Formation.' *Comparative Studies in Society and History,* Vol 41 (2), pp. 374–411.

Buisseret, D. (ed.) 1992. *Monarchs, Ministers and Maps. The Emergence of Cartography as a Tool of Government in Early Modern Europe.* The University of Chicago Press, Chicago & London.

Buisseret, D. 1992. 'Monarchs, Ministers and Maps in France before the Accession of Louis XIV.' In Buisseret, D. (ed.) *Monarchs, Ministers and Maps. The Emergence of Cartography as a Tool of Government in Early Modern Europe.* The University of Chicago Press, Chicago & London (1992), pp. 101–107.

Buisseret, D. 2003. *The Mapmakers' Quest. Depicting New Worlds in Renaissance Europe.* Oxford University Press, Oxford.

Constable, G. 2006. 'Frontiers in the Middle Ages.' In Merisalo, O. & Pahta, P. (eds.) *Frontiers in the Middle Ages.* Brepols, Louvain-la Neuve (2006), pp. 3–28.

Cuomo, S. 2000. 'Divide and Rule. Frontinus and Roman Land-Surveying.' *Studies in History and Philosophy of Science*, Vol. 31 (2), pp. 189–202.

Davies, R. 2003. 'The Medieval State: The Tyranny of a Concept?' *Journal of Historical Sociology,* Vol. 16 (2), pp. 280–299.

Delano-Smith, C. 1985. 'Cartographic Signs on European Maps and their Explanation before 1700.' *Imago Mundi*, Vol. 37, pp. 9–29.

Ehrensvärd, U. 2006a. *Pohjolan kartan historia. Myyteistä todellisuuteen.* John Nurmisen säätiö, Helsinki.

Ehrensvärd, U. 2006b. *The History of the Nordic Map. From Myths to Reality.* Trans. Roy Hodson. John Nurminen Foundation, Helsinki.

Enckell, C. 1951. 'The Representation of the North of Europe in the Worldmap of Petrus Plancius of 1592.' *Imago Mundi*, Vol. 8, pp. 55–69.

Goetz, H.-W. 2001. 'Concepts of Realm and Frontiers from Late Antiquity to the Early Middle Ages.' In Pohl, W. & Reimitz, H. (eds.) *The Transformation of Frontiers from Late Antiquity to the Carolingians.* Brill, Leiden, pp. 73–82.

Gustafsson, H. 1998. 'The Conglomerate State. A Perspective on State Formation in Early Modern Europe.' *Scandinavian Journal of History*, Vol. 23 (3–4), pp. 189–213.

Gustafsson, H. 2002, 'The Eighth Argument. Identity, Ethnicity and Political Culture in Sixteenth-Century Scandinavia.' *Scandinavian Journal of History*, Vol. 27 (2), pp. 91–114.

Hardt, M. 2000. 'Linien und Säume, Zonen und Räume an der Ostgrenze des Reiches im Frühen und Hohen Mittelalter.' In Pohl, W. & Reimitz, H. (eds.) *Grenze und Differenz im Frühen Mittelalter.* Verlag der Österreichischen Akademie der Wissenschaften, Vienna, pp. 39–56.

Hardt, M. 2001. 'Hesse, Elbe, Saale and the Frontiers of the Carolingian Empire.' In Pohl, W. & Reimitz, H. (eds.) *The Transformation of Frontiers from Late Antiquity to the Carolingians.* Brill, Leiden, pp. 219–232.

Hooke, D. 1998. *The Landscape of Anglo-Saxon England.* Leicester University Press, Leicester.

Iwańczak, W. 2006. 'Borders and Borderlines in Medieval Cartography.' In Merisalo, O. & Pahta, P. (eds.) *Frontiers in the Middle Ages.* Brepols, Louvain-la Neuve (2006), pp. 661–672.

Järvinen, J. 1998, 'Mappamundien maailmankuva.' In Niiranen, S. & Lamberg, M. (eds.) *Ihmeiden peili. Keskiajan ihmisen maailmankuva.* Atena, Jyväskylä. pp. 9–30.

Kagan, R. L. & Schmidt, B. 2007. 'Maps and the Early Modern State. Official Cartography.' In Woodward, D. (ed.) *The History of Cartography*, Vol. 3: *Cartography in the European Renaissance*, Part 1. The University of Chicago Press, Chicago & London, pp. 661–679.

Katajala, K. 2004. 'Against Tithes and Taxes, for King and Province.' In Katajala, K. (ed.) *Northern Revolts. Medieval and Early Modern Peasant Unrest in the Nordic Countries.* The Finnish Literature Society, Helsinki, pp. 32–52.

Katajala, K. 2006. 'The Origin of the Border.' In Gustafsson, H. & Sanders, H. (eds.) *Vid Gränsen. Integration och indentitet i det förnationella Norden.* Makadam, Stockholm, pp. 86–106.

Lilley, K. D. & Lloyd, C. D. 2009. 'Mapping the Realm. A New Look at the Gough Map of Britain (c. 1360).' *Imago Mundi*, Vol. 61 (1), pp. 1–28.

Marino, J. 1992. 'Administrative Mapping in the Italian States.' In Buisseret, D. (ed.) *Monarchs, Ministers and Maps. The Emergence of Cartography as a Tool of Government in Early Modern Europe.* The University of Chicago Press, Chicago & London, pp. 5–25.

Mead, W. R. 2007. 'Scandinavian Renaissance Cartography.' In Woodward, D. (ed.) *The History of Cartography.* Vol. 3: *Cartography in the European Renaissance*, Part 2. The University of Chicago Press. Chicago & London (2007), pp. 1781–1805.

Mickwitz, A.-M. & Miekkavaara, L. (eds.) 1979. *The A. E. Nordenskiöld Collection in the Helsinki University Library. Annotated catalogue of maps made up to 1800*, Vols. 1–2. Almqvist & Wiksell International, Stockholm.

Mikoś, M. J. 1989. 'The Polish Kings and Cartography.' *Imago Mundi*, Vol. 41, pp. 76–86.

Morse, V. 2007. 'The Role of Maps in Later Medieval Society. Twelfth to Fourteenth

Century.' In Woodward, D. (ed.) *The History of Cartography*. Vol. 3: *Cartography in the European Renaissance*, Part 1. The University of Chicago Press, Chicago, pp. 25–52.

Parker, G. 1992. 'Maps and Ministers. The Spanish Habsburgs.' In Buisseret, D. (ed.) *Monarchs, Ministers and Maps. The Emergence of Cartography as a Tool of Government in Early Modern Europe*. The University of Chicago Press, Chicago & London, pp. 126–134.

Pohl, W. 2001. 'Conclusion. The Transformation of Frontiers.' In Pohl, W. & Reimitz, H. (eds.) *The Transformation of Frontiers from Late Antiquity to the Carolingians*. Brill, Leiden, pp. 247–260.

Power, D. 1999. 'French and Norman Frontiers in the Central Middle Ages.' In Power, D. & Standen, N. (eds.) *Frontiers in Question. Eurasian Borderlands, 700–1700*. MacMillan, Basingstoke & London, pp. 105–127.

Reed, M. 1984. 'Anglo-Saxon Charter Boundaries.' In Reed, M. (ed.) *Discovering Past Landscapes*. Routledge, London, pp. 261–306.

Reynolds, S. 2003. 'There Were States in Medieval Europe: A Response to Rees Davies.' *Journal of Historical Sociology*, Vol. 16 (4), pp. 550–555.

Selart, A. 1997. 'The Formation of Estonian Eastern Border during the Middle Ages.' In Landgren, L.-F. & Häyrynen, M. (eds.) *The Dividing Line. Borders and National Peripheries*. University of Helsinki, Helsinki, pp. 27–41.

Serchuck, C. 2006. 'Picturing France in the Fifteenth Century. The Map in BNF MS Fr. 4991.' *Imago Mundi*, Vol. 58 (2), pp. 133–149.

Tollin, C. 1999. *Rågångar, gränshallar och ägoområden. Rekonstruktion av fastighetsstruktur och bebyggelseutveckling i mellersta Småland under äldre medeltid*. University of Stockholm, Stockholm.

Vann, J. 1992. 'Mapping under the Austrian Habsburgs.' In Buisseret, D. (ed.) *Monarchs, Ministers and Maps. The Emergence of Cartography as a Tool of Government in Early Modern Europe*. The University of Chicago Press, Chicago & London (1992), pp. 49–67.

Wigal, D. 2006. *Historic Maritime Maps 1290–1699*. Grange Books, Hoo.

Wilford, J. N. 2002. *The Mapmakers. The Story of the Great Pioneers in Cartography from Antiquity to the Space Age*. Pimlico, London.

Woodward, D. 1990. 'Roger Bacon's Terrestrial Coordinate System.' *Annals of the Association of American Geographers*, Vol. 80 (1), pp. 109–122.

Woodward, D. 2007. 'Cartography and the Renaissance. Continuity and Change.' In Woodward, D. (ed.) *The History of Cartography*. Vol. 3: *Cartography in the European Renaissance*, Part 1. The University of Chicago Press, Chicago, pp. 3–24.

Woodward, D. & Howe, H. M. 1997. 'Roger Bacon on Geography and Cartography.' In Hackett, J. (ed.) *Roger Bacon and the Sciences. Commemorative essays*. Brill, Leiden, pp. 199–221.

PART II

MOVEMENTS IN SPACE

CHAPTER 3

In Deep, Distant Forests

Jukka Korpela

Scandinavian–Baltic field agricultural societies were based on land road connections. Scholarly literature has tended to assume that this was also the primary form of travel across the entire medieval Finnic inland area. This area has usually been regarded as having been an unpopulated wilderness until late medieval colonization and the adoption of extensive cultivation. It seems, however, that the theory of colonization has been based on a misinterpretation of the sources. The area had earlier been settled by other kinds of people; the colonization recorded in written sources reflects only the formation of the realms of Sweden and Muscovy and their administration of the area, which began in the late fifteenth century. The process resulted in changes to the economic system, which developed from a semi-nomadic hunter-fisher economy into a system based on permanent cultivation in a fixed location. This change also had crucial implications for other aspects of life. Previously travelling had taken place on water roads which connected the research area to the south-east. However, the new permanent form of administration required connections to the west and south-west, which increasingly led to the use of land roads and the subsequent deterioration of traditional connections.

Time and space

We measure time in order to plan, predict and organize life. Time is thus the basic dimension of history. The modern Finnish language is in great trouble because it has no future tense, and we can hardly comprehend the world of Pirahã speakers in the Brazilian rainforest because they have no form to speak about the past.

Christian history is a linear development from Genesis to the Second Coming. The Bible is a history book that counts years and describes the linear history of a religion. However, the passing years are largely similar: nature is very stable in itself (even though seasonal changes in nature are a basic precondition for all biological existence). Progress and change in linear meaning only occur when new generations are born or old ones die: therefore, linear extension has only a genetic meaning. Indigenous populations follow the seasonal cycle and in linear meaning only recognize the general categories of the past and the distant past.[1]

Time and space should not be separated from each other: they must be studied together. The concept of 'reach' refers to the area which a person can reach both physically and mentally. 'Reachability' is dependent on the experiences and understanding of the person or group of people involved. In addition to its concern with the physical possibilities of travelling, the concept of reach also has social, economic, psychological and mythical dimensions. Dick Harrison divides space into 'micro space' and 'macro space'. According to Harrison, micro space is the area from which an individual's experiences originate, although he or she not need have physically visited or even seen this space. Macro space is not necessarily connected to physical geography: it refers to a cosmological category to which deities, the dead and mythical phenomena belong.[2]

Indeed, because it is only a measure, it is impossible to discuss time as an independent concept. We need to know what has happened or will happen, or what is possible, within a time extension. Thus our primary interest is in reach rather than duration. Reach is concerned with communication, that is, physical travel or mental comprehension. Communication and possibilities to communicate organize the world. Today, the general reachability is global, thanks to the internet, email communication and long-distance air connections. The twentieth century was the world of railways, land roads, big ships and the telephone. Eighteenth-century Europe was a continent with sea connections and hostelries. For a sixteenth-century king 'reach' meant extension into all the corners of his realm.

Indigenous world

Forest areas in late medieval East Fennoscandia (modern-day eastern Finland and Russian Karelia) have been considered wilderness areas by traditional studies. However, it seems probable that heterogeneous hunter-fisher populations – whose culture differed from that which scholars have traditionally associated with permanent settlements – had been settled in the region for some time. The pattern of village societies and progressiveness of agriculture have led theorists to believe that the

Map 3. In the map of Ptolemy, published in 1477, the Pyrenees and rivers make the borders of the territory that is known as France today. Ptolemaus, Claudius, *[Cosmographia,] Tabula Tercia* (1477), The Nordenskiöld Collection, no. 196:3, Helsinki University Library, Finland.

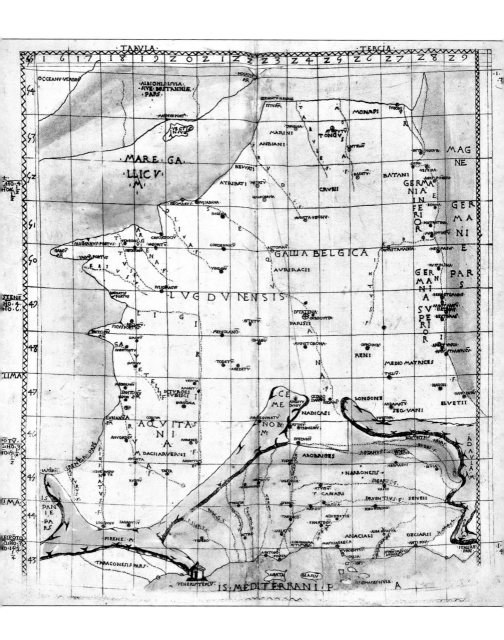

Map 5. The map of Germany ('Teutschland') in Johan Stumpff's atlas of Europe from the year 1548 shows clearly how map drawing was still entwined with the medieval tradition of understanding the borders. The duchies and dukedoms are separated from each other with rivers, forests and mountains. Stumpff, Johan, *Gemeiner loblicher Eydgnoschafft Stetten/ Landern und Völkeren…Germania Teutschland / die ander Landtafel des anderen buchs* (1548), The Nordenskiöld Collection, no. 289:11, Helsinki University Library, Finland.

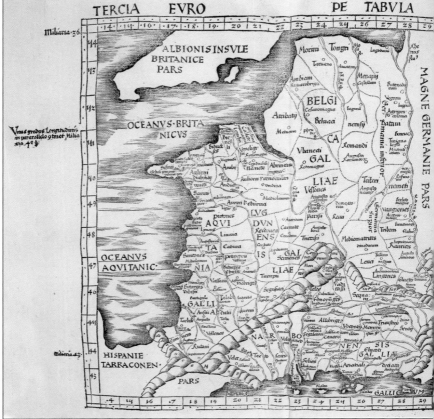

Map 4. The historical presentation of 'France' on the map of Ptolemy from the year 1513 divides the territory to separate smaller areas with abstract linear boundaries (dotted lines). However, the mountains and rivers are still bordering the French territory. Ptolemaus, Claudius, *Claudii Ptolemei viri Alexandrini Mathematice discipline Philosopi doctissimi Geographica, Tercia Evrope Tabula* (1513), The Nordenskiöld Collection, no. 205:4, Helsinki University Library, Finland.

Map 6. The corridor-like border in the map of Swedish commissaries examining the Swedish-Russian border in 1595 is a kind of transitional form between the pictures of natural border markers and presenting the border as an abstract line. Note the pictures of the border markers carved to the stones and cliffs and the 'Warpawuori' which is drawn as a picture of a mountain. The 'corridors' are endowed with legends telling about the course of the border. Gränsk., Sv (F) – R komm. 1595–1596, nos. 1–8, The National Archives of Sweden, Stockholm, Sweden.

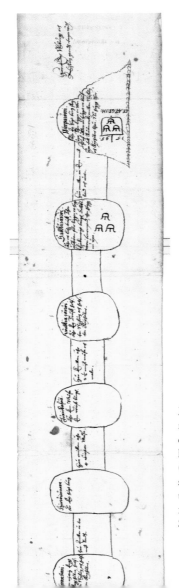

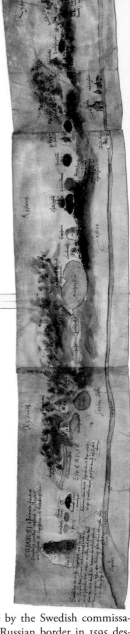

Map 7. The final map made by the Swedish commissaries examining the Swedish–Russian border in 1595 describes the border as a row of pictures of natural formations like mountains, lakes, rivers and ponds. East and Russia ('Rysslandh') is in the upper side of the map. Cf. the presentation of 'Warpawuori' and the border markers carved to the cliff with the picture 4. Gränsk., Sv (F) – R komm. 1595–1596, nos. 1–8, The National Archives of Sweden, Stockholm, Sweden.

Map 8. The divisions between the Scandinavian kingdoms and Russia are presented as a dotted line in the atlas of Barendt Langenes from the year 1599. The form of Finland is influenced in this map by the famous map of Simon von Salingen who mostly was interested in the Barents region. Langenes, Barendt, *Chart-Thresoor Inhoudende dee tafelen des gantsche Werelts Landen* (Amsterdam, 1599), The Nordenskiöld Collection, no 131:61, Helsinki University Library, Finland.

Map 9. Andreas Bureus marked the borders of peace treaties in 1595 and 1617 on his famous map of Scandinavia, known as *Orbis Arctoi*. Bureus himself was a secretary of the Swedish commission examining the border with Russians after the peace treaty of Stolbov. The examination was finished in 1621 and Bureus published the map in 1626. Bureus, Andreas, *Orbis Arctoi Nova Accurata Delincatio* (Stockholm, 1626), Uppsala University Library, Sweden.

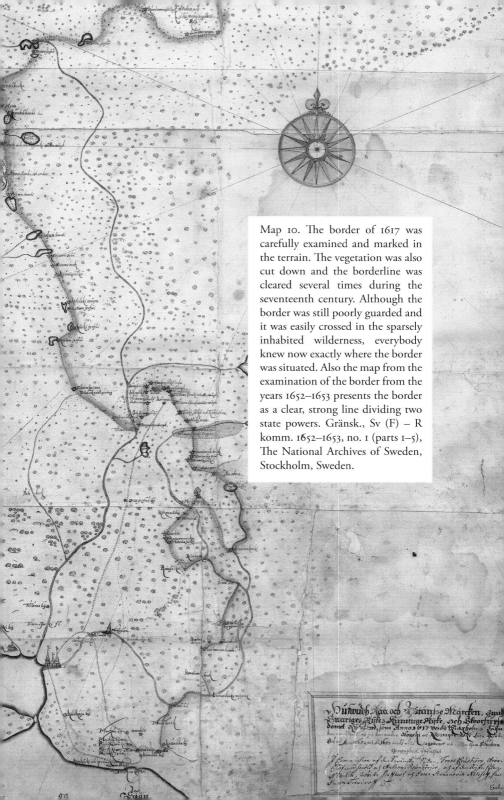

Map 10. The border of 1617 was carefully examined and marked in the terrain. The vegetation was also cut down and the borderline was cleared several times during the seventeenth century. Although the border was still poorly guarded and it was easily crossed in the sparsely inhabited wilderness, everybody knew now exactly where the border was situated. Also the map from the examination of the border from the years 1652–1653 presents the border as a clear, strong line dividing two state powers. Gränsk., Sv (F) – R komm. 1652–1653, no. 1 (parts 1–5), The National Archives of Sweden, Stockholm, Sweden.

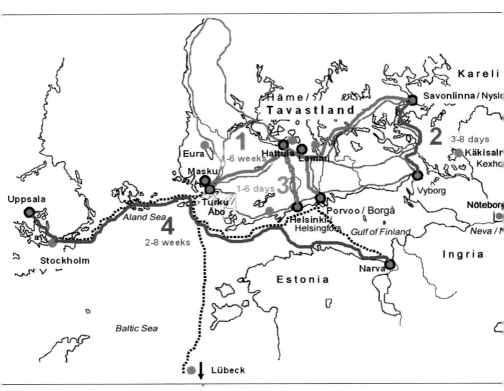

Map 16. Travel times of some letters to and from Arvid Henriksson Tawast. Drawing by Ulla Koskinen.

Route 1. From the south-west coast to Savo: Turku (Åbo) / Masku – Savonlinna (Nyslott): 12 letters; travel time 5–39 days (5, 6, 8, 9, 9, 11, 11, 15, 17, 19, 25 and 39 days).

Route 2. From Vyborg to Savonlinna: 18 letters; travel times 3–8 days (8 times 3 days, 5 times 4 days, 3 times 5 days, 6 and 8 days).

Route 3. From southern coast towns Helsinki (Helsingfors) and Porvoo (Borgå) to the parishes of Hattula and Lammi in Häme (Tavastland): 5 letters; travel times 1–6 days (1, 2, 3, 4, 6 days).

Route 4. From Narva, Estonia, to the centre of the realm (Uppsala): 4 letters; travel times 15–56 days (15, 31, 37 and 56 days).

Other routes:

From the centre of the realm to Häme (Tavastland): Stockholm–Hattula 19 days (1 letter).

From the south-western coast to Häme (Tavastland): Turku (Åbo)–Hattula 9 days (1 letter).

From Germany to Häme (Tavastland): Lübeck–Lammi 45 days (1 letter).

From Estonia to Karelia: Narva–Käkisalmi (Kexholm) 20 days (1 letter).

Sources: Information is based on 43 letters from the following archives: SRA AHTs1-2; SRA Avskrift-samlingen efter 1520: Gödik Finckes registratur 1598–99; SRA Muscovitica: Gränskommission 1595; SRA Livonica II:1, 193. Roads on the map based on Masonen 1999, p. 137; Viertola 1974, p. 107.

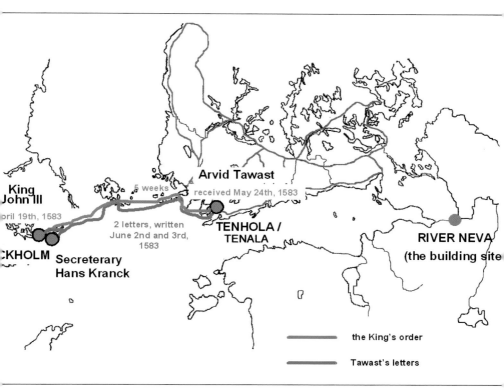

Map 17. Correspondence between Arvid Henriksson Tawast and the central power, spring 1583. Drawing by Ulla Koskinen.

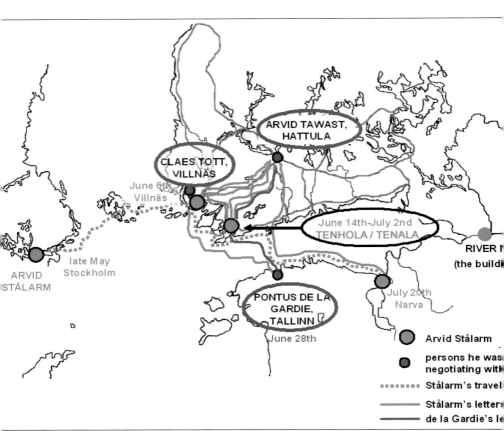

Map 18. Arvid Eriksson Stålarm's travels and letters, summer 1583. Drawing by Ulla Koskinen.

Map 23. The area of baronial fiefdom of Kajaanipori (Kajanaborg) in a map drawn by Claes Claesson in 1650. MH 107, The National Archives of Finland, Helsinki.

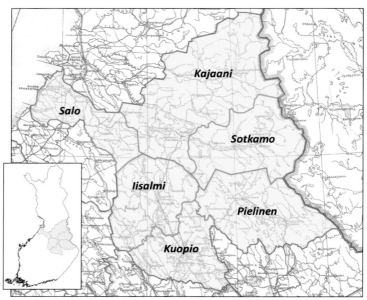

Map 22. The baronial fiefdom of Kajaani (Kajana). The administrative districts of the fiefdom were Kajaani, Iisalmi, Sotkamo, Kuopio (1650–1681), Salo, and Pielinen (1652–1681). Drawing by Jari Järvinen.

Map 24. The residences of the Cajanus family members: Anders Eriksson (Säräisniemi), Erik Cajanus (Sotkamo), Johan Cajanus (Paltamo), Anders Cajanus (Nurmes and Lieksa), Jeremias Andersson (Kajaani), Samuel Andersson (Iisalmi), Beata Andersson (Raahe), Felicia Andersson (Kajaani), and Agneta Andersson (Kajaani). Drawing by Jari Järvinen.

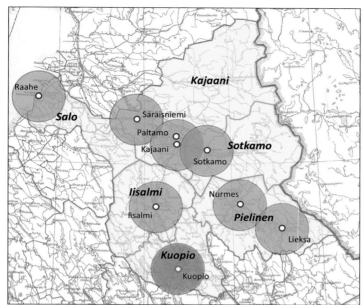

Map 25. The Cajanus family members' sphere of influence: walking range (approximately 30 km). Drawing by Jari Järvinen.

Map 26. The Cajanus family members' sphere of influence: mobility by horse-drawn cart or sledge (approximately 60 km). Drawing by Jari Järvinen.

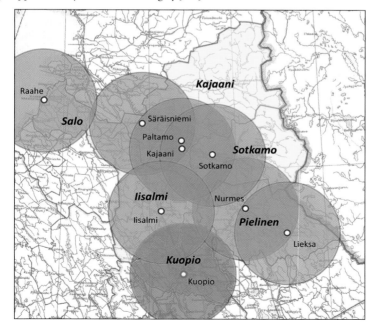

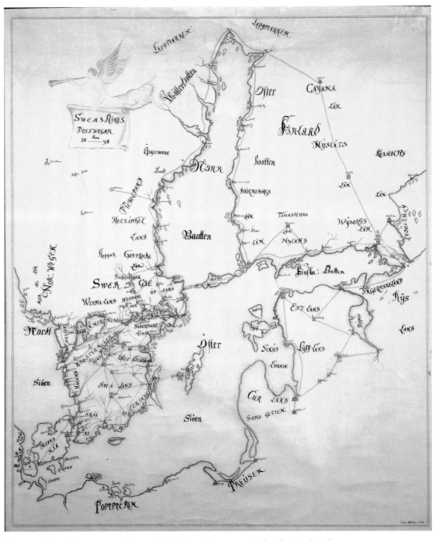

Map 27. Postal route map from 1698. Post Museum, Helsinki, Finland.

Map 28. Road map from 1757. Georg Biurman, *Vägvisare til och ifrån alla städer och namn-kunniga orter, uti Svea- och Götariken, samt Stor-Furstendömet Finland* (Stockholm, 1776, Map appendix no. 2.

Map 30. The area controlled by the Cajanus family. Drawing by Jari Järvinen.

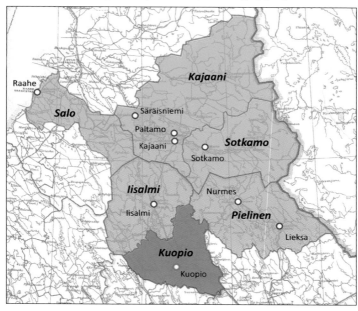

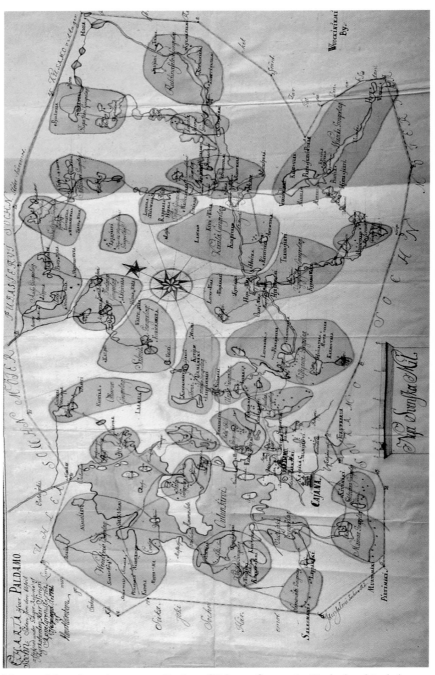

Map 29. Map of catechism exam districts of Paltamo from 1762. Finska handritade kartor, Pf 154, The Military Archives of Sweden, Stockholm.

forests were externally colonized and that the population grew during the late medieval and early modern period. This has been at the expense of understanding how the expansion of state administration and taxation both changed the production system and economic forms and led to the emergence of written documents: the invisible world transformed into a visible one.[3]

The medieval source texts use the term 'Lapp' to refer to the heterogeneous Finnic-speaking hunter-fisher populations who lived in the forest areas of (present-day) eastern Finland, Karelia (Fi. Karjala, Sw, Karelen) and Lapland (Fi. Lappi, Sw. Lappland). The modern meaning of the word is exclusively limited to the Sámi people. The Royal Dapifer (Steward) Knut Jonsson on 5 September 1328 described the population as '*homines siluestres et vagi, vulgariter dicti Lappa*'. Some time later an unknown German chronicler similarly counted the Lapps and Finns among the 'savage peoples' ('*de Lappen unde de Vynnen unde vele andere wilde lude*'). These populations used local resources and lived in ecological niches.[4]

The creation story of Finnic Folk Poetry describes a closed world, an island which was surrounded by endless waters. This was probably the micro space of the populations. People living in such circumstances had little outside contact. They did not need sophisticated tools for the organization of their spaces of communication and thus their understanding of time was cyclical.[5]

Mental mapping was primarily used to describe seasonal circulation routes and locate hunting and fishing places. The daily reality consisted of an area that a person could reach on foot or by boat. Over the course of a year, seasonal migration took place over a wider area. Individuals would seek out a spouse from neighbouring co-resident groups, that is, outside their own seasonal circulation areas.

It is very difficult to estimate the size of area covered during an annual cycle. Ylva Stenqvist has studied the extent of reach in medieval agricultural societies of Central Sweden (also a semi-peripheral forest area) and has concluded that there were significant local variations.[6] According to anthropologists, variations in the extent of reach were even greater among nomadic populations, whose movements were entirely determined by local resources, climate, geography etc. Nevertheless if we assume that the radius of the daily area of a co-resident group in the East Fenno-scandian forests was generally about 10 kilometres, seasonal migrations would have taken place within an area that was about 50 kilometres wide and spouses would have been found within a larger area that may have been around 100 kilometres large. The distance from one end of an individual's seasonal circulation to the most distant point reached by his spouse's family was at least 150 kilometres. Two sisters, for example, could reach an area of 300 kilometres, a huge distance. However, this reach was dwarfed by the distances covered in Siberia: reindeer nomadism and Arctic fishing meant that a single household in Siberia could cover several hundred kilometres.[7]

Travel was usually connected to securing nourishment and related resources. However, three types of 'exceptional' travels are described in Finnic folklore:

1. *Marriage.* Family formation did not take place inside one's own group as far as was genetically reasonable. The standard pattern of the poems describes how long it took to go wooing.
2. *Mystic travel to 'Pohjola' ('the realm of North' or the realm of the deceased).* This refers to shamanistic trips to the world of the deceased and to the land of otherness.
3. *Social gatherings, as described in the poem 'Oluen synty' ('Birth of Beer').* These were casual get-togethers of relatives and people from an area beyond the reach of everyday communication. It is possible that such gatherings were connected to regional cults or decision making. However, the role of such gatherings in East Finnic societies remains obscure because we have no information about regional cults or decision making. The cult places (*seita*) were located within the daily area of each co-resident group. On the other hand, seasonal gatherings of households took place for other reasons, such as elk hunting or salmon fishing, and were also important for family formation.[8]

We can attempt to reconstruct the areas of daily life on the basis of toponymic and geographic information. Although very few old placenames remain in use, the old form culture persisted in peripheral areas. We can use this information to build a model that can shed light on the old toponymic forms and types of travel. The following are important categories of toponyms:

1. Fishing and hunting placenames (Kutulahti ('spawning bay'), Siikajärvi ('whitefish lake'), etc.)
2. Seasonal placenames (Talvisalo ('winter island'), Kevätlahti ('spring bay'), etc.)
3. Travel placenames (Kulkemusjärvi ('travel lake'), Metsätaipale ('forest way'), etc.)

4. Mystic placenames (toponyms that are derived from pagan cult names)
5. Sámi placenames

Table 2. Distribution of various toponym types within a 10 km radius of selected seasonal toponyms[9] in the lake district of eastern Finland.

	Mystic names	Lapp/Sámi names	Spring-spawning fish names	Autumn-spawning fish names	Travel names	Total
Winter (21 pc)	193 (39%)	76 (15%)	153 (31%)	30 (6%)	46 (9%)	498 (100%)
Spring (2 pc)	9 (26%)	5 (15%)	17 (50%)	1 (3%)	2 (6%)	34 (100%)
Summer (7 pc)	70 (42%)	23 (14%)	60 (36%)	7 (4%)	8 (5%)	168 (100%)
Autumn (4 pc)	34 (31%)	23 (21%)	38 (35%)	7 (6%)	8 (7%)	110 (100%)
TOTAL (34 pc)	306	127	268	45	64	810

Table 3. The relative number of the relevant (above-mentioned, cf. Table 1) toponyms in close proximity to selected seasonal placenames (average number of names per square kilometre, absolute number in parentheses).

	Radius 0–5 km	Radius 5–10 km	Radius 10–15 km	Radius 15–20 km	Average 0–20 km
Talvisalo/Nyslott	0.08 (6)	0.09 (21)	0.12 (46)	0.06 (33)	0.08 (106)
Kesälahti	0.17 (13)	0.11 (26)	0.07 (29)	0.03 (18)	0.07 (86)
Talvilahti/Pieksämäki	0.08 (6)	0.1 (24)	0.08 (33)	0.06 (31)	0.07 (94)
Talviranta/Anttola	0.23 (18)	0.03 (7)	0.10 (38)	0.10 (56)	0.09 (119)
Syysjärvi/Mikkeli	0.03 (2)	0.11 (27)	0.09 (35)	0.1 (56)	0.10 (120)
Kevätsalo/Joutsa	0.10 (8)	0.06 (14)	0.07 (28)	0.04 (20)	0.06 (70)
Talvisuo/Mäntyharju	0.06 (5)	0.10 (23)	0.06 (25)	0.07 (37)	0.07 (90)
Kesämäki/Sulkava	0.10 (8)	0.08 (20)	0.12 (46)	0.11 (58)	0.11 (132)
Average	0.11 (8.3)	0.07 (20.3)	0.09 (35)	0.07 (38.6)	0.08 (102.1)

There is a clear indication of seasonal circulation in many places. A cluster of mystic names and various fishing or hunting names are concentrated around one or two of the same type of seasonal names (e.g. winter). Ten kilometres or so from this area we find a new concentration located near

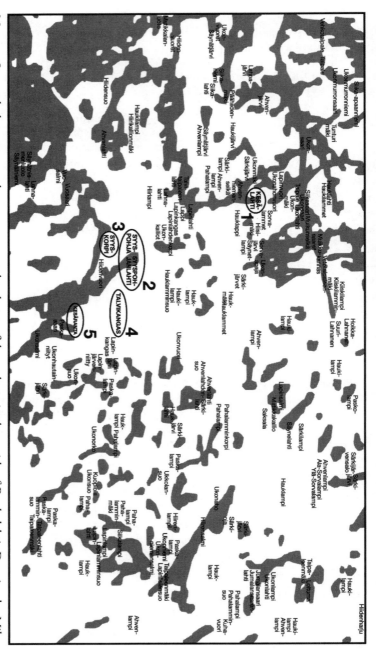

Map 11. Seasonal placenames and names connected to hunter-fisher culture in the parish of Ruokolahti. Drawing by Mika Saarelainen.

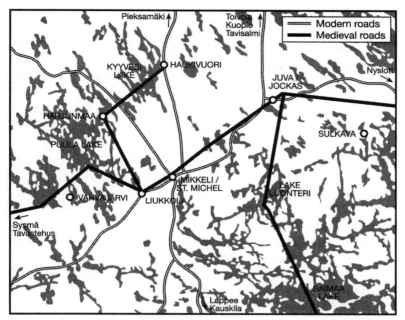

Map 12. Medieval and modern main roads in southern Savo. Drawing by Mika Saarelainen.

another kind of seasonal name (e.g. autumn). The parish of Ruokolahti in south-eastern Saimaa (Sw. Saimen) serves as an illustrative example of this pattern (Map 11). Within a ten-kilometre radius of Kesälahti ('summer bay') there are twelve mystic toponyms, seven names that refer to Lapps or Sámi, nineteen fishing names and three travel toponyms. Syyspohja ('autumn bay') and Syyskorpi ('autumn forest') are located twelve kilometres from Kesälahti; in this area we find one travel, five mystic, eight Lapp/Sámi and eight fish toponyms. A further six kilometres from Syyspohja one comes to Talvikangas ('winter forest') with eight mystic, four Lapp/Sámi and five fish names.

Travel

The water systems in the region form natural communication routes, which have been in use since the Stone Age. One can easily travel along them both in summer and in winter (when they are frozen). Growing and fallen trees, rocky soils, lakes and marshes make the forests of East

Fennoscandia seem impenetrable in comparison to southern and western parts of Finland. Historically the topography of East Fennoscandia certainly hindered the construction of land roads (Map 12). Although travelling on foot was, in fact, the most important form of communication until the nineteenth century, small paths only connected areas that were a short distance apart.[10]

Old folkloric poems offer descriptions of travel, and the following is a fairly typical example: 'Laski päivän maan vesiä, päivän toisen suon vesiä, kolmannen merenvesiä' ('sailed a day through land-waters, another through marsh-waters, a third day through sea-waters'). In most descriptions, travelling means following water routes (either moving across the ice or sailing). Väinämöinen, the mythical shaman hero, drove a sledge 'on an open lake' and travelled to Pohjola 'by boat'. There are very few references to land roads in the poems, and these seem to have been collected in West Finland or in Ingria (Fi. Inkeri, Sw. Ingermanland). The poem *Luojan virsi* describes travel in Vuokkiniemi: '*Kesällä kevyisin purjein, talvella lylyin lipein*' ('in summer in a light craft, in winter on sliding skis'). However, in a version of the same poem from Kopor'e (Ingria), there is a sequence about riding a horse along a rocky road. It is possible that even the famous sea poems of the Sampo complex had their origins not in western Finland but in the east. The sea motifs may in fact provide better accounts of the Finnish lake district than the Iron Age culture found on the shores of the Baltic Sea, which has traditionally been seen as a possible subject or inspiration for the complex.[11]

The lake systems east of Lake Päijänne largely run from north to south. Thus east–west connections are rare and occur in areas where two water systems are close to each other. These kinds of watersheds are known as *taipale* in Finnish (*volok* in Russian) and have traditionally been very important communication areas.

A '*taipale-volok*' is not only a communication connection: it is also a border region and encounter area of two 'water worlds'. Such areas were already dwelling places in the Stone Age. Many rock paintings have been discovered around taipales, which reflects the significance of such areas for the indigenous culture. Their strategic importance for the new European power is also evident: the first parishes and control centres were established in the taipale areas.[12] Mikkeli (Sw. S:t Michel), Joroinen (Sw. Jorois) and the passages from Valkeala to Lappee (Sw. Lappvesi) and Valkeala to Savitaipale are the most significant connections between the Kymijoki (Sw. Kymmene) and Vuoksi-Saimaa water systems. An important connection takes a route from Ladoga (Fi. Laatokka) to

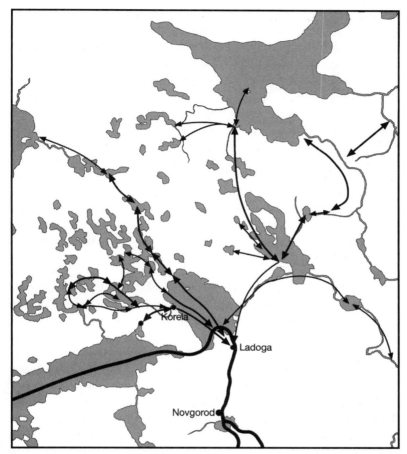

Map 13. Routes following waterways (marked with piles) between the Ladoga area and the Gulf of Bothnia as well as the White Sea. The old sailing and rowing route between Scandinavia and the Russian areas is also marked on the map. Drawing by Mika Saarelainen.

Saimaa along the river Vuoksi (Sw. Vuoksen) and the river Hiitolanjoki to Lake Simpeleenjärvi. Saimaa is also connected to the White Sea by Lake Pielinen (Sw. Pielis) and the river Lieksanjoki, although the main connection to the White Sea from the world of Ladoga passes through Lake Onega. A medieval route connects Saimaa via Lake Pielinen to the lake system of the river Oulujoki (Sw. Ule älv) and then to the Gulf of Bothnia (Map 13).

Forms of communication in peripheral areas have been overlooked in scholarly literature. The only text relating to Finland deals with land roads and concentrates on areas south of the Salpausselkä hills. Russian scholars have discussed northern water roads, but their main focus has been the identification of archaeological finds rather than the composition and analysis of the system itself. Although Petr Sorokin and Nikolai Makarov have recently published comprehensive texts that fill these gaps in a substantial way, their studies are concerned with more eastern and southern regions and with people who had regular contact with merchants and the representatives of Christian power.[13]

A new publication by Jussi-Pekka Taavitsainen, Janne Vilkuna and Henry Forssell about the village of Suojoki is a highly important case study. Suojoki is situated in the remote wilderness of Central Finland, to the west of Lake Päijänne. The river Suojoki takes a route that connects the water system of Kymijoki with that of Kokemäenjoki (Sw. Kumo älv). Over the years tens of boats, the remains of winter vehicles and other organic objects have been found in the river. These finds date from the late thirteenth century through to the 1700s. It seems that Suojoki may have been a 'centre' in the transition zone between the peasant culture and the world of nomadic 'Lapps'.[14]

The only written medieval reference to vehicles in the inland area refers to Savonlinna (or Olavinlinna) Castle (Sw. Nyslott, Olofsborg). A *pråm* (barge) is mentioned in connection with the building of the stone castle in 1477. Rock paintings also depict the various kinds of boats, canoes, sledges and skis that were used on the waterways. The remains of wooden items such as skis, boats, paddles and sledges have been preserved in lakes and marshes for hundreds, or even thousands, of years. They are an important sample of historical sources that relate to Finnish history before the time of written sources. The remains of these items have been restored and kept in local museums or private houses. However, we still lack a general analytic overview and scholarly analysis of these important artefacts. Perhaps they may support the idea that travel/transport routes and connection places like Suojoki existed and that roads were primarily routed across water and ice.[15]

Despite some technical developments, the basic solutions to the problem of transportation and communication remained largely unchanged from the Stone Age through to the nineteenth century, because local needs had not altered significantly. The sewn boats found in Mekrijärvi and Hartola (Sw. Gustav Adolfs) were introduced in the Viking Age. Because such boats had oars instead of paddles, they could carry larger loads and make longer journeys. The barge at Nyslott was typical of Swedish navy vessels of the period. Both of these innovations indicate that there was a need for improved reachability and transportation; however, we should bear in mind that this need came from outside the area.[16]

Although rock paintings are rather common in the Finnish lake district, they have not been recorded systematically. Mark Hoppál views them as records of the shamanistic extensions of mental experiences and travels to 'the other world'. The paintings date from the Neolithic period, the time at which Shamanism took hold. Cults, cult places and shamanistic practices survived, however, for hundreds or thousands of years – as long, in fact as the local culture (economic and social system) remained unchanged. New rock paintings have been found in Siberia, and at least one rock drawing in Lapland dates back to the Middle Ages. We should also take note of the fact that the figures found on Sámi shaman drums are very similar to those found in rock paintings. Overall it seems that we can largely equate the world of the rock paintings with that of the semi-nomadic forest-dwellers. Thus the messages of the paintings remained relevant to everyday life in the lake district until the Middle Ages.[17]

It is perhaps difficult for us, from our modern point of view, to fully appreciate the primary role that travel from this world to the other world played (and continues to play) in indigenous societies. Reaching the other world was extremely important. Such journeys were living forms of travel and reach. The world of the deceased was as real as the visible world, and travel beyond the everyday sphere always meant crossing a border. In this way the mystic extension and the path from one's daily area to the macro space (of the deities, the dead and the future) was an essential form of travel and communication. The shaman was able to make this journey and sought to reach information vital for the survival of his people. Cult stones, holy hills and other sites were visible markers of mystical borders. These mystical borders and their markers formed part of a traveller's mental map of an area.[18]

Veikko Anttonen has explained that in western Finland the toponym *pyhä* ('sacred') was a concept which marked the border area between the everyday and the otherness.[19] Lotte Tarkka has described the forest as another world and travel to the hunting area from one's dwelling place as a border crossing. The idea of a border between forest and home also prevailed in the mythology of agriculture.[20]

The conceptualization of geographically distant areas must have been very unspecific (from our point of view) but also unimportant. To some extent, the spatial dimensions of folklore also belong to the economic system. The land of Pohjola (the North) was cold and dark and thus a poor area for cultivation. This was of course essential information for agricultural purposes, but this statement had another more essential meaning, because Pohjola was also the mythical realm of the dead. In fact the Finnic Epic is based on travel between two distinct spaces: the home area and the distant Pohjola. There is a dichotomy both between home and the unknown other and between this world and the world of the dead. However, the division between the known and the unknown was not limited to the most peripheral societies: it was also a part of conceptualizations of the world in more international and developed medieval cultures. According to John McKinnell, 'most Norse mythological narrative shows a dualism of outlook which divides living beings between us and them [...] and this antagonistic dualism is one of the basic assumptions of Norse myths.'[21]

In the conceptualization of borders one must pay special attention to the symbolic meanings of the surroundings. Kindred relations, hunting and fishing, trade routes and the mystical meanings of various geographical objects (bad water, holy water, holy hill, stone of god, *hiisi*, *ukko*, etc.) were all part of the sacral landscape. One division was between the everyday living place of home and forest; while the sacral meanings of various geographical objects such as hills, peninsulas and lakes – the living places of the idols – formed the second level of the division. Other kinds of meanings in the surroundings formed internal borders: the Hanti people (a North Siberian Finnic-speaking population), for example, also define space according to the spheres of males and females.[22]

The mental geography of the shamanistic world must have been an essential element in the conceptualization of space. The places where the ancestors lived and the cosmic world (the stars, sun and moon) belonged to both the macro space and the everyday world. An important distinction was made between *tämänilmainen* (the visible world – literally 'this air space') and *tuonilmainen* (the invisible world – literally 'that air space'). The idea of the world beyond the visible did not, however, mean something absolutely supernatural: above all it meant the space beyond society. As previously discussed, the dichotomy between one's home surroundings and Pohjola also encompassed the difference between the visible and invisible worlds. Thus long-distance travel also implied '*extra societatem*', that is, going outside one's own ecological niche. Anna-Liisa Siikala has connected the understanding of the mythic Pohjola or 'that air space' to the understanding of time. The mythic conception of history does not make a clear and unambiguous distinction between this world and the world of the deceased. In contrast to our way of conceptualizing the world, indigenous cultures composed their mental map of symbolic meanings in a way which resulted in conceiving physical geography (the micro space) differently. The concept of space consisted of many levels rather than long distances.[23]

Mauno Koski refers to the connection between certain *hiisi* toponyms with toponyms prefixed by *nais* ('woman') along water routes. The *hiisi* places had formed taboos that were forbidden for women. The *nais* toponyms provided women with another route. For example, in Sortavala women would get out of their boats in Naislahti ('women bay') and take a land road while men would continue on Lake Ladoga and sail around Hiidenniemi ('peninsula of *hiisi*').[24]

Eero Kiviniemi has stressed that this worldview has influenced the way the landscape has been named: certain animal names, like 'the bird of Shaman' (black-throated diver), are commonly found even on modern maps. In the study of the Lapp village of Sompio written by folklorist Samuli Paulaharju (1875–1944), there is an illustrative description of a journey along a river. It provides details of how the traveller chose his route and venerated certain places and stones as the dwelling places of idols.[25]

New world

The increasing number of foreign objects found among archaeological material dating from the tenth century onwards provides evidence of the gradual penetration of a supra-local European cultural influence and the beginning of Christianization in the region. A trade area was formed around the basin of Lake Ladoga, which connected it to the Viking trail to the north Russian rivers and finally to the river Volga. The influence of trade soon extended to Lapland, Norrland and Finnmarken. Trade connections followed the waterways from the north and the north-west to the south and south-east. However, as Richard Hodges argues, the logic of early trade differed from that of present-day trade. The need to travel lay with the new world. Indigenous hunters and fishers did not travel to distant markets: instead buyers came to the forests. This influenced understanding of the world and reachability. The expansion of trade did not automatically expand the micro space of forest-dwellers because, in part, trade was more successful when it took the form of a mystic gift-exchange ritual.[26]

Trade led to the development of a consciousness about the wider world and made distant regions physically reachable, thus extending micro space. Urbanization had a strong impact in this regard. While the reach of an agricultural society was limited to village society or the seasonal movement area of a co-resident group, the urban way of life led to the division of labour and the formation of social structures. Craftspeople required raw materials which had to be imported from the surrounding areas and later on from distant countries. This resulted in the integration of the local economic area and also the integration of the townspeople with Baltic and Central European cultures.[27]

Although the first Christian fingerprints had already been visible in the time of the Vikings, the expansion of the new world into indigenous everyday life and the proper formation of private churches and primitive parishes only began from the eleventh century onwards in the south-west and west of Finland and along the shores of Lake Ladoga. The first Christians were new settlers and formed the elite of the local agricultural society, also connected to the expansion of European power. The realm was formed as a network between the parish centres and was represented by royal castles, but the influence of the new culture extended only to those people who were physically reachable. By the end of the Middle Ages, this meant the agricultural societies who lived in southern and western Finland, along the Baltic coast and on the shores of Lake Ladoga. State formation did not reach the inland area of the Ladogan water system before the late medieval European economic crisis. Therefore, the building of parish network and control centres (castles) and the expansion of taxation had halted by the early fourteenth century and only resumed among the forest-dwellers in the last years of the fifteenth century.[28]

The situation was described in a very concrete way when, on 15 October 1504, the State Council authorized Laurentius, the Bishop of Turku (Sw. Åbo), to found new parishes in Karelia and Savo (Sw. Savolax). Furthermore new taxes were to be levied in order to support these parishes: the State Council regarded these areas as part of the Swedish realm and thus belonging to the Bishopric of Turku. According to the letter, the rural inhabitants neither knew the Christian teachings nor attended the churches but instead were living like Lapps and other pagans. The reason for this was the scarcity of churches: some people lived more than 15 Swedish miles (150 kilometres) from a church. Canons Michael Agricola and Canutus Johannis Raumensis expressed similar worries when they described the religious situation in North Savo in a letter (dated 7 February 1549) addressed to Bailiff Gustaf Fincke.[29]

In a modern sense, the establishment of the border was part of the conceptualization of space. The local border institution of fixed borders of land areas developed in West Finland during the Middle Ages, as Seppo Suvanto has shown.[30] This way of thinking only spread to the eastern region alongside progress in field agriculture, village formation and urbanization: the indigenous way of life was semi-nomadic and did not include the concept of landownership. One of the first examples of a fixed border may be the ditch around the church of Kappelinmäki (Kauskila/Lappee). Perhaps it had a mental influence on the surrounding. Apart from this, the first known land borders in the area date from the fifteenth century. However, the first real maps to depict the landscape were drawn up only from the seventeenth century onwards. These first traces of European-style landownership also came from the circles of the local Christian upper class.[31]

Long-distance trade, a monetary economy and the development of state and administrative structures required a linear understanding of time. The transformation of the concept of time among forest-dwellers began with their increased contacts with the outer world. A trip to a distant marketplace necessitated a conceptualization of the future. The linear way of thinking became even more important in connection with production for markets: planning also required timing.

A slight change in the understanding of the concept of time was already visible in the Iron Age world. The Scandinavian pre-Christian religion had a concept of the end of the world ('*Ragnarok*') and the Finnic Epic recounts the story of creation. On the other hand, these kinds of stories still had a more mystical rather than real linear extension. The description of creation had a symbolic meaning and formed a stable part of the poems rather than being a dogmatic recitation of history. Thus Ob-Ugrians, like other forest-dwellers, continued to be unable to offer precise answers about the source of creation (i.e. who or what had created the world), because, as they said, they only followed the customs of their ancestors.[32]

The parallel lives of the new and old worlds continued to co-exist for some time. Because names and their value/meaning are two different things, the new world may have adopted old holy names and simply ascribed new meanings to them. The myths were tied to certain places in the landscape, because these were important cult objects. Although the Christian Church did not consider such places holy, it is probable that new holy institutions were founded, at least to some extent, on the same sites. Places that inspired fear because of some taboo rules might have retained their ancient horror within the new explanations. In the nineteenth century people still experienced Lapp cairns as frightening. It seems that something from their indigenous meaning as sacred places had been preserved. In the same way, other 'sacred' places might have been transformed into Christian holy places in the explanations of the new power. Locals probably did not consider the explanations but rather just considered the places to be sacred or denied. In this way placenames that took certain prefixes such as *pyhä*, *paha* ('evil') and *hiisi* may reveal traces of the old society in the new surroundings.[33]

New ways

The expansion of European society and the formation of the royal realm changed not only the economic system, but also the conceptualization of the surroundings and the communication system. The ability to reach into a larger territory was necessary in order to exert control. As a result planning took on an increasingly important role and thus strengthened the need for a linear understanding of time. Moreover, the new Scandinavian administration was based on land roads and approached the area under study from the west (against the natural water connections). Therefore, the new power also meant a new orientation in all means of communication. The last Catholic Archbishop of Uppsala, Olaus Magnus, wrote an extensive description of the history, geography, culture and political life of the Nordic people in the middle of the sixteenth century. According to Magnus, both the administration's and the army's connections were largely concentrated along land roads. Although the Archbishop describes warfare at sea, he also outlines the way in which rivers, lakes and the sea seem to have been obstacles within everyday life and activities. Magnus viewed the way in which the Muscovites used waterways and carried their light boats over stretches of land as an odd and alien phenomenon.[34]

The new road history of Finland (and related studies) emphasizes the role of historical land connections and underestimates the importance of waterways. Its criticism is levelled at local histories and their inclination to exaggerate the importance of rather small rivers and lakes as means of communication. The criticism is justified: traditional accounts have not used proper sources to explain their views. However, both the new road history and local histories have discussed the formation of European society. The road history describes the construction of a road network from the perspective of the new power; local histories have not drawn any distinction between the new administration and the indigenous world in this respect.[35]

The new administration had new reasons to extend its reach: in order to increase its resources through taxation, transportation had to be organized. The concept of sovereignty also entailed an obligation to be able to control the territory of the realm and to define its borders. Earlier this had not been necessary, but now there was a need to be able to physically reach the more distant areas of the realm. The obligation for physical reach required the strengthening of the realm's power within the forest areas – that is, more travel, more transportation and a stronger presence of military troops and administrative officials (as well as the support and sustenance of these personnel). The presence of foreign elements in the forests also created consciousness about the 'other' and a sense of self-identification; an idea about a supra-local identity formed among the local inhabitants. This stimulated travel, trade (goods exchange) and the formation of local contacts, all of which brought together the loosely organized hunter-fisher populations and resulted in the formation of pre-national regional entities ('regional bands' in the vocabulary of anthropologists).

According to the sixteenth-century list of pagan 'Finnish' deities collected by Bishop Michael Agricola, the 'West Finns' had a special idol for the protection of travellers, Ilmarinen, but 'East Finns' had no equivalent deity. This may reflect social developments, which resulted in increased travel and the formation of a supra-local reality in western areas.[36]

In general the primary reason for long-distance travel by ordinary people in Christian Europe was pilgrimage. South-western Finland was, in this respect, part of the new world. Medieval sources concerning pilgrimage in the eastern area are scarce: only one document describes a specific pilgrimage. Pope Bonifacius IX issued a letter (dated 9 May 1403) in support of the pilgrimage to the Franciscan church of Vyborg (Fi. Viipuri, Sw. Viborg). The situation was similar in the Orthodox Church. The hagiographists describe the pilgrimage of the saints, but we cannot know whether the stories were based on historical facts or were only a part of the stereotypical narration. It seems probable that the pilgrimages of ordinary people only became more common during the modern period.[37]

The first reorientation of the eastern contact landscape took place when castles were built at Hämeenlinna (Sw. Tavastehus), Vyborg, Korela, Oršek and Tiuri and parishes were established in Eastern Häme (Hollola, Hauho, Lammi, Sysmä), Eastern Nyland (Porvoo, Sw. Borgå), Helsinki (Sw. Helsinge), Pyhtää (Sw. Pyttis), Pernaja (Sw. Pernå) and Sipoo (Sw. Sibbo), Swedish Karelia (Kymi, Lappee, Vehkalahti (Sw. Veckelaks),

Vironlahti (Sw. Vederlaks), Vyborg, Jääski (Sw. Jääskis) and Äyräpää), Savo (Mikkeli) and Novgorodian Karelia (Korela (Ru. Priozersk), Kurki-joki, Sortavala (Sw. Sordavala), Sakkola, Salmi (Sw. Salmis) and Rautu (Sw. Rautus), as well as the monasteries of Valamo and Konevica (Fi. Konevitsa, Sw. Konevits) from the middle of the thirteenth century to the late 1300s. This stopped or limited trade from East Häme and South Saimaa to Ladoga. Instead these areas (East Häme and South Saimaa) formed connections with Vyborg, Hämeenlinna and the south-west. This contributed to the creation of a de facto southern border and consolidated that border after it was officially defined in the Treaty of Nöteborg (Fi. Pähkinäsaari).[38]

The first land roads connected the new type of castle centres with the parishes of eastern Fennoscandia. The road from Vyborg to Hämeenlinna had an influence on dwelling sites on the southern coast of Saimaa and contributed to the growth of Kauskila. Another important land road followed the coast of the Gulf of Finland from Vyborg to Turku and connected parish centres along its route. As well as the famous bridge order from the 1260s (which refers to the southern coast of Lake Ladoga), we also have information about drivers and ferrymen from many places in Karelia. Such details can be found in the first written documents of the late fifteenth century, but we have no real information about specific roads in Russian Karelia before the modern period. However, in all probability Korela was connected to the core area of Novgorod not only by the route over Lake Ladoga and along the river Volhov, but also from the fourteenth century by land roads through Ingria. The new connections created a new geographical understanding among local inhabitants and led to the marginalization of old routes and orientations.[39]

The new phase of Christian administration building began in earnest at the end of the fifteenth century with the construction of the castle at Savonlinna in the middle of the Saimaa area. Parishes were established in Juva (Sw. Jockas), Sääminki (Sw. Säminge) and Ilomantsi (Sw. Ilomants); the chapel of Kitee (Sw. Kides) was also founded. In the sixteenth century the parishes of Kuopio and Pieksämäki were founded and the Lapp pogosty were organized. This second period resulted in the precise definition of the Swedish–Muscovite border at the end of the sixteenth century and the realization of royal power and the levying of taxes among the societies of eastern Finland and Karelia. The formation of controversies between local populations was a part of the regional identity formation. The final transformation from an economic system based on semi-nomadic fishing and hunting to a system based on agriculture (slash-and-burn cultivation) also affected reach and travel.[40]

Permanent settlements form the basic precondition for a permanent network of roads. The traditional way of living resulted in a flexible system in which only certain key points were fixed. These locations were important for crossing over land areas or had some cultic meaning or practical significance in orientation. Otherwise the (water) road itself was open (i.e. not fixed). Permanent field-based agriculture was introduced to the area largely after the late medieval period and led to a transition from semi-nomadism to permanent dwelling sites. Therefore road formation also belongs to the later period and the establishment of foreign administrative power.[41]

The more permanent way of life also increased overall travel. It became possible for the early modern administration of the realm to submit the local population to obligations and control. This integrated the region into the realm but also meant that administrative centres had to be visited (which had not been the case earlier). Individuals had to bring items from the market to their homes, and opportunities to take one's own produce to market were increasing. Whereas old cult places were connected to dwelling places, the new Christian churches, which individuals had to visit from time to time, were located in parish centres. Under the new administration, royal legislation extended into various spheres of daily life: for example, marriages had to be conducted in parish centres and judges held court sessions in their mansions. The need for such travel had not previously existed in this area.

There are very few existing records that refer to early long-distance travel. We can identify two stories that date from 1442. The formation of parishes required communication with the Bishop of Turku's administration. Bishop Magnus Tavast claimed that the road between the parishes of Sysmä and Mikkeli was 18 Swedish miles (180 kilometres) long and that travellers had to rest overnight on ice or land. For this reason Tavast founded a staging house ('*hws*') in Vahvajärvi. In another document a '*nath bool*' in Juva is mentioned in connection with an episcopal visit. This perhaps also referred to an exact place or house in the area. These kinds of arrangements connected the roads to fixed places and created administrative roads between churches, mansions and castles, routes that were alien to the traditional way in which travel was conceptualized.[42]

The document about the foundation of the parish of Juva also provides what seems to be an odd description of travel routes in the area. When returning from his visit to Juva, the Bishop had two options: either travel back to Mikkeli or continue on to Lappee. From a modern geographical perspective, there is only one option: the shortest route from Juva to Lappee passes through Mikkeli. However, perhaps in the fifteenth century the road over Lake Saimaa was more appealing. In this case one would have travelled from the centre of Jockas to Lake Luonteri (passing the Ihantsalo hill fort) or to Sulkava and then on to Saimaa.[43]

The Muscovite-Finnic merchant Nousia Rydz's famous description of trade routes from Lake Ladoga to the Arctic Ocean and the Gulf of Bothnia was recorded by Jacob Teitt, a Swedish royal scribe. Nousia describes the route from Ladoga to Saimaa and then on to Lake Oulunjärvi (Sw. Ule träsk) and another route to the White Sea. The Swedish officials assumed that Russians used waterways: they asked Nousia to tell them the names of the lakes between Ladoga and the Gulf of Bothnia ('*hvadh träsk som rydzerne farads ifrå Kexholmm och til Norboten, hvadh the heetha, huru longe, och huru bredhe the äre?*'). Moreover they were curious about the shape and the length of the White Sea ('*huru longt Hvitehaffvedh löper in udi Rydzlandh, um the kunne komme med skep til Nogårdh ther utaff, szå att the icke skole drage utöffver land?*'). The merchants' routes took them across large lakes and along rivers, but they also had to carry their goods along rather long land roads. It seems that land roads were viewed as obstacles in their journeys.[44]

In 1556 Ture Bjelke described the journey between Swedish administrative units in his letter to Jakob Bagge. He notes with pleasure that land roads can be used on the route from Vyborg through Savilahti (Sw. Savilaks) near Mikkeli and Juva to Joroinen (Sw. Jorois), but then goes on to say that the journeys to Tavisalmi near Kuopio and to Oulu (Sw. Uleåborg) are more complicated due to lakes and moors.[45]

Having defeated rebelling peasants in Mikkeli in the winter of 1597, the knights of Savonlinna, under the leadership of Gödick Fincke, moved from Mikkeli to Liukkola (some 10 kilometres south of the parish centre) and continued on to Haukivuori (approximately 45 kilometres north of Mikkeli) via Harjunmaa. The route taken by the knights seems totally incomprehensible from a modern perspective. The main railway from the south to Mikkeli passes by Liukkola before reaching the town and then continues on to Haukivuori. A highway also follows this route. Today travelling via Harjunmaa would mean taking a long diversion into the western wilderness area. The old route has ceased to exist and no longer seems to make sense to us.[46]

However, when we examine the map more closely the rationale behind the decision to take such a route becomes clear. Liukkola lies at the edge of Lake Puula, which is part of the Kymijoki water system and thus connected to Lake Kyyvesi in Harjunmaa. Haukivuori lies in the north-eastern corner of Kyyvesi. The modern route follows a hill chain, which is also the watershed between the Saimaa-Vuoksi and Kymijoki water systems. While modern people operate in a world dominated by land roads, it was still natural for sixteenth-century knights to travel south from Mikkeli along the easiest route to the Kymijoki water system and then to follow the waterway (ice road) to the north. The direct path to the north from Mikkeli was blocked by impenetrable forests and rocky terrain.

Sources reveal that when the king called the Bailiff of Savo, Jören Nilsson, home (on 9 September 1551) another bailiff of the same stature, Jacob Pederssen, was within the jurisdiction area surrounding Savonlinna Castle. The title 'redfougte' indicates that the official was 'riding' through the area of the bailiwick (i.e. he was not appointed to a specific location).[47]

According to the register of grievances compiled by Jacob Teitt, three (riding) bailiffs worked in the Saimaa area. Alongside Simon Andersson (Savonlinna) and Jacob Pedersson (Juva, Rantasalmi (Sw. Randasalmi), Tavisalmi, Liistensaari), Mats Raffweldson worked as a bailiff in Store-Sawlax (Mikkeli). The royal mansions were local centres, of which there were four in the bailiwick of Savonlinna: Kiiala (Mikkeli), Liistensaari (Sulkava), Rantasalmi and Tavisalmi (Kuopio). As a matter of fact, the reorganization of royal mansions in Savo increased the number of bailiffs from two to six. There were three mansions on the road from Vyborg to Savonlinna: Lappee (Kauskila), Taipale and Sulkava (Liistensaari). The road from Savonlinna to Hämeenlinna went through three or four stations: Rantasalmi, Juva, Mikkeli (Kiiala) and Kuopio (Toivola).[48]

Flexibility was not the only difference between the travel geography of the new and old worlds. Perhaps the greatest difference was the change from the world of water roads to the world of land roads. As we saw in the letter by Ture Bjelke, the route from Vyborg to Oulu through eastern Finland was easy only as long as it went across land. When the route took them over lakes and along waterways, the officials faced difficulties. This was in sharp contrast to the descriptions of travel found within Finnic Folk Poetry.[49]

The new administrations in Sweden and Muscovy exerted their authority in the forest inland areas from the middle of the fifteenth century. Their presence led to the organization of land roads, hostelries and ferries (which met the needs of officials rather than those of the indigenous populations). Roads became fixed in certain places, thus creating 'small permanent centres'. All of this contributed to a new connection geography that favoured land areas and avoided natural water chains. The first information about these changes in the lake district dates back to 1442 (as discussed above). Later sources also mention ferries, hostelries and bridges, which indicates the importance of land roads. However, such features were uncommon and were largely connected to roads that led to castles.[50]

The sources also refer to the drivers and peasants who took care of ferries and boats. Peasants had a duty to undertake this work and so some of the sources that mention boat workers are court protocols. The needs of the royal administration were the primary reason for the organization of otherwise unknown practices among local inhabitants. Only later did peasants take on hostelry-keeping and driving as their own businesses.[51]

Jacob Teitt also provided details of the hostelries found alongside public roads. Hostelries were the houses of bailiffs ('*gårder, som Kon:ge M:t wår alder nådligaste herre will, haffwe fougter opå, ther almänne wager är*'). Moreover, Teitt refers to the '*natläger*' used by John (Johan), Duke of Finland: the accommodation of soldiers in ordinary houses owned by peasants and burghers. With regard to the area of our study, the text only mentions the few mansions of bailiffs found along the road from Savonlinna to Hämeenlinna and those from Vyborg to Savonlinna and Hämeenlinna.[52]

The changing relationship with water routes is also visible in the new cartography of the sixteenth and seventeenth centuries. The traditional communication routes were transformed into borders and border markers (that is, division markers rather than connections). Cartographers used lakes and rivers to mark the borders of the realms, either real or imagined. These borderlines on maps and in the terrain meant a totally new conceptualization of one's surroundings. This way of thinking was introduced into the forests alongside the establishment of the new royal state power.

The degeneration of water routes is visible in eighteenth- and nineteenth-century documents. At this time increased trade required better transport connections, and the state administration started to assess the waterways in this light. Between 1738 and 1741, *kolleegiiassessor* Ulrik Rudenschöld evaluated the connections between Päijänne and Saimaa. The aim was to use the waterways to form a connection from the Gulf of Bothnia to the Gulf of Finland. According to Rudenschöld, the connection between Mikkeli and Sysmä was hardly ever used anymore and the one between Lappee and Valkeala was unsuitable because of the low water levels. The connection over Mäntyharju to Savitaipale was deemed the most feasible route. In general Rudenschöld was not very optimistic about the usefulness of water connections.[53]

Conclusion

The indigenous populations of inland eastern Fennoscandia lived within separated ecological niches and thus seldom undertook long-distance travel. In this context travel meant short trips to fishing or hunting places and seasonal circulation between dwelling areas. The most important forms of travel were shamanistic journeys to the other world of the deceased and the deities. Contact with the outside world began to increase in the age of the Vikings but remained rather limited. The communication system was based on waterways and was only fixed in a few places that were important for orientation or crossing from one water system to another.

The first reorientation of the eastern contact landscape took place between the mid-thirteenth century and the late 1300s as a result of the medieval formation of the Swedish and Novgorodian realms and the beginning of Christianization. This limited the trade connections from East Häme and South Saimaa to Ladoga and the south-east. Instead these areas (East Häme and South Saimaa) formed connections with Vyborg, Hämeenlinna and Turku. This contributed to the creation of a de facto southern border and consolidated that border after it was officially defined in the Treaty of Nöteborg.

The first land roads connected the new type of castle centres with the parishes of eastern Fennoscandia. The land road from Vyborg to Hämeenlinna reoriented the dwelling places on the southern coasts of Saimaa. Another important land road followed the coast of the Gulf of Finland from Vyborg to Turku and connected parish centres along its route. It seems probable that Korela had already been connected to the core area of Novgorod by this route in the fourteenth century. Overall, these land connections created a new geographical understanding among local inhabitants and led to the marginalization of old routes and orientations.

The formation of the early modern territorial states of Sweden and Muscovy prompted the development of a new Christian administration by the end of the fifteenth century. The new centres were connected to each other by means of communication, and the realm's presence was felt at a local level. The new permanent administration preferred land roads to the old water connections. This second period resulted in the definition of the Swedish–Muscovite border at the end of the sixteenth century, the realization of royal power and the taxation of local societies in eastern Finland and Karelia. The transformation of the local economic system from semi-nomadic fishing and hunting to agriculture (slash-and-burn cultivation) also had an impact upon reach and travel. The settled living pattern enabled a more permanent way of life, but at the same time it also required increased travel to churches and markets or for tax collection and administration, for example. Thus the old loosely defined waterway systems were transformed into fixed locations, and the role of land roads became increasingly important.

Notes

1. Siikala 1992, p. 145.
2. Hägerstrand 1991, pp. 53–54, 187–188; Harrison 1998, pp. 50–56; Stenqvist Millde 2000, pp. 65–66, 73–74.
3. Korpela 2008, passim.
4. FMU I 360; 'Ex prima continuatione Detmari, a. 1395–1400'and 'Ex chronico Hermanni Korneri ceterisque continuatioribus Detmari', both published in SRS III. Cf. Lamberg, 2006, pp. 121–125; Korpela 2008, pp. 137–150.
5. Korpela 2004, p. 20; Korpela 2008, p. 205.
6. Stenqvist Millde 2000, p. 73.
7. According to Jari Mäki (2004, p. 144), the distance between the summer and winter camps of the indigenous peoples of Siberia was several hundreds of kilometres (300 or even 600), while according to Petri Halinen (2005, p. 87, pp. 92–93), the nomadic reindeer herders travelled about 250 kilometres a year. This can be explained by the alternation between Arctic Sea fishing, reindeer hunting and pasturing. As Halinen (2005, p. 87) states, the Fennoscandian hunter-gatherer-fishers needed only to move from one ecological environment to another, and thus the annual journey was not so long. See also Stenqvist Millde 2007, pp. 113–114, 118, 177–184 and passim.
8. Korpela 2008, pp. 55, 65.
9. The Finnish language contains two words for summer: *kesä* and *suvi*. The latter originated in western Finland. However, in eastern parts of Finland the meaning of some toponyms with the prefix *suvi* may in fact refer to *susi* ('wolf'), e.g. Suvensaari ('wolf island'). Thus placenames with the *suvi* prefix are not included. See Parviainen, 1976, pp. 123–126.
10. Sorokin 1997, pp. 5–23, Nenonen 1999)(a), p. 19; Masonen, 1999(a), p. 29; Masonen 1999(b), pp. 94–103; Masonen 1999(c), pp. 53–54.
11. Kuusi, Bosley & Branch (eds.) 1977, pp. 106, 110, 115–116, 167–169, 224–230; Kuusi 1949, pp. 311–325, 330–335, 347–356; Korpela 2005, pp. 25–26.
12. Makarov 1997, pp. 48–50, cf. also pp. 50–104.
13. Makarov 1997; Sorokin 1997.

14 Taavitsainen,Vilkuna & Forssell 2007, pp. 103–116, 129–146 and passim.

15 Taavitsainen 2001, pp. 72–74; Vilkuna 1999, pp. 46–49, 62–70; FMU IV 3733; Halinen 1999, pp. 42–51; Huurre 1979, p. 59; Sirkiä 1999, p. 96.

16 FMU IV 3733; Vilkuna 1998, pp. 256–267.

17 Hoppál 2003, pp. 42–46; Bolin 1999, pp. 140–141, 158–160; Pentikäinen 1995, pp. 62, 159–193; Mulk 1998, pp. 23–25. Taavitsainen has critically paid attention to the fact that paintings are not found in places that would have been natural for medieval water conditions but impossible to reach from a Stone Age perspective.

18 Korpela 2008, pp. 206–207.

19 Anttonen 1996, pp. 108–116.

20 Lönnrot, Kalevala; Anttonen 1996, pp. 108–116; Tarkka 2005, pp. 258–266, 275–282, 286–292.

21 Tarkka 2005, pp. 168–169, 300–302; McKinnell 2005, p. 4.

22 Siikala & Uljašev 2003, p. 142.

23 Tarkka 2005, p. 287, pp. 300–302, 313–323, 328–329; Siikala 1992, p. 145.

24 Koski 1967, pp. 176–179.

25 Kiviniemi 1990, pp. 139–140; Paulaharju 1979, pp. 24–26; Tarkka 1998, pp. 95–97, 104.

26 Hodges 1982, pp. 53–57; Gustin 2004, pp. 219–221 and passim; Mulk 1996, pp. 47–76.

27 Suhonen 2005, pp. 156–159.

28 Korpela 2008, pp. 217–225, 255–285.

29 Novgorodskaja četvertaja letopis' (spisok Dubrovskago) 7042 (1534); Materialy po istorii Karelii XII–XVI vv. Pod redakciej V. G. Geimana, Petrozavodsk, 1941, no. 52, pp. 127–131, no 64, pp. 154–159: Registrum ecclesiae Aboensis, no 694; Handlingar till upplysning af Finlands häfder VIII, no 15; Väänänen 1975, pp. 457–458.

30 Suvanto pp. 1972, 1–13, 23–54, 119–135, 171–182, 197–206.

31 Korpela 2008, pp. 29–31, 299–302.

32 Kalevala, 1:177–288; Holtsmark, pp. 649–652; Sarmela 1994, pp. 190–193; Tarkka 2005, pp. 160–163, p. 198; Glavatskaya 1996, pp. 374–380.

33 Above pp. XXX and Anttonen 1996, pp. 122–125; Salo 2004, pp. 145–146.

34 Olaus Magnus 1555, lib. 7–11 and especially 10.1., 10.23 and 11.3.

35 Nenonen 1999(a), pp. 16–19; Sirkiä 1999, pp. 94–103; Nenonen 1999(b), pp. 144–148; Masonen 1995, pp. 21–23.

36 'Alcupuhe Psaltarin päle.' In Mikael Agricolan teokset, Vol. 3, c. III.211.

37 FMU II 1165; Krötzl 1994, pp. 100–135; Heikkilä 2005, pp. 74–81, 87 and passim.

38 Palola 1996, pp. 89, 92–94, 97; Korpela, 2008, pp. 26–27, 256–259.

39 Masonen 1999(a), pp. 65–70, 82–83; Hiekkanen 1999, p. 122; Ustav knjazja Jaroslava o mosteh. 60-e gody XIII v. Zakonodatel'stvo Drevnej Rusi, Vol. 1., pp. 233–238; Korpela 2008, pp. 283, 315–316.

40 Korpela 2008, pp. 255–259.

41 FMU IV 3733; Masonen 1999(a), p. 23.

42 REA, no 506 and 510.

43 REA, no 506.

44 Jakob Teitts klagomålsregister emot adeln i Finland år 1555–1556, pp. 154–155, 157–160.

45 Handlingar till upplysning af Finlands häfder IV, no. 148; Nenonen 1999(b), pp. 144–145.

46 Puntanen & Särkkä 1995, pp. 48–50.

47 Konung Gustaf des förstes registratur, Vol. 22, pp. 312–313, 342; Nilsen Herluf 1981, p. 464; Suvanto 1981, p. 461.

48 Jakob Teitts klagomålregister, pp. 87, 92–93, 98–99; Soininen 1961, p. 231.

49 Handlingar till upplysning af Finlands häfder IV, no 148.

50 Masonen 1999(b), pp. 66–72, 88–93, 137.

51 Masonen 1999(b), pp. 72–73; Korpela 2008, pp. 283, 315–316.

52 Masonen 1990(b), p. 90; Jakob Teitts klagomålsregister, pp. 84–89, 125–127; Salminen 1999, pp. 139–141.

53 Ulrik Rudenschölds berättelse, pp. 2–6; Sirkiä 1999, p. l 95.

Bibliography
Source editions

Finlands medeltidsurkunder (FMU), Vols. I–VIII. Edited by R. Hausen. The National Archives of Finland, Helsinki, 1910–1935.

Handlingar till upplysning af Finlands häfder, Vols. I–IX. Edited by A. I. Arwidsson. Norstedt & Söner, Stockholm, 1846–1857.

Jakob Teitts klagomålsregister emot adeln i Finland år 1555–1556. Edited by K. Grotenfelt. The Finnish Historical Society, Helsinki, 1894.

Konung Gustaf des förstes registratur, Vol. 22. Edited by J. A. Almquist. The National Archives of Sweden, Stockholm, 1904.

Kuusi, M., Bosley, K. & Branch, M. (eds.) 1977. *Finnish Folk Poetry. Epic. An Anthology in Finnish and English.* The Finnish Literary Society, Helsinki.

Lönnrot, E. 1995. *Kalevala.* 28th edition. The Finnish Literary Society, Helsinki.

Materialy po istorii Karelii XII–XVI vv. Edited by V. G. Geimana. Petrozavodsk, 1941.

Mikael Agricolan teokset, Vol. 3. Uudistettu näköispainos, WSOY, Porvoo, Helsinki & Juva, 1987.

Novgorodskaja četvertaja letopis' (spisok Dubrovskago). Polnoe sobranie russkih letopisej IV. Moskva, 2000.

Olaus Magnus, *Historia de gentibus septentrionalibus* (Romae, 1555). Introduction by J. Granlund. Rosenkilde og Bagger, Copenhagen, 1982.

Registrum ecclesiae Aboensis eller Åbo domkyrkas svartbok med tillägg ur Skoklosters codex Aboensis (REA). Edited by R. Hausen. The National Archives of Finland, Helsinki, 1890.

Scriptores rerum Svecicarum medii aevi (SRS), Vol. III, Edited by C. Annderstedt. Uppsala, 1871.

Ulrik Rudenschölds berättelse om ekonomiska o.a. förhållanden i Finland 1738–1741. Edited by J. W. Ruuth. The Finnish Historical Society, Helsinki, 1899.

Ustav knjazja Jaroslava o mosteh. 60-e gody XIII v. Zakonodatel'stvo Drevnej Rusi, Vol. 1: *Rossijskoe zakonodatel'stvo X–XX vekov v devjati tomah pod obščej redakciej doktora juridičeskij nauk, professora O. I. Čistjakova. Otvetstvennyj redaktor toma členkorrespondent AN SSSR doktor istoričeskih nauk, professor V. L. Janin.* Moscow. 1984.

Literature

Anttonen, V. 1996. *Ihmisen ja maan rajat. 'Pyhä' kulttuurisena kategoriana.* The Finnish Literature Society, Helsinki.

Bolin, H. 1999. *Kulturlandskapets korsvägar. Mellersta Norrland under de två sista årtusendena f.Kr.* University of Stockholm, Stockholm.

Glavatskaya, E. 1996. 'Christianization = Russification? On preserving the religious and ethnic identity of the Ob-Ugrians.' In Pentikäinen, J. (ed.) *Shamanism and Northern Ecology.* Mouton de Gruyter, Berlin & New York, 1996, pp. 373–386.

Gustin, I. 2004. *Mellan gåva och marknad. Handel, tillit och materiell kultur under vikingatid.* University of Lund, Lund.

Hägerstrand, T. 1991. *Om tidens vidd och tingens ordning. Texter av Torsten Hägerstrand.* Edited by G. Carlestam & B. Sollbe. Byggforskningsrådet, Stockholm.

Halinen, P. 1999. 'Suomen liikenteen esihistoria: kivi- ja pronssikausi.' In Mauranen, T. (ed.) *Maata, jäätä, kulkijoita. Tiet, liikenne ja yhteiskunta ennen 1860.* Edita, Helsinki, pp. 36–51.

Halinen, P. 2005. *Prehistoric Hunters of Northernmost Lapland. Settlement patterns and subsistence strategies.* The Finnish Antiquarian Society, Helsinki.

Harrison, D. 1998. *Skapelsens geografi. Föreställningar om rymd och rum i medeltidens Europa.* Ordfront, Stockholm.

Heikkilä, T. 2005. *Pyhän Henrikin legenda.* The Finnish Literature Society, Helsinki.

Hiekkanen, M. 1999. 'Keskiajan kirkot ja tiet.' In Mauranen, T. (ed.) *Maata, jäätä, kulkijoita. Tiet, liikenne ja yhteiskunta ennen vuotta 1860.* Helsinki, Edita, pp. 122.

Hodges, R. 1982. *Dark Age Economics. The Origins of Towns and Trade A. D. 600–1000.* Duckworth, Bristol.

Holtsmark, A. 1981. 'Ragnarok.' In *Kulturhistoriskt lexikon för nordisk medeltid,* Vol. 13. Rosenkilde og Bagger, Copenhagen, pp. 649–652.

Hoppál, M. 2003. *Šamaanien maailma.* Translated by J. Huotari. Atena, Jyväskylä.

Huurre, M. 1979. *9000 vuotta Suomen esihistoriaa.* Otava, Keuruu.

Kiviniemi, E. 1990. *Perustietoa paikannimistä.* The Finnish Literature Society, Helsinki.

Korpela, J. 2004. *Viipurin linnaläänin synty.* 'Viipurin läänin historia II.' Karjalaisen Kulttuurin Edistämissäätiö ja Karjalan Kirjapaino Oy, Joensuu & Lappeenranta.

Korpela, J. 2005. 'Aspects Concerning Communication and Contact Landscape of Medieval North-Eastern European Subarctic Forest Zone.' In Paškov, A. M. (ed.) *Vostočnaja Finljandija i Rossijskaja Karelija. Tradicija i zakon v žizni karel. Materialy meždunarodnogo seminara istorikov posvjaščennogo 65-letiju PetrGU.* Izdat. PetrGU, Petrozavodsk, pp. 23–42.

Korpela, J. 2008. *The World of Ladoga. Society, Trade, Transformation and State Building in the Eastern Fennoscandian Boreal Forest Zone ca. 1000–1555.* LIT Verlag, Münster.

Koski, M. 1967. *Itämerensuomalaisten kielten hiisi-sanue. Semanttinen tutkimus,* Vol. I. University of Turku, Turku.

Krötzl, C. 1994. *Pilger, Mirakel und Alltag, Formen des Verhaltens im skandinavischen Mittelalter.* The Finnish Historical Society, Helsinki.

Kuusi, M. 1949. *Sampo-eepos. Typologinen analyysi.* The Finno-Ugrian Society, Helsinki.

Lamberg, M. 2006. 'Finns as aliens and compatriots in the late Medieval Kingdom of Sweden.' In Merisalo, O. & Pahta, P. (eds.) *Frontiers in the Middle Ages.* Brepols, Louvain-la-Neuve, 2006, pp. 121–132.

Makarov, N. A. 1997. *Kolonizacija severnyh okrain Drevnej Rusi v XI–XIII vekah. Po materialam arheologičeskih pamjatnikov na volokah Belozer'ja i Poonežja.* Skriptorij, Moscow.

Mäki, J. 2004. 'The Annual Cycle of the Settlements of the Circumpolar Peoples.' In Lavento, M. (ed.) *Early in the North*, Vol. 5. Finnish Antiquarian Society & Archaeological Society of Finland, Helsinki, pp. 131–153.

Masonen, J. 1995. 'Ura, polku ja tie. Suomalaisen infrastruktuurin synty ja varhaisvaiheet 800–1500.' *Historiallinen Aikalauskirja*, 93 (1), pp. 20–33.

Masonen, J. 1999(a). 'Meri ja maa.' In Mauranen, T. (ed.) *Maata, jäätä, kulkijoita. Tiet, liikenne ja yhteiskunta ennen 1860*. Edita, Helsinki, pp. 22–33.

Masonen, J. 1999(b). 'Kirkon, kruunun ja kansan tiet keskiajalla.' In Mauranen, T. (ed.) *Maata, jäätä, kulkijoita. Tiet, liikenne ja yhteiskunta ennen vuotta 1860*. Helsinki, Edita, pp. 57–108.

Masonen, J. 1999(c). 'Rautakauden reitit.' In Mauranen, T. (ed.) *Maata, jäätä, kulkijoita. Tiet, liikenne ja yhteiskunta ennen vuotta 1860*. Helsinki, Edita, pp. 52–56.

McKinnell, J. 2005. *Meeting the Other in Norse Myth and Legend*. D. S. Brewer, Cambridge. Mulk, I. M. 1996. 'The Role of the Sámi in Fur Trading during the Late Iron Age and Nordic Medieval Period in the Light of the Sámi Sacrificial Sites in Lapland, Northern Sweden.' *Acta Borealia*, Vol. 13, pp. 47–76.

Mulk, I. M. 1998. 'Nyfunna hällristningar avbildar samiska segelbåtar.' *Populär Arkeologi* 1998:4, pp. 23–25.

Nenonen, M. 1999(a). 'Rajojen piirtämisestä rajojen ylittämiseen.' In Mauranen, T. (ed.) *Maata, jäätä, kulkijoita. Tiet, liikenne ja yhteiskunta ennen 1860*. Edita, Helsinki, pp. 16–19.

Nenonen, M. 1999(b). 'Maitse vai vesitse. Kulkemisen peruskysymys 1550–1800.' In Mauranen, T. (ed.) *Maata, jäätä, kulkijoita. Tiet, liikenne ja yhteiskunta ennen vuotta 1860*. Helsinki, Edita, pp. 144–167.

Nilsen, H. 1981. 'Fogde. Danmark.' In *Kulturhistoriskt lexikon för nordisk medeltid*, Vol. 4. Rosenkilde og Bagger, Copenhagen, pp. 462–466.

Palola, A.-P. 1996. 'Yleiskatsaus Suomen keskiaikaisten seurakuntien perustamisajankohdista.' *Faravid – Acta Societatis Historicae Finlandiae Septentrionalis*, Vol. XVIII–XIX, pp. 67–104.

Parviainen, L. 1976. *Suomen vuodenaikanimet*. Unpublished MA thesis, University of Helsinki, Finnish Language; Library of the Archive of Names of Research Institute for the Languages of Finland, Helsinki.

Paulaharju, S. 1979. *Sompio. Luiron korpien vanhaa elämää*. WSOY, Porvoo, Helsinki & Juva.

Pentikäinen, J. 1995. *Saamelaiset. Pohjoisen kansan mytologia*. The Finnish Literature Society, Helsinki.

Puntanen, P. & Särkkä, T. 1995. *Nuijasota Savossa. Kaskiviljelijän kannanotto yhteiskunnan murrokseen*. Mikkelin läänin maakuntayhtymä, Mikkeli.

Salminen, T. 1999. 'Jaakko Teitin luettelo.' In Mauranen, T. (ed.) *Maata, jäätä, kulkijoita. Tiet, liikenne ja yhteiskunta ennen vuotta 1860*. Helsinki, Edita, pp. 139–141.

Salo, U. 2004. *Sastamalan historia*, Vol. I: *Esihistoria*. The Town of Vammala, Vammala.

Sarmela, M. *Suomen kansankulttuurin kartasto*, Vol. 2: *Suomen perinneatlas*. The Finnish Literature Society, Helsinki.

Siikala, A.-L. 1992. *Suomalainen šamanismi. Mielikuvien historiaa*. Finnish Literature Society, Helsinki.

Siikala, A.-M. & Uljašev, O. 2003. 'Maailmojen rajoilla. Muuttuvaa hantikulttuuria kohtaamassa.' *Kalevalaseuran vuosikirja*, Vol. 82, pp. 130–147.

Sirkiä, A. 1999. 'Hämäläisten vesitiet ja Tallinna.' In Mauranen, T. (ed.) *Maata, jäätä, kulkijoita. Tiet, liikenne ja yhteiskunta ennen 1860*. Edita, Helsinki, pp. 108–112.

Soininen, A. M. 1961. *Pohjois-Savon asuttaminen keski- ja uuden ajan vaihteessa*. The Finnish Historical Society, Helsinki.

Sorokin, P. E. 1997. *Vodnye puti i sudostroenie na severo-zapade Rusi v srednevekov'e*. University of Sankt-Peterburg, Sankt-Petersburg.

Stenqvist Millde, Y. 2000. 'Vägar inom räckhåll. Olika nivåer av kommunikation med exempel från Dalarna och Hälsningland.' *Bebyggelsehistorisk tidskrift*, Vol. 39, pp. 65–82.

Stenqvist Millde, Y. 2007. *Vägar inom räckhåll. Spåren efter resande i det förindustriella bondesamhället*. University of Stockholm, Stockholm.

Suhonen, M. 'Way of Life. A Useful Concept in Archaeology?' In Mäkelä, S. (ed.) *Rituals and Relations. Studies on the society and material culture of the Baltic Finns*. The Finnish Academy of Science and Letters, Helsinki, pp. 149–168.

Suvanto, S. 1972. *Satakunnan ja Hämeen keskiaikainen rajalaitos*. University of Tampere, Tampere.

Suvanto, S. 'Fogde. Finland.' In *Kulturhistoriskt lexikon för nordisk medeltid*, Vol. 4. Rosenkilde og Bagger, Copenhagen, pp. 459–462.

Taavitsainen, J.-P. 2001. 'The Heritage Management of Wetlands: 9: Finland.' In Coles, B., Olivier, A. & Bull, D. (eds.) *The Heritage Management of Wetlands in Europe*. Europae Archaeologiae Concilium und WARP, Exeter, pp. 71–80.

Taavitsainen, J.-P., Vilkuna, J, & Forssell, H. 2007. 'Suojoki at Keuruu. A Mid-Fourteenth- Century Site of the Wilderness Culture in the Light of Settlement Historical Processes in Central Finland.' The Finnish Academy of Science and Letters, Helsinki.

Tarkka, L. 1998. 'Sense of the Forest. Nature and Gender in Karelian Oral Poetry.' In Apo, S., Nenola, A. & Stark-Arola, L. (eds.) *Gender and Folklore. Perspectives on Finnish and Karelian Culture*. The Finnish Literature Society, Helsinki, pp. 92–142.

Tarkka, L. 2005. *Rajarahvaan laulu. Tutkimus Vuokkiniemen kalavalamittaisesta runokulttuurista 1821–1921*. The Finnish Literature Society, Helsinki.

Väänänen, K. 1975. 'Kuopion maaseurakunnan vaiheita 1552–1917.' In Rytkönen, A. (ed.) *Kuopion pitäjän kirja*. The Town of Kuopio, Kuopio, pp. 457–508.

Vilkuna, J. 1998. 'Suomen esihistoriallisen ajan veneet – Finska båtar från förhistorisk tid.' *Sjöhistorisk årsbok 1998–1999: Människor och båtar i Norden*, pp. 256–267.

Vilkuna, J. 1999. 'Keski-Suomen esihistoria.' In Jokipii, M. (ed.) *Keski-Suomen historia*, Vol. I: *Keski-Suomen vanhin historia*. Keski-Suomen liitto, Jyväskylä, pp. 32–77.

CHAPTER 4

A Travelling Governor

Piia Einonen

Introduction

One day in September 1654 as the sun rose, Governor Johan Rosenhane climbed into the saddle in the courtyard of Vyborg (Fi. Viipuri, Sw. Viborg) Castle. Together with his bookkeeper and secretary he began to ride to Lappeenranta (Sw. Villmanstrand), where he was to preside over the opening of the market and at the same time take care of some important administrative tasks. The party fed their horses on their way and arrived in Lappeenranta late the same afternoon. The governor opened the market the next day and spent the following week in Lappeenranta. On his way back to Viipuri, Johan Rosenhane found himself in great danger: his horse fell and he was trapped beneath it until his servants managed to get both horse and master up again. So it was time to praise God, for not even a single bone was broken.[1]

Johan Rosenhane (1611–1661) was a member of the nobility, and thus he had a certain amount of prestige wherever he travelled. As a governor[2] he was also a significant civil servant of the Crown. He exerted political power, given by the king, over the towns of Vyborg (1645–1655) and Linköping (1655–1658), and the surrounding counties.[3] Within this chapter, the main focus is on Johan Rosenhane's time as the governor of the Finnish county of Vyborg and Savonlinna[4] (Sw. Nyslott), although his later appointment in Eastern Götaland (Sw. Östergötland) in Sweden is also examined to some extent.

Sweden was at its largest geographically in the mid-seventeenth century. The Kingdom of Sweden was sparsely populated and there were long distances between population centres. This was especially true of Finland and during this period the eastern parts of Finland can be described as peripheral. Territory was already a significant feature of Swedish government ideology during the reign of King Gustavus I in the sixteenth century.[5] He concentrated power for himself and reorganized central government, as well as local administration. This work was later continued by his successors.[6] In spite of the development of an administrative system during the sixteenth and the first half of the seventeenth century, Johan Rosenhane found himself governor of a remote and peripheral[7] area with unsatisfactory connections and under constant threat from Russia. Nevertheless, due to the region's military, economic and political significance, there was importance and prestige attached to the office of governor of Vyborg and Savonlinna.

The state formation process, structure of the realm and functioning of the administrative system have been thoroughly studied,[8] but in this chapter mapping is used to enhance our understanding of how this system functioned. A certain degree of power is seen as having been invested in the office of governor. Presence and the diminishing of distance were crucial to the process of establishing, maintaining and asserting status. The governor exercised power over his territory. He became acquainted with it as he travelled to take care of his duties.[9] Here, this presence is analysed through mapping. Maps are used to analyse where the governor spent his time and how long he stayed in various places as he travelled across his administrative territory, and thus how central power extended its dominion to the farthermost corners of the realm. Correspondence and gift-exchange were essential aspects of 'office-holding', even if the letters cannot be analysed because they are rarely mentioned in the governor's diary.

In general, the authority of office-holders was tightly bound to a specific place and province, and so it is reasonable to use mapping techniques when researching civil servants and their everyday work. An early modern governor would establish his power through his presence.[10] Travelling around the county, as well as proximity to official sites of government, was crucial for a governor. In this chapter, the authority of an office-holder is explored through his spatial power. Mapping Rosenhane's official duties in his county is the basis for the analysis. Additionally, in this context different kinds of ceremonial and spatial welcomes and farewells were used to diminish distance and create power. This also includes the giving and receiving of gifts in order to create and reassert authority.

How did spatial elements affect the office-holding of a high-ranking Swedish nobleman of the late seventeenth century, and how were geographical, social and cultural distances manifested? The hypothesis is that such distances can be discerned through a comparative examination of Johan Rosenhane's periods of service in the provincial Finnish town of Vyborg and in Linköping in Sweden.

Rosenhane's period in Vyborg is more interesting from the perspective of mapping. He was a stranger in eastern Finland, and so there were marked cultural as well as social distances[11] between the governor and his subjects. The geographical distances between the Finnish counties and the Crown were also significant. Rosenhane's time as a governor in Eastern Götaland is thus considered only for comparative purposes. It is also important to address the more general ways in which difficulties relating to information and office-holding were overcome.

Diary as a source material

The source of this case study is the diary of Johan Rosenhane, which has been utilized in few historical studies.[12] Rosenhane's office-holding in Vyborg has been outlined in Pekka Toivanen's works[13] and Arne Jansson puts his diaries in a wider historical context in his foreword, but otherwise Rosenhane's experiences have not been studied.[14]

When did Johan Rosenhane start to keep a diary and for whom did he write? Was the diary written as a notebook for himself, or did he think that future generations would read and interpret his notes as immensely valuable sources of an individually experienced past? It seems likely that he had also written a diary before 1652 (the first surviving entry). His laconic expressions and notions of his official duties imply that he wrote his diary as a memorandum for himself. Arne Jansson shares this view. Rosenhane's notes were likely to have been written daily, and so his experiences and feelings in the diary are presented almost immediately without distortion due lapses of time or memory.[15] Nevertheless, the reliability of a diary as a source material should not be so easily assumed. Conscious or unconscious selection, as well as interpretations, would have guided his writing.[16] When memoirs are researched as historical source material, we need to keep in mind that we are not reading the memory itself but a written transformation of it.[17] The same is also true of diaries.

Rosenhane made notes of his daily experiences in the form of a diary. It seems likely that he inherited the habit of registering events in writing from his father, who had also kept a kind of diary ('*chronologiskt diarium*'). Johan's diary largely focuses on his various duties as a governor, but it also provides some descriptions of family life and social events.[18] The period he spent as the governor of Vyborg is mainly devoted to details about holding office; whereas his time as the governor of Eastern Götaland is portrayed in a more lively way, as though his whole life had changed from an office-centred obligation to a noble lifestyle filled with hunting and social engagements. The business of office-holding plays a minor role in Rosenhane's diary entries during his time in Sweden. This chapter explores why office-holding was so much more central during his earlier period in Vyborg.[19] In his introduction to the published diary, Arne Jansson attributes this to less demanding tasks in Eastern Götaland, diminishing ambition and the effect of war on the office-holding of governors, but it may well have had more to do with familiar networks and environment.[20]

Could Rosenhane's diary-writing be seen as part of a wider tradition of travel journals? This seems unlikely: other than occasional distances, he did not record the circumstances relating to his travel, only those connected to his official duties. He also noted details about family births, deaths and sicknesses (as well as those of close relatives and friends); the weather; and some economic details.[21] This also suggests that he was writing for himself alone. He was familiar with the academic culture[22] and his family were literary. Johan's elder brother, Schering Rosenhane, wrote two famous books – *Hortus Regius* and *Oeconomia* – and his younger brother, Gustaf Rosenhane, was an established poet. It seems that for Johan Rosenhane writing was a way of expressing himself.[23]

Only a few letters remain from Johan Rosenhane's periods as governor of Vyborg and then Eastern Götaland. Letters to the Crown describe both his own official duties and, to some extent, more general circumstances in the eastern part of Finland. Only two of Johan Rosenhane's letters written in Linköping have survived in the National Archives of Sweden (Riksarkivet; SRA).[24] In addition, two letters from Count Per Brahe to Johan Rosenhane have been researched, but essentially they simply relate to Rosenhane's formal relations with Brahe.[25] Personally, Johan Rosenhane had strong and negative feelings towards Per Brahe. Unfortunately, even though the personal diary represents an exceptionally rich source material, in this case it can only occasionally be supplemented by other sources, such as official records or correspondence.[26]

Distances and office-holding

Spatial thinking and the defining of spatial borderlines reflect general social ideas, statuses and norms. When society changes, our views of the surrounding space and our place in it are also transformed. Concepts and conceptions of space are created within social interaction between individuals and their surroundings. Spatial categories are connected with cultural phenomena and time.[27] For early modern individuals and societies, invisible cultural and geographic borders were more important than largely hypothetical political boundaries.[28] Rosenhane acted as a governor in a period when such political and administrative border-lines were explicitly manifested, and thus his travels across the county were not only purely administrative trips, but also demonstrations of the presence of the state. The need for regional cohesion increased the need for travelling in order to undertake administrative duties.[29] When this is connected to the ongoing 'project' of civilizing the subjects,[30] the significance of his presence and absence is highlighted.

With his academic education, Johan Rosenhane represented a new kind of governor. Johan Rosenhane's grandfather, Jöran Johansson, and his father, Johan Jöransson Rosenhane, had themselves acted as *ståthållare* (a kind of governor). Johan's brother, Schering Rosenhane, had earlier been the governor of Eastern Götaland (1637–1645). During Schering's final two years in the post Johan had served as his vice-governor. When the governors were occupied with other duties (Schering, for example, attended the peace negotiations in Germany), suitable office-holders would serve as their deputies.[31] In this sense it is interesting that after serving in Götaland Johan Rosenhane was sent to the eastern border of the realm. This was probably because someone with at least some office-holding experience was needed in Vyborg. It may have also been an opportunity for Rosenhane to gain further merit, which could lead to him holding office in the central areas of the kingdom.[32] In any case, when combined with social and cultural factors, Rosenhane's previous experience probably made it easier for him to take care of his new duties in Linköping.

During the seventeenth century, the career of a single office-holder would have generally developed quite gradually, even though the highest elite of the realm had an unquestioned right to certain posts. Visions of evolving careers existed and some posts were certainly perceived to be springboards for offices of a higher grade. Representatives of central government were sometimes sent to remote and challenging regions; if they succeeded they could be rewarded with posts in the heartland.[33] Life, as well as office-holding, was often a lot easier in central areas than was the case in the peripheries. In addition, seventeenth-century noblemen viewed certain offices and locations as laborious and saw such appointments almost as forms of punishment. These fears were not entirely without substance: on occasion noblemen who found themselves in trouble or political disfavour really would be sent to remote areas.[34]

The distance between an office-holder and the central power could have an enormous effect on the administrative duties attached to an office.[35] In the provincial areas practical details required more consideration than was the case in the heartland of the empire. Long distances separated the central places of the county, and so the governor had a duty to travel across his county to hold court meetings as well as to gather men for the king's army. Speed of travel was influenced by both direct factors (such as condition and route of the road; intensity, aim and length of journey; means of travel; socio-cultural background of the traveller; geography of construction; and communication and weather) and indirect factors (such as topography, geology and hydrology).[36]

In the county of Vyborg and Savonlinna, subjects were scattered across a large and sparsely populated area, and travelling was both time-consuming and laborious for the governor. Roads were often more like paths. However, the seventeenth century did see improvements in the road network of Finland, despite the long distances involved and the wide dispersal of the population.[37] Both horseback-riding and coaches were used for transportation, as were boats.[38] Usually Rosenhane would ride, but he once travelled from Lappeenranta to Savonlinna and even further by boat. Lake Saimaa (Sw. Saimen) functioned as the main passage of waterborne traffic towards the north (to Kuopio and North Karelia), but in general Finnish water-routes were not particularly suitable for smooth travel.[39] As the governor of Vyborg, Rosenhane needed to travel as far as Kuopio and Pieksämäki.

Although Johan Rosenhane travelled to take care of his administrative duties and arriving at his destination was vital, the journey itself was important. Travelling quickly was not the ideal. In the chapters that follow, travelling will be researched further as a manifestation of power and status.[40] Other office- and power-related aspects (such as ceremonies and the giving and receiving of gifts) will also be studied.

Mapping office-holding in a periphery

>...so that if I, with others from this distant area, could not arrive within the specified time because of the contrary wind and poor weather, the Queen should be merciful and forgive us, and not interpret our delay unmercifully.[41]

Johan Rosenhane acted as the governor of Vyborg from 1645 until 1655. Vyborg was a significant staple town and was the second largest town, after Turku (Sw. Åbo), in the eastern part of the realm. It was located in the border area of the Swedish realm, and so it was also important militarily. However, Vyborg had earlier been even closer to the border. With the Treaty of Stolbovo in 1617 the border had been redrawn and Vyborg was now 20 rather than 8 Scandinavian miles from Russia.[42] Vyborg was an original town with special features: strong national parties and severe inner power struggles, but it was first and foremost a border town. It was also an administrative centre for the geographically large county of Vyborg and Savonlinna.

The types of duties undertaken by a governor were in practice identical to those undertaken by the general county administration: military, political, economic, judicial and administrative. In 1635 these tasks were defined in the *landhövdingeinstruktion* (instructions for the governors), which provided previously unknown stability for the office of a governor. The governor represented the ruler in his county. He took care of the financial administration and collection of taxes (and other payments to the Crown); of recruiting and maintaining soldiers (as well as those troops who marched through the area)[43]; of policy relating to economic life and order; and of supervising justice and its execution.[44] The governors' instructions also provided them with quite far-reaching authority over the towns under their governance. Giving the governors a free hand to act as they saw fit was supposed to motivate them to improve towns in line with the general trend of economic activation of the urban system. The governor had a duty to supervise the appointment of a town burgomaster and scribes, and later he also oversaw the appointment of magistrates. Governors controlled crafts, trade, administration and the economy in their towns. The latter half of the seventeenth century saw a steady increase in the powers of governors.[45]

Johan Rosenhane largely worked from his residence in the castle of Vyborg. He took part in city court meetings and dealt with petitioners in the castle.[46] Being posted far from the central government involved a great deal of writing and receiving letters. The postal services of the period were not advanced, and letters were carried also by couriers, tradesmen and their agents. Vyborg and Turku were the administrative centres in the eastern part of the realm and also served as junctions for the mail services. Although there were functioning postal connections with Vyborg in the 1650s, Rosenhane occasionally failed to receive his post. A letter to Turku would take from five to seven days to reach its destination; one to Stockholm, twelve to eighteen days. Rosenhane usually received his letters on a Saturday and wrote his replies the following Friday.[47] Likewise, it often took weeks to receive information from Stockholm.

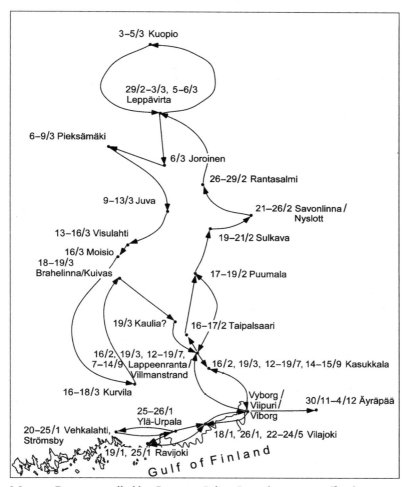

Map 14. Routes travelled by Governor Johan Rosenhane in an official capacity in 1652, according to his diary. One place, Kaulia, is marked with a question mark, even though it could not be identified. The diary index has been used to help to identify places. Drawing by Jari Järvinen.

Furthermore, many of Rosenhane's political and economic activities required him to travel.[48] Rosenhane planned his travels as efficiently as possible: he tried to take care of all his tasks in a particular area at the same time, and later shared information with others.[49]

Map 14 illustrates how burdensome travelling in eastern Finland could

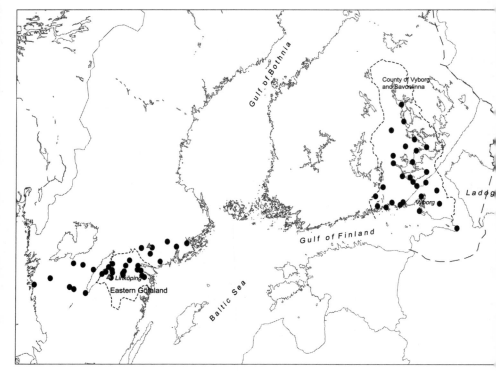

Map 15. The counties ('län') of Vyborg and Savonlinna and Eastern Götaland, as well as the most significant places where Johan Rosenhane paid official visits during his period as governor. Rosenhane's own manors are marked with triangles. Drawing by Jari Järvinen.

be. The travels of governors in the Swedish part of the realm seem to have been shorter in both duration and distance in the mid-seventeenth century.[50] This is also evident when we compare Rosenhane's travels in the county of Vyborg and Savonlinna with those during his time as the governor of Eastern Götaland (Map 15).[51]

The most visible of the governor's duties were his responsibility to convene district court sessions and his recruitment of soldiers. During the Middle Ages, governors were legally required to make a circuit of their region three times each year. This meant that officials would choose the shortest possible route when touring their counties. However, in the seventeenth century the governors inspected the district court sessions less frequently.[52] Vyborg was quite inconveniently situated: although it was accessible by sea, its inland connections were problematic. The only 'easy' land route to Vyborg was to take the Great Coastal Road (Fi. *Suuri rantatie*; Sw. *Stora Strandvägen*).[53] During his lengthy travels Rosenhane would often also strengthen social relations and address economic concerns.

Roads were peopled with various travellers including representatives of the Crown, troops, couriers from the castles and circuit judges (along with their companions). Tradesmen and those involved in transportation could also be seen travelling along the roads.[54] The local administration or subjects themselves had a responsibility to provide a representative of the Crown with lodgings and to facilitate his travel. Office-holders would also frequently stay overnight in rectories. The regal right to free hospitality and transportation applied to official travelling only. Nevertheless, it was easy for a single nobleman – especially when he was an office-holder of the Crown – to obtain fresh horses and fodder and thus travel quite long distances in a single day. Although Rosenhane usually changed at inns, on occasion he even exchanged horses with troops.[55] Relatives would sometimes provide a vehicle during private excursions: when Johan Rosenhane and his wife, Brita, travelled to Nevanlinna Carl Mörner sent his carriage for them. Brita Ribbing was a regular traveller. She would occasionally accompany Johan on an official visit, and sometimes visited her relatives without her husband. Brita Ribbing's freedom to travel was probably connected to her marital status. Johan's sister, Christina Rosenhane, expressed envy of her brothers' opportunities to travel ('...*haft den plaisir som kan vanka på landet...*').[56]

Johan Rosenhane seems to have been quite pedantic by nature: each day he recorded the weather in his diary, and sometimes after travelling he would also note down the number of miles he had covered.[57] He was clearly fond of measuring and accuracy. On one occasion he noted that the dangerous boat-trip from Stockholm to Vyborg (his seventh such crossing) had taken only five days, when previously it had always taken at least three weeks.[58] This comment illustrates not only the distance between Vyborg and the central areas, but also the significance of distance and proximity in early modern society.

Realm of estates and power relations

In 1654 Johan Rosenhane was introduced to the House of Nobility (*Riddarhuset*) and appointed governor of Eastern Götaland. Rosenhane moved from almost the furthermost border of the Swedish Empire to

Linköping, in the heartland of Sweden. His own manor, Stenhammar (formerly Slädhammar), was located in Flen, Södermanland.[59] Besides Stenhammar, the other manor that Johan Rosenhane called home was Mossebo[60] in Rinna parish. The area around Linköping and Nyköping was filled with manors, and many important Swedish noble families had some kind of an estate nearby.[61] Flen and Linköping were also situated close to the central power, both geographically and symbolically. Rosenhane enjoyed regular contact with representatives of the political elite in both official and unofficial contexts. The Swedish capital, Stockholm, was close to Linköping, where Rosenhane spent his last years. He died in Ryd in 1661 at the age of fifty.[62] Even though both Schering and Johan Rosenhane are referred to as being among the most influential governors in Eastern Götaland, Linköping's history only records Johan Rosenhane's efforts relating to regulation.[63]

In the Swedish part of the realm the situation relating to office-holding was reversed. In contrast to the burdensome period he spent in Vyborg, Johan was among his own kind – noblemen – and he enjoyed an active social life in Linköping. Johan Rosenhane's wide social network was positioned just below the highest strata of Swedish society. Schering Rosenhane was as member of the political elite and so he sought to help his younger brother's career. Although it was generally easier for an elder brother to ascend through the ranks, work and intelligence, not birth, had secured Schering's post. During his time in Vyborg Johan Rosenhane had himself striven for years to secure an office in the Swedish part of the realm and to achieve the status of baron. Johan Rosenhane's dedication to an aristocratic lifestyle was probably the result of this long process and may have compensated for his comparatively 'low' status within the inner social order of the nobility. Hunting was a manifestation of a royal or aristocratic lifestyle, rather than simply some sort of leisure activity.[64]

In Sweden, Johan Rosenhane enjoyed hunting parties[65] and sat at the dinner table with the Queen. It would seem that office-holding in Eastern Götaland was less fraught than had been the case in Vyborg. Rosenhane also had to travel much shorter distances than had been the case in eastern Finland. Almost all of the realm's important events took place nearby. Moreover, he no longer needed to travel about the county for weeks simply in order to fulfil his basic duties; he could now devote time to maintaining the social contacts suitable for a nobleman of his rank. This does not mean that he failed to take care of his duties: it was simply easier to govern a county with a functioning town government and accessible spaces. The distances between central places (his manor, official residence, the estates of relatives and allies, and the capital city of Stockholm) were of course shorter than they had been in Finland. In addition, the roads were probably better[66] and the environment of everyday life more closed. Travel was clearly much easier: most significant locations could be reached within a day.

The roads of seventeenth-century Södermanland were largely identical to the present road network. However, there were many places where the 'roads' were suitable only for riding, and were impassable by coach or cabriolet. During summer and winter, waterways often offered a more comfortable and faster route (for transporting both goods and people). The region also boasted a well-established system of inns.[67] Water roads and land roads were used during summertime and winter roads across icy lakes and snowy lands during the coldest months. Travel in the winter (by sleigh) was often easier and faster than travelling during the summer. However, it could also be more dangerous: Brita Ribbing once almost drowned when the ice she was travelling across broke. Partly because peasants were free to travel in winter, there were many important wintertime markets, particularly in places where winter roads crossed.[68]

Every high-ranking traveller required a couple of horses for himself and often travelled with servants.[69] The cortege of a traveller was an indication both of his prestige and of his social, political and economic power. Kings and high-ranking noblemen travelled with large entourages and many horses and carriages.[70] Office-holders often travelled with only their secretary and book-keeper, but they were able to demonstrate their power not through the size of their group, but through the way in which they were received and sent off. Like the size of one's cortege, greetings and farewells could be interpreted as signs of prestige.

Cultural distance and closeness

In an early modern society office-holding was an all-inclusive task.[71] It was not a specialized and differentiated 'job' as was later the case. An early modern office-holder would represent and be defined by his office at all times. Securing an office was dependent on personal and social networks, as well as individual capabilities. In order to fulfil his duties, an office-holder required contacts, and these contacts were often created through unofficial social interaction. This meant that social events (such as weddings) were vital to the creation and maintenance of social networks. Such contacts were also established over dinner or during other forms of hospitality. Attempting to attract prestigious guests was a distinctive feature of the festival culture.[72]

Both because office-holders (as representatives of the Crown) were entitled to free hospitality and because of the dubious reputation attached to inns, officials often preferred to stay overnight in manors or vicarages. Routes were often planned around such locations. Hosts also benefitted from this system: they would hear news and gossip from their guests.[73] This view emphasizes the social and economic aspects of travelling. When moving from place to place was laborious, it was important to take care of business and social relations at the same time. Thus these visits were used to conduct economic transactions and also (intentionally or unintentionally) to maintained or strengthen vital social connections.

It is obvious that, whether or not this was his intention, Johan Rosenhane did not successfully create a functioning network of other office-holders and individuals of his rank in Vyborg. This probably stems from the political culture in the town. Rosenhane was seen as a stranger and there was often particular animosity towards Swedes. Many Swedish incomers who came to the area were office-holders or magistrates – representatives of the Crown, although there were also some Swedish merchants and craftsmen.[74] A Swedish governor thus began from a difficult position. Even after ten years as governor of Vyborg, Johan Rosenhane was still treated as an outsider. His interactions, especially with the burgomasters and magistrates, were marked by a lack of confidence and, to some degree, mutual disrespect.[75]

The inconveniences of travelling were not the only problems that faced a foreign office-holder in the border areas of the realm. As an outsider, the opportunities to create and maintain power relations were quite limited. Even though the governor had been appointed by royal order, he could have enormous difficulties establishing a functional role as the highest office-holder. In Vyborg the all-powerful (as they regarded themselves) town court continued to function as it always had. There were ongoing struggles between factions, and political fights between different nations (namely German, Swedish and Finnish) tore the town apart. Burgomasters and magistrates neglected their governor in many ways, and the governor was literally treated as an outsider despite his superior role in the power hierarchy.[76] It has been argued that a governor's position in the middle of urban struggles for power between the burghers and the town court could often strengthen his status,[77] but this does not seem to have been the case in Vyborg.

Even though social relations and power were demonstrated according to prevailing convention, in reality the governor of Vyborg would have often been ignored. Rosenhane's life was socially quite limited. There was significant social and mental distance between the governor and local office-holders in Vyborg, and this was reflected in Rosenhane's office-holding.[78] Although Johan Rosenhane enjoyed high political and social status while stationed and living in Vyborg, he was nevertheless shut out of local social groups. In Sweden his social standing was lower, but in general his life was easier.

Differences in religion, language, climate and customs created a feeling of cultural distance for travellers.[79] Rosenhane provided an unflattering description of the Karelian population: he claimed that there could be ten idle men living on a farm that could not provide a livelihood for them all.[80] This illustrates the difficulties Rosenhane perceived when working in eastern Finland rather than the Swedish heartland. Rosenhane's diary entries can thus also be interpreted as traces of cultural shock. Rosenhane represented the new ideal: a nobleman with a good education, who was appointed to office. However, office-holding in places like Vyborg and Karelia had probably not been in Rosenhane's mind when he undertook his peregrination in Holland, France, England and Germany.[81] This also explains his eagerness to return to Sweden.

Official duties were thus closely intertwined with social life, especially during Rosenhane's time in Sweden.[82] Individuals seem to have generally travelled frequently, often staying overnight with their relatives and friends. As they travelled they also transferred information, which was comparatively more accessible than was the case in the more peripheral areas of the realm. Wining and dining guests (and their large entourages) was a social obligation. Although it could prove to be expensive and laborious from time to time,[83] it was also an essential means of maintaining vital social relationships. Rosenhane often socialized with relatives, particularly his brothers and sisters and their families (who were themselves closely connected to the highest elite of society).[84] Rosenhane's active socializing during his period as an office-holder in Sweden can also be interpreted as a manifestation of a noble lifestyle: he was an experienced, established and wealthy Swedish nobleman, and this needed to be demonstrated to his contemporaries. This was particularly important because the family of Rosenhane had only been introduced in the *Riddarhuset* in 1654, and their position in the map of noble power relations had not yet been established.[85]

Travelling: farewells and welcomes

Distance was a reality that early modern office-holders needed to take into consideration in their everyday work. Letters were the easiest, and most frequently used, tool by which distance could be diminished. During his period as governor of Vyborg, Johan Rosenhane often needed to rely on letters, but naturally he also wrote letters whilst in serving in Sweden.[86] Constant travelling and meetings with established noble families diminished the need to specifically gather and share information. When Johan Rosenhane was located in the central areas of Swedish society, he was in the middle of the information networks. His social and political contacts provided necessary news, and often different tasks could be taken care of personally. Under these circumstances letters played a less vital role than had been the case in Vyborg, where the governor had needed to rely on letters in both an official and a personal capacity.

Power and status was demonstrated visually and expressed in speech and the written word, but rituals of welcomes and departures were also an important element in creating and maintaining power hierarchies. When Johan Rosenhane travelled from Sulkava to Savonlinna, the commander of the castle *(slåtz Haubtman)* of Savonlinna (who was probably accompanied by his entourage) met the governor half a mile outside the castle. Other townspeople were also sometimes part of such welcoming parties.[87] Rosenhane often noted that he was met by his hosts half a mile from the castle and town. This was a ritual of respect and honour, which were to be shown for those superior in office and overall status. The governor was escorted out of the town in the same manner: the commander of the castle, burghers and bailiffs travelled with him for a mile.[88] Sometimes Rosenhane described how he had himself welcomed and escorted a higher-ranking office-holder for a quarter of a mile. This distance could have been some sort of an indicator of political and social status, and of the power relations between the host and his guest.[89] It is noteworthy that this procedure was not simply a manifestation of a hierarchical society: it was often a natural part of ordinary office-holding.[90]

Bidding farewell was an essential element in social life. These rituals were vital to the maintenance of social relations and possibilities. In early modern society there was heavy reliance on hierarchical relations and networks. It was also a society in which organizational structures were being formed. Staying on the spatial and social map, being known and recalled were vitally important. It would have been easy for Johan Rosenhane to be totally forgotten during his period as the governor of Vyborg, had he not been so attentive towards his contacts and relatives in the central areas of the realm. Information was valuable and farewells were, in addition to their role in social relations, part of sharing and gathering information.

These kinds of rituals were seen as protection against evil,[91] but bidding farewell properly was also a token of realism: journeys took a long time and travelling was both insecure and dangerous. So it was possible that the two parties might never meet again.

When various office-holders returned to Sweden or changed their posts, they would visit the castle of Vyborg with their families before their departure.[92] In the same manner Johan Rosenhane also went to the court house of Vyborg to bid farewell ('*och där medh valedicerade*'), when he left for the Riksdag of the Estates. The day he left, Rosenhane also held some kind of a reception in the castle for the town's most important burghers and office-holders, both local and royal ('*dee förnämbste uthi staden*'). After the reception, the guests sailed away with the governor before later riding back to town.[93] The situation was totally different in Sweden, where Rosenhane's ranking in the social hierarchy was often lower than had been the case in the more peripheral areas. When Johan Rosenhane returned to Vyborg for the last time, he bid farewell to the king and a number of privy councillors (Sw. *riksråd*), but only his brother Schering and his family escorted Johan out of Stockholm.[94] The meaning of farewells is clearly evident from Rosenhane's indignantion when Schering left without saying a word ('*Reste bror Skiäring uth till Säby och sadhe ingen till*').[95] Burdensome and even dangerous travels would often be followed by happy reunions.[96]

Gifts

Interaction was an important element of office-holding. This involved, for example, taking part in weddings or being a godfather, and also giving and receiving gifts.[97] Gifts were a form of interaction as well as a means of securing influence.[98] A gift could be an instrument for gaining information and creating authority. The giving of gifts was an important gesture, which for its part kept social relations active and functioning. It seems that the actual gifts themselves were not quite as important as the gesture of giving. This was an 'economy of mutual favours', where every small favour reinforced the bonds of friendship and trust, also making it more likely that help would be forthcoming in a major crisis. Gifts were material objects: wine, food, clothes, money or something else of value. There was no clear scale of value for gifts, but of course it was important that the gift itself was sufficiently valuable. There were simultaneously existing and overlapping urban publics, and as Valentin Groebner writes: 'Gifts served as media within these social spaces, as means of transmitting and multiplying information.'[99] Thus, gifts were a form of creating and diminishing distance.

When Rosenhane returned from Vyborg to Sweden for the final time, he stopped in Turku. The members of the royal court of Turku paid him a visit and so Rosenhane felt that he was obliged to provide them with dinner in return. As he noted in his diary, he was honoured by this gesture, and it needed to be reciprocated (even though he was in a hurry to get back home).[100] This reciprocal manifestation of a relationship can be compared with the giving of gifts. Like a gift, the visit demanded a return gift or requital.[101] Often received gifts would be accurately registered in order to identify those who had donated them.[102] It is possible that Johan Rosenhane wrote down the gifts and favours he was given so that he could duly respond. Gifts were (and are) predicated on an idea of goodwill; a refusal to give therefore denied the idea and created ill will, which in turn could lead to a fear of retribution.[103]

Different kinds of gifts were necessary elements in this reciprocal system. In Vyborg the governor received gifts even when he was simply taking care of his ordinary duties. On one occasion after Rosenhane had helped some of the wealthiest burghers in their struggle with a reluctant magistrate, he received a gift of Spanish wine (*'Ohm spansk wijn'*).[104] Gifts were tools of political culture and conflict. Gifts that contained alcohol were often regarded as characteristic of personal and informal relationships, but urban office-holders also gave wine as a gift.[105] It is important to notice that in Vyborg this receiving of gifts was a part of office-holding: gifts were probably given explicitly to the governor, not to Rosenhane himself.

Some have argued that Johan Rosenhane was used to giving precious gifts[106] and that the burghers of Vyborg had perhaps just adopted his custom and learned to give presents when the governor showed them good will.[107] However, during his time in Sweden, Rosenhane did not give or receive presents so often.[108] It seems that the explanation could probably be reversed: Johan Rosenhane adopted the custom of giving presents in Vyborg. This would emphasize the difference between his office-holding in Finland and in Sweden even further. Gift-exchange was different between insiders and outsiders,[109] and one probable explanation for this activity in gift-exchange might be that the burghers of Vyborg acted in a way that they thought Rosenhane would expect. Or perhaps it was a calculated strategy: giving gifts softened the otherwise problematic relationship between the burghers, the town council and the governor. Interaction and mutual reciprocity did not operate in Vyborg in the same way as they did in Sweden, where hospitality and favours played an essential role. In Vyborg gifts were needed in order to balance the subtle system of social, political and power relations.

Conclusion

Johan Rosenhane was a governor wavering between the old and the new world: he demonstrated and exercised the power of the Crown by constantly travelling around his county and taking care of his duties just as his successors had done for decades. The office-holding of a governor was, however, changing in the late seventeenth century: the need to travel gradually diminished and governors increasingly acted from their residences. Information that had previously been gathered personally was received from bailiffs and the clergy. The county government was only established in the 1630s. By the latter half of the century the system had begun to function in a more regular manner and the subjects, too, found their way into county offices. The amount of written administration also increased, and this needed to be taken care of by the office-holder in his own residence. Previously governors had often, to some extent, kept up their correspondence whether they were travelling or staying in their manors, but eventually they became more or less bound to their residences. This was at the same time an indication of a functioning local government: information delivered by the lower office-holders was considered trustworthy.[110]

For Johan Rosenhane, the spatial dimensions of power were concrete and essential. He spent weeks on horseback and in remote venues taking care of his duties. Sometimes he even recorded the distance or duration travelled. Spatial distance was a determining element in early modern office-holding also because the power of the governor had an effect on the local populace: the longer he stayed the greater the public attention. In consequence, the institution of counties and governors was strengthened, as was, indirectly, the authority of the king.

Spatial categories in the Swedish heartland were different from those in the remote Finnish parts of the realm due to geographic, social and cultural differences. This was emphasized when a Swedish nobleman was sent to eastern Finland and different kinds of instruments were required to mediate between authorities, estates and individuals. In a way, gifts diminished these social distances, just as letters were used to overcome the spatial distances of early modern society and office-holding. In addition, 'welcomes' and 'departures' were used to control social and power relations in a ritualized manner. In general many such activities, which in Sweden were invisible and taken care of by different kinds of networks, needed to be carried out openly in Vyborg. This meant that the role of gifts, rituals and symbolic acts was emphasized.

Closed and overlapping circles of the power elites in the peripheral areas did not allow an outsider to take a full advantage of his position as the highest office-holder in his town and county. On the other hand, close and intertwined networks of relatives and friends in the central areas of the realm provided the opportunity to concentrate on social life of a noble kind; holding office was not such a burdensome and laborious duty. Johan Rosenhane's periods in Vyborg and Linköping were so fundamentally different that the explanation cannot be found in the office itself or in his personal ability. Rather, the differences seem to have stemmed from external and spatial factors. Office-holding in a peripheral area was essentially defined by the periphery itself: the geographic, social and cultural distances were immense and needed to be bridged using gifts and rituals.

Acknowledgements

The archival research for this article has been supported by the Swedish–Finnish Cultural Foundation. Acknowledgements are due to my colleagues within the project, as well as members of the Early Modern Practice and Thought (now renamed as Early Modern Morals) community in the Department of History and Ethnology at Jyväskylä University for their valuable commentaries.

Notes

1 Diary 7–14 September 1654, pp. 119–120; Toivanen 1999, p. 24. On the personnel of county administration in general, see Asker 2004, pp. 341–373.

2 This is a translation of (Sw.) *landshövding* and (Fi.) *maaherra*. See also Asker 2004, pp. 52, 88 on the Swedish title *guvernör*.

3 Later, he acted as a member of the Privy Council of Sweden (*riksrådet*) and the Svea Court of Appeal (*Svea hovrätt*). See Jansson 1993, pp. 89–118 and Toivanen 1999 for detailed desciptions of Rosenhane's life and career.

4 Vyborg (Fi. Viipuri, Sw. Viborg) was a medieval fortified town, but it was also understood as a larger region and part of the county of Vyborg and Savonlinna

(Sw. Nyslott). Savonlinna was a newly established town (1639), which had also given its name to the county. Savonlinna was also spoken of as Olavinlinna or Olofsborg; however, such usage usually referred to the castle itself.

5 Katajala 2005, pp. 13–21; Katajala 2006, p. 104.

6 Karonen 1999, pp. 79–83, 85–87, 92, 185–194.

7 Harrison 1998, p. 38; Katajala 2005, pp. 20–21.

8 See, for example, Karonen 1999 and Eng 2006, pp. 122–123.

9 Björn Asker (2004, especially p. 164) acknowledges the importance of geography and spatial elements, but his approach is more general in nature.

10 Compare the importance of an office-holder's presence both with the idea of 'Eriks-gata', in which the ruler travelled across the realm and reasserted his authority by presence, and with Per Brahe's travels. Hytönen 2004, pp. 55, 57; Karonen 1999, pp. 241–242; Lappalainen 2009, pp. 146–147.

11 On social distance, see Krausman Ben-Amos 2000, pp. 333–334.

12 Peter Englund refers to Rosenhane's diaries, see Englund 2000, pp. 781, 784–786. Björn Asker also refers to Rosenhane's diary and his experiences on some occasions, see Asker 2004, pp. 42, 71, 90, 94, 181–182, 184, 219. See also Jansson, 1993; Jansson 1995, p. 10; Nenonen 1999(a), pp. 330–332; Mäkinen 2000.

13 Toivanen 1991, pp. 64–72; Toivanen 1999.

14 I will research love and affection within the seventeenth-century family with Rosen-hane's diary as partial source material in my forthcoming article 'Huolehtivaa rak-kautta huoneentaulun hengessä' (working title), in a collection of essays preliminary entitled *Esimoderni rakkaus*, edited by Emmi Lahti & Hanna Kietäväinen-Sirén.

15 Compare with Stenbock & Stenbock 1920, p. v; Stanley 1992, p. 62; p. 562; Mortimer 2002, pp. 982–983, 997–998; Paperno 2004, pp. 982–983, 997–998. *Abraham Brahes Tidebok* is quite similar in style to Rosenhane's diary. See also Elaine McKay's interpretations about the underlying motives behind the diaries of officials (McKay 2005, pp. 203–204).

16 Compare with Stanley 1992, p. 128–131; Smyth 2008, p. 209; Paperno 2004, p. 562.

17 Burke 1997, p. 47. See also Stanley 1992, pp. 7, 10–11, 62, 85–86, 93, 128, 135.

18 Elgenstierna 1931, p. 482. Diaries have been connected to chronicles and annals as well as personal and household account books (Paperno 2004, pp. 562–563). Even though Rosenhane wrote a great deal about his office-holding and related travelling, diaries probably were for him also memoranda of his official duties, one may presume that he did not consider diary-writing to be an official act.

19 See also Toivanen 1999, p. 21.

20 Jansson 1993, pp. 95–96; Jansson 1995, pp. 8–9. Compare with Asker (2004, pp. 181–182), who is a little sceptical of Jansson's view. Asker puts forward the possible explanations that the social network of Eastern Götaland, provided Rosenhane with more opportunities for private traveling. Compare this with the career of Ernst Johan Creutz (Lappalainen 2005, pp. 208–209).

21 See Smyth 2008/2, p. 205. According to Smyth, the annotations refer to the same topics 'with particular frequency'.

22 Andersson, Carlsson & Sandström 1900–1911, p. 35.

23 Jansson 1995, pp. 4, 21; Toivanen 1999, pp. 13–15.

24 See SRA, Landshövdingens skrivelser till kungl. Maj:t, Viborgs län, Vol. 1: 1635–1671; SRA, Landshövdingens skrivelser till kungl. Maj:t, Östergötlands län, Vol.

1: 1638–1678. The latter volume also contains some letters relating to a criminal case that was investigated in 1645, during Johan Rosenhane's period as a vice-governor of Eastern Götaland.

25 SRA, Skoklostersamlingen II, E8167, 24 May 1657 and 3 June 1657; Jansson 1993, p. 105. It is well known that Per Brahe and Axel Oxenstierna had an antagonist relationship (see, for example, Karonen 1999, p. 240). This would probably have affected Johan Rosenhane's attitude towards Brahe if there was a patron–client relationship between the families of Oxenstierna and Rosenhane, as has been claimed. Schering Rosenhane was himself related to Axel Oxenstierna by marriage (see Jansson 1993, p. 90; Haggrén 2006). On the client system in general see, for example, Lappalainen 2005, pp. 53–55; Hakanen 2006, pp. 100–102, 104–112. See also Sundborg 1967, p. 18 and Einonen, 'Huolehtivaa rakkautta' on Axel Oxenstierna's role in the love affair of Johan's sister (which was carefully handled in order to minimize its effect on the family's reputation).

26 See also SRA, Rosenhaneska familjepapper, E5185. Naturally the court record books of Viipuri provide a precise record of Rosenhane's presence in the court house, but they are not relevant to his office-holding as such.

27 Harrison 1998, pp. 19–20.

28 Harrison 1998, pp. 46–47.

29 Masonen 1999, p. 70. Compare this with the nationalizing process within the Swedish county of Skåne after the Danish period, and particularly the role played by governors in this process (Ericsson 1984, pp. 32–62).

30 Karonen 1999, pp. 246–248.

31 Elgenstierna 1931, pp. 481–482; Lindberg 1946, p. 165; Jansson 1993, pp. 89–90; Asker 2004, pp. 215–225; Asker 2007, p. 106. It has been suggested that the Rosenhane family's success in securing appointments can be seen as results of their patron–client relationship with the Oxenstierna family (see Arne Jansson, Johan Rosenhane, p. 90; Georg Haggrén, Rosenhane).

32 Ruuth (Halila), 1974, pp. 274, 276. See also Lagerstam 2007, pp. 184–185.

33 See, for example, Lappalainen 2005, pp. 206–207. Compare with the royal burgomasters, who were likewise able to ascend through the ranks. On royal burgomasters, see Karonen 1995, pp. 40–83.

34 Some of the Rosenhane's successors did not even accept their nomination to the office in Vyborg. Compared to the considerable turnover of governors, Rosenhane's period in Vyborg was relatively long (Haggrén 2006; Ruuth (Halila) 1974, pp. 273–274, 276; see also Lappalainen 2005, pp. 185–187, 192, 206, 270; Lagerstam 2007, pp. 186–188).

35 See Asker 2004, pp. 70–71 about the significance of distance to Finnish participation in the Riksdag of the Estates (Sw. *riksdag*, Fi. *valtiopäivät*). Johan Rosenhane also took part in the Riksdag (Toivanen 1999, pp. 71, 73–85).

36 Retsö 2007(b), pp. 35–36.

37 See also Mörner 2001, p. 263; Lappalainen 2005, p. 128. On medieval roads and their effect on velocity, see Retsö 2007(b), pp. 44–49.

38 Toivanen 1999, p. 11. He even once mentions a sleigh (Diary 13 January 1652, p. 17) See also Retsö 2007(b), pp. 36–39, 44, 85–91; Nenonen 1999(a), pp. 274–277, 315.

39 Nenonen 1999(b), pp. 144, 146, 149, 163–167; Nenonen 1999(d), p. 356.

40 Compare with Stanley 1992, p. 107.

41 '..*där iagh och dhe flere ifrå denne widt aflägne orthen, icke kunne till efwentyrs för mootwind och owäder så precise oppå föresagde termin tillstädes komma, det då H:s K. Maÿ:tt wille hafwa oß i nåder excuseradhe och en sådan wår drögzmåhl icke till onåder optaga*' (RA, Landshövdingens skrivelser till kungl. Maj:t, Viborgs län, Vol. 1: 1635–1671, 17 March 1654).

42 Toivanen 1999, p. 29; Ruuth (Halila) 1974, p. 9.

43 For example, RA, Landshövdingens skrivelser till kungl. Maj:t, Viborgs län, Vol. 1: 1635–1671, 24 November 1654.

44 New instructions were issued in 1687 (Lindberg 1946, p. 163); Karonen 1999, pp. 102, 193, 236; Asker 2004, pp. 43–58, 126–130; Lappalainen 2005, pp. 191–192; Asker 2007, pp. 106–107. Royal statutes defining the tasks of governors have also been traced with the help of C.U. Leyonmarck (ed.) *Register öfwer den utaf framledne herr cancellie-rådet och riddaren Anders Anton v. Stjerneman gjorde samling af Riksdagh-beslut, bewillningar, arffdreningar, Regements-former, resolutioner på ståndens allmänna besvär m.m., ifrån år 1521 til år 1731 inclusive*, författadt af Stockholm 1820. About Rosenhane's office-holding in this context see Jansson 1993, pp. 91–97. See also Mörner 2001, p. 21.

45 Lindberg 1946, pp. 163–165.

46 See also Asker 2004, pp. 92, 179–180, 186–189.

47 Nenonen 1999(c), pp. 179–180; Nenonen 1999(a), pp. 275–276; Ruuth (Halila) 1974, pp. 279–281. See also Jansson 1993, pp. 117–118.

48 See, for example, Diary 25 October 1653, p. 86.

49 Diary 1 December 1653, p. 89.

50 Asker 2004, pp. 200–205.

51 See also Jansson 1993, p. 96, on Rosenhane's travelling in general, pp. 97–98.

52 See Toivanen 1999, pp. 44–56. Compare with Asker 2004, pp. 182–186, 199–200. On official periods of district court sessions, see Masonen 1999, p. 88.

53 Nenonen 1999(c), pp. 203–207; Salonen 1999, pp. 82–83. See also Jansson 1993, p. 96.

54 Salonen 1999, pp. 82–83. About roads, which were used by Vyborg travellers see Nenonen 1999(c), pp. 168, 185–189, 209–210.

55 Diary 19 January 1654, 95; Masonen 1999, p. 72; Nenonen 1999(a), pp. 279, 281, 284–290; Retsö 2007(b), p. 43. See also Lappalainen 2005, p. 128.

56 See, for example, Diary 16 February 1653, 4 July 1653, 1 July 1653, 28 September–6 October 1653, 13 February 1654, pp. 59, 75–76, 84, 97; Sundborg 1967, p. 36; Toivanen 1999, pp. 18, 24, 32–33, 49. See also Hytönen 2004, pp. 16–17, 19. Compare with Retsö's 2007 article on women's/one woman's travelling in the Middle Ages.

57 Compare with medieval views concerning 'long' and 'short' distances, and reliability of measurement (Retsö 2007(b), pp. 21–23, see also p. 91). See also Toivanen 1999, p. 48; Nenonen 1999(a), p. 293.

58 Diary 21 August 1654, p. 118. See also Rosenhane's comments concerning Gustaf Kurck's journey from Elbingen (Diary 12 April 1656, p. 171).

59 Diary 6 June 1654, p. 110. On this and other estates owned by the family Rosenhane, see von Malmborg et al. 1971, pp. 307–308, 320; Almquist 1935, pp. 674–675; Mörner 2001, p. 129.

60 Almquist 1947(b), pp. 930–932, see also 988–989. About Johan Rosenhane's landed property in general see Almquist 1947(a), pp. 219, 233–234, 262, 283–

284, 382–383, 428, 437, 576–577, 607–608, 641; Almquist 1935, pp. 512–513, 515–516, 634–636.

61 Nisbeth & Selling 1971, p. 193; Christiansson 1985, pp. 99, 101. See also Mörner 2001, pp. 21–25, 41–42. About manors as manifestations of symbolic power see Lappalainen 2005, p. 273; Englund 1994, pp. 70, 73; Emery 2005, pp. 141, 160.

62 Toivanen 1999, pp. 13, 20–21. About political geography in the Swedish Realm see Asker 2004, pp. 110–113.

63 Lindberg 1946, p. 165, 464.

64 Christiansson 1985, pp. 99–100; Mörner 2001, p. 231. See also Krausman Ben-Amos 2000, pp. 306–308; Lappalainen 2005, pp. 45–50. On networks compare with Stanley 1992, p. 10. On Johan Rosenhane's family and extended 'kinship', and their significance, see Jansson 1993, pp. 111–114; Einonen, 'Huolehtivaa rakkautta' (forthcoming). Compare with Cressy 1986, pp. 44–53, 66–67.

65 See, for example, the following entries from 1655: 16 August, 18 August, 2 September, 6 November, 4 and 5 December, pp. 153–154, 159, 161.

66 Twice Johan complains about the road *(ilack vägh)*, see Diary 19 and 20 December 1659, p. 269.

67 Edvardsson 2001, pp. 8–13; Mörner 2001, pp. 20, 258, 260, 262–263, 283; Retsö 2007(b), pp. 29, 31–32, see also 106–113; Nenonen 1999(d), pp. 348–350.

68 Edvardsson 2001, pp. 16, 18; Mörner 2001, pp. 251–252.

69 See, for example, Diary, 3 March 1652, p. 25; Mörner 2001, p. 256.

70 Retsö 2007(b), pp. 40–41; Nenonen 1999(a), p. 293. Compare with Edvardsson 2001, p. 92.

71 Groebner 2002 (2000), p. 68. See also Kopczynski 1994.

72 See, for example, Diary 11 April 1653, 13 April 1653, 16 April 1653, 1 May 1654, 19 September 1654, pp. 65–66, 105, 121; Jansson 1993, p. 110; Lappalainen 2005, pp. 278, 336–337. See also Heal 1984, pp. 66–93; Emery 2005, p. 144; Krausman Ben-Amos 2000, pp. 314–315, 319 on the importance of hospitality.

73 Edvardsson 2001, p. 25.

74 See for example Diary 17 and 18 August 1652, p. 40; Ruuth (Halila) 1974, especially pp. 77–78, 86, 95–96, 240; Toivanen 1999, pp. 64–66. See also Katajala 2005, p. 64. On ethnic groups and their characteristics (as defined by researchers and contemporaries) within the eastern county of Käkisalmi, see Katajala 2005, pp. 42–58, 238–244.

75 See, for example, Diary 10 November 1652 and 22 November 1652, pp. 47–49; see also Ruuth (Halila), 1974 pp. 233, 239–245, 324–325.

76 See, for example, Diary 10 June 1652, 21 June 1652, 10 November 1652, pp. 34–35, 47; Ruuth (Halila) 1974, pp. 82, 85–91; Toivanen 1999, pp. 33–35, 64–66, 87, 98.

77 Lindberg 1946, p. 165.

78 See also Jansson 1993, p. 111.

79 Burke 1997, p. 99.

80 SRA, Landshövdingens skrivelser till kungl. Maj:t, Viborgs län, Vol. 1: 1635–1671, 12 July 1647. Compare with Lappalainen 2005, pp. 128–129.

81 Jansson 1995, p. 4; Lappalainen 2005, pp. 146–148, see also 318–319.

82 See for example 7 February 1655, 4–6 March 1655, pp. 136, 138–139.

83 Diary 22 February 1655, p. 167. Von Malmborg, B. et al. 1971, p. 308.

84 See, for example, 9–19 August 1655, p. 153; Jansson 1993, pp. 111–113. See also Heal 1984, pp. 66–93; Emery 2005, p. 144.

85 Jansson 1995, p. 8; Toivanen 1999, p. 13. See also Englund 1994, pp. 74–76.

86 See, for example, 17 July 1655, p. 151

87 See, for example, Diary 22 February 1653, 11 July 1653, 19 February 1654, pp. 60, 75, 98. According to Dag Retsö (2007(b), p. 41) kings had usually large entourages and prominent persons were received and met before they reached their destination. Likewise they were escorted on their departure. Entourages could become quite large from time to time. Even though Rosenhane usually travelled with his closest servants, some governors had large entourages (see Lappalainen 2005, p. 128; see also Hytönen 2004, p. 16, on Per Brahe's entourage). On welcoming ceremonies, see also Korhonen 1996, pp. 93–94.

88 Diary 27 February 1653, p. 61, see also 16 February 1653, 59.

89 Diary 6 October 1654, 14 October 1654, 21 November 1654, 23 November 1654, pp. 122–123, 127.

90 See also Diary 30 January 1654, p. 96. There are only a few such references during Rosenhane's Swedish period, see Diary 8–9 August 1655, 8 September 1659, 19 December 1659, pp. 152–153, 263, 269. In September 1659 it was the king who was escorted.

91 Burke 1994 (1978), p. 177.

92 See for example Diary 26 May 1653, p. 70.

93 Diary 8 May 1654, 14 April 1654, pp. 106–107, see also 2 December 1654, p. 128.

94 Diary 15 August 1654, 16 August 1654, p. 117.

95 Diary 8 July 1654, p. 113.

96 See, for example, Diary 22 August 1654, p. 118.

97 Compare with Groebner 2002 (2000), pp. 2–3, 7.

98 On bribes see, for example, Groebner, 2002 (2000), pp. 71–75, 89; Einonen 2005, p. 162, 164–165.

99 Groebner 2002 (2000), pp. 3, 33, 66 (citation); Capp 2003, pp. 56–57; Krausman Ben-Amos, 2000, p. 299. See also Mauss 1999, p. 28.

100 Diary 18 December 1654, pp. 130–131. See also Groebner 2002 (2000), p. 7, 13; Krausman Ben-Amos 2000, p. 300. On complimentary calls, see also Diary 10 April 1657, p. 199.

101 Groebner 2002 (2000), pp. 3, 7, 71; Krausman Ben-Amos 2000, p. 315.

102 Groebner 2002 (2000), p. 19.

103 Stewart & Strathern 2004, p. 18.

104 Diary 3 January 1653, p. 53. See also Toivanen 1999, pp. 90–91. A similar gift of wine was given to the governor by burghers only a few weeks later because of some letters of recommendations (Diary 28 January 1653, p. 56). Arne Jansson (1993, p. 101) suggests that some of the gifts Rosenhane received were quite questionable, and can almost be seen as bribes.

105 Groebner 2002 (2000), pp. 18, 23.

106 Suolahti 1949, p. 235.

107 See for example Diary 28 October 1654, p. 124.

108 Diary 26 March 1655, 16 January 1657, 6 September 1658, pp. 169, 192, 235. These are the only gifts mentioned in the diary during Rosenhane's Swedish period except for the royal donations (see Diary 18 May 1658, p. 232; Jansson 1993, p. 100).

109 Wickham 1998, p. 14.

110 Asker 2007, pp. 106–107.

Bibliography
Archival sources

The National Archives of Sweden (Riksarkivet), Stockholm (SRA)
Landshövdingens skrivelser till kungl. Maj:t, Viborgs län, Vol. 1: 1635–1671
Landshövdingens skrivelser till kungl. Maj:t, Östergötlands län, Vol. 1: 1638–1678
Rosenhaneska familjepapper, E5185
Skoklostersamlingen II, E8167

Source editions

Diary = Jansson, A. (ed.), *Johan Rosenhanes dagbok 1652–1661.* Kungl. Samfundet för utgivande av handskrifter rörande Skandinaviens historiam Stockholm, 1995.
Leyonmarck, C. U. (ed.), *Register öfwer den utaf framledne herr cancellie-rådet och riddaren Anders Anton v. Stjerneman gjorde samling af Riksdagh-beslut, bewillningar, arffdreningar, Regements-former, resolutioner på ståndens allmänna besvär m.m., ifrån år 1521 til år 1731 inclusive.* Stockholm, 1820.

Literature

Almquist, J.A. 1935. *Frälsegodsen i Sverige under storhetstiden med särskild hänsyn till proveniens och säteribildning,* Vol. 2:2: *Nyköpings län och livgedingets Södermanlandsdel. Säterier.* Riksarkivet, Stockholm.
Almquist J.A. 1947(a). *Frälsegodsen i Sverige under storhetstiden med särskild hänsyn till proveniens och säteribildning,* Vol.3:1: *Östergötland. Inledning och tabeller.* Riksarkivet, Stockholm.
Almquist J. A. 1947(b). *Frälsegodsen i Sverige under storhetstiden med särskild hänsyn till proveniens och säteribildning,* Vol. 3:2: *Östergötland. Säterier.* Riksarkivet, Stockholm.
Andersson, A., Carlsson, A. B. & Sandström, J. 1900 – 1911. *Uppsala universitets matrikel,* Vol. 1. Berling, Uppsala.
Asker, B. 2004. *I konungens stad och ställe. Länsstyrelser i arbete 1635–1735.* Stiftelsen för utgivande av Arkivvetenskapliga studier, Uppsala.
Asker, B. 2007. *Hur riket styrdes. Förvaltning, politik och arkiv 1520–1920.* Riksarkivet, Stockholm.
Burke, P. 1994 (1978). *Popular Culture in Early Modern Europe.* Revised reprint. Scholar Press, Aldershot.
Burke, P. 1997. *Varieties of Cultural History.* Polity Press, Cambridge.
Capp, B. 2003. *When gossips meet: women, family, and neighbourhood in early modern England.* Oxford University Press, Oxford.
Christiansson, H. 1985. 'Herremannens hus.' In Christiansson, H. et al. (eds.) *Ett stycke Sörmland. Flens kommun i tiden och historien.* Flens kommun, Flen.
Cressy, D. 'Kinship and Kin Interaction in Early Modern England.' *Past & Present,* No. 113, pp. 38–69.
Einonen, P. 2005. *Poliittiset areenat ja toimintatavat. Tukholman porvaristo vallan käyttäjänä ja vallankäytön kohteena n. 1592–1644.* The Finnish Literature Society, Helsinki.
Edvardsson, I. 2001. *Hästskjuts. Vägar, fordon och människor förr i tiden.* Wahlström & Widstrand, Stockholm.

Elgenstierna, G. 1931. *Den introducerade svenska adelns ättartavlor*, Vol. 6. Norstedt, Stockholm.

Emery, A. 2005. 'Late-Medieval Houses as an Expression of Social Status.' *Historical Research*, Vol. 78, No. 200, pp. 140–161.

Eng, T. 2006. 'Sweden as State, Realm and Sphere of Dominion in Early Modern Time.' In Gustafsson, H. & Sanders, H. (eds.) *Vid gränsen. Integration och identitet i det förnationella Norden*. Makadam, Stockholm, pp. 122–131.

Englund, P. 1994. *Det hotade huset. Adliga föreställningar om samhället under stormaktstiden*. Atlantis, Stockholm.

Englund, P. 2000. *Den oövervinnerlige. Om den svenska stormaktstiden och en man i dess mitt*. Atlantis, Stockholm.

Ericsson, L. 1984. 'Absolutism eller nationalism? Till frågan om försvenskningen av magistraterna i de erövrade danska städerna under 1600-talet.' *Karolinska Förbundets Årsbok*, 1984, pp. 32–62.

Groebner, V. 2002 (2000). *Liquid Assets, Dangerous Gifts. Presents and Politics at the End of the Middle Ages*. Translated by Pamela E. Selwyn. University of Pennsylvania Press, Philadelphia, pp. 2–3, 7.

Haggrén, G. 2006. 'Rosenhane, Johan.' In Klinge, M. et al. (eds.) *Suomen Kansallisbiografia*, Vol. 8. The Finnish Literature Society, Helsinki, pp. 361–363.

Hakanen, M. 2006. 'Klienttijärjestelmäroolit identiteettien muokkaajina 1600-luvun Ruotsin valtakunnassa.' In Moilanen, L.-M. & Sulkunen, S. (eds.) *Aika ja identiteetti. Katsauksia yksilön ja yhteisön väliseen suhteeseen keskiajalta 2000-luvulle*. The Finnish Literature Society, Helsinki, pp. 98–116.

Harrison, D. 1998. *Skapelsens geografi. Föreställningar om rymd och rum i medeltidens Europa*. Ordfront, Stockholm.

Heal, F. 1984. 'The Idea of Hospitality in Early Modern England.' *Past & Present*, No. 102, pp. 66–93.

Hytönen, J. 2004. 'Matkalla jossain suuriruhtinaskunnassa.' In *Pietari Brahe matkustaa*. Turun maakuntamuseo, Turku, pp. 7–61.

Jansson, A. 1993. 'Johan Rosenhane. Ämbetsman i Kristinas och Karl X Gustavs tid.' *Karolinska Förbundets Årsskrift*, 1993, pp. 89–118.

Jansson, A. 1995. 'Inledning.' In Jansson, A. (ed.) *Johan Rosenhanes dagbok 1652–1661*. Kungl. Samfundet för utgivande av handskrifter rörande Skandinaviens historia, Stockholm.

Karonen, P. 1995. 'Raastuvassa tavataan'. *Suomen kaupunkien hallinto- ja oikeuslaitoksen toimintaa ja virkamiehiä suurvalta-aikana*. University of Jyväskylä, Jyväskylä.

Karonen, P. 1999. *Pohjoinen suurvalta. Ruotsi ja Suomi 1521–1809*. WSOY, Porvoo, Helsinki & Juva.

Katajala, K. 2005. *Suurvallan rajalla. Ihmisiä Ruotsin ajan Karjalassa*. The Finnish Literature Society, Helsinki.

Katajala, K. 2006. 'The Origin of the Border.' In Gustafsson, H. & Sanders, H. (eds.) *Vid gränsen. Integration och identitet i det förnationella Norden*. Makadam, Stockholm, pp. 86–106.

Kopczynski, M. 1994. 'Service or Benefice? Officeholders in Poland and Sweden in the Seventeenth Century.' *European Review of History*, Vol. 1 (1), pp. 19–28.

Korhonen, T. 1996. *Tervehdys ja hyvästely*, Helsinki, Suomen Antropologinen Seura.

Krausman Ben-Amos, I. 2000. 'Gifts and Favors. Informal Support in Early Modern England.' *The Journal of Modern History*, Vol. 72, (2), pp. 295–338.

Lagerstam, L. 2007. *A Noble Life. The Cultural Biography of Gabriel Kurck (1639–1712)*. University of Turku, Turku.

Lappalainen, M. 2005. *Suku, valta, suurvalta. Creutzit 1600-luvun Ruotsissa ja Suomessa*. WSOY, Helsinki.

Lappalainen, M. 2009. *Susimessu. 1590-luvun sisällissota Ruotsissa ja Suomessa*. Siltala, Helsinki.

Lindberg, F. 1946. *Linköpings historia*, Vol. 2: *Tiden 1567–1862*. Westman & Wernerska Fonden, Linköping.

Mäkinen V. 2000. *Säädynmukaista elämää? Henkilökohtaiset lähteet 1600-luvun ihmisten maailmankuvan heijastajina*. Unpublished MA thesis. University of Jyväskylä, Department of History (and Ethnology) 2000.

von Malmborg, B. et al. 1971. *Slott och herresäten i Sverige*, Vol. 2: *De kungliga slotten*. Allhems, Malmö.

Masonen, J. 1999. 'Kirkon, kruunun ja kansan tiet keskiajalla.' In Mauranen, T. (ed.) *Maata, jäätä, kulkijoita. Tiet, liikenne ja yhteiskunta ennen vuotta 1860*. Edita, Helsinki, pp. 57–108.

Mauss, M. 1999. *Lahja. Vaihdannan muodot ja periaatteet arkaaisissa yhteiskunnissa*. Translated by Jouko Nurmiainen & Jyrki Hakapää. Tutkijaliitto, Helsinki.

McKay, E. 2005. 'English Diarists. Gender, Geography and Occupation, 1500–1700.' *History*, Vol. 90, pp. 191–212.

Mörner, M. 2001. *Människor, landskap, varor & vägar. Essäer från svenskt 1600- och 1700-tal*. Atlantis, Stockholm.

Mortimer, I. 2002. 'Tudor Chronicler or Sixteenth-Century Diarist? Henry Machyn and the Nature of His Manuscript.' *The Sixteenth Century Journal*, Vol. 33 (4), pp. 981–998.

Nenonen, M. 1999(a). 'Kulkijan taival.' In Mauranen, T. (ed.) *Maata, jäätä, kulkijoita. Tiet, liikenne ja yhteiskunta ennen vuotta 1860*. Edita, Helsinki, pp. 274–334.

Nenonen, M. 1999(b). 'Maitse vai vesitse. Kulkemisen peruskysymys 1550–1800.' In Mauranen, T. (ed.) *Maata, jäätä, kulkijoita. Tiet, liikenne ja yhteiskunta ennen vuotta 1860*. Edita, Helsinki, pp. 144–167.

Nenonen, M. 1999(c). 'Vesiltä pyörille. Suuret maantiet 1550–1800.' In Mauranen, T. (ed.) *Maata, jäätä, kulkijoita. Tiet, liikenne ja yhteiskunta ennen vuotta 1860*. Edita, Helsinki, pp. 167–273.

Nenonen, M. 1999(d). 'Tien synty.' In Mauranen, T. (ed.) *Maata, jäätä, kulkijoita. Tiet, l iikenne ja yhteiskunta ennen vuotta 1860*. Edita, Helsinki, pp. 334–367.

Nisbeth, Å. & Selling, G. 1971. *Slott och herresäten i Sverige. Östergötland*, Vol. 1: *Adelsnäs–Ljung*. Allhems, Malmö.

Paperno, I. 2004. 'What Can Be Done with Diaries?' *The Russian Review*, Vol. 63, pp. 561–573.

Retsö, D. 2007(a). '"Instängdhetens nytta." Kvinnors geografiska mobilitet under medeltiden och Mätta Ivarsdotters resor 1504–1511.' *Scandia*, Vol. 73, pp. 39–56.

Retsö, D. 2007(b). *Människans mobilitet och naturens motsträvighet. Studier kring frågan om reshastighet under medeltiden*. University of Stockholm, Stockholm.

Ruuth, J. W. (Halila, A.) 1974. *Viipurin kaupungin historia*, Vol. 2: *Vuodet 1617–1710*. Torkkelin säätiö, Helsinki.

Salonen, K. 1999, 'Ylinen Viipurintie.' In Mauranen, T. (ed.) *Maata, jäätä, kulkijoita. Tiet, liikenne ja yhteiskunta ennen vuotta 1860*. Edita, Helsinki, pp. 82–83.

Smyth, A. 2002. 'Almanacs, Annotators, and Life-Writing in Early Modern England.' *English Literary Renaissance*, Vol. 38 (2), pp. 200–244.

Stanley, L. 1992. *The auto/biographical I. The theory and practice of feminist auto/biography.* Manchester University Press, Manchester & New York.

Stenbock, C. M. & Stenbock, R. 1920. '(untitled preface).' In Stenbock, C. M. & Stenbock, R. (ed.) *Abraham Brahes Tidebok,* Norstedt, Stockholm, pp. III–VIII.

Stewart, P. J. & and Strathern, A. 2004. *Witchcraft, Sorcery, Rumors and Gossip.* Cambridge University Press, Cambridge.

Sundborg, B. 1967. *Den skiten Per Andersson. En lycksökare från Christinas tid.* Bonniers, Stockholm.

Suolahti, G. 1949. 'Barokkiajan kirjeitä ja muistelmia.' *Valvoja,* Vol. 69 (6), pp. 230–235.

Toivanen, P. 1991. 'Landshövding Johan Rosenhanes diarium från åren 1652–1655.' In Åström, A.-M. & Nordlund, I. (eds.) *Kring tiden. Etnologiska och folkloristiska uppsatser. Vänskrift till Bo Lönnqvist 29.9.1991.* Svenska litteratursällskapet i Finland, Helsinki, pp. 64–72.

Toivanen, P. 1999. *Viipurin maaherran Johan Rosenhanen diarium päiväkirja 1652–1654. Mahtimiehen elämää itäisessä Suomessa.* Etelä-Karjalan museo, Lappeenranta.

Wickham, C. 1998. 'Gossip and Resistance among the Medieval Peasantry.' *Past and Present,* No. 160, pp. 3–24.

PART III

INFORMATION FLOWS

CHAPTER 5

Distance as an Argument

Ulla Koskinen

Introduction

This chapter is based on a short case study of a fortress that was to be built in the eastern part of the Swedish realm in the 1580s on the orders of King John III. At the same time it is a story of the everyday life, or struggle, of the noble office-holders who took care of administration on the edges of the kingdom. The focus is on the process of executing decisions made by the central power. Office-holders needed a relatively free hand, particularly in geographically remote areas, because communication with the central power was a lengthy process.[1] The office-holders were not the king's puppets: they had their own networks, interests and views about what was profitable for them and the realm.

Although the nobility in the peripheries of the realm, especially in Finland, have long been attributed an 'independent' position regarding the central power,[2] it is not clear what this actually meant in terms of administration. The dynamics of the relationship between office-holders and the king, strategies used in mutual negotiation and office-holders' practices of executing commands remain largely unexamined.[3] Political power has traditionally been seen as something directed from top to bottom; the possibility that members of the lower political tiers might have exercised some form of power has been hidden beneath their seemingly passive role as obedient subjects. Other researchers have stressed the way in which subjects might have been able to negotiate and exert influence through societal institutions. The informal aspects of power have started to attract attention only recently.[4] Still, most research on political culture takes an unproblematic view of the role of office-holders as representatives of the Crown.[5] This ignores the contradiction inherent in their position: they were at once authorities and subjects of the king.[6] Thus office-holders, like all other subjects, had their own solidarity groups, interests and wishes, which could be opposed to the demands of the Crown.[7]

In this case study I examine the significance of distance from two different perspectives. I consider distance both as a geographical fact that determined a framework for the administration and as a legitimizing argument, which office-holders used to justify their sometimes arbitrary actions.[8] My central question is if and how office-holders on the edges of the realm could take advantage of the distance, the slow speed at which information travelled and the central power's lack of local knowledge in their execution of decisions taken by the Crown. I will pay special attention to the importance of office-holders' cooperation and networks in the administration of distant areas.

Flow of information: carrying letters

Sweden was a large kingdom. In the late 1500s it was engaged in constant warfare with the neighbouring Russian realm. The recent successful expansion to the east – into Karelia (Fi. Karjala, Sw. Karelen), Ingria (Fi. Inkerinmaa, Sw. Ingermanland) and Estonia – meant that the distances of the Swedish realm grew considerably. The distance from the capital Stockholm to the war zone was over 600 kilometres (cf. Maps 1 and 2). The actual sea and land routes were of course even longer than this. It is not surprising that in the late sixteenth century it could take several months to send a message and receive an answer. The time required depended on weather conditions and the season, among other factors.

Yet these remote areas were borderlands of the realm and there was a pressing need to keep them under the central power's control, especially as they were central to the war efforts against Russia. Castellans and other noblemen who held offices in these areas had to maintain correspondence networks with each other and with the central power in Sweden.

Map 16 (see colour plate section 1, p. 8) shows how long it took to deliver letters within different parts of the realm. It is based on the correspondence of Arvid Henriksson Tawast (c. 1540–1599), a nobleman living in the Finnish part of the realm. Tawast, like other office-holders, would habitually note down the date letters had arrived. This makes it possible to calculate travel time by comparing the date of writing with the date of arrival, if the places of origin and receipt are also known.

For instance, during the summer of 1579 a letter from Stockholm seems to have been delivered to Hattula nineteen days after it was written. This letter was labelled 'Cito Cito', which indicated that it was to be delivered as quickly as possible. In this particular case we have detailed information about the actual travel route. The letter was written in Stockholm on 23 June. A Finnish nobleman carried it across the sea to Porvoo (Sw. Borgå), where he arrived by 9 July at the latest. This sea voyage took about two weeks. This seems a good speed when one considers that in the 1650s the approximate travel time for mail from Stockholm to Turku (Sw. Åbo) was between one and two weeks[9] (the sea route to Porvoo is almost twice as long as that to Turku). It is possible that the nobleman landed in Turku and then travelled to his mansion in Porvoo by horse, but even in this case he would still have made good time. In Porvoo he wrote another letter to Tawast and then sent the two of them with his servant to Häme (Sw. Tavastland). This shorter trip over land (perhaps 130 kilometres by road) took only three days and the letters reached Arvid Tawast on 12 July.[10] The servant must have covered over forty kilometres per day on average (probably changing horses), which compares well with the maximum distances covered by the mail-carriers of the next century.[11]

This journey took place in summertime with apparently favourable weather conditions and a courier who was travelling as quickly as possible. From other letters we can see that the travel time could vary a great deal even on the same routes: the longer the distance, the greater the variation. It took three to eight days to travel from Vyborg (Fi. Viipuri, Sw. Viborg) to Savonlinna (Sw. Nyslott), between five and thirty-nine days from Masku to Savonlinna and fifteen to fifty-six days from Narva to Uppsala. These times can be compared with the speed of mail-carrying in the 1650s. At that time it took between three and five days from Vyborg to Savonlinna, from Turku to Savonlinna eight to eleven days, and between sixteen and twenty-one days from Stockholm to Narva.[12] On longer routes Tawast's messengers could be delayed considerably longer than was the case after the postal service had been founded.[13] This variation was an inevitable part of the process of administration. The consequent uncertainty involved in correspondence was a fact that could also be exploited.

For instance, a letter that had arrived just 'a couple of days ago' might have actually been received a couple of weeks earlier.[14] Similarly the slow pace of travel could be exaggerated: in 1595 the Swedish peace negotiators told their Russian counterparts that some of them were many weeks late for the appointed meeting because they had been delayed by bad weather and difficulties in crossing the sea. In reality these men had not even begun their journey, because they were attending the funeral of a family member.[15]

The time needed to deliver a letter was the sum of many factors. In addition to distance, geographical conditions, the quality of roads and the weather were decisive factors.[16] Riding was the fastest way of travelling, but wintry conditions or a multitude of lakes and rivers on a route could present serious difficulties. On the other hand, during the winter travel within the Swedish realm was very fast in comparison with journeys in other European countries. Rivers, marshes and lakes froze to form winter-ways along which a horse and sleigh could be driven. This was the fastest way of travelling by land in early modern times.[17] It was the duty of peasants to maintain the main roads, which on the Finnish side ran between the biggest towns and castles: from Turku via Hämeenlinna to Vyborg and Savonlinna and on the southern coast from Turku to Vyborg.[18]

The fastest connections from Sweden to Finland, Ingria and Estonia went over the Baltic Sea. A familiar but unsubstantiated notion has been that waterways were also the primary travel routes in inland areas.[19] Even on open seas, it was nearly impossible to travel in spring and autumn because of the ice conditions. Long-distance messengers were dependent upon ships coming and going, favourable winds and so on. When the winds were adverse, a ship may have had to wait for days, but with favourable winds the journey proceeded quickly: 'We could not arrive with speed, but had to march and row until the uttermost point of Koivisto (Sw. Björkö). But on the 21st of August God gave us wind, [and] then we sailed the same day all the way to the river Neva (Sw. Nyen)'.[20] Seasonal conditions affected travelling. Given the poor conditions, it was difficult to travel at all during spring and autumn. Military campaigns were planned for the summer, when the roads were dry, and the transportation of taxes and other heavy loads was undertaken during the winter months, when it was possible to use sledges. 'Sledge conditions' are repeatedly mentioned in administrative correspondence: matters could be taken care of only when sledge time arrived, or they had to be taken care of before it was over.[21] On the other hand, the northern realm had the advantage of up to twenty hours of daylight in the summertime,[22] when it was possible for messengers to travel 'through night and day', as was requested for urgent matters.[23]

Office-holders had to organize letter-carrying themselves: at this time there was no postal service.[24] The name of the letter-carrier has sometimes been marked on the outside of the letter, for example, 'arrived with my servant Olof Andersson'.[25] The letters in the Tawast collection along with letters to and from Tawast held in other archives contain information about forty-six letter-carriers, of whom fifteen can be identified as servants of the sender, receiver or some other nobleman. The identities of a further third remain unknown, while most of the remaining carriers appear to have been guard soldiers or other servants with positions in the castles. Some craftsmen also acted as carriers, as did Tawast's own brother on one occasion. Two letters were carried by a special 'postman' (*brefdragare*) who was stationed in Vyborg Castle in 1599.[26]

A messenger did not only carry letters: he was often a spokesman for the writer and would converse with the person who received the letter. The letters sometimes stated that the letter-carrier would discuss the subject matter further.[27] In cases of urgency the messenger might remain at the recipient's house and wait for a reply, which he would then carry back with him. Sometimes there was nothing to report: 'no news came during the time that your letter-carrier stayed here'.[28]

Uncertainty and waiting

Because of the aforementioned factors, the flow of information was perceived as being slow and to some extent unpredictable. This was due to the variation of the seasons, weather conditions and other variables beyond human control. This was a normal part of communication that had to be taken into account whenever messages were sent. My argument is that the unpredictable flow of information had a significant influence on the practical organization of administration. Strict plans were not rational: flexibility was required in order to adapt to changing circumstances.

In many cases the exact whereabouts of an addressee would not be known. A messenger sometimes had to search for the recipient over a large area and, of course, this could add considerably to the time it took for a letter to be delivered.[29] In other cases office-holders often had to wait a considerable time for people to arrive. A letter from Henrik Claesson (Horn), an old nobleman and knight, to Arvid Tawast shows that planning one's timetable in advance was not worthwhile:

> Henrik Mattsson lingered so long that I waited for his arrival eight weeks in Vyborg. Now last Tuesday he left Vyborg for Kaprio, where he is planning to stay for a while. I cannot wait there longer, but have departed and am going to leave for home. But as soon as I get information about his returning from Kaprio and beginning the court sessions, I will hasten back again to wherever I may find him.[30]

Henrik Claesson lived on the western coast of Finland in Masku (several hundreds of kilometres from Vyborg). Travelling between Vyborg and Turku (close to Masku) was estimated to take eight days in the 1540s,[31] but as seen above road conditions could significantly increase the length of time the journey took. An old nobleman who travelled with a big company would require more time, effort and organization for his journey.[32]

However, practical difficulties and personal adversities were not the only consequences of the slow pace of travel: it also led to better opportunities for independent action by office-holders. It was possible to promote one's private interests – even to act against the king's orders and avoid being confronted by him – because the central power had no established mechanisms of control. Let us take the wooden fortress on the river Neva as an example of an instance in which office-holders on the eastern borders successfully resisted the king's orders.

The king's plan: 'a fortress is to be built'

In 1582 John III of Sweden drew up a plan to build a fortress in Ingria. It was to be situated on the river Neva, opposite the fortress of Nöteborg (Fi. Pähkinälinna), which was in enemy hands. The area played a central part in the war. Swedish troops had been very successful in the last few years and had conquered a number of fortresses in Karelia, Ingria and Estonia, largely thanks to the famous commander-in-chief Pontus De la Gardie.[33] From John III's point of view, the new fortress was necessary to ensure Sweden's continued success in the war. He wrote to Pontus De la Gardie: 'a fortress is to be built, and we do not want to know of any excuses in that matter', adding that if the army had already built the fortress the previous summer, as soon as they first arrived in enemy territory near Nöteborg, 'it would have been more valuable for the Swedish Crown than a barrel of gold'.[34]

John III assigned the building task to two Finnish noblemen, Arvid Henriksson Tawast and Arvid Eriksson Stålarm. The order was dated 3 January 1583 and was renewed on 19 April. Their task was first to collect the necessary troops and supplies and then to travel with them to the building site and finally to organize the actual construction of the fortress. When choosing these two men, John III probably saw their personal networks as an asset. Both were experienced military commanders and administrators, and they had already served the Crown for many years and cooperated successfully. In fact they called each other 'dear brother of my heart' – they had long been confidants. Their earlier careers and landed properties had given them an insight into local conditions, and they were well-known figures in the eastern parts of the realm.[35] They had already achieved a recognized status and established networks, which were vital for any administrative tasks in distant areas.[36] In theory they were capable of cooperating and carrying out the demanding task.

John III gave no detailed instructions for how his plan should be implemented.[37] He left those decisions in the hands of the noblemen, who best knew the local conditions. The king could not be in constant contact with Tawast and Stålarm, since it took so long for letters to travel, nor could he monitor the building work. He had to entrust the process to the noblemen who were on the spot.

The problem was that Tawast and Stålarm were completely opposed to the king's plan. They thought it was utterly impracticable, given the scarce resources at hand. Because Tawast and Stålarm were unwilling to implement John III's plans, the noblemen's networks turned out to be a threat to the king's authority. As soon as Tawast and Stålarm received information about their assignment, they began to take action against it with the help of their personal contacts.

Arvid Tawast finds excuses

The king's renewed order reached Arvid Tawast, who was visiting his south-coast mansion in Tenhola (Sw. Tenala), only a month after having been sent from Stockholm on 24 May 1583. Travelling in springtime over the Sea of Åland (Fi. Ahvenanmeri) had taken a very long time. But as soon as he got the order, Tawast swiftly began to utilize his network against it. He wrote two letters in the days that followed. The first was addressed to the royal secretary Hans Kranck and the other, to John III himself. The letters are interesting as they reveal the way in which Tawast chose to present his arguments to different recipients. His purpose was the same: to rid himself of an unpleasant assignment. The argumentation shows the kind of tone that Tawast considered appropriate when writing to the secretary and to the king (Map 17 see colour plate section 1, p. 9).

Although they lacked official power, the royal secretaries were in a key position within the Swedish central administration. They worked in the Chancellery and were in daily contact with the king. In practice they were his counsellors and had real possibilities to exert influence.[38] Tawast had already succeeded in creating a reciprocal relationship with Secretary Hans Kranck, who was also of Finnish origin.[39] They had some shared business matters and Tawast called Kranck 'his dear brother'. He adopts a confidential tone when writing about the building plan:

> My brotherly request to you, dear brother, is that you would *make things go so that I would not receive that kind of a task*, because I am not able to take care of it because of my weakness and illness. *I trust you, dear brother of my heart, that you will help me to get rid of this assignment*, because I cannot make the soldiers obey and I do not know by which means to do it, because there are no clothes, no money, not even provisions to support them tolerably. I have also sent a letter to His Royal Majesty with this servant of mine. I ask you, my brother, that I would be worthy of a favourable and graceful reply as soon as possible so I can act accordingly [...]⁴⁰ (Italics added)

Tawast sent Kranck's wife a roll of cloth as a gift and assured Kranck of his future services, promising to compensate 'your benevolent brotherly goodwill with all good'.⁴¹

In his letter to the king, Tawast goes into much more detail. He underlines his willingness to obey the king but makes clear that this task is beyond his capabilities. He attributes this to local circumstances and a lack of resources. Moreover, he not only makes complaints, but also provides an alternative solution. He suggests a more suitable person take his place:

> *I am obliged to obey Your Royal Majesty's mind and will if only all those things that are needed there would be now available here.* First, Most Gracious King and Lord, there are no more than four companies of soldiers left here in Finland [...] And I have now, Most Gracious King and Lord, written to the captains that are here in Finland that they should ... depart with them to Vyborg so that they would be there by Saint John the Baptist's Day at the latest, because *they cannot be collected sooner and the troops are widely scattered around the country, especially as one of the companies is in Ostrobothnia* [...] But those troops, Most Gracious King and Lord, that are left here, *complain bitterly that they do not want to go on any campaign before they get clothes and money and provisions*, with which they could support themselves as many months as Your Royal Majesty wants them to stay in the enemy's territory, because they have many times before retreated because of hunger. Most Gracious King and Lord, although I would write to the cavalrymen that they should take off, *they do not care about me. If the Noble Lord, Lord Pontus cannot get the military to build the fortress, there is no one*

else who can make it happen and obey Your Royal Majesty's mind and will […] But now, Most Gracious King and Lord, I have intended to leave, in the name of the Holy Trinity, to Vyborg at the aforementioned time. *If the troops are gathered together and they get enough to support themselves with, I will gladly follow them* and do whatever is possible to me. But, Most Gracious King and Lord, *I do not trust myself capable of taking the responsibility of organizing the whole thing. I beg Your Royal Majesty most humbly and subserviently that Your Royal Majesty would write to the Noble Lord, Lord Pontus, that he would take on the task.* I do not know anyone, who can fulfil Your Royal Majesty's mind and will in this matter, nor anyone else, whom Your Royal Majesty could order to this job.[42] (Italics added)

These two letters serve as examples of argumentation strategies that were tailored to the addressee. In his letter to Kranck, Tawast could directly state that he did not want to take the job; John III required a more discrete approach, both an assurance of obedience and a demonstration that the task was beyond Tawast's capabilities. He also employs arguments that relate to distance: gathering the scattered troops and transporting them to the eastern border would take a considerable amount of time. In both letters Tawast mentions the disobedience of the soldiers as though it was an everyday matter, well known to the king and his secretary. Although he was the commander-in-chief of the Finnish infantry, he portrays the failure of his soldiers to obey him as a normal occurrence. Tawast states that only one man, the commander-in-chief of the entire military, could command their obedience, thus making clear that it was largely personal authority that mattered, not the king's commission. This further validates the notion that the central power could not efficiently control local networks and that this was an administrative fact of which everybody was aware. Tawast also argues that his responsibility is to obey the king only if the required resources are at hand. Thus he does not consider himself obliged to obey unconditionally, only if certain prerequisites are met.

The tangle of power relations

Meanwhile, Arvid Stålarm had visited Stockholm at the end of May. By the beginning of June, before Tawast's letters had arrived at the Chancellery, he had already returned to the south coast of Finland. Because Tawast had travelled from the south to the north-east (to Häme, where his main mansions were located), Stålarm had to negotiate with his colleague in writing (Map 18 see colour plate section 1, p. 10). During his visit to Stockholm, Stålarm had discussed the matter in person with John III, who held firmly to his plan: 'His Royal Majesty does by no means want to hear anything from you or me, but ordered that we have to leave as soon as possible to Pähkinälinna with 1,000 men and build a fortress there'.[43] Peace negotiations with Russia were imminent. Stålarm was a member of the negotiating committee and there was a chance that the building plan might be forgotten if the negotiations proved successful. However, a week later in mid-June Stålarm reported the king's latest dictate to Tawast: the fortress was to be built regardless of whether or not a truce was agreed.[44]

John III was well aware that the noblemen were opposed to the project and that their networks could pose a threat to his authority. However, there was little he could do, given that he did not want to negotiate or make any compromises about his building plan. Instead he attempted to weaken the networks by explicitly forbidding Stålarm to mention the plan to Claes Åkesson (Tott) and Pontus De la Gardie (members of the Council of the Realm and peace negotiators), who were strongly opposed to his plans. This did not, of course, have the desired effect. Stålarm immediately contacted both men: Tott in person and De la Gardie (who was in Tallinn) in writing.[45]

Although the noblemen could not alter the king's decision, they could hinder and delay the execution of it. Having read the details from Stålarm's letter, Pontus De la Gardie explicitly advised Tawast and Stålarm to postpone the building plans. He listed the possible dangers and difficulties that could be expected and concluded:

> I leave to your consideration what will follow hereafter. *I withdraw myself from responsibility* should any of these aforementioned misfortunes fall upon the fortress. *Do not let me be found, good men, to be against His Royal Majesty's gracious and high opinion* about this building project, but, taking into consideration the time that has passed, *I advise* that, if such a task shall be undertaken, work should begin in spring as soon as the ice breaks so that the summertime, when Russians can do no harm to the building project, may add to the fortress's better endurance.[46] (Italics added)

In practice De la Gardie forbade Tawast and Stålarm to obey the king's orders. He had already written to the king and given his advice that the plan should be abandoned, but Stålarm 'hardly believed' that the letter would have any effect on the notoriously stubborn John III, as 'His Royal Majesty was terribly obstinate and furious about this matter'.[47] De la Gardie was careful to state that he did not by any means wish to oppose the king's will. He only advised the noblemen to postpone the project, using the dwindling summer as his strongest argument. He left ultimate responsibility with Tawast and Stålarm, who were now forced to choose between the king's orders and De la Gardie's advice and, in doing so, take a stand against one or the other. Stålarm wrote of the tricky situation 'God knows whom one should obey',[48] voicing his confusion over the manifold administrative authorities.

This indicates how unclear power relations actually were. The king had power over everybody, but he had also delegated his power to various office-holders, who had the right to give orders to their subordinates. However, the scope and chain of command between the different offices were not defined.[49] Which lord should subjects obey, if their nearest superior and the king disagreed? In fact it seems that this lack of clarity in the end proved to be the salvation of Tawast and Stålarm. It gave officials the opportunity to choose the more agreeable option and try to legitimize it through the use of proper argumentation. Obedience could convincingly be used as a justification for either choice: *the king ordered and I had to obey* or *my superior ordered and I had to obey*.

This is exactly what Stålarm did when he received Pontus De la Gardie's letter. De la Gardie's advice was of course more agreeable to him than John III's orders, and Stålarm regarded the letter as a licence to reject the king's orders:

> Dear brother Arvid Henriksson, I have received Lord Pontus' letter that is addressed to both you and me. Therein we may find Lord Pontus' understanding and announcing. I send you a copy of the letter, and *Lord Pontus' original letter we will readily keep safe so that we can plead to it when the time comes.* My brother can well arrange his matters according to Lord Pontus' letter.'[50] (Italics added)

De la Gardie had written his letter on 28 June in Tallinn. At this time Stålarm was at home in Tenhola busily preparing to leave for the peace negotiations in Narva, Estonia. Luckily he had not yet left and so he was made aware of De la Gardie's opinions very quickly. As Stålarm's letter to Tawast is dated 2 July, it could only have taken four days at most for De la Gardie's letter to reach Tenhola. Had Stårlarm not been at home, it might have taken many weeks before the messenger could locate him.

The passing of time gave the noblemen an advantage. It was already July. The more they wrote and pondered, the less feasible the building plan would become, as it would be too late to begin the project in the autumn. The length of time correspondence took to arrive was an integral part of the administrative process, but in this case it was in the office-holders' interests to lengthen it as much as possible.

Finally in late July 1583, Arvid Stålarm saw it was time to give up the whole project. He had arrived in Narva and reported to Tawast:

> *I have cast away the commission which His Royal Majesty gave us* about tasks here upon Neva, according to Lord Pontus' and Lord Claes Åkesson's orders and otherwise because of the ice situation and the shortness of the summer.[51] (Italics added)

This strikingly illustrates how the king's own office-holders could discard orders they received from their sovereign. There are many similar examples of noblemen 'casting away' commissions or at least attempting to avoid unpleasant duties the king wanted to give to them.[52] This means that they believed that they had the right of discretion; they did not feel they had to blindly accept the king's decisions.

In this case, Stålarm dared to ignore the king's orders with the support of his network and by invoking the adverse conditions. Having received Pontus De la Gardie's letter, he felt confident that he could discard the assignment and still appear to be a loyal subject, who was only doing what his commander told him to. The final outcome was that the plan was never implemented.

Conclusion

In the 1540s the Swedish chronicler Olaus Petri wrote:

> Sweden is a country so fortified with marshes, mountains and forests that common people can no longer be dominated with force and power, because they have a good opportunity to take their stand against their lord. Therefore Sweden is better reigned through good will than through great strictness.[53]

Olaus Petri's idea reflects the experience of the Neva fortress affair: the king could not force his subjects to obey his wishes, because they had real opportunities to oppose him. Olaus Petri suggests that cooperation and negotiation ('good will') was a more effective tactic than attempts to stubbornly enforce the royal will; John III refused to engage in negotiation and the whole plan failed, which, in this case, seems to support Olaus Petri's argument. Without good will from the office-holders, the king could not realize his plan. The central power was dependent on the networks, and it needed to do its best to make such networks work for its benefit, not against it.

Great distances, combined with the slow speed at which information travelled, complicated office-holders' relations with the king. Although the king took practically all the important decisions, in order for the administration to work more effectively he had to render independent power to execute decisions to local office-holders on the borderlands. The limits of the noblemen's authority were vaguely defined, and the central power lacked the means to control how authority was exercised.

Local noblemen would often stretch their freedom a little too far. In cases where their actions were not in line with the king's orders, distance could serve as a practical, legitimizing excuse. The noblemen could claim that they had not received information from the king in time, that it was already too late to do anything because winter was approaching or that circumstances had changed since the king's letter had been written.

Thus noblemen beyond the king's reach could utilize distance as a legitimizing argument. However, they rarely mentioned distance directly, preferring to discuss the amount of time it would take to travel, carry information or transport resources from one place to another. The shortness of summer was often used as a reason for postponing one's actions. Officials would argue that nothing could be started because winter would arrive before the project in question could be finished. Sub-zero temperatures and ice effectively halted war efforts and building activities; after the onset of winter any unpleasant tasks could easily be postponed for over half a year. Local conditions also served as another legitimizing argument. Office-holders described how a lack of resources or the advancing enemy had prevented them from following their orders. This was possible because the king had no other means by which he could effectively monitor the information provided by his local representatives.

In an analysis of the Neva fortress case, it is useful to draw a distinction between the power to make decisions and the power to execute them. Although on a formal level the king had supreme undivided power, in practice the execution of his orders depended on local agents. These agents needed to be given a relatively free hand in order to apply the king's orders within local circumstances. They could make a number of choices and delay the projects that they did not consider relevant. However, at all times they had to be able to present legitimate explanations for their actions and decisions. Local agents had to ensure that they were seen as obedient subjects.

This seems to have been easier in remote locations, where it was difficult to determine what was actually going on. The king might have had suspicions about the activities of his local agents, but even when he imposed a direct ban on communication, he was unable to stop the networks operating against him. In addition to the remote location, there were other factors that helped local noblemen to be disobedient. Thanks to the unclear power relations, they could invoke contrary orders given by their superiors. Their knowledge of the local circumstances allowed them to present solid-sounding reasons why a plan could not be carried out: there was not enough building material or food, autumn was already approaching, the river would freeze over or the enemy was too close. Neither the king nor we know the truth of these excuses, but they certainly served as legitimizing arguments.

The slow speed at which information travelled often served the interests of local agents, but this was not always the case. Office-holders could be posted to distant garrisons and be desperate to contact the central power in order to get more provisions or money.[54] Depending on the circumstances, the fact that correspondence took some time to arrive could be utilized by different agents, including the king. It seems that the party who wanted to slow things down usually had the advantage in the letter game, because it was much easier to delay things than to make them actually happen. The difficulty for the king was that he had to take the initiative and be active. His role demanded that he make plans and try to realize them with the help of local office-holders. In this respect he was, to a great degree, dependent upon them.

Office-holders' networks could be either an asset or a threat to the central power, depending on the interests of the different agents involved. They were not yet 'Crown's office-holders' in the sense that the king could unquestionably rely on them and their obedience. Noblemen were not solely dependent on the king: they had their own networks to rely on.[55] Further research would be needed to show whether this was a variant of the noblemen's honour communities, which in early sixteenth-century England gave way to unconditional obedience to the king. Earlier, noblemen had been able to maintain their honour even if they had opposed the king, as long as they had justified their actions by reference to the common honour code of the group of knights. The duality of honour was possible because the king was also regarded as one member of the honour community.[56]

Peasants' passive resistance of the central power's demands has been recognized as a common feature of the political culture of the early modern Swedish realm.[57] It seems clear that office-holders could also resort to various methods of passive resistance, such as delaying or justifying their actions. After all, the officials were also members of the local elite and attended to their own interests.[58] The impact of geographical factors on the interaction between the central power and the office-holders' networks would merit further research. Even in the vicinity of the central power, as was the case in Stockholm, subjects could use tactics of delaying and trying to slow down the execution of unpleasant commands. This was a part of the informal political culture.[59] The scope, forms, potential and limitations of these tactics must have been very different when used by peasants and Crown's office-holders respectively. As the case of Neva also shows, the central power could not easily control the office-holders' networks. Great distances contributed to this: the king could not effectively monitor what was happening in the borderlands. Orders were not simply given from above; there was continuous reciprocal negotiation going on within the administration, and it was never quite clear how things would turn out.

Acknowledgements

This chapter is written thanks to funding from the Academy of Finland (as a part of the research project 'Politics of Brothers, Neighbours and Friends: Political Culture and Strategies of Influence in Early Modern Sweden c.1500–1700') and it is based on papers presented to 26:e Nordiska historikermötet, Reykjavik 8–12 August 2007 and Mapping Early Modern Interaction and Relationships, University of Jyväskylä, 23–24 November 2007. I am grateful for all the valuable comments I have received.

Notes

1 Herlitz 1928, p. 73.
2 See, for instance, Renvall 1949, pp. 304–317 with a strong nationalistic tendency; Karonen 1999, pp. 101–103; Lappalainen 2002, pp. 255–256.
3 However, there are insightful analyses of the general organization of administration in older studies, such as Herlitz 1928, pp. 68–81 and Renvall and Roos 1934, pp. 136–156.

4   For a summary of recent studies on political culture, see Cederholm 2007, pp. 36–42 and Einonen 2005, pp. 9–17, 23–25, and for examples of innovative research on informal networks, Einonen 2005, Lahtinen 2007 and Haikari 2005.

5   Harnesk and Taussi Sjöberg 2001, p. 11; Haikari 2006, p. 33; Gustafsson 1985, pp. 17–21. A rare example of studies about the practical work of office-holders can be found in the Swedish anthology *Mellan makten och menigheten: ämbetsmän i det tidigmoderna Sverige* (2001), which however does not deal with noble office-holders in the sixteenth century. For the Icelandic context, see Gustafsson 1985 and for Germany, Rublack 1997.

6   This has been pointed out by Einonen 2005, pp. 15–16.

7   Chittolini 1995, p. 40; Supphellen 1985, pp. 364–365; Frohnert 1985, p. 270.

8   On the need to legitimize demands and petitions through proper argumentation and common arguments used by the Crown and the peasants, see Harnesk 2003, pp. 42–74.

9   Pietiäinen 1988, p. 52.

10 Svenska Riksarkivet (SRA), Arvid Henriksson Tawasts samling (AHTs), Vol. 1, Henrik Claesson (Horn) to Arvid Tawast, 23 June 1579, Stockholm and Svante Eriksson (Stålarm) to Arvid Tawast, 9 July 1579, Porvoo.

11 About 50 km according to Nenonen 1999b, p. 276. A synthesis of European data from the Middle Ages has suggested a daily achievement of 50–60 km by horse without much luggage. Berings 1992, p. 70. A day's journey could be a lot longer if the rider was able to change horses. There is evidence that day trips of over 400 km were sometimes undertaken in medieval England. Retsö 2002, pp. 313–314, 319.

12 Pietiäinen 1988, p. 52.

13 Retsö 2002, pp. 314, 325 provides examples of medieval letters which were significantly delayed because of bad weather and other unknown reasons.

14 Retsö 2002, p. 325.

15 SRA, Muscovitica, Gränscommissioner 1595–1596, 2: Gränsen från Varpavuori till Pisamäki. Commissariernes bref till Hertig Karl: Arvid Tawast to Gödik Fincke, 7 July 1595, Kurjala and Gödik Fincke to the Russian peace negotiators, 14 July 1595, Savonlinna.

16 Retsö 2002, 329.

17 Nenonen 1999a, pp. 52, 57.

18 Viertola 1974, pp. 39–50; Pietiäinen 1988, p. 21; Masonen 1999, pp. 65–66; Salonen 1999, p. 82.

19 Nenonen 1999c, pp. 144–149.

20 SRA, AHTs1, Arvid Tawast to John III, 25 August 1582: 'wij kundhe iche fortt framkomes wdan huad som wij togedh oss fram och rodde alt in till ytt:ste vdden i Biörcköön Men dhn 21 Augusti fogede gud oss vind:n, thå seglade wij same dag:n in till Nyen'.

21 To give one example, in SRA, AHTs1, Claes Åkesson (Tott) to Arvid Tawast, 10 December 1582, Sjundby, the writer refers to travelling by sledge twice.

22 Nenonen 1999a, p. 52.

23 For instance SRA, AHTs2, Mårten Boije to Arvid Tawast, 17 May 1592, Isnäs: 'the skyndhe sigh till wijborgh Genom natth och dagh'. There are even some specific pieces of information about travelling through the night in medieval Swedish letters. Retsö 2002, 328.

24 Special couriers were already used to deliver the king's letters and ecclesiastic mail, but the general postal service in Sweden was only founded in 1636. Pietiäinen 1988, pp. 20, 31.

25 SRA, AHTs1, Henrik Claesson (Horn) to Arvid Tawast, 26 November 1578, Kankainen: 'Ahnkom ... mz mijn Tienare Oleff Andersson'.

26 SRA, AHTs1-2; SRA Avskriftsamlingen efter 1520: Gödik Finckes registratur 1598–99; SRA, Muscovitica: Gränskommission 1595–96, 2.

27 Clanchy 1993, p. 263; SRA, AHTs1, Pontus De la Gardie to Arvid Tawast, 28 June 1583, Tallinn: 'Effther min Lägenheett Nu gudh bettre ichke sigh så begiffuer att iagh till eder mere tillskriffue kan haffuer Jagh ofthe:be Bengtt Söffringhson munttligen befaltth att Eder berette'.

28 SRA, Avskriftsamlingen efter 1520, Gödik Finckes registratur 1598–99: Gödik Fincke to Arvid Tawast, 5 August 1599, Savonlinna: 'på den tijdh inga Kunskap kome som Eder brefdragare her Stadder war'.

29 Retsö 2002, pp. 326–327.

30 SRA, AHTs1, Henrik Claesson (Horn) to Arvid Henriksson Tawast, 24 February, 1581, Asikkala: 'Henrich Madzson drögde så lenge, och iach förtöffuede hans Ahnkompst i Wijburg i otto wekor, Och medan han drog nw vm förgange- tissdag iffro Wijburg till Coporie, ther han åther enn tiidh förtöffue warder, derfföre kunne iach icke förbijdhe ther lenger, vthan är åstadhdrage- och will begiff:e mig hem till mitt, Men så snart iach fhår spörie att han kommer tillbake iffro Coporie, och begynner tingte, Tho will Jach skynde mig tillbake igenn, ehuar Jach hono- tho finne kan'.

31 Nenonen 1999d, p. 168.

32 Retsö 2002, p. 319.

33 Tawaststjerna 1918–20, pp. 273–336.

34 Tawaststjerna 1918–20, pp. 374–375.

35 Tawaststjerna 1920, pp. 21–23; Tawast's and Stålarm's correspondence in SRA, AHTs1.

36 Lappalainen 2002, p. 259.

37 Tawaststjerna 1918–20, pp. 374–375.

38 Svalenius 1991, p. 51.

39 Svalenius 1991, pp. 100–101.

40 SRA, AHTs1, Arvid Tawast to Hans Kranck, 2 June 1583: 'är min brodlige begärn til dig käre b[ror] du wille dher så lagedh at vpå mig motte inthz bliffue sådant opå lagt till at bestelle, effter iag förmo inthet för min suaghett och siuchdom at tage på Jag förseer mig och till tig min h[järtats] käre broor attu är behielplig thet iag motte blifue aff mz dhetta kalledh aldenstundh iag kan inthz kome knichtarn til velluillighett, ty iag weet inthet mz huadh wilkor iag dher göre kundhe, effter dhet varker inthz klede och pnr eij hellr fetalie dher mz the kune nödtorfftlig:n ware försörgdt Dernoch k.b. haff:r iag och mz denne min dreng scriffuit til K:mtt beed iag dig min bror at iag motte bethiene gunstligt och nodig:tt swar mz thet försthe til bache ig:n dher iag wett sedan Rette mig effter'.

41 SRA, AHTs1, Arvid Tawast to Hans Kranck, 2 June 1583: 'din welwillig brod:ligit benegenhett mz alt gott förskylle och förtiene'.

42 SRA, Skrivelser till konungen, Johan III:s tid 5: Arvid Tawast to John III, 3 June 1583, Karsby: 'iag haffuer bechomit EK: mtz breff ... huilchit iagh tess plictigh ähr och effterkomme, E:K: mtz meaning och wilie, så frampt ath al den deell

våre nhu her förhanden som thertil behöffdes, först Aller nodigs:te Konung:n och Herre, är her vdi finlandh nhu inthz mere qwarre en fyre fenicker knichtar ... Och nu haff:r iagh Aller nod:ste Konungh och Herre, scriffuit Knichthöfuitzmen til, her äre i findlandh dhet the skulle ... begifue mz dem till Wiborgh at the äre allesenest om Sancti Iohannis baptiste tijdh i Wiborg, effter the kune inthet blifue snarar försambledh och krigsfolckedh liggie wijdt wtsprijdhtt i Landet Besynner-ligh att then ene fenichen ligg i Östb:en ... Men thet Krigzfolck Aller N. K: och Herre, som her quarre äre beswäre sig swårlige uinthet vijle nogot togh göre för the bechome Kledhe och pnr-, och fetalie hwar mz the kune vntholle sigh på så monge månadher som E:K:M: vil ath dhe skulle ware i fiendelandh, Efther the äre offta tilförenne affdragne för hunger skuldh Aller nod:ste Konung och Herre, dher en iag wille scriffue Rytt:ne till at the skulle opryckie, dog blifue the inthet Achtat aff mig der som den Ädle Herre her pontus kan inthet kome krigzfolck-edh ther til at opbyggie för:ne befestning, dog är ingen Annan heller sosom dhet kan vtrette eller eftherkomme, effter E:K: Mtz mening och vilie ... Men nu Aller nod:ste Konung och Herre, haffuer iag actat begifue mig i dhe helge trefaldighettz nampn til wiborg til försagden tid, der sosom Krigzfolket bliffue försambledh och the bechome den deell the kune vppeholle sig medh, wil iag gierne vore dhem följactig och göre til saken huad mig mögligt ähr, Endog Aller nodg:ste Konung och Herre, iag tröster mig inthet ther opå tage eller vtrette, vtan beder EK: mtz ganske ödmiucheligen och vnd:donligen E.K: mtt wille scriffue den ädle herre-till her Pontus thil ther han wille sigh tage opå och vtrette, J althen stundh iag vett ingen som kan effterkome E:K: mtz mening och wilie dher om, eller nogon Anna- sosom E:K: mtt synes thertil förordne'.

43 SRA, AHTs1, Arvid Stålarm to Arvid Tawast, 6 June (year missing, but the content clearly indicates 1583), Villnäs: 'hans KM uill inthet endeligen höra hwarcken utaf dig eller mig uthan befalthe att wij medh thet första skulle begifua oss till Nöthbårg medh nogre 1000 ma- och ther upsättia en befästning'.

44 SRA, AHTs1, Arvid Stålarm to Arvid Tawast, 14 June 1583, Lindö.

45 SRA, AHTs1, Arvid Stålarm to Arvid Tawast, 20 June 1583, Lindö. Stålarm dis-cussed this in a letter dated 20 June, and so he must have already contacted the aristocrats before this date. He probably met Tott in early June at Villnäs mansion in Askainen, where Stålarm stayed for the funeral of his father-in-law Herman Persson Fleming. Fleming was also the father-in-law of two sisters of Tott's wife, and so presumably Tott attended the funeral too. Both men were members of the peace committee. Elgenstierna 1934, pp. 339–340; Ramsay 1909–16, pp. 116–124, 181–187, 444–450.

46 SRA, AHTs1, Pontus De la Gardie to Arvid Stålarm and Arvid Tawast, Tallinn, 28 June 1583: 'steller wdi Eders bethenkiande huadh Effther följe will, iagh framdels endttskyllige hwar huadh Någre aff thesse för:ne olegenheter samme Befestningh weder henda kunde Ichke Lather iagh migh godhe Men Emoth Kång:e Maitz Nådige och höge Meningh stridig befinne om samme bygningh wthan förlåpne tiden Achtandes rådhr thill Att ther som Sådantt Arhbethe schulle tages före, så bör thedh Mz förste isslossedh Åmm wåren begyntt Att påthagetth warde på thz Att sommarsens tillräckningh på huilken Ryssen ingen förhindringh same Bygh-ningh göre kan Måtte belempa befestningens större warachtigheett'.

47 SRA, AHTs1, Arvid Stålarm to Arvid Tawast, 20 June 1583, Lindö: 'Kong:e Maiitz:n war gruffligh inkin och iligh ther wppå.

48 SRA. AHTs1, Arvid Stålarm to Arvid Tawast, 20 June 1583, Lindö: 'gudh weett
    hwäm man skall göre i Lagh'.
49 Renvall & Roos 1934, pp. 136–138, 147–148.
50 SRA, AHTs1, Arvid Stålarm to Arvid Tawast, Lindö, 2 July 1583: 'Khäre bror
    Arfuedh Hendrichson är migh her ponti schriffuelse till honde komitt som Lyder
    tigh och migh till, ther wthaff ui warder förnimande her ponti mening och föregi-
    fuelse, aff hwilkett bref iagh för skickar tigh en Copie, och här ponti organal bref
    will man gärna haffua i förwar, ther wppå wij och wethe på en Anna tidh ware oss
    endtskylig, så warder mi- bror wäll berättandes sin saker Effther här ponti bref'.
51 SRA, AHTs1, Arvid Stålarm to Arvid Tawast, Narva, 20 July 1583: 'then full
    machthen som Kong:e Maittz oss giffuit haff:r wedh Nyienn att bestellas haffuer
    iagh thet aff slagett Effther här ponti och här Claes åkessons befalningh och Eliest
    för iidzens Legen hetter schuldh och sommarssens Korttheett'.
52 See, for instance, SRA, AHTs1, Arvid Eriksson Stålarm to Arvid Tawast, 8 August
    1584 (about his appointment as commander-in-chief of the navy), Henrik Claesson
    (Horn) to Arvid Tawast, 3 February 1576 (about the order to organize an inves-
    tigation into the privileges of the Finnish nobility) and Arvid Tawast to John III,
    10 May 1590 (about his appointment as commander of Narva castle in Estonia).
53 Villstrand 2005, p. 115: a direct quote from *Olai Petri krönika*, Edited by G.E.
    Klemming, Stockholm 1860, pp. 176–177: 'Swärige är itt sådana land som med
    mosar bergh och skoghar så befestat är, at almoghen icke lenge kan med twång
    och macht vnderkuuffuas, ty tee haffua stoor tilfelle at settia sig vp emoot theras
    herra. Ther före regeras Swerige myckit bätter med weluiliogheet, en med mykin
    strengheet.'
54 See for instance Tawast's letters to John III from the time he was commissioned
    as the commander of Narva castle in SRA, Livonica II:1, 193 and SRA, AHTs1,
    Arvid Tawast's letter register.
55 Reinholdsson 1998, p. 97.
56 James 1986, pp. 375–383.
57 See for example Villstrand 1992; Katajala 1994, pp. 135–139; Linde 2000.
58 Compare Gustafsson 1985, pp. 278–279 and Supphellen 1985, pp. 364–365 for
    similar features in the eighteenth century.
59 Einonen 2005, pp. 210–211, 279.

Bibliography
Archival sources

The National Archives of Sweden (Riksarkivet), Stockholm (SRA)
    Arvid Henriksson Tawasts samling (AHTs), Vols. 1–2.
    Avskriftsamlingar efter 1520: Gödik Finckes registratur 1598–99.
    Livonica II:1, Vol. 193.
    Muscovitica, Vol. 543: Gränscommissioner 1595–1596, Vol. 2:
    Gränsen från Varpavuori till Pisamäki.
    Skrivelser till konungen, Johan III:s tid, Vol. 5.

Literature

Berings, G. 1992. *Transport and Communication in the Middle Ages. Kommunikation und Alltag in Spätmittelalter und früher Neuzeit. Internationaler Kongress, Krems an der Donau 9. bis 12. Oktober 1990.* Österreichische Akademie der Wissenschaften, Vienna.

Cederholm, M. 2007. *De värjde sin rätt. Senmedeltida bondemotstånd i Skåne och Småland.* Historiska institutionen vid Lunds universitet, Lund.

Chittolini, G. 1995. 'The "Private", the "Public", the State.' *The Journal of Modern History*, Vol. 67, Supplement, pp. 34-61.

Clanchy, M. T. 1993 (1979). *From Memory to Written Record: England 1066–1307.* Blackwell, Oxford.

Einonen, P. 2005. *Poliittiset areenat ja toimintatavat. Tukholman porvaristo vallan käyttäjän ja vallankäytön kohteena n. 1592–1644 (with English summary).* The Finnish Literature Society, Helsinki.

Elgenstierna, G. 1934. *Den introducerade svenska adelns ättartavlor.* Vol. 8. Norstedts, Stockholm.

Frohnert, P. 1985. 'Administration i Sverige under frihetstiden.' In Frohner, P. (ed.) Administrasjon i Norden på 1700-talet. Universitetsforlaget, Oslo, pp. 185–275.

Gustafsson, H. 1985. *Mellan kung och allmoge. Ämbetsmän, beslutsprocess och inflytande på 1700-talets Island.* Stockholms universitet, Stockholm.

Haikari, J. 2006. *Kreivin aikaan, kreivin valtaan. Vallankäytön arki satakuntalaisissa maaseutuyhteisöissä 1651–1657.* Unpublished licentiate thesis. Department of History and Ethnology, University of Jyväskylä.

Haikari, J. 2009. *Isännän, Jumalan ja rehellisten miesten edessä. Vallankäyttö ja virkamiesten toimintaympäristöt satakuntalaisissa maaseutuyhteisöissä 1600-luvun jälkipuoliskolla.* The Finnish Literature Society, Helsinki.

Harnesk, B. 2003. 'Konsten att klaga, konsten att kräva. Kronan och bönderna på 1500- och 1600-talen.' In Harnesk, B. (ed.) *Maktens skiftande skepnader. Studier i makt, legitimitet och inflytande i det tidigmoderna Sverige.* Umeå universitet, Umeå.

Harnesk, B. & Taussi Sjöberg, M. 2001. 'Inledning.' In Harnesk, B. & Taussi Sjöberg, M. (eds.) *Mellan makten och menigheten. Ämbetsmän i det tidigmoderna Sverige.* Institutet för rättshistorisk forskning, Stockholm, pp. 7–16.

Herlitz, N. 1928. *Grunddragen av det svenska statsskickets historia.* Norstedts, Stockholm.

James, M. 1986. *Society, Politics and Culture. Studies in Early Modern England.* Past and Present Publications, Cambridge.

Karonen, P. 1999. *Pohjoinen suurvalta. Ruotsi ja Suomi 1521–1809.* WSOY, Helsinki.

Katajala, K. 1994. *Nälkäkapina. Veronvuokraus ja talonpoikainen vastarinta Karjalassa 1683–1697.* The Finnish Historical Society, Helsinki.

Lahtinen, A. 2007. *Sopeutuvat, neuvottelevat, kapinalliset. Naiset toimijoina Flemingin sukupiirissä 1470–1620.* The Finnish Literature Society, Helsinki.

Lappalainen, M. 2002. 'Aatelisvallan kulmakivet ja aateliskulttuurin murros.' In Lehtonen, Tuomas M.S. & Timo Joutsivuo (eds.) *Suomen kulttuurihistoria*, Vol. 1: *Taivas ja maa.* Tammi, Helsinki, pp. 254–264.

Linde, Martin 2000. *Statsmakt och bondemotstånd. Allmoge och överhet under stora nordiska kriget.* Uppsala universitet, Uppsala.

Masonen, J. 1999. 'Kirkon, kruunun ja kansan tiet keskiajalla.' In Mauranen, T. (ed.) *Maata, jäätä, kulkijoita. Tiet, liikenne ja yhteiskunta ennen vuotta 1860.* Edita, Helsinki, pp. 57–108.

Nenonen, M. 1999(a). 'Before Cars. The Horse as a Means of Transport and Status Symbol.' In Mauranen, T. (ed.) *Traffic, Needs, Roads. Perspectives on the Past, Present and Future of Roads in Finland and the Baltic Area*. The Finnish National Road Administration (Finnra), Helsinki, pp. 51–63.

Nenonen, M. 1999(b). 'Kulkijan taival.' In Mauranen, T. (ed.) *Maata, jäätä, kulkijoita. Tiet, liikenne ja yhteiskunta ennen vuotta 1860*. Edita, Helsinki, pp. 274–334.

Nenonen, M. 1999(c). 'Maitse vai vesitse. Kulkemisen peruskysymys 1550–1800.' In Mauranen, T. (ed.) *Maata, jäätä, kulkijoita. Tiet, liikenne ja yhteiskunta ennen vuotta 1860*. Edita, Helsinki, pp. 144–167.

Nenonen, M. 1999(d). 'Vesiltä pyörille. Suuret maantiet 1550–1800.' In Mauranen, T. (ed.) *Maata, jäätä, kulkijoita. Tiet, liikenne ja yhteiskunta ennen vuotta 1860*. Edita, Helsinki, pp. 167–273.

Pietiäinen, J.-P. 1998. *Suomen postin historia*, Vol. 1. Posti- ja telelaitos, Helsinki.

Ramsay, J. 1909–16. *Frälsesläkter i Finland intill stora ofreden*. Söderström, Helsinki.

Reinholdsson, P. 1998. Uppror eller resningar? Samhällsorganisation och konflikt i senmedeltidens Sverige. Uppsala universitet, Uppsala.

Renvall, P. 1949. *Kuninkaanmiehiä ja kapinoitsijoita Vaasa-kauden Suomessa*. Tammi, Helsinki.

Renvall, P. & Roos, J. E. 1934. 'Keskitetyn hallintolaitoksen kehitys.' In Suolahti, G. et al. (eds.) *Suomen Kulttuurihistoria*, Vol. 2. Gummerus, Helsinki, pp. 136–168.

Retsö, D. 2002. 'Hur mäta en dagsled? Senmedeltida brev som källa för beräkning av restider och rekonstruktion av itinerarier.' In Gejrot, C., Andersson, R. & Abukhanfusa, K. (eds.) *Ny väg till medeltidsbreven. Från ett medeltidssymposium i Svenska Riksarkivet 26–28 November 1999*. Svenska Riksarkivet, Stockholm, pp. 313–336.

Rublack, U. 1997. 'Frühneuzeitliche Staatlichkeit und lokale Herrschaftspraxis in Württemberg.' *Zeitschrift für historische Forschung*, Vol. 24 (3), pp. 347–376.

Salonen, K. 1999. 'Ylinen Viipurintie – valtaväylä Hämeestä Karjalaan.' In Mauranen, T. (ed.) *Maata, jäätä, kulkijoita. Tiet, liikenne ja yhteiskunta ennen vuotta 1860*. Edita, Helsinki, pp. 82–83.

Supphellen, S. 1985. 'Administrasjon og avgjersprosess i dei nordiske landa på 1700-talet i komparativt perspektiv.' In Frohert, P. (ed.) *Administrasjon i Norden på 1700-talet*. Universitetsforlaget, Oslo, pp. 345–368.

Svalenius, I. 1991. *Rikskansliet i Sverige 1560–1592*. Svenska Riksarkivet, Stockholm.

Tawaststjerna, W. 1918–1920. *Pohjoismaiden viisikolmattavuotinen sota. Vuosien 1570 ja 1590 välinen aika*. The Finnish Historical Society, Helsinki.

Tawaststjerna, W. 1920. *Arvi Henrikinpoika Tawast*. The Finnish Historical Society, Helsinki.

Tawaststjerna, W. 1929. *Pohjoismaiden sota 1590–95 ja Täysinän rauha*. The Finnish Historical Society, Helsinki.

Viertola, J. 1974. 'Yleiset tiet Ruotsin vallan aikana.' In Fogelberg, P. & Viertola, J. *Suomen teiden historia*, Vol. 1: *Pakanuudenajalta Suomen itsenäistymiseen*. Tie- ja vesirakennushallitus & Suomen tieyhdistys, Helsinki.

Villstrand, N. E. 1992. *Anpassning eller protest? Lokalsamhället inför utskrivningarna av forfolk till den svenska krigsmakten 1620–1679*. Åbo Akademis förlag, Turku.

Villstrand, N. E. 2005. 'Från morgonstjärna till memorial – politisk kultur i det svenska riket 1500–1800.' *Sphinx 2004–2005*. Societas Scientiarum Fennica, Helsinki.

CHAPTER 6

Shaping a Political Network

Christian Kühner

Introduction

Network analysis has long been a method used by researchers of early modern interpersonal relationships.[1] The visualization of results has always figured among its tools; in most cases, however, this has meant drawing diagrams rather than maps. I do not want to enter here into a discussion about the advantages and disadvantages of network diagrams; I intend to discuss how maps can be used to depict networks. I shall try to demonstrate this using the example of the correspondence of the Grand Condé, one of the most important leaders of the Fronde uprising and the great antagonist of Cardinal Mazarin. My thoughts in this chapter thus relate to France in the seventeenth century. However, before considering this example, it is necessary to reflect upon the map as a tool of network analysis. This reflection will form the first part of this chapter; I will then turn to look more closely at the Condé network itself.

In this chapter the role of the map is clearly an instrumental one. The map is not the *explicandum* (which is the network), but part of the *explicans*. Thus, what is undertaken here is not an inquiry into the nature of the map, but rather a sketch of how maps can be used to show new aspects in interaction networks. The term 'map' shall be understood here in a traditional sense, that is, two-dimensional and non-interactive. One needs to be precise about this because some of the specific constraints of maps do not apply if computer-based technology is used to create three-dimensional and interactive maps. Given this, one could argue that reflections on the traditional map are already anachronistic. However, researchers in the humanities continue to work with books, that is, printed information, alongside electronic material. As long as researchers have to cope with the fact that only the fixed and the two-dimensional can be printed (i.e. as long as electronic displays cannot be applied onto the pages of a book) the traditional map will retain its importance for researchers. In this context scholarly discussions about the characteristics of maps (including their specific strengths and constraints) are still relevant and necessary.

Unlike texts, maps are not linear. On the one hand, this is an advantage, because it allows things to be displayed simultaneously that could only be described sequentially in a text. For example, a map can at once display a number of the prince of Condé's contacts in various countries, whereas a text must enumerate the countries and the partners with whom the prince exchanged letters.

However, this characteristic of maps also imposes certain limitations that do not apply to texts. A text can be extended by adding new paragraphs without disturbing existing paragraphs. A map, on the other hand, can only be made more complex by superimposing elements onto the same map, but the more elements one adds to a map, the more difficult it becomes to read. Thus, drawing a map always entails selection and rejection of data.

Moreover, not every subject is suited to mapping, and among those which are, some are easier to show on a map (again understood in the traditional sense) than others. In the case of interpersonal relations, the extent (or reach) of a network can more easily be shown on a map than the power relations within that network.

Hierarchical power relations can be better illustrated through the use of diagrams rather than maps: maps always privilege the horizontal over the vertical dimension. One could, of course, modify the lines between the points on a map to show different levels of hierarchy or equality, but it is clear that such an approach cannot show hierarchy as clearly as a diagram could (which, in turn, would have to leave aside the geographical dimension in order to concentrate on hierarchy).

Another important point is that maps have the general characteristic of being synchronic; the temporal dimension can only be added by drawing a sequence of different maps. One could object that maps which show itineraries are diachronic; they are indeed, but only because they show an individual's movements in a mapped space which is fixed in time. Where structures are to be mapped, the demonstration has to be divided into several 'pictures', if change is to be depicted.

Mapping often means simplifying facts in order to visualize them. Where a text could make a digression, the map cannot. Here, we are concerned with mapping the geographic scope of a network. This means that the individuals involved are hypothetically tied to a single place – even if they moved away periodically or wrote letters from different locations.

As discussed above, the number of elements a map can show without becoming unreadable is limited. In this case, Condé's numerous correspondents have been sorted into various groups. Mapping each correspondent individually would have led to a map that would have been confusing in its excessive complexity.

Two important aspects have been left out of the maps, a decision that needs to be justified. First, the maps do not show the direction of correspondence. The prince's family archive holds Condé's entire passive correspondence along with some of the notes he made for his secretaries, but it does not contain copies of all the letters he ever sent. In order to build a complete record of his outgoing correspondence, one would need to locate these letters in the archives of all his partners across Europe. (This would be an enormous task even if all of letters still existed, which is far from certain.) Often, however, there are notes that indicate that the prince did in fact answer the letters or personally write to his partners. In any case, the overwhelming majority of correspondents wrote several times, which in all probability indicates bilateral correspondence.

Second, the maps do not show the number of letters that were exchanged. An analysis of this is beyond the scope of a study of the geographic reach of the network. However, leaving out the quantity of exchanges is also a methodological statement: I will argue here that the number of letters exchanged does not directly indicate the intensity of a relationship (something that would be implied by, for example, using thicker lines between partners who exchanged letters more often). Those partners who lived near the prince wrote less often, because some of the information that was transmitted in letters could be discussed in person with Condé. Furthermore, not every letter carries the same symbolic value. Monarchs did not write letters very often, even to those they wished to distinguish; in fact, a royal letter was such a high distinction that it was only rarely granted. Servants or diplomatic agents wrote more often, of course, but this was part of their duties.

The Prince of Condé

Louis II de Bourbon, known as the Grand Condé, was one of the most interesting figures of seventeenth-century France. Born in 1621, the son of the First Prince of the Blood, he bore the title of Duke of Enghien and was a possible successor to Louis XIII until the birth of the future Louis XIV in 1638. He undertook a military career and won spectacular battles in his early twenties, most notably the battle of Rocroi in 1643. In 1646, his father died, and he himself became Prince of Condé and First Prince of the Blood, the highest-ranking nobleman after the royal family. He was one of the leading French generals during France's participation in the Thirty Years' War. In the Fronde, he at first kept out of the revolt. However, this changed after 1650 when Cardinal Mazarin had him imprisoned as a preventative measure; the experience turned Condé into an implacable adversary of the cardinal. After he left prison in 1651, he took the lead of the Fronde. When this last noble uprising against the strengthening monarchy collapsed in 1652, Condé was the only one of the leaders of the insurgents who chose exile rather than submission. Having left France, he joined the Spanish side and resumed his military struggle against Mazarin, whom he viewed as a wicked counsellor who was manipulating the young king. When the Peace of the Pyrenees was signed, Condé was granted amnesty by the French crown and even resumed his career as a French general in the late 1660s. He died in bed in 1686.[2]

It is not surprising that such a career should bring Condé into contact with a great number of individuals across Europe. Fortunately, Condé's correspondence has been preserved at the family's seat, the Château de Chantilly (35 kilometres north of Paris in southern Picardy). The names of his various correspondents can be found in the registers of this correspondence.[3]

The role of Condé's network in the history of seventeenth-century France has recently been examined by Katia Béguin.[4] She concentrates on the political relationship between Condé and the French monarchy and on Condé's patron–client relationships within France. Here I will attempt to build upon Béguin's work and address two additional aspects: the international dimension of the network and the spatial dimension (i.e. I will try to map the network).

Of course, this poses the question of how the temporal dimension should be handled. Networks change over time: sometimes old links fall into disuse and sometimes new contacts are formed. For my purpose, however, attempting to trace the evolution of the network would be too complicated. Thus, I have chosen to examine Condé's network from the 1640s to the 1660s, that is, during the period when he was politically most active. For reasons of clarity I have treated the network in a synchronic way; treating it in a diachronic fashion would not only lead to the aforementioned problems of mapping, but also largely exceed the scope of this chapter. For the same reason, I will only give brief hints about how and why Condé contacted each partner; in many cases this information is missing. What can be said, though, is that a sizeable number of his correspondents had already exchanged letters with his father, Henri II de Bourbon. Sometimes, correspondents even wrote two letters at a time: one to the father and one to the son. The immense reach of the network might thus be partly explained by the fact that the Grand Condé did not need to build it from scratch.

Condé's French partners

The network can be divided into three spheres: those in the immediate vicinity of the prince, contacts within the kingdom of France and the European contacts. It goes without saying that the study of this network cannot be a comprehensive one; I intend to present the structures of the network, not provide a full list of all the individuals who ever exchanged letters with Condé. It could be argued, furthermore, that this method can only trace those relationships that produced letters. This is indeed the case. However, early modern aristocrats often communicated by letter, the most important means of long-distance communication. Of course, the oral transmission of information by messengers was also used to carry information from one place to another, but the abundance of letters and the fact that even sensitive information was written down (in enciphered form) allows us to conclude that the bulk of information was channelled through letters. So even though there may have been individual (perhaps even important) relationships that did not produce letters, it is extremely unlikely that this was the case for whole groups of people or whole regions within the network. We can thus assume that the general picture of Condé's network can indeed be inferred from the letters.

The 'domestic' and the 'foreign' parts of the network are not clearly separated; the separation, thus, is a heuristic one. People travel and networks intermingle: the formation of networks does not respect frontiers. Moreover, French was the lingua franca among seventeenth-century nobles throughout Europe. So even on the linguistic plane, there is no clear divide between 'inlanders' and 'foreigners': letters from partners outside France were often written in French. One could, thus, view the network as a continuum that extended from Condé's relationships in the immediate vicinity of Chantilly to his contacts in Stockholm, Warsaw or Rome. However, as distance also influences the nature of exchanges – by privileging face-to-face communication within the immediate vicinity

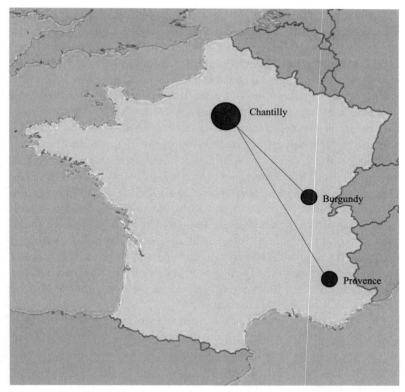

Map 19. The Grand Condé's French provincial networks. Modern state borders. Drawing by Christan Kühner.

and epistolary exchange with the more distant regions – the introduction of subdivisions seems justifiable. Different geographic spaces also pose different problems of mapping.

Those within the immediate vicinity form the first category of Condé's contacts. This group of individuals can hardly be mapped. Of course, one could consider drawing a map showing Ile-de-France and Picardy, with strong links between Paris, Chantilly and other royal residences in the region. The problem, though, would lie in connecting specific individuals to one of these places. In fact, French high nobles tended to own a city palace or great townhouse in Paris and a rural castle (in Condé's case this was in Chantilly). Mapping only the rural castles would be misleading, as it would suggest that the nobles spent most of their time at the place whose name they bore. This might have been the case in earlier epochs but was no longer true in seventeenth-century France. Enumerating even a substantial proportion of the members of the French high nobility with whom Condé exchanged letters would result in a huge list. Besides Louis XIV and the royal family, Condé's partners include dukes (among them La Rochefoucauld[5] and Saint-Simon[6]), counts (Créqui[7]), marquises (Lusignan[8]) and marshals (Schomberg[9] and Turenne[10]). However, as discussed above, this was a circle in which face-to-face interaction dominated. The absence of letters between Condé and another high French aristocrat should thus not be understood as proof that there was no contact between them. More interesting is the fact that any letters prove the existence of exchanges. In our case, letters indicate that, in spite of the great difference of rank, Condé did not neglect the powerful ennobled leaders of the administration. Condé exchanged letters with Colbert at least since 1660,[11] when Condé had just been pardoned but well before Colbert was appointed controller-general of finances. The voluminous correspondence with Louvois began in 1663 at the latest;[12] at that time Louvois was just twenty-two years old, but it was already apparent that he was likely to succeed his father Michel Le Tellier as secretary of state for war.

The second group is made up of contacts within France but outside *la cour et la ville* (the court and the city), in other words beyond Paris and the other royal residences (Map 19). These contacts were often lesser nobles. The provincial nobility consisted of people whose rank and fortune did not permit them to spend most of their time at the royal court – in the seventeenth century this was a necessary condition for higher administrative, ecclesiastic or military careers. Burgundy was the Condé's provincial stronghold. At first sight this seems surprising as the family's seat, Chantilly, is located in Picardy, a considerable distance from Burgundy. However, the Condé's power in Burgundy was not based on the family's permanent presence. Instead, it derived from important offices (the office of governor of the province, in particular) and networks of clients. Provence was another region in which Condé's network was active, even though, unlike the situation in Burgundy, the prince did not hold the governor's charge there. The count of Alais was a very eager correspondent of the prince.[13] Condé's provincial contacts also included officeholders' corporations and cities across France. The first category notably includes the *parlement* of Metz,[14] that of Provence at Aix,[15] that of Toulouse,[16] and of course that of Burgundy in Dijon.[17] In the second category, one can cite his contacts with the consuls of Marseilles[18] and notably his exchanges with several institutions in Dijon (the capital of

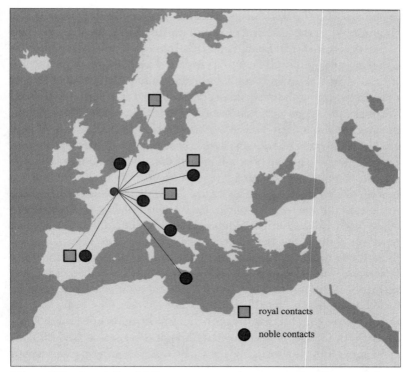

Map 20. The Grand Condé's European networks. Drawing by Christan Kühner.

Burgundy) including those with the *vicomte majeur* and the *échevins*,[19] the *cour des comptes*[20] and the *chambre des comptes*.[21]

Condé's European partners

The Grand Condé also had a European network (Map 20). This network, however, was not an accidental mass of single contacts without links between each other; on the contrary it was a structure with regional concentrations and involved distinct groups of people. Condé's European network extended across western and central Europe. The easternmost point from which he received letters was, in fact, the city of Lwów in the kingdom of Poland (present-day Lviv in Ukraine). There seem to have been no correspondents from Russia or the Ottoman Empire.

More puzzling than the lack of correspondents from the two great empires of eastern and south-eastern Europe is the nearly complete absence of contact with the British Isles. This may be tentatively explained by a circumstance of the historical moment: the English Revolution. The lack of partners from Great Britain and Ireland might be due to the prince's opposition to Cromwell's republic; indeed, Condé was in contact with the exiled Stuarts[22] (which could have made him a dangerous individual to be in contact with for members of the elite of the Commonwealth). We might also suppose that the prince himself did not have much interest in entering into a lively exchange with the British. At this time Condé was not a devout Catholic: in sharp contrast to his father (a converted Protestant who became a Catholic *dévot*) the Grand Condé was known as a *libertin* and only became a devout observer of the Catholic faith in the 1680s, shortly before his death. Nevertheless, it is hardly imaginable that the First Prince of the Royal Blood of France should have felt at ease with the Puritan republicans in London. Unlike the English rebellion, Condé and the other leaders of the Fronde never intended to dethrone the king. When Condé rebelled, he did so as an ally of the Spaniards, who were, of course, monarchists. He did not want to rebel against his king; his intention was to oppose Mazarin, the evil counsellor.[23] Early modern French aristocrats attested that they had a 'duty to revolt'[24] if they found that the monarch was being manipulated by his counsellors. Condé, in his own view, did not rebel against his king, but in favour of him. This explains why Condé found common ground with the exiled Stuarts rather than with Cromwell and to a greater extent the republicans.[25] A letter from a 'Milord Crofts' in London supports this explanation: it dates from 1662,[26] which seems to suggest that contacts with nobles in Britain were re-established after the Restoration.

Most, though not all, of Condé's foreign partners were nobles. Although there is no strict causal link, we might infer that these networks correspond more or less to the reach of European noble culture at the time.[27] The 'Grand Tour',[28] a voyage that a young nobleman was expected to undertake in his youth, was a characteristic feature of this culture. Young men would visit courts in several countries, as well as attending so-called gentlemen's academies (institutions whose task it was to teach specifically aristocratic skills such as riding, hunting, dancing or proficiency in foreign languages). This is not the place to develop this hypothesis further, but one could imagine that international contacts developed much more easily among countries whose nobles undertook the Grand Tour. Russian noblemen, for instance, did not normally visit western Europe in the seventeenth century. Neither did they marry western European nobles as easily as the elites of those countries intermarried (within confessional limits, of course). Moreover, many material and non-material cultural forms were found in countries across western and central Europe: styles of clothing, dancing, court ceremonial and duelling. The Grand Tour, intermarriage and common cultural forms may have facilitated exchanges between the elites of the Occident.

When we take a closer look at Condé's European network, four categories of partners can be distinguished: first, royal contacts; second, European noble contacts; third, private diplomatic 'agents'; and fourth, non-noble contacts. Condé was in contact with the Austrian Habsburgs. In 1653 he wrote a letter to Emperor Ferdinand III,[29] and in 1663 he received a letter from Leopold I,[30] whom he wrote again in 1664.[31] Queen Christina of Sweden corresponded directly with Condé.[32] Her letters were, of course, written by a secretary, but they sometimes feature a postscriptum added in her own hand.[33] This was a sign of distinction widely used across Europe: the honour to the addressee directly corresponded to the proportion of a royal letter that was written by the monarch himself. To receive a letter written entirely by the king was an extraordinary distinction. Condé's contacts with the Polish royal court reached their apogee in the 1660s when Condé – a pardoned rebel living on his own estates and in a state of disgrace – tried to have himself or his son elected successor to the king of Poland. This idea had been first raised by an old friend of Condé, the Polish queen Marie-Louise de Gonzague. She was a member of the French branch of the Gonzaga (the ducal family of Mantua), which held the duchy of Nevers.[34] She left France only after her marriage to Władisław IV Vasa. The contact between Condé and the Polish court was thus grounded on an old French friendship transported to Poland by means of a dynastic marriage. Geographically speaking, contacts could be stretched: when individuals moved to another country, they retained at least some of their contacts (which were necessarily transformed from face-to-face-interactions into long-distance contacts). High-ranking acquaintances at home could provide a precious resource of power when one moved abroad.

The prince's contact with the Spanish monarch was, of course, most intense during Condé's time as a rebel in Spanish service (between the end of the Fronde and the signing of the Peace of the Pyrenees). Interaction was not always direct: Spanish aristocrats would act as go-betweens between Condé and the Spanish king. Links with the Spanish crown were not totally severed after Condé's return to France in 1659: he received a letter from the queen of Spain in 1665.[35]

Four spaces of interaction with European noble partners can be emphasized. First, Condé had many correspondents from the Holy Roman Empire. At least some of these contacts stem from his experience as a general in the Thirty Years' War. When Condé moved his army into a German territory that was an ally of France, the rulers of this territory entered into contact with him. For example, in 1644 the lower clergy of Mainz requested that Condé mediate with the higher clergy, who wanted to impose a 'contribution' on them (most probably in order to supply the French garrison).[36] Some of these contacts went beyond mere military affairs: Countess Amalie Elisabeth of Hessen-Kassel, for example, sent a letter of condolence to Condé when his father died.[37] The three ecclesiastic Electors, the prince-bishops of Cologne,[38] Mainz[39] and Trier[40] numbered among Condé's partners in the Empire; moreover, the prince also exchanged letters with the Elector of Bavaria, Ferdinand Maria,[41] the Elector of Brandenburg[42] and the Palatine Elector.[43] Condé was in contact with a number of imperial princess, including Duke Ulrich of Württemberg-Neuenbürg,[44] the duke of Zweibrücken,[45] the duke of Neuburg,[46] and the duke of Holstein.[47] Moreover, it seems probable that 'M. de Schwerin'[48] was Christian Ludwig I, duke of Mecklenburg-Schwerin. Expelled by Wallenstein, who took over his territory, he went into exile to Paris and, after returning to his lands in 1659, married Isabelle-Angélique de Montmorency-Boutteville, the widow of the Duke of Coligny-Châtillon. (The duke had fought alongside Condé in many battles until he was killed in the battle of Charenton in 1649.) Among the German counts, Condé was in contact with the Rheingraf,[49] the Count of Fürstenberg,[50] and the aforementioned Countess Amalie Elisabeth of Hessen-Kassel. This list is by no means exhaustive. Besides these numerous connections with electors and imperial princes, Condé was also in contact with the German Habsburgs: he received letters from Archduke Leopold Wilhelm, governor of the Spanish Netherlands,[51] and Archduke Sigismund of Further Austria.[52] Raimondo Montecuccoli, a fellow general in the Thirty Years' War, also maintained contact with Condé.[53]

Second, his connection to the Polish royal court also brought Condé into contact with many other noble and ecclesiastical partners in Poland. His noble contacts included the governor of Warsaw;[54] Count Dönhoff (an important family among the German-speaking nobility of East Prussia, with branches in both Prussia and Poland);[55] Stanislas Lubomirski, great marshal of Poland;[56] and Prince Radziwiłł.[57] The Bishop of Cracow, also Chancellor of Poland;[58] the Archbishop of Gniezno;[59] and the Countess of Manderscheid-Blankenheim, Abbess of Toruń, were among his ecclesiastical partners.[60] Condé's Swedish contacts were far less numerous. Apart from Queen Christina, only two Swedish correspondents have been identified, but both of these were significant. The first was General Lennart Torstensson. He came into contact with Condé in 1645;[61] at that time Torstensson commanded the Swedish army in Germany and Condé led one of the French armies. Their contact began as generals of two allied armies in the Thirty Years' War. Torstensson was in contact with Condé even after the war, writing to him again from Stockholm in 1651, the year of his death.[62] The other Swedish contact was Magnus Gabriel de la Gardie, favourite of Queen Christina and extraordinary envoy to France.[63] It seems probable that he became acquainted with Condé during his mission. He wrote to Condé in French, unlike Torstensson, who wrote in German, which Condé then had translated (the archives retain the translation alongside Torstensson's original letter).

Third, Condé had many contacts with Spanish nobles, especially during the 1650s when he served the Spanish crown. Two correspondents exchanged a particularly large number of letters with Condé. The first was Luis Menéndez de Haro y Sotomayor,[64] the nephew of Count Olivares and his successor as *valido* (favourite) of Philip IV; he later became one of the chief Spanish negotiators in the process that led to the Peace of the Pyrenees. The other was John of Austria the Younger,[65] natural son of Philip IV and governor of the Spanish Netherlands (as successor of Archduke Leopold Wilhelm), and later prime minister of Spain.

Other Spanish partners included Luis Francisco de Benavides Carillo de Toledo, Marquis of Caracena,[66] a Spanish general and John of Austria's successor as governor of the Spanish Netherlands; Francisco de Moura Cortereal, Marquis of Castel-Rodrigo,[67] who was in contact with Condé from 1654 onwards and who in 1664 became governor of the Spanish Netherlands as Caracena's successor, and Gaspar de Bracamonte y Guzmán, Count of Peñaranda,[68] who had been the Spanish plenipotentiary during the negotiations that led to the Peace of Westphalia. A particularly interesting case is Condé's correspondence with the *deputats* (the representatives of Catalonia);[69] this shows that also on the level of estates, Condé had contacts outside France.

Fourth, Condé also had contacts in Italy, which can be subdivided into two groups. On the one hand, he exchanged letters with several Italian princes, among which were Ferdinando II de' Medici, Grand-duke of Tuscany;[70] Ranuccio II Farnese, Duke of Parma;[71] Charles II Gonzaga, Duke of Mantua;[72] the Duke of Bracciano (a branch of the mighty Roman Orsini family);[73] a Duke Sforza, most probably the duke of Onano, (this was a branch of the Sforza family whose Milanese line had already died out by Condé's time);[74] and the Duke of Sabbioneta (a branch of the Gonzaga family whose main line was reigning in Mantua).[75] Condé was also in contact with Christine de France, the Duchess of Savoy.[76] She was the daughter of Henry IV of France and Marie de' Medici; this explains why she called Condé her cousin when writing to him.

After having returned to France and having been forgiven for his rebellion, in 1663 Condé received a letter from the Duchess of Modena, the widow of Alfonso IV d'Este and regent of the Duchies of Modena and Reggio in the name of her infant son. This may not be the first letter she ever wrote to him, but perhaps this contact would not have been possible during Condé's rebellion: the duchess was no other than Laura Martinozzi, Cardinal Mazarin's niece.[77] However, she was also the sister-in-law of Condé's brother. (Condé had earlier forced his younger brother, Armand de Bourbon, Prince of Conti, to break off his engagement with Mademoiselle de Chevreuse, daughter of the Duchess of Chevreuse.[78] Unlike Condé himself, Conti made his peace with Mazarin after the Fronde was over and in 1654 married the cardinal's niece Anne Marie Martinozzi.) Thus, even the families of the great antagonists Condé and Mazarin were linked through marriage ties; on a more general level, this particularly striking example illustrates that the vast European network Condé maintained was reinforced by kinship ties. Unless a noble family was divided by an internal conflict, contacts with one member certainly facilitated approaches to others in the same family; this was all the more important because the high nobility often married someone from another realm.

This can be further illustrated by looking at Condé's connections with the Holy See. They include partners from some of the most important cardinal families.[79] Some of these cardinals came from families whose princely members were also in contact with Condé, for example the Este. Among his partners were the cardinal-nephew Pamphili,[80] nephew of Pope Innocent X, and Cardinal Chigi, nephew of Innocent's successor Alexander VII.[81] Moreover, Condé was also in contact with Cardinal Rospigliosi, Alexander's Cardinal Secretary of State, who in 1667 succeeded Alexander and took the name Clement IX.[82] Condé was also in contact with other families whose members included popes, namely several cardinals of the Barberini family,[83] but also cardinals Carafa,[84] Colonna,[85] Orsini[86] and Piccolomini.[87] Other cardinal partners included cardinals Albizzi,[88] Azzolini,[89] Bichi,[90] Boncompagni,[91] Celsi,[92] Corradi,[93] Este,[94] Franciotti,[95] Ginetti,[96] Maidalchini,[97] Pallavicino,[98] Panziroli,[99]

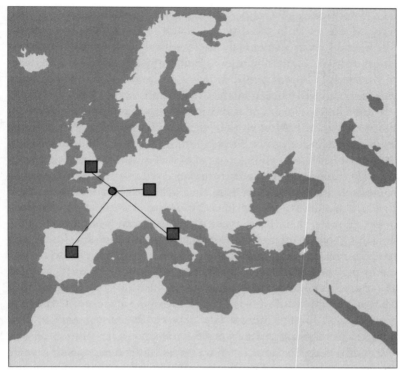

Map 21. The Grand Condé's network of agents. Drawing by Christan Kühner.

Sachetti,[100] Sforza,[101] Spada[102] and Trivulzio,[103] as well as the cardinal of Hessen-Darmstadt.[104] Given these extensive connections with the cardinal college, it is not surprising that Condé's contacts at the Curia went beyond the group of the cardinals. He was also in contact with other high-ranking priests, notably Goswin Nickel, general of the Jesuits.[105] Taken together, the partly overlapping circles of princely and cardinal families among Condé's Italian contacts cover a great number of Italy's most important aristocratic houses in the seventeenth century.

Contacts with other partners, especially Swiss and Dutch correspondents, complement the network. The Chantilly archive contains a sketch for a letter Condé wrote to the Swiss Cantons in 1652;[106] his father had already been in contact with the Thirteen Cantons (in the early modern period, the Swiss Confederation still had only thirteen members),[107] and in particular with the republic of Geneva.[108]

In 1645 Frederick Henry, Prince of Orange and Stadtholder of Holland, wrote twice to Condé's father;[109] the year before, he had also received a letter from the Estates-General of the United Provinces.[110] The Grand Condé maintained contact with the Netherlands, receiving letters from the Count of Egmont[111] and from the council of the Duchy of Guelders.[112] The southernmost point of Condé's network was Malta, whence he received letters from the Grand Master of the Order of Malta.[113]

Condé had a network of agents in the important capitals of western Europe (Map 21). Most of these agents were nobles, but of a much lesser rank than the prince himself – if this had not been the case, they would not have been willing to serve him in a clearly subordinate position. He corresponded with them and received not only letters, but also *nouvelles* (reports which can be likened to those of diplomats or spies). In fact, if one leaves aside the official titles, this network of 'ambassadors' possessed many characteristics of a diplomatic service of the period; the only thing that distinguishes these agents from ambassadors is that they served a private person rather than a monarch. These private ambassadors included Saint-Agoulin at Philip IV's court in Madrid, Barrière at Cromwell's residence in London, the Abbé Montreuil in Rome, and Marigny in Frankfurt, who was charged with the affairs concerning the Holy Roman Empire (he was later replaced by Saint-Estienne, who stayed in Regensburg at the Imperial Diet).[114]

Condé was also in contact with non-noble individuals outside France. Two principal groups of contacts can be identified. There were many contacts from city councils outside France. These included partners in a number of imperial cities: the mayor and council of Frankfurt;[115] the 'praetors, consuls, and senate of the Republic of Strasbourg' (which was still a free imperial city at the time of Condé's active political and military role);[116] the mayor and senate of Landau;[117] and the consuls and senate of Cologne.[118] Defining these contacts as non-noble is, of course, problematic: members of oligarchic city governments often tended to consider themselves as nobles. However, the noble quality of these officials depends on how nobility is defined, and other city governments were often made up of individuals who could not be described as nobles (in particular members of craftsmen's corporations and guilds). Condé also had contacts who were clearly not noblemen. These individuals often lived in cities and formed a second network of informants. Perhaps the most notable of these was Monsieur Frischmann, who reported to Condé from Strasbourg in the 1670s. Similarly, in the 1640s Hubert Bleymann from Frankfurt had written to the Grand Condé's father.[119] One could suppose that this was a method by which Condé could obtain information from places that were not great centres of power without having to place permanent private ambassadors there. Of course, as the foreign informants were in a less formalized relationship with Condé than were his French noble agents, the flow of information from them was more irregular and often did not last for many years.

Conclusion

Two conclusions can be drawn from the analysis of the geographic and social characteristics of this network. First, it clearly shows the interweaving of the French and foreign connections. There is no clearly demarcated difference between those partners who are 'compatriots' and those who are not. Second, the interactions do not clearly distinguish 'official' contacts from 'private' friendships; Condé's network of private agents, which was almost a diplomatic service, is only the most distinct feature of a general structure. Early modern nobles often used their personal networks abroad to promote interests of their king. Thus, neither the dichotomy of the domestic and the foreign nor that of the public and the private are suitable ways of interpreting these kinds of networks. In the seventeenth century, a noble culture that was pan-European still persisted; society was structured hierarchically from the most noble to the most humble, not according to the binary models of sovereign versus subject and domestic versus foreign. This does not entitle us to describe early modern Europe as entirely exotic or to deny the existence of continuities; but it is a characteristic feature that, in the field of social relationships, clearly distinguishes early modern Europe from the Western world of today.

Notes

1 There is an abundant literature about networks and especially patronage in early modern history. In the French case, the starting point of the debate was Mousnier 1990 [originally 1974]. Criticism of Mousnier can be found in Reinhard 1979 and in Kettering 1986. Sharon Kettering's conception has been criticized by Kristen B. Neuschel, (1989). Since then, many studies about networks in early modern Europe have been published; some of the most notable include Mączak (ed.) 1990; Reinhardt 2000; Emich 2001; Wieland 2004; and Boltanski 2006. For a sociological view see Eisenstadt & Roniger 1984.

2 There are several biographies of the Grand Condé, the most recent of which is Pujo 1995.

3 Archives du Musée Condé, Chantilly. As many of the correspondents frequently exchanged letters with the prince, I do not list every letter individually in the

footnotes. Instead, for each partner, I cite one of the earliest letters he or she wrote to the prince, which can serve as a starting point from which to track their correspondence. I use the abbreviation AC for Archives de Chantilly, followed by the letter indicating the series, the number of the volume and that of the letter.

4 Béguin 1999.
5 AC M XXIX 426f.
6 AC M XXXIII 106–109.
7 AC P XXV 260f.
8 AC P XI 334.
9 AC P XIII 378f.
10 AC M XXXII 112.
11 AC P XXIII 209.
12 AC P XXVIII 13.
13 For the count of Alais and for the micro-political mechanisms in the parlement of Aix-en-Provence, see Kettering 1986.
14 AC M XXXI 358.
15 AC P X 135.
16 AC P X 184.
17 AC P XXIII 189.
18 AC P X 234.
19 AC P XXIII 233f.
20 AC P XXIV 57.
21 AC P XXX 277.
22 AC P XXIII 261.
23 The notion of 'evil counsellor' has become frequent in historiography to describe the phenomenon of favourites who were accused of manipulating the king. The term may have become prominent as it was already a catchphrase in early modern English texts, see Walker 2005, p. 8
24 For this concept of revolt as an act of loyalty, see Jouanna 1989.
25 In fact Condé wrote a personal letter to Cromwell in December 1653. Cf. Pierre Lenet, Mémoires, in Michaud, & Poujoulat, (eds.) 1838, p. 612. Significantly, the purpose of this letter is to congratulate Cromwell for adopting the title of Lord Protector and thus returning to a de facto monarchy.
26 AC P XXVII 14.
27 This does not mean that this culture existed as such. Instead, it is the large number of shared features in the way of life of European nobles that allows us to speak of such a culture as a heuristic concept.
28 For the Grand Tour see Boutier 2000.
29 AC P XIII 56.
30 AC P XXX 184.
31 AC P XXXI 166.
32 AC M XXXIII 138.
33 For example AC P X 151.
34 For the establishment of the Gonzaga as dukes of Nevers see Boltanski 2006.
35 AC P XXXIII 439.
36 AC M XXXI 282.
37 AC P I 1.
38 AC P X 186.

39 AC P XXII 237.
40 AC P XV 39.
41 AC P XXXI 226.
42 AC P XXII 63.
43 AC P XXXIX 253. This letter was only written in 1672. However, the Palatine
    Elector had already received a letter from Condé's son, the duke of Enghien, in
    1663 (P XXX 117).
44 AC P XII 339.
45 AC P X 415f.
46 AC P XVII 79.
47 AC P XV 41f.
48 AC P XXII 65.
49 AC P XX 123f.
50 AC P XXXIII 45.
51 AC P XIV 377.
52 AC P XIX 449.
53 AC P XXVIII 165.
54 AC P XXV 316.
55 AC P XXV 35.
56 AC P XXVIII 472.
57 AC P XXXI 244f.
58 AC P XXV 114.
59 AC P XXV 117.
60 AC P XVII 311.
61 AC M XXXII 388.
62 AC P XII 122f.
63 AC P III 374.
64 AC P XVI 392.
65 AC P XVI 99.
66 AC P XIX 261f.
67 AC P XIV 16.
68 AC P XIX 23.
69 AC P III 11.
70 AC P XV 124.
71 AC P XX 198.
72 AC P XXIII 263.
73 AC P XXIII 390.
74 AC P XXX 210.
75 AC P XXV 358.
76 AC P X 417.
77 AC P XXIX 410.
78 Coste 1748, pp. 203–205.
79 For prosopographical information on cardinals, see the Humboldt University of
    Berlin's REQUIEM database: http://www2.hu-berlin.de/requiem/db/default.
    php?comeFrom=prosopo and also the Florida International University's bio-
    graphical dictionary of Roman Catholic cardinals: http://www.fiu.edu/~mirandas/
    cardinals.htm.
80 AC P 289.

81 AC P XVII 164.
82 AC P XVII 81.
83 AC P II 297. For the great Italian noble houses, see Reinhardt 1992.
84 AC P II 250.
85 AC P XXIII 307.
86 AC P II 305.
87 AC P XXXI 103.
88 AC P XXIII 265.
89 AC P XXIII 21.
90 AC P X 149.
91 AC P XXXI 59. This letter was written on the very day of Boncompagni's promotion to the College of Cardinals and announced the news of this to Condé. One might thus suppose that their relationship predates Boncompagni's obtaining the Red Hat.
92 AC P XXXI 65.
93 AC P XVII 15.
94 AC P X 299.
95 AC P XXIII 406.
96 AC P XI 15.
97 AC P XXVII 458.
98 AC P XXIII 35.
99 AC P X 287.
100 AC P XXVII 466.
101 AC P XXIII 203.
102 AC P II 311.
103 AC P XIII 102.
104 AC P XVII 88.
105 AC P XXIV 242f.
106 AC Q I 45f.
107 AC M XXXII 520.
108 AC M XXXIV 135–140.
109 AC M XXXI 449 and M XXXII 423.
110 AC M XXXI 333.
111 AC P XXI 263.
112 AC P XXI 399.
113 AC P XXVII 342.
114 Pujo 1995, pp. 214–215.
115 AC M XXXI 68.
116 AC M XXXI 92. Strasbourg became a French city in 1681.
117 AC M XXXI 261.
118 AC P XX 11.
119 AC M XXXI 490.

Bibliography
Archival sources
Archives du Musée Condé (AC), Chantilly.
Correspondence the Grand Condé

Literature

Ago, R. 1990. *Carriere e clientele nella Roma barocca.* Laterza, Rome.

Béguin, K. 1999. *Les princes de Condé. Rebelles, courtisans et mécènes dans la France du Grand siècle.* Champ Vallon, Seyssel.

Boltanski, A. 2006. *Les ducs de Nevers et l'Etat royal. Génèse d'un compromis (ca 1550–ca 1600).* Librairie Droz S. A., Geneva.

Boutier, J. 2005. 'Le Grand Tour des gentilshommes et les académies d'éducation pour la noblesse. France et Italie, xviᵉ–xviiiᵉ siècle.' In Babel, R. & Paravicini, W. (eds.) *Grand Tour. Adeliges Reisen und europäische Kultur von 14. bis zum 18. Jahrhundert.* Jan Thorbecke Verlag, Ostfildern, pp. 239–255.

Coste, P. 1748. *Histoire de Louis de Bourbon, Second du Nome, Prince de Condé, et premier prince du sang. Contenant ce qui s'est passé en Europe depuis 1640, jusques en 1686 inclusivement.* 3e édition, revue, corrigée et augmentée par l'auteur, The Hague 1748.

Eisenstadt, S. H. & Roniger, L. 1984. *Patrons, Clients and Friends. Interpersonal Relations and the Structure of Trust in Society.* Cambridge University Press, Cambridge.

Emich, B. 2001. *Bürokratie und Nepotismus unter Paul V. (1605–1621). Studien zur frühneuzeitlichen Mikropolitik in Rom.* Hiersemann, Stuttgart.

Jouanna, A. 1989. *Le devoir de révolte. La noblesse française et la gestation de l'État moderne (1559–1661).* Fayard, Paris.

Kettering, S. 1986. *Patrons, Brokers, and Clients in Seventeenth-Century France.* New York & Oxford, Oxford University Press.

Mączak, A. (ed.) 1989. *Klientelsysteme im Europa der Frühen Neuzeit.* Munich, Oldenbourg.

Michaud, J.-F. & Poujoulat, J.-J.-F. (eds.) 1838. *Nouvelle collection des mémoires pour servir à l'histoire de France,* Third series, Vol. 2. Paris.

Mousnier, R. 1990 (1974). *Les institutions de la France sous la monarchie absolue, 1598–1789,* Vols. 1–2. Presses universitaires de France, Paris.

Neuschel, K. B. 1989. *Word of Honor. Interpreting Noble Culture in Sixteenth-Century France.* Cornell University Press, Ithaca & London.

Pujo, B. 1995. *Le Grand Condé.* Albin Michel, Paris.

Reinhard, W. 1979. *Freunde und Kreaturen. "Verflechtung" als Konzept zur Erforschung historischer Führungsgruppen. Römische Oligarchie um 1600.* Voegel, Munich.

Reinhardt, N. 2000. *Macht und Ohnmacht der Verflechtung. Rom und Bologna unter Paul V. Studien zur frühneuzeitlichen Mikropolitik im Kirchenstaat.* Bibliotheca Academica Verlag, Tübingen.

Reinhardt, V. (ed.) 1992. *Die großen Familien Italiens.* Kröner, Stuttgart.

Walker, G. 2005. *Writing under Tyranny. English Literature and the Henrician Reformation.* Oxford University Press, Oxford.

Wieland, C. 2004. *Fürsten, Freunde, Diplomaten. Die römisch-florentinischen Beziehungen unter Paul V. (1605–1621).* Böhlau, Cologne, Weimar & Vienna.

PART IV

LOCAL POWER

CHAPTER 7

The Reach of Power

Marko Hakanen

Introduction

The concept of power has been much debated in historical studies, but the spatial dimensions of power remain less well explored. This lack of interest is all the more noteworthy when we take into consideration the fact that the exertion of power has always had a geographic aspect: how far in physical space the power-wielder's influence was able to reach. My aim in this chapter is to examine the intersections between power, social space, and the physical environment. The study of landscape is relatively new in history studies,[1] and in some ways it has failed to consider the social aspect of human life. More recently, historians have started to examine the actual spaces in which people lived. This 'spatial turn'[2] has given rise to an interesting perspective, one which can provide us with new information about many different aspects of social life. I examine how far-reaching the scope of social networks could be. Here, I map out the social range of one family's influence, to see how large an area could be controlled in the seventeenth century through social interaction and physical presence alone.

In my analysis of the reach of social power, I build my approach on four previous studies[3] which examine the use of space in everyday life. Using the results of these studies as a starting point, I map out the social reach of Anders Eriksson and his family in the baronial fiefdom of Kajaani (Sw. Kajana).

Swedish historian Dick Harrison states that space is socially relative and that different individuals view it differently, depending on their social status and their idea of the function of space. For instance, a king's perception of his castle would surely have been very different from the way in which it was viewed by his peasants. Concepts relating to space are created through the contest of social actions.[4] Harrison uses the concepts of 'microspace' and 'macrospace' as tools:

> Microspace can be described as the empirically known world around us including areas that we think of as being empirically known (even if we have not been there personally). Its size varies according to cultural situation, social structure, age, sex, personal habits, etc. Macrospace, on the other hand, has nothing to do with geography. Rather, it is a cosmological category potentially embracing God, religion and human beings within what on the surface looks like a geographical context.[5]

Using Harrison's concepts of microspace (how people understood the environment in which they lived) and information about their activities from a spatial point of view, I am able to restructure the Cajanus family's reach of social space.

Finnish historian Marko Lamberg has ideas that are similar to Harrison's, but he defines his concept of space somewhat differently. Instead of using the concept of microspace, Lamberg speaks of 'information environments'. By these he means geographical areas that can be clearly specified, in which people are socially active and in interaction with other people.[6]

Both Harrison and Lamberg have studied mobility in medieval Sweden,[7] especially during the fourteenth century, but they draw upon different source materials. Harrison uses the collection of Swedish charters *Diplomatarium Suecanum*,[8] and Lamberg uses similar documents issued by secular and religious authorities in medieval Finland.[9] Both study the distances people travelled in order to appear as witnesses and thus are able to define the area of social interaction. In other words, they use the authorities' official documentation to assess how far people travelled to participate in an action.

Swedish historian Örjan Simonson's study of the Torstuna juridical district in seventeenth-century Sweden concentrates mainly on the problem of local society. Using court records from three different periods (1599–1608, 1644–1653, and 1690–1699), he tries to assess to what extent the local society was in fact local and whether the local court carried the same meaning across the Torstuna juridical district.[10] The objective of Simonson's study is to determine the interaction among the contact fields of the local people, because these social actions simultaneously defined social space and separated the contact fields from the surrounding world. One way to define these contact fields is to track the movements of individuals.[11]

Taking roads as a starting point, Swedish archaeologist Ylva Stenqvist Millde has focused on mobility in seventeenth-century Sweden. Her main concern is the way in which people related to roads and travel. What makes her approach interesting is the combination of archaeology and history as a research method. She divides her study into four different areas: local (use of land and roads), economic, social, and political. Each viewpoint has been studied using different kinds of source material. At the local level, Stenqvist Millde has largely employed archaeological methods. Once the road has been charted, she concentrates on the functional level of the roads, studying the reasons why people used roads and what caused people to move. This study then explores the other three categories. The first of these is economic and relies on old letters (diplomas). Next, Stenqvist Millde considers the social field, and here the focus is on marriage patterns, which can be traced from the parish registers. Finally, court records are the main source of information for the political field.[12] When the results of all these studies are combined we can form a relatively detailed picture of the way in which people moved around their localities in the seventeenth century.

The results of these four studies (Harrison, Lamberg, Simonson, and Stenqvist Millde) point in similar directions, and so we can gain a good idea of why people were mobile and the size of the social spaces within which they moved. Using this information as a point of departure, I will map out the social range of power enjoyed by officials in local society. It was possible for one individual's sphere of influence to cover an even broader area by utilizing social networks or family strategies to place people in strategic offices.

In this study I examine one early modern family, whose influence ranged over an entire baronial fiefdom. I attempt to map out the area that Anders Eriksson[13] was able to control with the help of his children (or their spouses), who held important local offices including bailiff, vicar, assistant vicar, rural police chief, and jurisdictional district judge. This exercise of power over a large area caused some restlessness among the inhabitants of the baronial fiefdom. People began to doubt whether justice always prevailed.

The area

This study deals with the baronial fiefdom of Kajaani in eastern Finland, then part of the Kingdom of Sweden (Map 22 see colour plate section 1, p. 12). The fiefdom covered some areas only recently officially acquired by the Swedish realm. In a letter dated 18 September 1650, Queen Christina donated the fiefdom of Kajaani to Per Brahe the younger (1602–1680). At that time Brahe already held a number of titles: Member of the Council of the Realm; Lord High Chancellor of Sweden; Count of Visingborg; Lord of Rydboholm and Lindholmen;

Chief Judge of Wessmanland, Bergslagen, and Dahlerne; and General Governor of Finland, Aland (Fi. Ahvenanmaa, Sw. Åland) and Ostrobothnia (Fi. Pohjanmaa, Sw. Österbotten). His new baronial fiefdom included the parishes of Kajaani, Sotkamo, Iisalmi (Sw. Idensalmi), and Kuopio. In 1652, as a result of various bargains, he was able to add the parishes of Salo and Pielinen (Sw. Pielis) to his fiefdom.[14]

We can use four major categories to describe the geography of the baronial fiefdom: swamps, lakes and rivers, forests, and mountains. Water and trees were dominant features of the area (Map 23 see colour plate section 1, p. 11). Lakes and rivers were used for travel and the population was largely settled close to the waterways. Because of the large forests, slash-and-burn methods were employed for cultivation; later, forests were used to produce tar. The fiefdom of Kajaani's proximity to the Arctic Circle meant that the climate was not favourable for cultivation and, for that reason, fishing and hunting were very important sources of food.[15]

Brahe became familiar with the area during several trips he made to Finland between 1639 and 1651. On these trips, he visited almost all of the important places in what later became his baronial fiefdom. He observed that the area had a lot of potential from an economic point of view, and it was no surprise that those areas were soon donated to him.[16]

The studies of Dick Harrison, Ylva Stenqvist Millde, and Örjan Simonson have concentrated on very similar environmental areas in Sweden. In his study Harrison describes the provinces of Småland and Dalecarlia (Sw. Dalarna), as heavily forested areas and central Östergötland and central Uppland as agricultural areas.[17] Ylva Stenqvist Millde's studies have concentrated only on the area of Dalecarlia, which she describes as rocky and richly forested.[18] Torstuna County in Uppland, studied by Simonson, is divided into two different types of landscape: open flat land in the south and in the north, mostly forests.[19] As was the case in the baronial fiefdom of Kajaani, waterways were also an important means of moving around locally in Torstuna and Dalecarlia. Because of these environmental similarities, it is easier to use these studies as a theoretical background.

When Anders Eriksson arrived in the area (around 1626) it was still in a phase of transformation. The borderline between Sweden and Russia had only been established thirty years earlier. Anders worked as a rural chief of police in the county of Kajaani from the beginning of 1630s and was the first professional officer in the area.[20]

Anders Eriksson was an educated man and it is believed that he was the oldest son of Erik Mickelsson from Kirkkonummi (Sw. Kyrkslätt) in southern Finland.[21] His move to the area of Kajaani might have been prompted both by the potential of the area and because his wife's family were settled in northern parts of Finland – she had relatives in the town of Oulu (Sw. Uleåborg) and in the parish of Sotkamo.[22] Perhaps with his background, he saw an opportunity to gain a good position in an area where there were few educated elites.

The family

Soon after the donation of the baronial fiefdom, Per Brahe appointed Anders Eriksson as bailiff of three northern counties, namely Paltamo (Sw. Paldamo), Sotkamo, and Pielinen.[23] From Brahe's perspective, Eriksson was a good choice because of his educational background and his knowledge of local living conditions. However, there were some mixed feelings among local people about the appointment. Niilo Kananen even said publicly that Anders Eriksson deserved to be hanged in front of his own gate. Nonetheless, the majority of the people considered him a well-respected man. On many occasions Anders acted as a guarantor for individuals who had taken over deserted farms. After his death, it emerged that many of these people had not paid enough taxes, which led to difficulties for his own family.[24]

It is believed that Anders Eriksson married more than once, but Agneta Laatikainen is the only spouse whom we can identify with any certainty: she was the daughter of Mathias Laatikainen, a burgher from Oulu, whose relatives also lived in Sotkamo. Anders had nine children.[25] His background supported the idea that an education was the key to securing better posts. Even the ability to write could open doors to offices that would have been completely closed to common people. It was probably for this reason that Anders Eriksson hired a tutor to teach all of his children at home. Later, almost all of the children either held office in the baronial fiefdom or were married to an office-holder.[26]

Three of his sons pursued ecclesiastical careers. After being educated at home, Erik Cajanus (1628–1691) continued his studies in the University of Uppsala in 1642 and in the University of Turku (Sw. Åbo) in 1646.[27] He then worked as a first assistant vicar in Sotkamo parish. The Chapter had promised that he would be appointed as the parish vicar when the position became available. In practice, Erik Cajanus had already taken on the duties of a vicar: the parish vicar was sick and frail. Finally in 1651 (the same year that his father was appointed bailiff), Erik was given the full rights of vicar. The appointment of the twenty-three-year-old was confirmed by Per Brahe. Erik served the people for forty years and became the second longest-serving vicar in the history of Sotkamo parish.[28] He also became one of the wealthiest people in the area and employed four maids and three hired men during his time at the vicarage.[29]

Anders Eriksson's eldest son Johan Cajanus (1626–1703) also studied first in the University of Uppsala from 1642, and was ordained as a priest in the University of Turku in 1648. He then returned to his home parish, Paltamo, as a church servant. In 1651, soon after Per Brahe had gained control over the area, Johan was appointed as assistant vicar. At the age of thirty-four he was appointed the vicar of Paltamo County. Johan Cajanus was a very capable man, a fact that was seized upon by Per Brahe, who in 1665 appointed Johan as dean of the entire baronial fiefdom. Johan eventually became one of the most influential Finnish clergymen of the seventeenth century. Johan Cajanus was not the most modest of vicars: he made the common people build a large church and vicarage for him, duly earning their resentment.[30] His church was one of the finest in the Nordic area, and his vicarage was no less grand. Johan employed ten maids and six hired men to work in his vicarage.[31]

Anders Eriksson's third son, Anders Cajanus, enrolled at the University of Uppsala, just as his older brothers had. After studying in Uppsala, he also attended the University of Turku, where was granted the right to be a vicar in 1650.[32] In 1652, Per Brahe appointed Anders as a vicar in the county of Pielinen. Pielinen, recently attached to the baronial fiefdom, needed a good vicar who could reorganize its ecclesiastical organizations. One of the most difficult decisions for the parish was where to site the new vicarage. Andreas Cajanus wanted it to be built close to the church, but the local inhabitants did not agree. They offered an alternative and, eventually, got their way. Anders Cajanus never really managed to perform well in his job. He was largely preoccupied with the reorganization process until his death in 1657. After his death, the Cajanus family tried, without success, to keep his office within the family circle.[33]

Two of Anders Eriksson's sons, Jeremias and Samuel, followed in the footsteps of their father. Jeremias Andersson was appointed rural chief of police in the county of Paltamo. He also acted for two years (1659–1661) as a bailiff in Kajaani and Sotkamo counties after the death of his father. Anders Eriksson had not collected enough taxes and the family was held responsible for doing so after he died. The family doubted that anyone other than a family member would be able to collect the unpaid taxes for them. In the end, even Jeremias was not able to collect the whole amount. He was forced to loan money from a tradesman in Oulu to prevent Brahe foreclosing on the family farm in Säräisniemi.[34] By all accounts, Jeremias was a very ill-natured man and was involved in many disturbances (mostly because of his heavy drinking). Even the baronial fiefdom's highest officer had difficulties with him, but he was unable to control Jeremias's actions, simply because the Cajanus family had so much power.[35]

Samuel Andersson was appointed rural chief of police in Iisalmi parish. One of his sons took up his father's office and another became a porter in the castle of Kajaani. The family traditions were carried on by Samuel's first son, who became the assistant vicar and schoolteacher in Kajaani.[36]

Anders Eriksson also had three daughters and was able to arrange good marriages for them all. Beata married the vicar of the town of Raahe (Sw. Brahestad). Felicia married the baronial district judge, Johan Curnovius. After her first husband died, she then married his successor, Nikolaus Petrellius. Both of her husbands also served as mayors of Kajaani. Agneta married the assistant vicar of Kajaani.[37]

Two of Anders Eriksson's sons did not remain in the baronial fiefdom. The youngest son became a seaman and did not return. The second youngest, Gustav Cajanus, had briefly held the post of schoolteacher in Kajaani, but his appointment only lasted a year and was fraught with difficulties. Gustav, who in temperament resembled his brother Jeremias, engaged in a constant war of words with the chief of Kajaani castle and the head of the whole baronial fiefdom. After his turbulent time in Kajaani, Gustav returned to the University of Turku and became a priest. Despite all the difficulties he had caused, Per Brahe still helped him to become the assistant vicar outside the Kajaani fiefdom in Lohtaja (Sw. Lochteå).[38]

The reach of social space

Kajaani's baronial fiefdom was divided into six smaller administrative parishes: Kajaani, Sotkamo, Iisalmi, Pielinen, Salo, and Kuopio. Secular and ecclesiastical administration in the Kingdom of Sweden tended to use the same borders, and this was the case in Kajaani's baronial fiefdom (Map 22 shows the administrative parishes of the Kajaani fiefdom).

Based on his own experience, Anders Eriksson knew that the key to power in society was the ability to read and write. He hired a tutor to educate all of his children and sent most of his sons to university. This meant that through his children he had a tremendous reservoir of resources for extending his social power.

Soon after the baronial fiefdom was established and Per Brahe took total control of the area, the Cajanus family began to spread out to all the major population centres. At the height of their power, the Cajanus family had at least one representative in five different parishes. They held the office of vicar, bailiff or rural police chief in seven different cities or villages (Map 24 see colour plate section 1, p. 12) shows the homes of Cajanus family members). Through Felicia's marriage to a baronial district judge, their reach extended into the parish of Kuopio, where they did not have a permanent presence. This means that their local network covered every major area in the baronial fiefdom.

In his studies of medieval microspace in rural Sweden (cities are not included in his study), Dick Harrison concludes that the active social space of an individual was, on average, approximately 20–25 kilometres. Nevertheless, he points out that in 22 per cent of cases the distance between witnesses and participants was less than 10 kilometres.[39] The same kind of results can be found in Marko Lamberg's studies of medieval people's knowledge of their environment. The average distance that people travelled to buy and sell land was 14 kilometres.[40] In both studies the variation in distances travelled is great: some individuals travelled only a few kilometres to attend a social occasion, while others could make a journey of up to 100 kilometres. However, when these extreme cases are excluded, the average active social space was an area with an approximate diameter of 20 kilometres.

These results point in same direction as those of studies by Ylva Stenqvist Millde and Örjan Simonson (of the fifteenth, sixteenth, and seventeenth centuries). The size of the average social space grew, but only slightly. Stenqvist Millde's studies of social and economic mobility show that the average distance travelled in the fifteenth and sixteenth centuries was approximately 30 kilometres. She also notes that most travelling was undertaken during winter and summer, because ice and open water were the best surfaces for travelling.[41] Örjän Simonson has studied mobility in three different periods (1599–1608, 1644–1653, and 1690–1699) in the seventeenth century, and his results indicate that there was no change at all in travel practices over the course of a century. Ninety percent of travelling remained under a distance of 30 kilometres. In some cases, people travelled as much as 100 kilometres, and it is these journeys that bring the average travelling distance up to around 30 kilometres. In most cases, the distance travelled remained inside 10 kilometres.[42] All of these studies points to the fact that people's normal social spaces remained approximately 30 kilometres in diameter.

Based on the results of these studies by Harrison, Lamberg, Stenqvist Millde, and Simonson, we may assume that the social space in which the Cajanus family was active comprised roughly 25 to 30 kilometres from their homes (Map 25 see colour plate section 1, p. 13). This is almost the same distance that a normal person is capable of walking in one day, and this means that the Cajanus family could directly control all the major residential areas of the baronial fiefdom.[43]

The covered areas of social space represent the areas that could be covered on foot. However, individuals belonging to the higher estates had more options and could travel farther and more frequently than those who were forced to travel on foot.[44] Because of the offices they held, it is almost certain that they would have travelled by horse or horse-drawn cart. The extensive waterways would have also provided them with the possibility of travelling by boat; in winter they would have been able to travel by sledge. With a horse or boat, it was possible to travel at least twice as far as by foot. Based on this assessment, we can widen each individual's domain of social space to cover an area roughly 60 kilometres in diameter.[45]

Because every member of the Cajanus family belonged to the higher estates, either by virtue of the office they held or by marriage, the social space within the family's sphere of influence covered almost the entire fiefdom (Map 26 see colour plate section 1, p. 13). If we examine their mobility, could this reach have been even greater?

Mobility

As part of his duties as bailiff and rural chief of police, Anders Eriksson had to move around his official district to collect information for court cases and taxes for his master (in this case Per Brahe). To perform his duties properly, he had to write reports and inform Brahe of how things were going in his jurisdiction. Through this personal correspondence and the court records, we are able to trace his movements.

Twice (or on occasion just once) a year Anders Eriksson attended court sessions in his jurisdictional districts (Table 4): Kajaani (sometimes held in Paltamo parish, where Sotkamo parish's matters were dealt with at the same time) and Pielinen parish. He also had to travel to Raahe several times, because some matters from Paltamo and Sotkamo were dealt with there. It is fair to say that Anders Eriksson moved around a lot in his jurisdictional districts: had he not, he would have been unable to perform his duties successfully.

Six of Anders's letters to Brahe were written in Kajaani.[63] This was natural, since the town of Kajaani and its castle constituted the administrative centre of the baronial fiefdom.[64] In addition, the eastern postal route of the realm passed through Kajaani (Map 27 see colour plate section 1, p. 14).[65] Four of his letters were sent from Oulu.[66] Although

Table 4. Court sessions in the baronial fiefdom of Kajaani, 1651–1659.[46]

Date	Location	Present	Date	Location	Present
17–18.2.1651	Kajaani	A. Eriksson	8–10.1.1655	Kuopio	
25–27.2.1651	Iisalmi		9 & 15–17.1.1655	Iisalmi	
5–7.3.1651	Kuopio		26.1.1655	Raahe	
26.3.1651	Kajaani	A. Eriksson	31.1.1655	Paltamo[47]	A. Eriksson
25–26.7.1651	Paltamo[48]	A. Eriksson	20.6.1655	Raahe	A. Eriksson
15–16.7.1651	Iisalmi		26–27.6.1655	Kajaani[49]	A. Eriksson
22–24.7.1651	Kajaani		9–12.7.1655	Kuopio	
5.2.1652	Kajaani	A. Eriksson	16–18.7.1655	Iisalmi	
12–14.2.1652	Iisalmi		Summer 1655[50]	Raahe	Curnovius
18–21.2.1652	Kuopio		Winter 1656[51]	Raahe	J. Curnovius
10–12.6.1652	Kuopio		[sig.]–12.1.1656	Kuopio	
16–18.6.1652	Iisalmi		16–17 & 19.1.1656	Iisalmi	
28–29.6.1652	Kajaani	A. Eriksson	6–7.2.1656	Paltamo	A. Eriksson
7–8.1.1653	Pielisjärvi	A. Eriksson	27–28.2.1656	Raahe	Curnovius
14–16.1.1653	Kuopio		16–17.1.1657	Kuopio	J. Curnovius
18–20.1.1653	Iisalmi		21–23.1.1657	Iisalmi	
26–27.1.1653	Raahe[53]		30–31.1.1657	Kajaani	A. Eriksson
5–7.2.1653	Kajaani	A. Eriksson	16–17.2.1657	Pielisjärvi	A. Eriksson
14–15.6.1653	Pielisjärvi	A. Eriksson	2 & 4.3.1657	Raahe	
22, 23 & 25.6.1653	Kajaani	A. Eriksson	27 & 30.6.1657	Kajaani[54]	A. Eriksson
12–14.7.1653	Kuopio		15–17.7.1657	Kuopio	
18–20.7.1653	Iisalmi	Curnovius sig.[55]	3–4.8.1657	Raahe	
27–28.7.1653	Raahe		Illegible	Illegible	Curnovius
7–8.1.1654	Pielisjärvi	A. Eriksson	11–14.1.1658	Kuopio	J. Curnovius
13–14.1.1654	Kuopio	Curnovius sig.	18–21.1.1658	Iisalmi	
17–18.1.1654	Iisalmi		10–11.3.1658[56]	Pielisjärvi	
24–26.1.1654	Raahe		21.6.1658	Iisalmi	
1–2.2.1654	Kajaani[57]	A. Eriksson	3.8.1658	Raahe	
16–17.6.1654	Raahe[58]	A. Eriksson	11–12 & 14.1.1659	Kuopio	J. Curnovius
20–21.6.1654	Iisalmi		4–5.2.1659	Kajaani[59]	Curnovius
23–27.6.1654	Kajaani	A. Eriksson	23.6.1659	Kajaani[60]	
12–14.7.1654	Kuopio		6–7.7.1659	Kuopio	Curnovius
31.7–1.8.1654	Raahe	Curnovius sig.	14–15.7.1659	Iisalmi[61]	
3–4.1.1655	Pielisjärvi	J. Curnovius[62]			

outside the area of the baronial fiefdom, Oulu (as one of the important coastal towns on the Gulf of Bothnia) was a significant marketplace. Furthermore, the service road from Oulu passed through Säräisniemi (Map 28 see colour plate section 1, p. 15).[67]

Anders Eriksson sent almost as many letters to Brahe from his home in Säräisniemi (3)[68] (which he always spelt 'Säresniemi'), where he owned a large house. Only one letter was sent from Raahe. This was an important town in the baronial fiefdom: most of the taxed goods from the fiefdom were transported through the town of Raahe to Brahe in Bogesund. Raahe was a newly-founded town (1652) and there was not even a decent riding trail leading to it from the interior. In 1653 and 1654 respectively, the district court sessions of Kajaani and Sotkamo took the decision to build a road from Säräisniemi to Raahe.[69]

When analysing the correspondence of Anders Eriksson and his sons (Table 5), my first impression was that the house in Säräisniemi would have been a remote place, far from the administrative centre of the fiefdom. However, Anders Eriksson's house was also a tavern on the only route to Kajaani, and so everyone, including important individuals, would have either had to pass by it on their way to Kajaani or even spend a night there. In this respect, the house can be seen as a gateway to the baronial fiefdom and was in an excellent location. In his second visit to the area, Per Brahe stopped in Säräisniemi on 3 March 1651.[70]

Table 5. Dates and locations of letters sent to Per Brahe by the Cajanus family.[71]

me	Date	Location	Name	Date	Location
ders Eriksson	18.2.1653	Säresniemi	Johan Cajanus	25.2.1661	Paltamo
"	30.9.1653	Säresniemi	"	21.9.1662	Paltamo
"	23.5.1653	Raahe	"	19.11.1662	Paltamo
"	15.2.1655	Kajaani	"	1.3.1663	Paltamo
"	25.4.1655	Oulu	"	1.5.1663	Paltamo
"	30.5.1655	Oulu	"	1.9.1669	Paltamo
"	6.7.1655	Säresniemi	"	26.3.1672	Paltamo
"	30.8.1655	Oulu	"	17.10.1674	Paltamo
"	28.5.1656	Oulu	Johan Curnovius	3.6.1653	Kajaani
"	18.6.1656	Kajaani	"	7.7.1654	Kajaani
"	19.7.1656	Kajaani	"	3.11.1654	Kajaani
"	26.7.1656	Kajaani	"	31.12.1654	Kajaani
"	11.11.1656	Kajaani	"	25.1.1661	Raahe
"	29.3.1657	Kajaani	"	18.2.1661	Kajaani
"			"	16.3.1661	Kajaani
k Cajanus	16.8.1667	Kajaani	"	23.4.1661	Oulu
			"	16.5.1661	Säresniemi
mias Andersson	20.3.1661	Säresniemi	"	29.6.1661	Kajaani

In contrast to those written by his father, the eight letters Johan Cajanus sent to Brahe were all written in his home village of Paltamo.[72] The fact that he was vicar of Paltamo does not in itself explain why all of the letters were sent from his home. Nor does it mean that he was not mobile. Because of the prevailing educational and ecclesiastical system, he had a duty to travel once a year around his official district accompanied by the assistant vicar and parish clerk. Later, when he was acting as dean of the baronial fiefdom, he had to inspect all the congregations in the area.[73] Every vicar's district was divided into smaller districts where the children had to gather together to be examined on their knowledge of the Catechism. In other words, they were tested on their ability to read to a limited level (Map 29 see colour plate section 1, p. 16) shows the catechism exam districts.) The parish clerk questioned the youngest children, the assistant vicar questioned the older children, and the vicar examined those whose turn it was to take confirmation during the current or following year.

Only one letter in the set of correspondence was sent to Per Brahe by Erik Cajanus, the vicar of Sotkamo. Interestingly this sole letter was written in Kajaani and not in Sotkamo, Erik's home village.[74] The reason for this might lie with the postal system, Kajaani's position as a central town of the area, or some other factor.

There is also only one letter from the other brother, Jeremias Andersson, the rural chief of police in Kajaani district. His letter was sent from Säräisniemi, the family home. At the time, he was taking care of his father's estate, since his father had died in 1657. All of Anders Eriksson's other sons had offices in different districts, and so it would have been natural for Jeremias to take care of the estate and help his widowed mother.

Anders Eriksson's daughter Felicia married Johan Curnovius, who was the judge of the whole baronial fiefdom. Most of his letters to Brahe (7) were written in Kajaani.[75] This was natural because Kajaani was the administrative centre of the baronial fiefdom; Johan Curnovius was also the mayor of the town. He sent three further letters from other locations: Oulu, Säräisniemi, and Raahe.[76] Säräisniemi was his wife's home, and so it seems probable that they would have made occasional visits. Oulu and Raahe were important coastal towns that were relatively close to Kajaani.

As a judge, Johan Curnovius had to hold court sessions every year in five different locations in the fiefdom: Kuopio, Iisalmi, Raahe, Pielinen (held in Lieksa), and Kajaani (matters relating to Paltamo and Sotkamo were also addressed in Kajaani). The old law from 1442 stated that the judge had to hold three court sessions every year: one in winter, one in summer, and one in autumn.[77] This was still the ideal in the seventeenth century, but in remote places it could not be upheld. In the baronial fiefdom, court sessions were usually held twice a year: once in winter and once in summer. Winter court sessions were usually convened in January, but some would take place in February. Similarly, although most summer sessions were held in June and July, some sessions were convened in August (Table 5).

The only clear pattern in Johan Curnovius's travels between the different court session locations is the fact the Kuopio and Iisalmi sessions were always held close together. Once (in the winter of 1655), he even travelled back and forth between these sessions. The reason for this was that Kuopio and Iisalmi were located quite a distance from Kajaani, the administrative centre of the fiefdom. (People from Kuopio and Iisalmi pleaded in 1664 that they should have their own civil court, which would convene in Kajaani once a year.)[78] There were probably several reasons why Johan Curnovius only held two court sessions per year. The population of the fiefdom was small, and so there might not have been enough cases for three sessions; or perhaps it was much easier to hold sessions during winters and summers when there were good weather conditions for travelling. In addition, three court sessions a year would have represented a substantial financial burden for the people, especially in poorer areas.

Anders Eriksson's other two daughters married clergymen. Beata married the vicar of Raahe, Kaspar Forbus; Agneta married the assistant vicar of Kajaani. Both of these marriages seem to show careful planning: both Kajaani and Raahe were strategic junction sites in the baronial fiefdom.

The human web

In this chapter, I have examined how far the direct social reach of personal power could extend in seventeenth-century Sweden. Building a strong family network or local patronage network was a means of increasing one's power in local areas. Of course, it was not possible to build these networks of power at the local level without external social power, which in the case of the Cajanus family meant belonging to the broad patronage network of Per Brahe. If we take into account all aspects of social reach – such as family ties, social status, and mobility – it is clear that the Cajanus family could control the entire baronial fiefdom (Map 30 see colour plate section 1, p. 15).

From the Cajanus family's point of view, filling official posts with family members was a good way to gain power in their home county; others were not always so happy about this. In 1661, when (following Anders Eriksson's death) it was time to choose the new bailiff for the Kajaani and Sotkamo parishes, the inspector of the whole fiefdom expressed his worries to Per Brahe. He explicitly hoped that Brahe would choose somebody from outside the Cajanus family, so that there would not be so many family members in various offices. He complained that they 'hang together like peas on stalks, and it's so difficult for me to get any of my decisions through'.[79]

This sentiment was felt even more strongly by local inhabitants, who felt that one family had gained so much power that it could do practically anything it pleased. In 1658, two peasants complained to the inspector that Bailiff Anders Eriksson had collected too many taxes from them. Inspector Samuel Palmboum told them that they should take their complaint about this misuse of the bailiff's power to Kajaani's convention.[80] The peasant replied: 'It is hard to complain when the father is the bailiff, the son-in-law is the judge, and the son is the vicar, meaning that both law book and church could be closed.'[81] These sentiments from local inhabitants convey how strongly family networks could influence life in local communities.

Acknowledgements

This research which forms the basis for this chapter was funded by the Academy of Finland as part of the research project 'Politics of Brothers, Neighbours and Friends – Political Culture and Strategies of Influence in Early Modern Sweden c. 1500–1700'. The author would like to thank his research assistant Pirita Frigren MA who collected the data for Table 4. The historical maps published here came to the author's attention through Adjunct Professor Heikki Rantatupa, whose knowledge about old maps is worthy of the deepest gratitude. The reader can find Heikki and his old maps on the Internet by visiting the following address: http:// www.vanhakartta.fi/.

Notes

1 One of the earliest historians to concentrate on the study of how mankind changed the physical appearance of the environment was W. G. Hoskins. His 1955 publication, *The Making of the English Landscape*, is one of the first books to concentrate on this specific topic. Landscape history uses approaches that are common in agrology, architecture, and historical geography. It concentrates mostly on physical

changes. The social connection between humans and objects was largely ignored until Simon Schama published his extensive *Landscape and Memory*. Schama demonstrates that even landscape (which at first might seem to be free from culture) can be seen as a product of culture.

2 For more information on the 'spatial turn': Kingston 2010. See also Marko Lamberg's introduction in this book.

3 Harrison 1998; Simonson 1999; Lamberg 2003; Stenqvist Millde 2007.

4 Harrison 1996, p. 1.

5 Harrison 1996, p. 2.

6 Lamberg 2003, p. 262.

7 Harrison also examines Andorra and England.

8 Harrison 1996, p. 177.

9 Lamberg 2003, p. 262.

10 Simonson 1999, pp. 18–19, 57.

11 Simonson 1999, pp. 18, 47–48.

12 Stenqvist Millde 2007, pp. 123–124, 125–164, 167–170, 206–207, 221–222.

13 In letters to Per Brahe he uses only this name. The National Archives of Sweden/ Riksarkivet (RA), Rydboholmsamlingen (Rs), E7451. Those of his children who studied in universities adopted the name of Cajanus as their family name; the other children used their father's patronymic name, Andersson.

14 Nordmann 1904, pp. 287–292; Vartiainen 1931, pp. 94–99.

15 Keränen 1984, pp. 37–45

16 Hytönen 2004, pp. 30–57.

17 Harrison 1996, pp. 24, 177–178.

18 Stenqvist Millde 2007, pp. 33–34.

19 Simonson 1999, pp. 74–79.

20 Keränen 1986, pp. 272–273, 279.

21 Vahtola 2003, p. 82.

22 Bergholm 1984, p. 249.

23 Jokipii 1960, p. 284; Bergholm 1984, pp. 249.

24 Keränen, 1986, pp. 172–173, 179, 420.

25 Vahtola 2003, p. 82.

26 Vartiainen 1931, p. 148.

27 Luukko 1946, p. 17.

28 Wilmi 1997, p. 228.

29 Keränen 1986, p. 482.

30 Virrankoski 2003, pp. 86–88.

31 Keränen 1986, p. 482.

32 Luukko 1946, p. 35.

33 Kilpeläinen, Hintikka & Saloheimo 1954, pp. 327–329.

34 Keränen 1986, p. 273; Jokipii 1960, p. 284.

35 Vartiainen 1931, pp. 203, 345–348.

36 Rissanen 1984, p. 259.

37 Bergholm 1984, p. 249.

38 Vartiainen 1931, pp. 200–208. Even though Gustav Cajanus's behaviour was somewhat less than perfect, he actually managed to increase the number of the students from 3 to 25 during his brief spell as a teacher.

39 Harrison 1996, p. 213.

40 Lamberg 2003, p. 266.
41 Stenqvist Millde 2007, pp. 179–184.
42 Simonson 1999, pp. 148–150, 237–239.
43 Lamberg 2003, p. 262. Simonson 1999, p. 238.
44 Harrison 1996, p. 19; Stenqvist Millde 2007, p. 183.
45 Nenonen 1999, pp. 164, 274–276.
46 The Provincial Archives of Jyväskylä (JyMA), ES 2113 (microfilm copy). Not all court documents from the baronial fiefdom have survived. Only those from 1651–1659, 1674–1676, and 1678–1680 are intact.
47 Also handled court cases from Sotkamo parish.
48 Also handled court cases from Sotkamo parish.
49 Also handled court cases from Paltamo parish.
50 No date available.
51 No date available.
52 Also had personal seal (Fi. *sinetti*).
53 Before June 1654, under the name of Saloinen.
54 Also handled court cases from Paltamo parish.
55 Curnovius has signed his name at the end of the court documents.
56 Partly illegible, not clear who has attended.
57 Also handled court cases from Paltamo parish.
58 Also handled court cases from Pielinen parish.
59 Also handled court cases from Paltamo and Sotkamo parishes.
60 Also handled court cases from Sotkamo parish.
61 List of participants illegible.
62 Johan Curnovius mentioned as a judge.
63 SRA, Rs, E7451.
64 The castle was located in Kajaani. It was here that the baronial fiefdom's inspector (a direct representative of Count Per Brahe) was based.
65 Nenonen 1999, p. 183.
66 SRA, Rs, E7451.
67 Nenonen 1999, p. 237.
68 SRA, Rs, E7451.
69 Toivonen & Forss 1990, p. 215.
70 Hytönen 2004, p. 50.
71 SRA, Rs. E7450, E7451; RA, Skoklostersamlingen (Ss), E8165.
72 SRA, Rs, E7451.
73 Lempiäinen 1967, 465.
74 SRA, Rs, E7451.
75 SRA, Rs, E7451; RA, Ss, E8165.
76 SRA, Rs, E7451.
77 *Kuningas Kristoferin maanlaki Herra Martin suomentamana* (King Kristofer's Law of the Land, 1442), p. 125.
78 Jokipii 1960, p. 58.
79 SRA, Rs, E7451; See also Jokipii 1956, p. 127.
80 The Kajaani convention was where the administrative personnel of the baronial fiefdom met regularly to make collective decisions.
81 SRA, Rs, E7451; See also Kilpeläinen, Hintikka & Saloheimo 1954, p. 211.

Bibliography

Archival sources

The National Archives of Sweden (Riksarkivet), Stockholm (SRA)
Rydboholmsamlingen (Rs)
Skoklostersamlingen (Ss)

The National Archives of Finland (Kansallisarkisto), Helsinki (KA)
The Archives of the National Land Survey (Maanmittaushallituksen arkisto) (MHA)

The Provincial Archives of Jyväskylä (JyMA)
The Baronial Fiefdom of Kajaani District Court, 1651–1659 (Mf ES 2113)

Source editions

Kuningas Kristoferin maanlaki Herra Martin suomentamana. Helsinki, Valtion paina-
tuskeskus, 1987.

Literature

Bergholm, A. 1901 (1984). *Sukukirja. Suomen aatelittomia sukuja*, Vol. I. Genealogical
Society of Finland, Helsinki.
Harrison, D. 1998. *Skapelsens geografi. Förestállningar om rymd och rum i medeltidens
Europa.* Ordfront, Stockholm.
Hoskins, W. G. 1965 (1955). *The Making of the English Landscape.* Hodder and
Stoughton, London.
Hytönen, J. 2004. 'Matkalla jossain suuriruhtinaskunnassa.' In Kostet, J. et al. (eds.)
Pietari Brahe matkustaa. The Provincial Museum of Turku, Turku, pp. 7–62.
Jokipii, M. 1956–1960. *Suomen kreivi- ja vapaaherrakunnat*, Vols. I–II. The Finnish
Literature Society, Helsinki.
Keränen, J. 1984. *Kainuun asuttaminen.* University of Jyväskylä, Jyväskylä.
Keränen, J. 1986. 'Uudisraivauksen ja rajasotien kausi.' In Kemppainen, H. et al. (eds.)
Kainuun historia, Vol. I. The Town of Kajaani, Kajaani, pp. 204–681.
Kilpeläinen, A. S. , Hintikka, A. L. & Saloheimo, V. A. 1954. *Pielisjärven historia*, Vol.
I. The Congregation and the Municipality of Pielisjärvi et al., Pielisjärvi.
Kingston, R. 2010. Mind Over Matter? History and the Spatial Turn, *Cultural &
Social History. The Journal of the Social History Society,* Vol. 7, Issue 1, pp. 111–121.
Lamberg, M. 2003. '1300-luvun suomalaisten tietoympäristöt.' In Ahonen, K. et al.
(eds.) *Toivon historia.* Department of History and Ethnology, Jyväskylä, pp. 261–272.
Lempiäinen, P. 1967. *Piispan ja rovastin tarkastukset Suomessa ennen isoavihaa.* The
Finnish Society of Church History, Helsinki.
Luukko, A. 1946. *Pohjalaisen osakunnan nimikirja*, Vol. I: *1640–1713.* Pohjalainen
valtuuskunta, Vaasa.
Nenonen, M. 1999. 'Juokse sinä humma.' In Mauranen, T. (ed.) *Maata, jäätä, kulki-
joita. Tiet, liikenne ja yhteiskunta ennen vuotta 1860.* Edita, Helsinki, pp. 144–369.
Nordmann, P. 1904. *Per Brahe, grefve till Visingborg, friherre till Kajana, herre till
Rydboholm, Lindholmen, Brahelinna och Bogesund, Sveriges rikes råd och drots samt*

lagman öfver Västmanland, Bergslagen och Dalarna. Svenska litteratursällskapet i Finland, Helsinki.

Rissanen, S. 1927. *Iisalmen entisen pitäjän historia*. The Municipality of Iisalmi, Iisalmi.

Schama, S. 1996. *Landscape and Memory*. Fontana, London.

Simonson, Ö. 1999. *Den lokala scenen. Torstuna härad som lokalsamhälle under 1600-talet*. Uppsala University, Uppsala.

Stenqvist Millde, Y. 2007. *Vägar inom räckhåll. Spåren efter resande i det förindustriella* bondesamhället. University of Stockholm, Stockholm.

Toivonen, P. & Forss, A. 1990. *Raahen tienoon historia*, Vol. I: *Salon emäpitäjän ja Raahen kaupungin historia esihistoriasta isonvihan loppuun*. The Town of Raahe et al., Raahe.

Vahtola, J. 2003. 'Cajanus suku.' In Klinge, M. et al. (eds.) *Suomen kansallisbiografia*, Vol. 2, The Finnish Literature Society, Helsinki, p. 82.

Vartiainen, A. 1931. *Kajaanin kaupungin historia*, Vol. I: *Isovihan loppuun*. The Town of Kaajani, Kajaani.

Virrankoski, P. 2003. 'Cajanus, Johan (1626–1703)'. In Klinge, M. et al. (eds.) *Suomen kansallisbiografia*, Vol. 2, The Finnish Literature Society, Helsinki, pp. 86–88.

Wilmi, J. 1997. *Sotkamon historia*. The Municipality and the Congregation of Sotkamo and the Sotkamo-Seura Society, Sotkamo.

CHAPTER 8

The Limits of Power

Janne Haikari

Introduction

During the winter court sessions of Huittinen (Sw. Huittis) in 1652, Valborg Jacobsdotter, the mistress of Hannula farm, was accused of adultery. According to widespread rumours, she had been sleeping with former soldier Erik Matsson, who was also married. Neither of them was present at the first court hearing of their case. One of the main pieces of evidence brought against the pair related to the everyday living arrangements within the farm. The mistress of the house and Erik Matsson slept in the same room, while Erik's wife slept in another room. Erik Matsson suffered from abscesses and felt more comfortable sleeping in the sauna because of its higher temperature. The sauna was warmed more often than the room in which his wife, Kaisa Hansdotter, slept. Valborg and Erik were not alone at night: one of the farm's maidservants also slept in the sauna.

Although the dwelling practices of the farm did not attract further attention during the court proceedings, the general preconditions for residing, moving and governing in a rural parish became major underlying themes. Three hearings were needed to review the case: the authorities had difficulties making contact with the suspects (not to mention catching them). In the summer sessions of 1653 the court sentenced both suspects to death. There was still no clear evidence of sexual impropriety; the sentence was pronounced on the basis that the suspects had fled the locality before the final hearing.[1]

By the middle of the seventeenth century, Sweden had become one of the major powers in Europe. The effective exploitation of the country's resources was one of the factors that underpinned Sweden's successful territorial expansion during the early seventeenth century. For this reason, Sweden has often been seen as a prime example of an early modern military state. The Swedish state administration was restructured during the first decades of the seventeenth century and, in addition to building up a powerful army, it also began to interfere with many norms of everyday life. Sexual behaviour was increasingly scrutinized and certain religious practices of ordinary people were now officially considered to be pagan rituals. Because of such actions, the era is known not only for its political greatness, but also for its religious fundamentalism and growing bureaucratic control.[2]

The Hannula case implies that the power of the victorious military state was not always absolute in local communities, however. Valborg Jacobsdotter and Erik Matsson escaped and were never caught by the authorities. Although there has been a great deal of research on seventeenth-century Sweden covering a wide range of social, cultural, military and administrative issues, little attention has been paid to a simple question closely related to the growth of the state: how did state officials operate in the local scene? Few researchers have studied the administrative practices that lay behind official tasks and normative duties.[3]

The might of the new state bureaucracy has not been critically reassessed in Nordic historiography,[4] at least not in the manner of historians who have questioned the epoch-making nature of early modern regimes in Central European countries. Instead of imposing its will on society, the state was forced to negotiate with other actors as it strove to achieve its own aims. At a local level the new bureaucrats could not operate without collaboration with local leaders, whose authority rested on various informal factors.[5] While there has been some debate about the status of the seventeenth-century peasantry in Sweden, there is still a strong consensus that it was largely the state that took initiatives in society. Peasants were forced to adjust themselves to the demands of increased taxation and conscription imposed upon them from above. Competing views, such as Eva Österberg's outline of interactional political culture, have been criticized for lacking sufficient empirical evidence.[6]

The main question of this chapter is concerned with the way in which the Swedish state exercised power in the localities. Rather than studying the norms and general standards of bureaucratic activities, the focus is on the practical realities faced by local state officials. To be precise, this chapter is concerned with the operational environment of Swedish local administration. What was it like to exercise power in a seventeenth-century rural parish? Were there limits created by the geography of an administrative district? Where did the information that shaped decision-making come from?

The adultery case involving Valborg Jacobsdotter provides a specific context in which we can examine the capabilities of Swedish state administration. Although the extent to which the case was typical (of its kind or within the crime structure in general) is not the subject of discussion here, it is obvious that adultery was not a common crime. However, the methods used by the court and its actors were by no means unexceptional in court investigations of crimes or other issues. The case has also been selected for its 'richness': it was a prolonged process that produced several pages of records. It must be stressed that these definitions of typicality and material breadth are based on an examination of all the records between 1651 and 1679 from the local courts of Huittinen and its two neighbouring parishes.[7]

In the courtroom

There were two dimensions to the Hannula case. It had a strong moral dimension: the suspects were accused of committing adultery and thus undermining marriage, one of the most sacred social institutions. On the other hand, the case can also be seen as an encounter between the machinery of government and the common people, during which the demands of the state collided with the social and economic resources of the peasantry. Although the court's focus was on the morality of two individuals, the justness of society was also being implicitly reviewed. The Thirty Years' War had exhausted the Hannula farm. Taxes were unpaid and the master of the household, Thomas Grelsson, had been recruited to the army in 1651. Erik Matsson was the only man left on the farm, where he lived alongside six women. The first hearing gave the impression that the work ethic on the farm was generally low.

During the court sessions it became apparent that some of those from the farm, including both suspects, used to drink heavily – that is to say, they consumed alcohol in a manner that was considered inappropriate by their neighbours. One of the witnesses told the hearing that the residents of Hannula farm frequently drank a great deal and that if they ran out of beer, they would buy more from wherever it was available. The witness reported that 'a lot has happened' because of the drinking. One of the farm residents described how they sometimes pooled their money to buy alcohol.

All of the witnesses at the first hearing stated that they had not seen any direct indication of a relationship between the suspects. Kaisa Hansdotter (Erik Matsson's wife) had first raised the incriminating evidence on which the case was founded. However, at the hearing she refused to blame her husband and was even ready to take an oath to clear him of all suspicion. Her comments were discounted because she had earlier publicly voiced her suspicions that her husband no longer loved her. Witnesses reported that Kaisa had, on several occasions, expressed various misgivings about her husband and described some of the reasons for her discontent. The matter was considered serious enough for the court to continue its investigation of the case.

The second hearing took place during the winter court session of 1653. The suspects were not present when the case was initially discussed and so the court again heard the accounts that had been given at the first session. Valborg Jacobsdotter arrived in the middle of the hearing. She defended her absence from the earlier session, and her claim that she had not received a summons was accepted. Valborg also stated that she had fled the Hannula farm out of fear that Bailiff Påwal Påwalsson would arrest her. After the first court hearing, the bailiff had confiscated all personal property from the farm because of its unpaid taxes. Valborg had moved to Kouvonoja farm, where she had largely remained since that time.

With the arrival of Valborg Jacobsdotter, the issues brought up at the first hearing were no longer the focus of attention. Instead, two new witnesses described the time Valborg had spent in Kouvonoja. One of them recounted how Erik Matsson had visited Valborg many times and further claimed that Erik had asked Valborg to leave the parish with him. The other witness reported that Erik and Valborg had stayed together for two weeks in a hay barn immediately after she had fled from Hannula.

The court also heard how on two occasions Erik Matsson had implied that the accusations of adultery were true. This information was provided by Mårten Markusson (witness) and Mårten Thomasson (juror). Mårten Markusson's testimony implied that he had met Erik face-to-face. Mårten Thomasson's description was indirect; he did not provide detailed information about who exactly had been with Erik at that time. No questions were raised in the court sessions about Erik's current whereabouts.

Valborg Jacobsdotter flatly denied all the accusations levelled against her. She claimed that she had seen Erik Matsson only once during her time at Kouvonoja. She admitted that she had stayed overnight in a hay barn on her arrival but claimed that Erik Matsson had not been with her. Valborg dismissed the significance of claims that Erik had not denied rumours about the adultery. As the court had heard, Erik had been drunk on both occasions and according to Valborg, he was 'out of his mind' whenever he was 'boozed up', a fact that was confirmed by all the jurors. At the end of her testimony, Valborg accused Erik of stealing grain from her hoard.

Valborg Jacobsdotter presented a rather successful defence. By the end of the second hearing, the jury were unwilling to pass a death sentence. Instead, she was ordered to clear her reputation with a 'purification oath' at the next court session. This oath was never heard: Valborg failed to appear before court during the summer sessions of 1653. Her absence was automatically interpreted as a confession and the death penalty was now handed down to both defendants. Erik's whereabouts were again waved aside without remark. Before pronouncing their verdict, the judge asked the jurors whether Valborg Jacobsdotter had previously been suspected of any similar crime. The answer was negative. She had been respectably married for thirty years, 'despite the fact that [her] man had not known or used (*kändt eller hävdat*) her because of the flaw in her genitals'.

Incriminated by neighbours

The court records do not in any way suggest that the authorities tried to arrest Erik Matsson. One could argue that this was related to gender: the control of morality primarily focused on the control of women. Yet, in this case the pressure on Valborg Jacobsdotter was not particularly intense either. She managed to remain at liberty for about a year after the first court session, and even when she arrived in court it appears to have been of her own volition and almost at random: she argued that she had not been aware that the case was being heard. Valborg's claims were accepted without objections; she was not blamed for hiding, and no questions were asked of any local officials who might have been obliged to act in the case. Whatever the reasons for this lack of interest were, the distance between the local officials and the locations at which events unfolded are of concern to this study.

The parish of Huittinen was located in the south-west of Finland,[8] in the middle of the province of Satakunta (Sw. Satakunda). At the time, the population stood at about 2,000 and there were around 300 farms in the province. Agriculture and cattle rearing were the primary means of earning a livelihood, and there were still sufficient backwoods to utilize the traditional slash-and-burn farming methods.[9] Settlements were largely located along the Kokemäenjoki (Sw. Kumo älv) and its many tributaries. In comparison with other Finnish regions, Satakunta, and the parish of Huittinen in particular, was rather prosperous. As a parish, Huittinen could not be considered a peripheral area. Generally speaking, the conditions in which the state functioned in Huittinen were almost as good as they could be at the time. Yet this seemed to be of secondary importance in the Hannula case.

The structure of the Swedish state administration at a local level can be described rather easily. The head of the local organization was the bailiff (Fi. *vouti*, Sw. *fogde*). His area of operation was a jurisdictional district (Fi. *kihlakunta*, Sw. *härad*), which incorporated several parishes. Huittinen belonged to the jurisdictional district of Lower Satakunta. The bailiff's main tasks were to take care of tax collection and to control the ability of the peasants to pay their taxes. Additionally, in the local court he would act as the prosecutor of any instances of possible illegality that he encountered. A bailiff was obliged to communicate regularly with the authorities above him: the governor and officials of the county administration (who controlled the collected taxes). Nevertheless, the position of a bailiff was rather autonomous. Within the local area there were no higher officials with control over him. A bailiff usually hired a number of servants, who would help him in all his practical tasks.[10] In the case of Huittinen, however, the bailiff at the time was not part of the crown administration. Huittinen and its neighbouring parishes formed the county of Pori (Sw. Björneborg) in 1651, but this did not change the pattern of governance at a local level. The county bailiff reported to the lord of the county, Field Marshal Gustaf Horn, about practical matters, but apart from this his basic duties were similar to those of a crown bailiff.[11]

Another major official institution at the local level was the court of justice. Despite the role of the bailiff in all legal proceedings, the judiciary was bureaucratically separate from the administration. The local court had a strong connection with geography, as the parish was primarily a judicial community. The residents of a certain area – a parish – had common court sessions (Fi. *käräjät*, Sw. *ting*), which were supposed to be led by a professional judge.[12] Furthermore, the seventeenth-century Swedish church is usually seen as having been a significant part of the state authorities. The church played a decisive role in legitimating the authority of the crown (and its growing demands for taxation) and undertook some administrative duties on its behalf.[13] Vicars would often be assisted by a chaplain. In Huittinen there were three churches: the main church and the chapel churches of Punkalaidun and Vampula. There was also a minor chapel in Kauvatsa (in the northern part of Huittinen) in which services were occasionally held.[14]

Finally, there was an informal sector of local administration. In all parishes there were certain posts whose holders were selected by the community. The most important of these was the *nimismies* (Fi.) or *länsman* (Sw.), a sort of rural police officer. Among other duties, he was obliged to maintain public order in any way possible, arrange the local court sessions (which were held in his house), take care of prisoners and provide transportation for crown officials who were travelling through the parish. Jurors not only played a key role in handling all criminal cases in the court sessions, but also often had some say in questions regarding people's ability to pay tax and were the executive body of the court in different kinds of cases. Although the criteria by which jurors were selected is not set out in any surviving official or unofficial documents, it seems that the main competence required was to hold an esteemed position within the community.[15]

These governing bodies form the network of the local authorities, which was supposed to exercise power in all its forms in the parish of Huittinen. The following table indicates the distances between the homes of various officials (which were also their 'offices') and the two farms where Valborg Jacobsdotter had lived.[16] There is no information about the personalities of all the officials from this time, for example the servants of bailiffs or various assistant church officials. The list includes fourteen jurors, but only twelve of these, at most, would have been present at any one court session (Table 6).[17]

Table 6. The individuals involved in the analysed case and the distances between their homes and Kouvonoja farm.

Person	Office	Home village	Distance to Hannula (km)	Distance to Kouvonoja (
Påwal Påwalsson	Rural police officer	Kiviranta	10	23
Henrik Påwalsson	Rural police officer	Mommola	11	22
Mats Tacku	Rural police officer	Sampu	12	24
Mathias Elg	Vicar of Huittinen	Pappila	11	23
Simon Kepplerus	Vicar of Punkalaidun	Kostila	12	10
Thomas Rajalenius	Chaplain of Huittinen	Mauriala	11	22
Knut Johannis	Chaplain of Vampula	Matkusjoki	16	17
Sigfred Jöransson	Juror	Raijala	16	26
Simon Hendersson	Juror	Leppäkoski	7	20
Mårten Thomasson	Juror	Sarkkila	13	11
Grels Jöransson	Juror	Mommola	11	22
Henrik Mårtensson	Juror	Jalonoja	24	37
Mats Clemetsson	Juror	Tamare	16	16
Jöran Thomasson	Juror	Löysälä	8	21
Mats Jakobsson	Juror	Sampu	12	24
Mats Eskilsson	Juror	Arikkala	17	30
Erik Andersson	Juror	Mäentaka	12	25
Sigfred Thomasson	Juror	Villilä	17	30
Jöran Jacobsson	Juror	Huittinen	10	22
Simon Jöransson	Juror	Rieskala	2	15
Anders Eriksson	Juror	Mäenpää	11	10

Sources: KA, The records of Huittinen district court 1652–1655.

The table also clearly demonstrates that moving from Hannula to Kouvonoja meant pulling away from the authorities. Most of the listed officials (seventeen out of twenty-one) lived closer to Hannula than to Kouvonoja. It should be noted that measurements have been taken 'as the crow flies', rather than by following roads or other routes. Thus some of the distances may differ from the range on the ground, but most are probably not too far removed from the 'real' travelling distance. One of the oldest maps to show the parish of Huittinen in detail and (almost) in its entirety dates back to the 1780s (Map 31 see colour plate section 2, p. 1).[18] Although parts of Huittinen remain unfinished, there are places where even minor paths have been marked on the map. Thereby it is possible to measure the probable length of the 'actual' path between some of the places included in the table. For example, using the paths indicated on the map the distance between Bailiff Påwal Påwalsson's house and Hannula farm is 10.7 km and it was a 24 km journey from the same bailiff's house to Kouvonoja. In these cases, the difference between the map measurement and the 'straight line' measurement is one kilometre.

In fifteen cases the distance between the two farms and the homes of the officials was twenty kilometres or more. Researchers have argued that Swedish peasants usually lived within a twenty to thirty kilometre radius.[19] Valborg Jacobsdotter seems to have been determined to keep her distance from authorities by moving away from them. The map from late eighteenth century further supports this idea: it shows the swamps and backwoods between Kouvonoja and the more densely populated northern part of the parish. It seems that Valborg moved to a periphery. However, this did not mean that she would have been beyond the reach of all the social control networks.

The official who raised the case was the bailiff Påwal Påwalsson. At this time, cases of sexual impropriety were usually brought before the Huittinen court sessions by the nimismies. However, this case was an exception due to its dual nature: moral decline was combined with a failure to pay taxes. The fiscal problems of the farm meant that the bailiff had to be active, at least to some extent. For Påwal Påwalsson, Valborg's capture was not necessary in order to get the Hannula farm up and running again. The farm's unpaid taxes gave the bailiff a legal right to seize the property and give it to another farmer, and Påwal exercised this right in the summer of 1652. The unpaid taxes could not be recovered, but at least someone who was considered reliable by the bailiff was now managing the farm. Yet, Påwal Påwalsson's role seems to have been somewhat passive, generally speaking. After the case had begun, the bailiff did not openly participate in the process, at least not in the courtroom.

The whole case began with Påwal Påwalsson's announcement that Lars Söfringsson and Jöran Pärsson had told him about the alleged adultery, but after this Påwal did not comment on the case. It seems that although the case was under court investigation, no particular examination was undertaken by any of the authorities outside the courtroom. The records do not include complaints by the authorities that their pursuit of the suspects had been in vain; instead there is an air of nonchalance about the progress of the case. The court record shows that when Påwal Påwalsson stepped aside, Lars Söfringsson and Jöran Pärsson 'took on the prosecuting'. This was not the standard course of action; neither of them held any official position at the time. However, the statement probably meant nothing more than that they were the first witnesses to give their evidence or that they were simply those who had the best information. This also suggests that the core of the case rested on personal reputations, rather than following the letter of the law according to principles of rational judgement.

The two men told the court about Kaisa Hansdotter's accounts of her husband's cold-heartedness. Neither specified exactly where they had met Kaisa and heard her accounts, but it was probably in the course of everyday life. Lars Söfringsson and Jöran Pärsson lived in the nearby village of Suttila. Nothing in the record indicates why Kaisa spoke to these particular men. Neighbourhood is the only apparent connection between them: Suttila was located about two kilometres south-west of Hannula and the same road was used by both villages when travelling to church, for example.

The following list (Table 7) details all the involved parties (the suspects, the authorities and the witnesses who are mentioned in the court records), the location of their homes and the distances between their homes and Hannula farm (the scene of the alleged crime).

Table 7. All the involved parties and the distances between their homes and Hannula farm.

Name	Role in the trial	Position/ Status	Home village	Distance to Hannula (km)
Valborg Jacobsdotter	Suspect	Mistress of the house	Hannula	0
Erik Matsson	Suspect	Farm worker, former soldier	Hannula	0
Kaisa Hansdotter	Witness	Wife of Erik Matsson, farm worker	Hannula	0
Brita Jacobsdotter	Witness	Farm worker	Hannula	0
Lisbet Olofsdotter	Witness	Farm worker	Hannula	
Agata Grelsdotter	Witness	Farm worker, sister of Valborg Jacobsdotter's husband	Hannula	0
Påwal Påwalsson	Prosecutor	Rural police officer	Kiviranta	10
Lars Söfringsson	Witness/ Prosecutor	Peasant		1.8
Jöran Pärsson	Witness / Prosecutor	Peasant	Suttila	1.8
Mårten Thomasson	Witness	Juror	Sarkkila	13
Simon Eskilsson	Witness	Peasant	Rieskala	2.4
Simon Jöransson	Witness	Juror	Rieskala	2.4
Michel Casparsson			Hurula	1.1
Markus Matsson	Witness	Peasant	Kouvonoja/ Talala	
Mårten Markusson	Witness	Peasant	Talala/ Kouvonoja	
Kaisa Michelsdotter	Not present in the court		Kostiala	

Sources: KA, The records of Huittinen district court 1652–1655.

As the table shows, neighbours, not the authorities, played a key role in reviewing the case. All the relevant information was provided by neighbours and the residents of the Hannula and Kouvonoja farms. It also seems as though there was a certain amount of additional inside knowledge about the suspects that was not recorded.

Escaping the threat of divine punishment

Whatever Valborg Jacobsdotter claimed in court was accepted. Reading the court records, it seems as though her opinions were considered accurate without hesitation. She rebuffed the claim that she had spent a night in a hay barn with Erik Matsson by declaring that the witness who made the allegation (Markus Matsson) was her foe and that his testimony was therefore biased. She was not asked to provide any details or evidence to verify her assertion. Whatever the relationship between them was like, Markus Matsson was generally known as a quarrelsome person. He had, in recent years, been involved in lengthy disputes over land with neighbouring villagers in Kouvonoja and this had certainly damaged his reputation.[20] This may explain why Valborg was able to discredit Markus Matsson's evidence so easily.

The obscurity of the case may be due to the way in which court records were written. During court sessions the scribe would prepare a manuscript, which would later be transcribed. Not all the information about a trial would necessarily be included in the final version of the record. It is possible that the unwritten and at the time seemingly self-explanatory information may explain the negligence in catching Erik Matsson. Astoundingly, throughout the entire case there seems to have been no interest at all in getting him to tell his side of the story.

Valborg Jacobsdotter provided the only recorded information about Erik Matsson's residence: she told the court that the only time she had met Erik again was when he was travelling from Punkalaidun (part of Huittinen with its own church) via Kouvonoja to the neighbouring parish of Loimaa (Sw. Loimijoki). This piece of information seemed to be of no particular interest to the court. No one asked questions about Erik's destination or the places he had stayed, and there seems to have been no interest in hearing his opinions. Given the local roads, his route was a logical path for anyone making this journey, but simple questions were not asked in court. What was Erik Matsson doing in Punkalaidun (Sw. Pungalaitio), and why was he heading for Loimaa? A simple explanation for this omission would be that this information was self-evident to those present: everybody knew all the essential details about Erik Matsson. When his drunken behaviour was discussed, one of the jurors stated that Erik was 'just like his father', meaning just as crazy when drunk. Thereby the failure to arrest him seems to stem from familiarity. The court might have believed that bringing Erik before the court would have been difficult and that his testimony would not have helped to resolve the case.

It may also be possible that this negligence and the authority granted to Valborg Jacobsdotter's testimony reflect the fact that there was no particular will to convict the defendants. The foregoing discussion supports the idea that in the court case the alleged crime was investigated primarily by the social network of a local community, not by the rational state bureaucracy. Honour and reputations counted in this case, not the law book alone. The final verdict was eventually pronounced according to law, but the process was not characterized by the cold, rational and efficient contemplation of facts within a machine-like investigation. The authorities seem to have been negligent in their duties outside the court, and personalities seem to have counted for a great deal within the court discussions.

The reference to Valborg Jacobsdotter's 'flaw' seemed to act as a vote of confidence. By emphasizing that she had lived honourably for a long time despite problems with the sex life within her marriage, the court (meaning the jurors) appears to have supported her, even though it was obliged to pronounce the death sentence. It also shows just how much the community knew about lives of its members. The most private details were known of a marriage that had lasted thirty years, and one can argue that the detailed information further supports the innocence of the suspects. If the court knew something so intimate about Valborg, then would they not also have known if there had been something between the mistress of Hannula farm and Erik Matsson?

The negligence of the authorities also seems to contradict the values of contemporary spiritual life. The crime itself was serious enough within the religious context of a marriage, but to leave the moral transgression unpunished could mean exposing the whole community to the wrath of God. One of the main teachings of the Swedish Lutheran church in the seventeenth century was that the sins of individuals could incur collective punishments (such as wars, famines or epidemics). Put simply, it was, therefore, always in the common interest to punish criminals in order to avoid endangering the everyday life of all members of the community.[21]

There are further indications that the geography of the parish influenced the exercise of power. Although Bailiff Påwal Påwalsson seems to step back from the court process, his role is interesting because his actions resulted in one of the major turning points of the case. Valborg Jacobsdotter fled the Hannula farm out of fear that Påwal Påwalsson would arrest her. In terms of geography and power this implies that the presence of the bailiff in the locality was strong enough to inspire fear among the residents involved in a conflict. At the same time it also suggests that a suspect was able to move outside the bailiff's grasp without moving outside his official sphere of authority. The threat of capture was not perceived to be imminent in the neighbourhood of Kouvonoja.

It should be stressed that, other than her own admission of fear of being arrested, no one suggested that Valborg Jacobsdotter had moved to Kouvonoja in order to distance herself from the authorities. No witnesses put forward this argument and nobody accused her of trying to remain undercover. Valborg Jacobsdotter herself did not provide any reason (either explicitly or implicitly) why she chose to move to Kouvonoja, but she may have had relatives there. Generally speaking it seems that Valborg was living in Kouvonoja in a normal fashion, as one of the servants or as a lodger (*itsellinen* (Fi.)), without any attempt to avoid being caught by the authorities. Although public opinion may have been against sentencing the suspects, because it had been brought before the court the bailiff and the other authorities were still responsible for advancing the case. It could not be completely neglected and so to some extent the slow progress of the court case resulted from the peripheral nature of Kouvonoja. Staying out of sight of the officials meant staying free: they did not routinely visit the peripheral neighbourhoods.

A further location that seems to have been beyond the reach of Påwal Påwalsson was the hoard mentioned by Valborg (when she accused Erik Matsson of stealing). She told the court that Erik had stolen one and a half barrels of grain from her hoard 'in a forest'. There is scant information about this secret store, as the theft was not discussed further. It is impossible to say whether there were more barrels than those that were stolen or to discover the exact location of the hoard. Yet this demonstrates that Valborg Jacobsdotter and the Hannula farm had some goods that were beyond the reach of the bailiff, even though the farm was burdened with enormous debts and unpaid taxes.

Conclusion

In this chapter mapping of social control has meant two things: 1) measuring distances between actors and 2) using an old map to understand the logic of actors. The sense of fear felt by the suspect highlighted the limits of micro-geopolitics. It made her move from one location to another, and the resulting shift of everyday spatial relations between a subject and the authorities granted the former some breathing space. Distance counted, and forests, rivers and roads did have at least some impact on the local exercise of power. In addition, the efforts of those responsible for maintaining public order seemed to be somewhat lethargic. It seems that little attempt was made to arrest the two suspects.

As a result, the case implies that the dynamics of local power were not dominated by an all-pervasive state machinery. Max Weber's definitions of the modern state have had a strong influence on views of the early modern period in Finnish and Swedish historiography since the early twentieth century, when seventeenth-century Sweden's administrative modernity needed to be placed within the long-term chronology with the contemporary rising democracy.[22] While it is obvious that certain characteristics of seventeenth-century administrative reforms had a modern 'essence' within them, it is equally evident that there were still plenty of non-modern elements at all levels of society.[23] There is a rather strong consensus among researchers about the long-term role of jurors in the local exercise of power and in the administration of justice. It is a common view that, incrementally, jurors became increasingly bound to the central power, as the judiciary and the administration were centralized and the local court sessions were transformed from an independent unit of local self-government to the first rung on a ladder of hierarchical judiciary controlled from above. Through the so-called 'judicial revolution', the state took hold of the reins of society during the course of the seventeenth century.[24]

Kimmo Katajala's findings from Karelia in the 1680s and the 1690s, for example, suggest that the jurors were primarily a local executive organ of the authorities. The peasants did not view them as a suitable channel for promoting their social demands when they questioned the local fief administration. Instead, they delivered their complaints to higher tiers of administration through unofficial channels. However, Katajala aptly remarks that whatever generalizations are made, empirical exceptions to rules regarding the role of jurors can always be found.[25] Similarly the case discussed in this article emphasizes the fact that the role of jurors should always be approached cautiously, because there were significant variations in their role both temporally and locally. The jurors contributed to the case against Valborg Jacobsdotter and Erik Matsson being brought to court, but they subsequently did little to conclude it and even voiced their support for Valborg when they finally sentenced her to death. It is very difficult to define who or what organization the two suspects were actually running away from. Was it the official bureaucracy: the authorities and the court? Or was it informal social control: their neighbours and the malicious rumours? Clearly it is difficult to answer which of these two 'sectors' was the main driving force in this case.

On the other hand, the case could be seen as an interactive episode in local political culture. However, the negotiations were not conducted between the state and the local community. In Valborg Jacobsdotter's case the local community seems to have had difficulties concluding its own 'negotiation': although it was accepted that Valborg Jacobsdotter was driven out of the farm, local people did not reach a unanimous agreement about her moral integrity. There was no consensus inside the local community. Some people supported Valborg; others felt she had lived dishonourably. When her reputation was contested, Valborg's foes felt it was a good time to come down hard on her, but her defence was convincing enough to delay the final judgement. At this point, the suspects were faced with two unappealing alternatives. Finding the men needed to give the purification oath would have proved difficult. Escaping from their home district helped the suspects to avoid the death penalty, but in practice it pushed them towards social death. To leave your home was to break off your social relations. Strangers had no reputation, and it has been argued that lack of reputation was worse than having a bad reputation.[26]

The tension between the crown and local communities has been a significant topic in Swedish and Finnish historiography for decades. In the latest research the contradictions between the concept of the interactional political culture and that of the all-controlling military state have been, to some extent, waved aside. Conflict and compromise can co-exist, it has been argued.[27] While most of the junior researchers seem to accept this, the understanding of local politics is still rather strongly tied to the twentieth-century ideal concept of the political: official structures and institutions, target-orientated forms of actions and formal means of influencing matters which are considered 'public'. The Hannula case suggests that the object of social mapping should not only be to put people on the map, but also to help to abandon our own modern mentality. It means that we should accept that while the new organizational structures of seventeenth-century Sweden had certain elements of modern rationality, society and local communities still followed social patterns that are familiar to us from the so-called stateless societies.[28]

Social mapping can also be seen as a path to understanding 'the social'. Bruno Latour has criticized the vagueness of 'social' as a concept by emphasizing that the social is not 'a specific domain of reality' which can as such explain things. Instead, the associations between 'domains' or things are the essence of the social, and according to Latour the goal of research should be to trace such associations without defining them or any larger 'aggregate' social as such.[29] By putting people, movements and incidents on a map, law, politics and administration are connected with space, and the associations between different spheres of life become discoverable. Social mapping can help us to see how a community is held together and what type of entity it actually is as a spatial set of human relations.

Notes

1 The discussion of the Hannula case is based on the following records of Huittinen district court: 26–28 February 1652 (pp. 345v–346v, The Finnish National Archives/Kansallisarkisto (KA) mm.7), 18–20 September 1652 (p. 509v, KA mm.7), 31 March and 1–2 March 1653 (p. 29v–32, KA mm.8), 2–5 July 1653 (pp. 108, 109v–110, KA mm.8) and 26–29 March 1655 (pp. 164–165, KA mm.9).

2 See, for example, Nilsson 1990; Aalto 1996; Jespersen (ed.) 2000; Eilola 2003.

3 Gustafsson 1994, pp. 98–100; Lennersand 1999, pp. 30–31; Einonen 2005, p. 14.

4 Hallenberg 2001, pp. 17–20; Hallenberg, Holm & Johansson 2008, pp. 1–4.

5 Beik 1988, pp. 13–17; Henshall 1992, pp. 155–162; Levi 1992, pp. 21–22, 76–77.

6 Österberg 1989; Österberg 1992. Critique: Harnesk 2002, pp. 80–81.

7 The case study is based on my dissertation (Haikari 2009), in which the local exercise of power is studied from the viewpoint of county officials.

8 At the time the area of modern-day Finland was part of Sweden, Stockholm was the capital of the realm and Swedish was the official language.

9 Viikki 1973, pp. 187–188.

10 Hallenberg 2001, pp. 97–122; Asker 2004, pp. 362–365.

11 Jokipii 1956, pp. 95–99.

12 Almquist 1917.

13 Forssberg 2005, pp. 23–38; Ihse 2005, pp. 16–22.

14 Viikki 1973, pp. 422–435, 484–512.

15 Viikki 1973, p. 333.

16 The distances have been measured using MapInfo with the help of a basic present-day map.

17 The listed jurors are those who were present at the court sessions where the adultery case was discussed.

18 This is one of dozens of detailed and coloured military maps (*rekognoseringskartor*) that are preserved at the Swedish Military Archives (Krigsarkivet) in Stockholm; they have been published as a cartographic atlas; see Alanen & Kepsu (eds.) 1989.

19 Harrison 1996, pp. 213–218; Simonson 1999, pp. 148–150, 237–238; Lamberg 2003, pp. 261–262.

20 Suvanto 1986, p. 73; Nenonen 1992, p. 57.

21 Juva 1955, pp. 61–65; Melkersson 1997, pp. 78–79; Eilola 2003, p. 194.

22 Simonsson 1999, pp. 24–25; Herlin 1996, pp. 93–100.

23 See, for example, Droste 2006, pp. 251–254, 287–288 and passim.

24 Österberg 1989; Österberg 1992.

25 Katajala 1994, pp. 230–233.

26 Matikainen 2002, pp. 162–164.
27 Lennersand 1999, pp. 30–31; Lerbom 2003, pp. 22–23; Forssberg 2005, 26; Holm 2007, p. 20.
28 Droste 2006; Eilola 2003; Matikainen 2002.
29 Latour 2005, pp. 1–9, 249–257.

Bibliography

Archival sources

The Finnish National Archives (Kansallisarkisto), Helsinki (KA)
The records of Huittinen district court 1652–1655, microfilmed volumes mm.7, mm.8 and mm.9.

Literature

Aalto, S. 1996. *Kirkko ja kruunu siveellisyyden vartijoina. Seksuaalirikollisuus, esivalta ja yhteisö Porvoon kihlakunnassa 1621–1700.* The Finnish Literature Society, Helsinki.

Almquist, J. A. 1917. *Den civila lokalförvaltningen i Sverige 1523–1630.* Vol. I. Norstedts, Stockholm.

Asker, B. 2004. *I konungens stad och ställe. Länsstyrelser i arbete 1635–1735.* Stiftelsen för utgivande av Arkivvetenskapliga studier, Uppsala.

Beik, W. 1988. *Absolutism and Society in Seventeenth-century France. State Power and Provincial Aristocracy in Languedoc.* Cambridge University Press, Cambridge.

Droste, H. 2006. *Im Dienst der Krone. Schwedische Diplomaten im 17. Jahrhundert.* Lit Verlag, Berlin & Münster.

Eilola, J. 2003. *Rajapinnoilla. Sallitun ja kielletyn määritteleminen 1600-luvun jälkipuoliskon noituus- ja taikuustapauksissa.* The Finnish Literature Society, Helsinki.

Einonen, P. 2005. *Poliittiset areenat ja toimintatavat. Tukholman porvaristo vallan käyttäjänä ja vallankäytön kohteena n. 1592–1644.* The Finnish Literature Society, Helsinki.

Forssberg, A. M. 2005. *Att hålla folket på gott humör. Informationsspridning, krigspropaganda och mobilisering i Sverige 1655–1680.* Stockholm University, Stockholm.

Gustafsson, H. 1994. *Political Interaction in the Old Regime. Central Power and Local Society in the Eighteenth-Century Nordic States.* Studentlitteratur, Lund.

Haikari, J. 2009. *Isännän, Jumalan ja rehellisten miesten edessä. Vallankäyttö ja virkamiesten toimintaympäristöt satakuntalaisissa maaseutuyhteisöissä 1600-luvun jälkipuoliskolla.* The Finnish Literature Society, Helsinki.

Hallenberg, M. 2001. *Kungen, fogdarna och riket. Lokalförvaltning och statsbyggande under tidig vasatid.* Stockholm University, Stockholm.

Hallenberg, M., Holm, J. & Johansson, D. 2008. 'Organization, Legitimation, Participation. State formation as a dynamic process – the Swedish example, c. 1523–1680.' *Scandinavian Journal of History,* Vol. 33 (3), pp. 247–268.

Harnesk, B. 2002. 'Den svenska modellens tidigmoderna rötter?' *Historisk tidskrift,* Vol. 2002 (1), pp. 78–90.

Harrison, D. 1996. *Medieval Space. The Extent of Microspatial Knowledge in Western Europe during the Middle Ages.* Lund University Press, Lund.

Henshall, N. 1992. *The Myth of Absolutism. Change & Continuity in Early Modern European Monarchy.* Longman, London and New York.

Herlin, I. 1996. 'Linjoilla ja linjojen takana. Historioitsijat sodassa.' In Ahtiainen, P. & Tervonen, J. (eds.) *Menneisyyden tutkijat ja metodien vartijat. Matka suomalaiseen historiankirjoitukseen*. The Finnish Historical Society, Helsinki, pp. 84–119.

Holm, J. 2007. *Konstruktionen av en stormakt. Kungamakt, skattebönder och statsbildning 1595–1640*. Stockholm University, Stockholm.

Ihse, C. 2005. *Präst, stånd och stat. Kung och kyrka i förhandling 1642–1686*. Stockholm University, Stockholm.

Jespersen, L. (ed.) 2000. *A Revolution from Above? The Power State of Sixteenth- and Seventeenth-Century Scandinavia*. Odense University Press, Odense.

Jokipii, M. 1956. *Suomen kreivi- ja vapaaherrakunnat*. Finnish Historical Society, Helsinki.

Juva, M. 1955. *Varsinais-Suomen seurakuntaelämää puhdasoppisuuden hallitsemina vuosisatoina. Varsinais-Suomen historia*. Vol. VII:3–4. Varsinais-Suomen historiantutkimusyhdistys, Turku.

Katajala, K. 1994. *Nälkäkapina. Veronvuokraus ja talonpoikainen vastarinta Karjalassa 1683–1697*. The Finnish Historical Society, Helsinki.

Lamberg, M. 2003. '1300-luvun suomalaisten tietoympäristöt.' In Ahonen, K. et al. (eds.) *Toivon historia*. Department of History and Ethnology, Jyväskylä, pp. 261–271.

Latour, B. 2005. *Reassembling the Social. An Introduction to Actor-Network Theory*. Oxford University Press, Oxford and New York.

Lennersand, M. 1999. *Rättvisans och allmogens beskyddare. Den absoluta staten, kommisionerna och tjänstemannen, ca 1680–1730*. Historiska Institutionen vid Uppsala Universitet, Uppsala.

Lerbom, J. 2003. *Mellan två riken. Integration, politisk kultur och förnationella identiteter på Gotland 1500–1700*. Nordic Academic Press, Uppsala.

Levi, G. 1992. *Aineeton perintö. Manaajapappi ja talonpoikaisyhteisö 1600-luvun Italiassa. L'eredità immateriale. Carriera di un esorcista nel Piemonte del Seicento*, translated by Kaisa Kinnunen and Elina Suolahti. Tutkijaliitto, Helsinki.

Melkersson, M. 1997. *Staten, ordningen och friheten. En studie av den styrande elitens syn på statens roll mellan stormaktstiden och 1800-talet*. Uppsala University, Uppsala.

Nenonen, M. 1992. *Noituus, taikuus ja noitavainot Ala-Satakunnan, Pohjois-Pohjanmaan ja Viipurin Karjalan maaseudulla vuosina 1620–1700*. The Finnish Historical Society, Helsinki.

Österberg, E. 1989. 'Bönder och centralmakt i det tidigmoderna Sverige. Konflikt – kompromiss – politisk kultur.' *Scandia*, Vol. 55 (1), pp. 73–95.

Österberg, E. 1992. 'Folklig mentalitet och statlig makt. Perspektiv på 1500- och 1600-talens Sverige.' *Scandia*, Vol. 58 (1), pp. 81–102.

Simonson, Ö. 1999. *Den lokala scenen. Torstuna härad som lokalsamhälle under 1600-talet*. Uppsala University, Uppsala.

Suvanto, S. 1986. 'Kylät ja niiden väki.' In Suvanto, S. & Niemelä, J. (eds.) *Punkalaitumen historia*, Vol. I. Punkalaitumen historiatoimikunta, Punkalaidun, pp. 51–90.

Viikki, R. 1973. *Suur-Huittisten historia*, Vol. II: *Punkalaitumen eroamisesta kunnallisen itsehallinnon alkuun n. 1639–1860*. Punkalaidun, Punkalaitumen historiatoimikunta.

PART V

RECONSTRUCTING BYGONE LANDSCAPES

CHAPTER 9

Landscapes of Power

Päivi Maaranen

Introduction

What is more impressive than the sight of the ruins of a medieval castle on a hilltop or the wide black roofs of stone churches on the shores of seas or inland lakes? These historical monuments still touch us and awaken our senses when we travel through present-day landscapes. They also evoked feelings in the past, although without written sources we can only guess something of those thoughts and visions. We should also consider those who planned and built such buildings. They would have had their own ideas and messages that they wanted their buildings to transmit to local people and passers-by. What were their intentions and how did those who designed and built such buildings exploit geographical features to achieve their aims?

Such questions challenge and encourage us to seek answers from different historical sources. Although many factors are connected to the study of the landscapes of the past, in this context the role of power in a medieval society is especially important. Here, I start from the dictionary definition of power as the ability to act or to affect something or somebody strongly.[1] In addition to the physical demonstration of power, there would also have been a need to affect the minds and activities of others. Because of the paucity of written medieval sources relating to such constructions in medieval Finland, we also need to consult other sources in our attempts to answer these questions. Thus, both archaeology and geography can play important roles in the research. Archaeological material allows us to fill in some of the gaps left by fragmentary written sources. Geographical methods enable us to identify the natural geographical features of the sites as well as help us to interpret the roles played by different elements of the landscape.

This study focuses on monuments within the landscape that can be

seen as expressions of authority, particularly sites of churches, fortifications and castles. The study attempts to examine three different areas of
inquiry. First, because the exact number of monument sites in Finland
has not been established, I have therefore attempted to compile details
about all known sites and gather together evidence that could provide
information about their character, age and use. Second, there has been
no specific discussion of these sites in the context of landscape and
thus this study examines the location of such sites in relation to natural
geographical features, different travel routes and landscape spaces. The
relationships between these sites and major settlement areas are also
explored. Third, I have sought to understand the role of these monuments from the perspective of medieval society and clarify whether they
played a part in interactions between people and the transmission of
messages from the authorities. However, I do not intend to critically
adjust existing interpretations of historical sources. My study merely
attempts to develop a multidisciplinary approach that combines historical, archaeological and geographical sources and methods.

One problem encountered during the study has been the landscape
itself. Unfortunately, we have very few pictorial sources that could provide some understanding of the Finnish medieval visual landscape.[2] The
analysis of later historical maps suggests that the agrarian landscape was
apparently open and mosaic-like, with plots or strips of small fields close
to villages. Larger meadows and woods surrounded these settlement centres, although woodlands close to settlements were less dense because of
felling and animal grazing. Larger forests and rocky areas, which used
to separate settled areas from each other, shrank as the agrarian settlement expanded. In addition, coastal landscapes and the sea were also
part of some people's 'activity spaces': many peasants had fishing and
trading connections around the Baltic Sea. The sea routes along the coast
increased the importance of the Finnish coast and archipelago.

Although the medieval agrarian landscape of southernmost Finland
differed in many ways from its current landscape, several existing elements
of the landscape do reveal something of the past. Many farms with fields
and pastures are located on medieval village sites and therefore provide
continuity with an agrarian way of life that has existed since the Middle Ages. In addition, medieval stone churches still stand in the middle
of villages and the ruins of medieval castles and other fortifications are
also visible. During the study, it became apparent that single elements of
the landscape were less important than their relationships with society.
Analysis of the data revealed that power was manifested differently by

secular and religious authorities. Whereas secular authorities engaged in controlling activities and were often distant from the people, religious authorities were located in the middle of settlements and the everyday activities of local society.

Power and the landscape

Power is connected to meanings attached to landscape and the ways in which people experience different spaces. This point of view originates in human cultural geography and its observation and differentiation of landscapes as social and cultural human environments. This perspective emphasizes the idea that those who experience the landscape also ascribe to it different collective and individual meanings. The values and meanings that are ascribed to landscapes are largely cultural agreements about what we can see, what we want to see and what we have to see.[3] Therefore, there is scope to study the messages and meanings that the landscape transmits from the past to the present day. From this point of view, the desired and intentional aspects and meanings of landscapes must be considered along with their concrete aspects and meanings.

Landscapes neither are inactive parts of the environment nor are they only experienced individually. Rather, landscapes reflect cultural beliefs, practices and technologies. They even reflect the coming together of members of society and can also exist socially. The social existence of landscape allows us to study landscapes as products of society and requires us to remember that landscapes are reproduced over time.[4] It is also important to understand that landscapes always have history attached to them and that we must, therefore, interpret landscapes from a historical point of view.[5] Thus, we can speak of a general history of landscape and a personal history that affect both the process of interpretation and the conclusions that emerge from this process. The conclusions drawn from this process are not absolutely 'true', but they can mirror something from the past mixed in with our present understanding. This already brings us very close to the idea that relics of the past play a double role: they help us to know and understand the past but also to bend it to our own uses.[6] This observation warns us to be cautious when presenting the results of our interpretation: we are not talking of the past as such, but rather we are placing the objects of our study in the given past. Thus, the landscape of power has connections to the experienced landscape, connections which allow us to interpret it based on our own experience. However, we cannot really know what people of the past felt or thought.

Some would also speak of the mind's deeper social intercourse with the landscape and even of the primitive relationship between mankind and nature.[7] This point of view reminds us that humans are not just objective and rational actors in the environment – they are feeling, thinking and experiencing creatures. Therefore, different man-made elements are in a process of continual and changing interaction with the landscape and the society that produces them. When people share a common understanding of certain values and experiences, they also seek to achieve these values and experiences even though they might not be very aware of their way of thinking. Simply making something together imbues the constructed object with common meaning. Therefore, when a society builds a monument that is meant not for private use but for public affairs, it is interesting to examine the motives behind the building project. If planners are aware of optional meanings that are associated, or should be associated, with their monuments, they will also try to create something that expresses those meanings that they view as most important.[8] Of course, because of society's necessarily limited resources, planners also have to balance practical, economic and ideological factors.[9]

Monuments such as churches and fortifications could be manifestations of many things, perhaps the most important being the exertion of power over a wider society and territory. From this point of view, such monuments present and clarify authority roles in the social system. Rulers who built monuments could express their authority over a geographical area beyond their immediate seat of power. In addition to demonstrating the importance of their role in social life, such rulers could also constitute societies through politically designed territories and control communication.[10] Thus, it seems that not only the type of the monument was important, but also its relationship to communication routes and spatial visibility. Tradition could also have an effect. However, if Finnish medieval society followed the general European trend of change, the whole system of communication would have undergone a transformation and old methods of interaction would have broken down. Through this social change, communities of kin were replaced by communities of place.[11] Communities of kin formed a society of rather small independent units spread over the land, in which interaction was largely controlled by the heads of kin. With the change from this kind of system to a society in which place was more important and social interaction was controlled in relation to the political system, the power of local authorities was transferred to the political authorities of the Church and state. In this context, monuments provided one way of organizing a changing society: they provided a reminder of the existence of the authority figure, even when he or she was not present.

An evaluation of medieval secular and religious power in the context of landscape should focus on the similarities and differences between these two kinds of power. One important meaning of the religious landscape could be the experience of sacredness.[12] Medieval texts, for example, give the impression that sacred landscapes were actively developed and that buildings could be both sacred centres and symbols that made Christianity visible in the landscape.[13] In addition, church buildings were symbols of a systematic organization that took care of members of the community.[14] This was in contrast to the role of secular authorities, which were merely concerned with controlling and getting benefit from the people. Thus, the symbols of secular power were perhaps more of a reference to the roles of maintaining internal order, taking care of economic redistribution and playing a part in military aggression.[15] In addition, they could underline the high social standing of the authorities.[16] One could almost claim that the state and the Church were ideological powers which took care of different parts of social life in medieval society. The Church looked after individuals in order to exert influence over their real lives, whereas the state took care of the cohesion of society in order to guarantee the continuance of kingdom.

Background, material and methods

This study of secular and religious power in the medieval landscape of southernmost Finland arose from an observation about the medieval church sites of Perniö (Sw. Bjärnå) and Karjaa (Sw. Karis). Both lie on the coast of Finland and were old historical districts long before the modern Finnish municipality system emerged. During the Middle Ages, the locations of the main churches of the Perniö region and the Karjaa region changed.[17] In both cases, the change of site seems to have been connected to changes in settlement. The church site appears to have been located in a central position in relation to the villages. This observation was developed into an idea that there might be more such cases which could be examined through the study of power and landscapes. Later, questions relating to church sites in general – their features, connections to travel routes as well as their role in the context of landscape – began to take precedence. Ideas about older church sites and the change of a main church site gradually appeared to be rather irrelevant. Instead, research revealed the existence of a variety of different church sites from different times and in various locations. From the perspective of landscape studies, the material began to provide the opportunity to study people and society in the context of the landscape. This perspective incorporates the idea that the landscape is a context for human activity and a space for interaction.[18] Not only was the church or fortification site itself of interest, but also the ways in which the construction and location of monuments could play a role in society.

As a result of expanding the core study questions, the research covered an area from Kemiönsaari (Sw. Kimitoön) to Virolahti (Sw. Vederlax) in southernmost Finland, including all districts in which a medieval stone church or ruins were located. In order to place them in a more appropriate social context, monument sites were considered within their historical districts rather than within present-day municipalities. Medieval sources and historical interpretations based on them in works of local history provided information about historical communes. Recent changes to the names and administrative borders of many historical communes presented some difficulties.[19] For this reason, older parish names and many old placenames have been used in preference to their newer counterparts.

As a whole, the study covers 71 church sites and 14 fortification sites (Appendices 1–3). Material relating to these sites is rather challenging from the perspective of source criticism. The researcher must accept that some interpretations can never gain firm ground but must stay as suppositions. A database compiled by the National Board of Antiquities,[20] various archive sources,[21] works of local history and other published archaeological and historical studies have provided information about these sites, as have historical maps. Certain Swedish maps from the late eighteenth century have played a particularly important role in geographical analyses because of their topographical accuracy and richness in placenames.[22] These maps were prepared for military purposes, which helps to explain the accuracy of natural geographical features, traffic routes and settlement sites. Moreover, the maps depict the general landscape before nineteenth-century changes in agriculture and the settlement system. In addition to these historical maps, modern digital maps have also proved important within the analysis of some sites and in providing the exact location of most sites.[23] Works of local history have also contributed to the study because they present both original historical sources and interpretations based on them. This study does not reinterpret original sources but tries to pursue a source-critical attitude to works of local history and acknowledge that the interpretations presented in such studies can affect discussions relating to church and fortification sites.[24] It was important to consult such works as part of the study in order to increase our understanding of historical contexts and the ways in which historians have approached the subject over the years.

Cross-comparison, reliability assessment and map analysis of the data were the main methods employed in the study. Cross-comparison involved studying original written sources and all existing historical interpretations of them. In this way, there was an attempt to test the reliability of an original source, as well as the plausibility of existing interpretations. The assessment of reliability connected to several stages of data handling, from the critical reading of archive sources and written sources to the assessment of data produced through map analysis. This method played an important role because it guaranteed that data and results were viewed critically throughout the research process. Map analysis provided specific information about sites: location, proximity to travel routes and points where travel routes crossed, geomorphologic relief and other formations, and visibility in the landscape. During the study, both cross-comparison and assessment of reliability prepared the data for the map analysis stage. Following the map analysis process, the data were then finally assessed before conclusions were formulated. In some cases, archaeological surveys provided additional information about the sites.

The choice of methods becomes more understandable when the source material is examined more closely. Lack of information, especially about church sites, presented a particular challenge. Medieval written sources relating to church sites were scarce or fragmentary and could sometimes only be connected to the sites through a process of interpretation. Historical interpretations could vary according to a particular historian's preferences and influences. In most cases there were no original sources; the only available sources were references to local traditions in works of local history. This resulted in problems in locating placenames and sites. Local traditions often mention placenames, but a name that had once been well known is not always necessarily known at all today. In some cases, it seems as though those who drew maps sometimes abandoned or changed names. Such exclusions or changes may have been connected to a cartographer's individual preferences or skills, or to more general changes in cartographical procedures.[25] Because of the problems associated with placenames, it was not possible to determine the precise location of all the church sites. As a result, our information about topography and other geographical features cannot be considered totally reliable.

Archaeological data presented various difficulties, largely connected to the number of surveyed sites and the quality of reports to be found in the archives. Many sites were not known to archaeologists and had not yet been surveyed. In several cases survey reports included documentation of the site, but these older reports were not as accurate as their modern counterparts. In addition, although there might be general information about sites, such reports failed to provide evidence that would enable accurate dating. In some cases, archaeological excavations had provided further knowledge of the site, but quality problems still remained with regard to reports and methods of older excavations. Sometimes no reports existed or existing material had not been researched to any useful degree.[26] In addition, in some cases a site that had existed during the nineteenth century had later vanished, which made reinterpretation rather difficult. All of these problems affected reliability. Although new surveys and excavations provided more accurate information, they could not entirely resolve such problems.

Analysis of natural geographical features and site locations provides us with data that describe sites more precisely: specific information relating to church and fortification sites, and an overall understanding of the site in a landscape space. In addition, the results of the analysis help us to consider the sites in the context of the landscape and, in this way, explore the relationships between such sites and past human activity and options of interaction. Each known site location was subjected to a process of map analysis, in which its location in relation to the coast, geomorphologic environments, special landforms and travel routes were recorded. In addition, visibility in the landscape and proximity to central settlement areas were also noted.

Whilst analysing the data severe weaknesses in the source materials and problems relating to the reliability of the results began to emerge. Thus, there will always be many unresolved questions about the number and distribution of medieval churches and chapels as well as accurate dating. Furthermore, some of the sites have been lost because of land use development and therefore survive only in the landscape of remembrance and as notes in the archives. The same challenges of accurate dating and even the destruction of archaeological structures also apply to fortifications. Those cases in which archaeological excavations have failed to uncover material that could help us to date a fortification, or even shed light on the functions of the assumed fortification site, are particularly challenging. However, despite all these problems, the study does provide some basis for interpretations relating to medieval landscapes of power in southernmost Finland. These interpretations largely present trends that can clarify something about medieval activity, spaces and ideas, thus raising new topics for general discussions of medieval phenomena.

Sites of churches and chapels

The study examined 19 sites of stone churches and 52 sites of other churches (Appendices 1 and 2), largely described in works of local history as medieval churches, 'sites for the first church' without medieval stone buildings, or 'very old church sites'. Of all the sites examined, stone churches have been perhaps the most intensely studied by researchers and there is a wealth of information about them.[27] Stone church construction within the study area largely dates back to the fifteenth century. Each parish in the area had its own stone church during the Middle Ages, which seems to suggest that all the churches that were planned were in fact built. However, not all of the churches were completed. In Virolahti and Kisko only the sacristies were constructed out of stone. There is also evidence that construction of the church in Vihti (Sw. Vichtis) was interrupted.[28]

The sites of churches constructed from materials other than stone have not been the focus of intense research and therefore offer both interesting and rather challenging research material. The lack of interest in other types of church sites seems understandable when we consider the uncertain sources and other problems discussed in some depth in the previous section. A closer examination of the other church sites reveals that there we can identify 12 'reliable' and 5 'fairly reliable' sites of churches or chapels. In these cases there is archaeological information or reasonably reliable notes that indicate some kind of religious use of the site. There are 18 'possible' church sites. This group forms a rather difficult study subject: there is no concrete evidence of religious use, but traditions or interpretations claim that these were church sites. In addition, there are some similarities between the locations of these possible sites and those of the reliable sites. Finally, there is a group of 17 'uncertain' sites located in unfavourable locations and based on sources whose reliability is questionable.

Only a few reliable sources can enable us to assess the age of the other church sites. For instance, stone foundations of buildings have been excavated in Kyrkön Kyrksundet ('church island church strait'), Kapell-backen ('chapel hill') and Hagnäs Kyrkogård ('Hagnäs church yard'). Stone foundations that seem to have later disappeared were apparently found in Kyrkstad ('church place'), Kyrkbacken ('church hill') and Tej-tom Malmgård ('Tejtom gravel manor'). Information about other stone structures, burial grounds or human bones has been obtained from many sites, including Bromarv Vanha kappeli ('Bromarv old chapel') and Kirkkomaan saari Kappelkangas ('churchyard island chapel heath') In addition, we also know something of the chapels of Kyminkartano (Sw. Kymmenegård), Vaalimaa and Raasepori (Sw. Raseborg), all of which later disappeared.

These sites are evenly distributed across the study area from the west to the east and from the archipelago to the inland. The only exception is the central part of the study area around the Helsinki region. No written sources or archaeological evidence indicate the existence of other types of church sites in this area. Loss of archaeological evidence may be connected to the development and ongoing expansion of the capital city.

Geographical analysis of the stone church sites reveals several interesting and characteristic features. In most cases, the site is situated on a plain or a plain on a ridge (79% of the analysed data) and often in marine relief (36%) or at the edge of a marine relief zone (47%). Visibility of the site in the context of landscape is largely good or very good (63%). Many sites are clearly inland sites (at least ten kilometres from the coast) (42%). However, a sea connection seems important: coastal sites (26%) and those close to the coast but separated from the shore by a broader land zone (32%) are more common. Most sites are located alongside the medieval Great Coastal Road or in its vicinity (63%), or alongside a route that leads to the Great Coastal Road (16%). Over a half of the sites (58%) can be found alongside a river or at the point where a tributary joins a lake. All the stone churches seem to be located at crossing points of different potential traffic routes. Only a minority of the sites (5%) are situated any real distance from a water route. It seems as though water routes played an important role in access to the sites.[29]

Geographical analysis of other church sites excluding very uncertain church sites also provides information about their characteristic features. Church sites are usually situated on an elevation (50% of the analysed data) or on a plain (48%) and most often in marine relief (39%) but are also found in polygenetic (28%) and glaciofluvial (25%) relief. In the majority of cases the visibility of the site in the context of the landscape is good or very good (69%).[30] Many sites are coastal (53%) or separated from the shore by a broader land zone (31%). A majority of sites are located close to the Great Coastal Road (55%), although only a few of them (11%) lie immediately alongside the road. In addition, a significant minority of sites lie on the shores of lakes or rivers (42%); the rest lie alongside sea routes (58%). This could be explained in part by the large number of sites in the archipelago. The crossing points of different travel routes would seem to be significant: over half of the sites (53%) are located at crossing points.

When the results of the analysis of the stone church sites and the other church sites are compared, some similarities and differences become apparent. In general, church sites are very visible in the landscape and most sites are coastal or close to the shore. Inland church sites are more likely to be stone church sites (42%) than other church sites (17%). Stone churches are more frequently located on plains; whereas other church sites can be found both on plains and elevations. This phenomenon may be connected to the fact that the construction of a stone church required more space or because larger scale religious activities took place at such sites. Further, it seems that proximity to the Great Coastal Road was more important for stone church sites (79%) than it was for other church sites (55%). Stone church sites are more likely to be located alongside rivers or lakes (58%); other church sites are more frequently found close to sea routes (58%). In general, proximity to the crossing points of water and land routes seems to have been significant for most church sites.

Sites of fortifications

Within the study area there are 23 different kinds of known fortification sites, of which 9 sites were excluded from the study because they are prehistoric. Prehistoric fortification sites would have been connected to a power system that must have differed in some ways from later systems. In addition, there are several sites in the study area that historians or archaeologists have assumed were fortification sites on the basis of placenames or natural features typical of fortified sites. These sites were also excluded from the study because of an absence of archaeological or historical evidence of their use as fortifications. In total, the study examined 14 known or suspected medieval fortification sites about which there were documents or other archaeological or historical evidence.

Seven of the studied fortification sites are hillforts: fortification structures consisting of more or less damaged stone and earth ramparts at the top or on the slopes of high, steep hills or rocks.[31] In some cases, the remains of stone foundations can be found on the hilltop and sometimes small outer baileys or moats on the slopes or lower hilltops. The small scale and perhaps the limited defensive role of the structures suggest that the steep slopes and height of hills were vitally important to their defence. Without excavations, the exact dating of individual hillforts is problematic, but the excavation of Vartiokylä ('guardian village') in Helsinki suggests that such sites could date back to the fourteenth century.

Five small castles form one subgroup of fortification sites. They are characterized by different kinds of earth ramparts and moats (with or without water) and, in some cases, outer baileys. In addition, the remains of building foundations can often be found in the middle of defensive structures. These fortifications do not resemble stone castles; they are merely a combination of hillfort structures and stone castle elements erected on hills or small rocks. Those who built such structures took advantage of suitable natural formations in the construction of the fortifications, and the defensive structures of these fortifications often follow natural topography. The various structures are largely visible and thus easy to study. These small castles appear to date back to the fourteenth century according to many archaeological excavations, such as those in Husholmen ('castle isle') and Junkarsborg ('nobleman's castle'). It is possible that some of these castles were built during the second half of the fourteenth century, when the king gave permission for the construction of fortifications.[32]

In addition, there are also the remains of a stone castle and another stone structure that is believed to have been a watchtower. The stone castle of Raasepori stands on a rock that was an island during the Middle Ages (Picture 2 see colour plate section 2, pp. 2–3). Raasepori Castle, once the seat of power in the Uusimaa (Sw. Nyland) region, consists of several stone structures. It seems that the stone castle itself was built no earlier than the end of the fourteenth century, but it is possible that there may have been some other kind of fortification on the site before this time.[33] Raasepori Castle, whose history is rather well known, was in use from the time of its construction until it was abandoned in the mid-sixteenth century. The watchtower in Horsbäck is more problematic. There is some archaeological evidence relating to the site, but we have very little information about the date of its construction or its historical role.

Geographical analysis of the fortification sites reveals that there are no significant differences in location between different fortification types. In general, most of the fortification sites can be found on or near the coast (64% of the analysed data). Half of the sites are located on capes and over a third on islands (36%) in marine or glasiogenic relief (79%). All the fortification sites could be easily reached by water routes, but only some of them (43%) seem to have a connection to the main land travel route, the Great Coastal Road. Most sites would have been found in the periphery of settlement centres (64%). In most cases visibility in the context of the landscape is moderate (57%); only just over a third of sites have good or very good visibility (38%). However, many of the sites are located at the border of two landscape spaces alongside water traffic routes and could not be avoided when travelling by water.

Elements of religious power

The study revealed various types of church sites, which can be divided into four groups according to location and construction materials. The first group includes all sites of existing stone churches or their remains. In many cases the stone church replaced a wooden church on the same site. Such sites are located in coastal as well as agrarian landscapes. The second group consists of a mass of different kinds of known or assumed inland church sites that may have served sites as for wooden churches. The third group includes known or assumed chapel sites in the maritime landscape, where they played a part in the lives of seafarers as well as the inhabitants of the archipelago. Finally, the fourth group consists of sites of known or assumed coastal chapels or small churches, which also seem to have played some kind of role in seafaring as well as coastal living.

In addition, during the study it became evident that there were a small number of local graveyards located on sites without church remains or any tradition as church sites (Appendix 2). These local graveyards were not the focus of this study but it seems possible that a thorough search could uncover more such sites. However, sources relating to the local graveyards are extremely scarce. Although archaeological excavations have obviously uncovered human bones as was the case in Kalmistonmäki ('graveyard hill'), hardly any material has been found which can help us to find out more about the sites themselves. It is possible that some of these local graveyards were in fact connected to chapels of which there are no longer any traces.

When the stone church sites were examined more closely, the supposition that they had been located in the centre of settlements was confirmed. The close proximity of churches to central settlements seems characteristic of church sites, particularly those located to the west of Porvoo. Although the case is somewhat different in the parish of Inkoo

(Sw. Ingå), this state of affairs could be explained by the important role that the sea played in settlement structure and means of livelihood. The church of Inkoo could thus serve both local people and seafarers because it was close to, or even alongside, an old medieval sea route.[34] The location of the church building on the sea shore could also explain the absence of chapels and local traditions relating to them in the archipelago off the Inkoo mainland. From Pernaja (Sw. Pernå) to the east, stone churches are found along the shore or at least on the same side of a settlement as the sea. This structure can perhaps be explained by the greater number of people living in and moving about the archipelago and coastal regions.

It is interesting that stone church sites are commonly situated either on or near the coast across the study area. However, some trends begin to emerge when we examine the age of church buildings in connection with proximity to the sea. It appears that stone churches were erected along the sea shores in the beginning of the fifteenth century, as was the case in Pernaja and Vehkalahti. In the mid-fifteenth century, the main building projects were connected to coastal zones and inland church sites. Later, at the end of the fifteenth and beginning of the sixteenth centuries, stone churches were built at the sea shore and inland, including Kisko, Inkoo, Lohja (Sw. Lojo) and Virolahti. It almost seems as though the newer stone churches filled the gaps in the whole system. A more detailed examination also reveals that stone churches were built slightly later in the old main settlement areas in the western part of the study area than was the case in the east between Karjaa and Helsinki (Sw. Helsingfors), construction of stone churches largely began somewhat later. Virolahti church, in the eastern part of the study area, is an exception to these clusters.

Significantly, stone church sites seem to be located close to what were the most important inland travel routes in medieval Finland: the Great Coastal Road, the Sea Road and the Old Porvoo Road. All of the stone church sites, except Lohja, Vihti, Kemiö (Sw. Kimito) and Kisko, are close to the Great Coastal Road and water route.[35] The Kemiö and Kisko sites seem to lie alongside smaller land routes that would have connected to the Great Coastal Road, but we cannot be sure that this was the case. In general, the church sites are characterized by the presence of several travel routes, including land routes and water routes. The case of Helsinki is interesting because the church site is located at the crossing point of the Vantaa River (Fi. Vantaanjoki; Sw. Vanda å), the Great Coastal Road and the Häme (Sw. Tavastland) Road. The situation in Porvoo is almost similar; its church site is close to the Great Coastal Road, the Old Porvoo Road and the mouth of the Porvoo River (Fi. Porvoonjoki; Sw. Borgå å).[36]

This connection between the stone church sites and major land routes is interesting. It raises questions about the importance of land routes in relation to the church sites in general. Did pre-existing land routes affect the choice of church sites or did the presence and importance of churches dictate the course of land routes? The history of the Great Coastal Road may shed at least some light on these issues. The Great Coastal Road is believed to be rather old, perhaps even dating back to the end of the thirteenth century, long before the first stone churches were built. The course of the road changed to some extent over the decades and summer routes sometimes differed from those followed in the winter.[37] The age and ongoing variation of the route suggests that perhaps church sites did not have to lie exactly alongside important roads but that sites should have ideally been close to major land routes. In fact ease of access to the church site by *both* land and water routes may have been a more important factor than absolute proximity to a major land route. However, great land routes may have been important to the process of constructing stone churches in Lohja, Vihti and Kisko. They were amongst the last stone churches constructed in the area and were some distance away from the Great Coastal Road.

Many church sites are believed to pre-date the stone church sites, at least in local traditions or even in scholarly works of local history. However, the results of the study suggest that some of these 'older' sites were in fact in use at the same time as the stone church sites – some are still in use today. Therefore, it appears that many existing ideas about the older sites or the sites of a first church are misleading. These older sites appear to be more independent church sites, whose role in religious activities had weakened. It is also possible that some of those sites traditionally considered to be older sites might, in reality, have been places reserved for church building or sites where churches were planned but never built.[38] Several of these 'church sites' may also have been retrospectively named in local traditions as sites of earlier churches.

The change of the main church site in Karjaa (Picture 3 see colour plate section 2, pp. 2–3) and Perniö is an interesting process, and one which may have taken place in Lohja. According to local tradition, Kyrkstad ('church town or church place') was an old church site. Indeed, the site is a very favourable location for a church building: it is clearly visible and was situated alongside the Sea Road and near the Great Coastal

Road. In addition, it is close to a supposed trading place in Virkkala (Sw. Virkby) and there is easy access to the site by water routes along Lake Lohja (Lohjanjärvi (Fi. Lohjanjärvi; Sw. Lojo träsk).[39] Old regional placenames such as Kirkkoniemi ('church cape') and Gerknäs ('church cape') seem to imply that these locations were associated with religious meanings and functions. Furthermore, we also have archaeological notes about the old stone foundation of the Kyrkstad ('church place').[40]

When viewed in a wider context, the Kyrkstad site would have been part of a chain of church sites that ran alongside the Great Coastal Road from Perniö via Tenhola (Sw. Tenala), Pohja (Sw. Pojo), Karjaa and Siuntio (Sw. Sjundeå) to Kirkkonummi (Sw. Kyrkslätt; literally 'church moor'). Other possible church sites that could be connected to changes of the main church sites include Espoo manor (Fi. Espoon kartano, Sw. Esbo gård) Kapellängen ('chapel meadow'), Norrkulla Kyrkbacken ('north mound church hill') and Tejtom Malmgård ('Tejtom gravel manor'). The latter may have been a church site of a great manor, which could connect it to the earliest stage of church building.[41] During that period, manor owners who were Christians, or who wanted to present themselves as such, built churches on their estates in order to demonstrate their important role in society.[42]

Chapels in the maritime landscape also emerged as an interesting group of religious sites. They are located on islands opposite the mainland or the outer border of an archipelago connected to the mainland. Therefore, the chapels largely served those who lived, worked and travelled in the seascape. There is evidence that some of these chapel sites were in use during the Middle Ages and it seems that they were connected to sailing routes.[43] In addition, links with trading sites may have influenced the location and building of chapels, as seems to have been the case in Kyrkön Kyrksundet ('church island church strait'). Some of the sea chapel sites, especially on the western part of the research area, clearly seem to have been connected to the sea travel routes that led seafarers to Reval, present-day Tallinn. There have been some problems ascertaining the age of many sites: historical sources suggest that most can be traced back to the seventeenth century, but local traditions and works of local history maintain that some sites were in use in the Middle Ages.

Sites of chapels or small churches in the coastal zone form a challenging and indefinite group. Some are known from historical sources and existed in the real world, but most appear only as stories within local tradition. The sites are located some distance from the stone churches of the region, mainly in the labyrinthine coastal zone and sometimes alongside rivers close to the sea. There is some reliable evidence about Kapellbacka ('chapel hill'); Kymenkartano, Vehkalahti, Vaalimaa, Virolahti and Raasepori. The site at Raasepori may have been connected to the castle of Raasepori, whereas Kapellbacka and Kymenkartano seem to have been manor chapels. The graveyard and chapel in Östersundom, also belonged to a manor, at least at a later date, but it is unclear whether the Östersundom site was in use during the Middle Ages. The ages and even the exact locations of several sites in this group are unclear. The coastal chapels could have served both seafarers and coastal people. However, they seem to have somehow lost their meaning and have largely vanished from the landscape. Perhaps the chapels were located in peripheral areas that later proved to be of little interest to either local people or seafarers.

In general, the large number of church sites in the study area seems to mirror some kind of functional system in time and space. It appears that there was a regional main church site and sites of local wooden village churches or chapels that were in use earlier, at the same time or later than the main church site. Sometimes the role of the church site seems to have changed, as was the case in Perniö. In other cases it seems that a wooden church had existed on the stone church site long before the stone building was erected. This process suggests that some sites of later medieval main churches might have originally been village church sites and that, with the growth of the settlement, the main church was placed permanently in the middle of the villages. In some cases, the main church site seems to have maintained its functional leading role throughout the Middle Ages. This seems to hold true especially for coastal stone church sites. Churches have perhaps had a wider role than merely providing religious services for the local population. Of course, the process of transformation from a village church to a main church must also have coincided with the complicated development from villages to parishes.

Taken as a whole, the sites of stone churches, sea chapels and coastal chapels seem to form a network-like system from the archipelago to the inland areas across the study area. From Porvoo to the east, the network connects to the seascape covering the archipelago and coastal zone; whilst from Sipoo (Sw. Sibbo) to the west, the network connects both to the seascape and to the agrarian landscape covering the inland area. The Karjaa region is a minor exception: there are no known sea chapels on the archipelago in front of the mainland and only the stone church of Inkoo and the chapel of Raasepori are found in the coastal area. We are also unaware of any sea chapels on the archipelagos of Helsinki and Sipoo. In some respects, this absence of sea chapels may be connected to the different character of the archipelago. Furthermore, the archipelago opposite the Helsinki mainland played a part in intensive land use activities during the eighteenth and nineteenth centuries, and it is therefore possible that the remains of earlier land use may have disappeared for ever.

Monuments of secular power

Fortification sites within the study area are less numerous than church sites, but they are still important to an analysis of power and landscape.[44] The various sites of hillforts, small castles, a stone castle and a watchtower seem to share surprisingly similar features. They are located in largely peripheral areas and close to the sea. In addition, ease of access via water routes and limited access from the main medieval land routes raise issues about the meaning and roles of the fortifications. Many sites were only moderately visible in the context of the landscape, but a number of the secular sites were located on a border of two landscape spaces alongside the water routes and thus guarded two spaces.

The fortification sites were not easy to reach, even though access via water routes was guaranteed. Most of the fortifications lie on capes or islands surrounded by water, and submerged wooden defence systems were used to prevent unwanted landings. This defended position suggests that security was as important as accessibility and that visibility did not play such an important role. In addition, many fortifications lay alongside the water routes that led to central settlement areas and only attracted notice when one passed by them. The fortification thus guarded and controlled activities and watched over important areas. Visibility in the space was less important than seeing the landscape and those who were active in it.

The most interesting feature was the limited visibility of the stone castle of Raasepori compared to the other fortification sites. This castle was located alongside the traffic route but could not be seen from a distance, even though it was the administrative centre of a larger region. Closer inspection revealed other explanations for its distance from the settlement centre and the coast. It appears that Raasepori was not a single fortification that controlled those travelling along the water route but was a defensive site that also had connections with trading activities. Some sources even suggest that there was town near the castle, but to date the character of the trading site has not been established. The importance and role of the castle seem to have been strongly connected to the Baltic Sea and the activities of merchants and peasants in Reval, a large trading centre.[45]

Thus, the study revealed the existence of some kinds of power complexes that included a church site and a fortification or a trading centre. The first type of complex consisted of a fortification and a church site, as was the case in Siuntio and possibly Karjaa. In Siuntio a church site and what may have been a medieval fortification are located side by side in the same spot on a border of the landscape space. In addition, a medieval manor, Suitia (Sw. Suidja slott), can be found on the opposite border of the same space. In Karjaa a possible church site on the north eastern part of Lake Läppträsket lies in the same region as a medieval fortification. The sites are close to one another on the borders of the landscape space. In addition, another possible medieval fortification lies a little further away on the shores of the same lake. The power complexes of Siuntio and Karjaa seem, in some ways, to have been broadly connected to developing settlement of the area: the fortifications are hillforts and the church sites might be rather old.

The second type of complex is that of a fortification, a trading place and a church site. The fortification, church site and trading place in Vehkalahti lie relatively close to each other on the borders of the same coastal space. The fortification lies at the mouth of a former sea bay, and the trading place and the church site on the shores of the bay. The type of the fortification is not clear, but it could even be a small castle.[46] A similar kind of complex can also be seen in Husholmen ('castle isle'), where a small castle and a trading place are located in the same landscape space. The trading place has been in use since at least the sixteenth century, but little is known about it before this time.[47]

In Porvoo the church site, fortification site and trading place which later received the privileges of a medieval town are close to one another.[48] All lie on a large geological formation at the border of two landscape spaces. The power complex of Raasepori is made up of a castle, a trading place and a chapel. The three sites are dispersed on small rocks in roughly the middle of the same space. The complexes of Porvoo and Raasepori exhibit similar features and differ from other complexes. Both were connected to town-like contexts and it is possible to date both back quite accurately to at least the end of the fourteenth century. Additionally, both complexes include quite remarkable monuments: the largest of the small castles lies in Porvoo and the only stone castle in Raasepori.

The number of power complexes is too small to allow more general conclusions to be drawn about them. It seems that they were clearly connected to important trading places and perhaps date back largely to the end of the fourteenth century. Interestingly, the combinations of monuments that form the power complexes include monuments of secular and religious power in the same landscape context. Some complexes form clusters around a central point of the same space, but other complexes are dispersed so that the monuments lie on different borders of the space. This seems to be largely connected to the particular geographical features of the area. The complexes appear to be extremely promising for further study but unfortunately there is a significant problem. In most cases it is extremely difficult to accurately ascertain the age of different monuments because of a lack of excavation results and historical written sources. Therefore, this discussion of power complexes is more like shifting the matter than stamping the facts.

Conclusion

Research of the analysed data and other study material provides a glimpse of the past and raises a number of ideas. The church sites generally differed from the fortification sites in many ways. In part, this appears to be connected to the messages transmitted by the monuments and the intended recipients of such messages. The site of a monument that served as manifestation of power to local people could be different from one whose demonstration of power was directed largely at passers-by. A monument that was intended to transmit messages to different groups would require a site that was visible to all of those groups. The monuments studied seem to have been impressive symbols, whether located in the central settlement areas or in the peripheries.

Many factors seem to have been important when selecting church sites. Relationship with settlement and other important activities of daily life seem to have been very important considerations.[49] In addition, the site had to be easily accessible, both for the congregation and, initially, for those who built the church. It seems that the visibility of the church building was also rather important: in most cases church buildings could be easily seen from a distance. This visibility seems to correlate with the value of the monument as some kind of symbol of religious power. This function appears to be very plausible if one accepts John Howe's assertion that during the Middle Ages there were attempts to mould more impressive religious landscapes.[50] The topography and soil of the site would also have been significant: such factors were of great importance when establishing burial grounds and could also affect building options.

Both the fortifications and the churches were tools for many different activities, but the fortifications played less of a role in everyday life than did the churches. The peripheral locations and moderate visibility of the fortifications seem to suggest that, unlike the Catholic Church, the secular authorities did not need to be visually present in everyday life. The physical and even psychological distance between local people and the secular authorities could, in fact, underline their controlling role. Secular authority seemed to be more active in townscapes in which non-local people were also present. This active role in relation to those who move from one place to another tends to be of importance for secular authorities.

The net-like system of church sites in the area suggests that those who travelled would inevitably notice church buildings. Therefore, churches and those meanings connected to them were continuously in the minds of everyone. Monuments were more prominent in the landscape of religious power on land because the stone churches of the agrarian open spaces were strikingly visible, with their larger size and dark-and-white colouring. Church buildings as monuments of the seascape were smaller in scale but perhaps, with the backdrop of the open sea, just as striking in their own way. In general, it seems that the Church wanted to remind everyone of its active role in everyday life.

The church sites dispersed over the study area seem to guarantee a very effective communication system that could have reached various groups and provided a physical reminder of the existence of religious power. This also encourages us to consider whether the stone church sites in particular might have mirrored the territory of a strong and established religious culture extensively in Finland. The stone churches were monuments of power that were visible and accessible and therefore formed permanent markers of the Catholic religion. In this way, Finland was connected to the larger European cultural circle of the Catholic Church. This interpretation gains strength from Markus Hiekkanen's assertion that during the fifteenth century the Church actively tried to influence the elite in Finland in order to launch stone church building projects.[51] Inspiration for this most likely came from northern Germany, where church building projects had already begun. Moreover, Finnish church art was influenced by that of the German-speaking world. During the fifteenth century, several members of the Finnish Catholic clergy studied in Germany, where they may have been influenced by the religious culture they encountered. It seems that strong and ongoing trading connections with Germany also played a role in the process. The ideas presented by Markus Hiekkanen provide general support for the notion that stone churches were held in particularly high esteem by Finnish representatives of the Church and that such building projects provided an important connection to European religious culture.

A church building must have awakened different images and ideas in the minds of those who observed them. Those who received the messages transmitted by the monument might even have had certain expectations of sacred or religious sites.[52] However, medieval travellers who came from other Catholic areas might have felt a sense of continuity and safety despite being foreigners. In addition, the building demonstrated that the local society was able to build and maintain a proper monument for the Church. Local people may have experienced togetherness in cultural and traditional matters, perhaps raising increasing engagement and giving strength to the local community. Local and non-local people alike might have had feelings of solidarity as members of the larger community of the Church. On an individual level, the church building would have evoked feelings about personal history and perhaps awoken the remembrance of mercy, hope, relief or fear. The Catholic Church was not just a guardian of souls: it also played an important role in society by taking care of the poor and the sick.

The net-like system of church sites and the power that it demonstrated was a part of a larger European system of religious culture. Under this system, societies interpreted and understood particular messages in rather similar ways. The manifestation of power strengthened the role of the Church in society, created a common identity for the community and bound members of the group together. The Church authorities in Finland appear to have had clear views about external markers of religious culture and commonly approved ways of transmitting religious messages. This was apparent in their systematic and planned construction of stone churches in certain locations. It seems that church buildings had several meanings, which were connected both to the religious culture and to the roles played by different social actors within that culture.

In conclusion, it seems that during the Middle Ages religious power was largely manifested in the central settlement areas and at the crossroads of important routes. Secular authorities, on the other hand, could manifest their power in the periphery. In addition, ways of manifesting one's power seem to have changed over time. It is possible that during the earlier period, when estate owners built their churches, secular and religious authorities strengthened each other. Later, the Church seems to have manifested its power through several village churches; whereas secular authorities built smaller fortifications. At this time castles started to take on a major role in the manifestation of secular power. The separation of religious and secular authorities may have contributed to the Church's decision to construct highly visible stone buildings.[53] The strengthening of the secular authorities led to a situation in which the Church also began to transmit messages of secular power. By bolstering secular power, the Church was able to strengthen its own role in society.[54] This role as a messenger of secular power was established during the sixteenth century when the Church lost much of its power as a result of the Reformation. Secular rulers gained a leading role in society, and during that time the religious and secular worlds of ordinary people began to change dramatically.

Notes

1 *Oxford English Dictionary.* Cf. Heidinga 1999, pp. 409–411.
2 For the main features of the Finnish Middle Ages, see, for example, Vahtola, 1993, pp. 188–194.
3 Raivo 1996, pp. 15–25, 281, 293–294.
4 Crang 1998, pp. 15–17.
5 Howe 2002, p. 92.
6 Lowenthal 1998, pp. xv, 2–4.
7 Porteus 1990, p. 8.
8 Louekari 2006, p. 22.
9 McMann 2000 (1994), p. 344.
10 Cf. Dodghson 1987, pp. 131, 138, 163.
11 Dodghson 1987, pp. 163–164; Fabech 1999, pp. 457–458.
12 Raivo 1996, p. 290.
13 Howe 2002, pp. 208–210, 214–215.
14 Johnson 2007, p. 133.
15 Mann 1997, pp. 67, 79.
16 Cf. Mileson 2007, pp. 11–26.
17 Maaranen 1997, pp. 17–26; Maaranen 2004.
18 Cf. Porteus 1990, 5–8; Crang, 1998, 15–17.
19 Because of the presence of a Swedish-speaking population, many Finnish places have both Finnish and Swedish names, sometimes in mixed and contaminated forms.
20 For example, Kulttuuriympäristö rekisteriportaali (a database of Finnish cultural heritage compiled by the National Board of Antiquities) <http://kulttuuriympar-isto.nba.fi/netsovellus/rekisteriportaali/portti/default.aspx>.
21 Except in some rare cases, Finnish archaeological studies do not provide references of archaeological archive sources. This article follows the Finnish tradition. Information about survey and excavation reports is often listed in the database of National Board of Antiquities.
22 These detailed maps, called *recognsceringskartor* in Swedish, are preserved at the Swedish Military Archives in Stockholm, but the maps depicting southern Finland

have been published in Alanen & Kepsu, *Kuninkaan kartasto Suomesta 1776–1805. Konungens kartverk från Finland*, The Finnish Literature Society, Helsinki, 1989.

23 See, for example, Kansalaisen Karttapaikka (a database of maps and aerial photographs by the National Land Survey of Finland) <http://kansalaisen.karttapaikka. fi/kartanhaku/osoitehaku.html?lang=FI>.

24 For more on this subject, see Maaranen 2007, pp. 35–45.

25 See, for example, Strang 2000, pp. 14–17.

26 During the process of writing this chapter, it emerged that archaeological material about the assumed church site Porvoo (Sw. Borgå) Sandholmen was held by the National Board of Antiquities. The material, which included iron nails with imprints of wood and human bones, had been found about 20 years ago but had not been studied. I surveyed the site immediately but unfortunately it had been almost totally destroyed by a development project and any further archaeological evidence had been lost.

27 For more on this subject see, for example, Hiekkanen 1994.

28 Hiekkanen 1994, pp. 250–254. Dating of stone churches in this study follows Hiekkanen, who has published a thorough analysis of these churches. See also Hiekkanen 2007.

29 According to Ilkka Leskelä water routes may have played an important role in the transportation of building materials, especially to the stone church sites. Ilkka Leskelä, in general conversation at the Dies Medievales conference in Tampere, Finland, 12 October 2008.

30 Visibility in the context of the landscape refers to the distance at which an object could be clearly discerned. Visibility on land was estimated in most cases from historical maps in relation to open landscape of fields, pastures and lakes. Visibility in maritime landscapes was also estimated with reference to historical maps in relation to open sea and islands. Woody and rocky areas as well as other high elevations were largely interpreted as barriers. When necessary, the accuracy of topographical information was ensured by also consulting modern maps.

31 For more on Finnish hillforts, see Taavitsainen 1990.

32 The small castle of Porvoo, Linnamäki, is discussed, for example, in Gardberg 1996, pp. 164–167.

33 Kerkkonen 1952, p. 120.

34 A medieval source describes an old travel route alongside the Swedish eastern and Finnish southern coast. For more on the subject, see, for example, Gallén 1993.

35 For more on the Sea Road, see Masonen 1999, pp. 103–106.

36 For more on the Old Porvoo Road, see Masonen 1999, pp. 106–108.

37 For more on the Great Coastal Road, see Viertola 1974, pp. 36–40; Salminen 1999, pp. 68–69.

38 Ylikangas 1973, pp. 90–96.

39 Rein 1944, p. 38.

40 Rein 1944, p. 26; Ylikangas 1973, pp. 92, 105.

41 Cf. Haggrén 2005, pp. 12–26.

42 Angler 1995, pp. 15, 183.

43 Nikula 1938, pp. 30–31.

44 For more on the functions of a medieval fortification, see, for example, Creighton 2002 (reprint 2005), pp. 1–5, 223.

45 For more on this subject, see, for example, Maaranen 2005, pp. 81–104.

46 Rosén 1936, pp. 4, 135–136, 273–274.
47 Selén 1996, p. 41.
48 See, for example, Gardberg 1996, pp. 172–176.
49 Liepe 1986, pp. 174–175.
50 Howe 2002, pp. 201, 215.
51 Markus Hiekkanen, Master builders and élite of the church. An overall plan behind the stone churches of the Diocese of Turku (Finland), a presentation at the Dies Medievales conference, Tampere, Finland, 11–12 October 2008.
52 Compare Raivo 1996, pp. 293–294; Howe 2002, p. 217.
53 Dodghson 1987, pp. 131, 138.
54 A short discussion with Christian Krötzl about the role of the Church in the transmission of messages from the secular authorities to the common people at the Dies Medievales conference, Tampere, Finland, 12 October 2008.

Bibliography

Primary sources

Alanen, T. & Kepsu, S. 1989. *Kuninkaan kartasto Suomesta 1776–1805. Konungens kartverk från Finland.* Helsinki, The Finnish Literature Society.
Kansalaisen Karttapaikka (A database of maps and aerial photographs by the National Land Survey of Finland). URL: <http://kansalaisen.karttapaikka.fi/>.
Kulttuuriympäristö-rekisteriportaali (A database of Finnish cultural heritage compiled by the National Board of Antiquities). URL: <http://kulttuuriymparisto.nba.fi/ >.
Oxford English Dictionary. URL: <http://www.oed.com/>.

Literature

Allardt, A. 1925. *Borgå Sockens historia*, Vol. I: *Till freden i Nystad.* Söderström, Helsinki.
Angler, M. 1995. *Från kristnande till sockenbildning i Skåne.* University of Lund, Lund.
Antell, K. 1956. *Pernå Socknens Historia*, Vol. I: *Tiden till år 1700.* The Municipality of Pernaja, Pernaja.
Antin, A.1997. *Luonnollisesti Artjärvi. Pitäjäkirja.* The Municipality of Artjärvi, Artjärvi.
Anttila, T. A. 1936. 'Vehkalahden kirkko.' In Kivenoja, Y., Lonka J. & Suikkanen, K. (eds.) *Vehkalahti. 600-vuotisjuhlan muistojulkaisu 8–9. VIII.1936.* Hamina, Maaseudun kirjapaino-osakeyhtiö, pp. 5–33.
Asplund, H. 1997. 'Kemiön suurpitäjän esihistoria.' In Suistoranta, K. & Asplund, H. *Kemiön suurpitäjän historia*, Vol. I. Sagalundin museon kuntayhtymä, Tammisaari, pp. 213–282.
Backmann, S. & Ihrcke-Åberg, I. 2003. *Det gamla Kyrkslätt.* Kyrkslätts hembygdsförening, Kirkkonummi.
von Born, E. 1949. *Pernåboken.* Söderström, Helsinki.
Brenner, A. 1936a. 'Namnet Ingå.' In Brenner, A. et al. *Ingå Fagervik Deggerby. En västnyländsk bygdekrönika*, Vol. I. The Municipality of Inkoo, Inkoo, pp. 37–39.
Brenner, A. 1936b. 'Prästerskapet.' In Brenner, A. et al. *Ingå Fagervik Deggerby. En västnyländsk bygdekrönika*, Vol. I. The Municipality of Inkoo, Inkoo, pp. 74–115.
Brenner, A. 1953. *Sjundeå sockens historia*, Vol. I. Hagö tryckeriaktiebolag, Hangö.
Crang, M. 1998. *Cultural Geography.* Routledge, London.

Creighton, O. H. 2002. *Castles and Landscapes. Power, Community and Fortification in Medieval England.* Equinox, London.

Dodghson, R. A. 1987. *The European Past. Social Evolution and Spatial order.* Macmillan, Basingstoke.

Fabech, C. 1999. 'Centrality in sites and landscapes.' In Fabech, C. & Ringtved, J. (eds.) *Settelement and Landscape. Proceedings of a conference in Århus, Denmark, May 4–7 1998,* Jutland Archaeological Society & Aarhus University Press, Århus, pp. 455–471.

Favorin, M. 1986. *Siuntion historia* I. The Municipality of Siuntio, Siuntio.

Fleege, U. A. & Rosberg, J. E. 1901. *Kyrkslätt socken. Dess natur, utveckling och historia,* Vol. II: *Kultur och utveckling.* Helsinki.

Forsén, B. & Moisanen, J. 1993. 'Svartån och den tidiga bebyggelsen runt denna.' *Finskt Museum,* Vol. 100, pp. 26–49.

Gallén, J. 1993. *Det Danska Itinerariet. Franciskansk expansionstrategi i Östersjön.* The Swedish Literature Society in Finland, Helsinki.

Gardberg, C. J. 1996. 'Medeltiden och 1500-talet.' In Edgren, T. & Gardberg. C. J. *Borgå stads historia,* Vol. I: *Borgåtraktens förhistoria, medeltiden och 1500-talet.* The Town of Porvoo, Porvoo, pp. 131–326.

Gardberg, J. 1981 (1944a). 'Bygden och folket.' In Nikander, G. (ed.) *Kimitöbygdens historia,* Vol. I. Faksimiltryck ur Kimitöbygdens historia, Vols. I–II. Sagalunds hembygdsmuseum & kommunalförbund, Tammisaari, pp. 27–62.

Gardberg, J. 1982 (1944b). 'Prästerskapet och det kyrkliga livet.' In Nikander, G. (ed.) *Kimitöbygdens historia,* Vol. I. Faksimiltryck ur Kimitöbygdens historia, Vols. I–II. Sagalunds hembygdsmuseum & kommunalförbund, Tammisaari, pp. 195–230.

Gardberg, J. 1970. *Karjaa ennen ja nyt.* Translated by V. Walin. Karjaan kotiseutulautakunta, Karjaa.

Haggrén, G. 2005. 'Moisio – kartano – kirkko. Suurtalot ja kristinuskon juurtuminen varsinaiseen Suomeen.' *SKAS* (1), pp. 12–26.

af Hällström, O. 1957. *Karis socken från forntiden till våra dagar,* Vol. IV: Karis och Svartå kyrkor. The Municipality and the Congregation of Karjaa, Karjaa.

af Hällström, Olof. 1964. 'Pitäjän kirkko.' In Edeman, N. et al. *Pohjan pitäjän historia osa* I. Translated by A. Haikonen, A. Haikonen & P. Linkola. The Municipality of Pohja, Pohja, pp. 159–247.

Hedengren, J. 1898. *Malmgård egendom. Pernå socken. Anteckningar till godsets historia.* Lovisa.

Heidinga, A. 1999. 'Transformations in the Landscapes of Power. Some Preliminary Reflections.' In Fabech, C. & Ringtved, J. (eds.) *Settelement and Landscape. Proceedings of a conference in Århus, Denmark, May 4–7 1998.* Jutland Archaeological Society & Aarhus University Press, Århus, pp. 409–411.

Hiekkanen, M. 1981. *Keskiajan kaupungit,* Vol. I: *Porvoo.* The National Board of Antiquities, Helsinki.

Hiekkanen, M. 1994. *The Stone Churches of the Medieval Diocese of Turku. A Systematic Classification and Chronology.* The Finnish Antiquarian Society, Helsinki.

Hiekkanen, M. 2007. *Suomen keskiajan kivikirkot.* The Finnish Literature Society, Helsinki.

Howe, J. 2002. 'Creating Symbolic Landscapes. Medieval Development of Sacred Space.' In Howe, J. & Wolfe, M. (eds.) *Inventing Medieval Landscapes. Senses of Place in Western Europe.* University Press of Florida, Gainesville, pp. 208–223.

Howe, N. 2002. 'The Landscape of Anglo-Saxon England: Inherited, Invented, Imagined.' In Howe, J. & Wolfe, M. (eds.) *Inventing Medieval Landscapes. Senses of Place in Western Europe.* University Press of Florida, Gainesville, pp. 91–112.

Hultin, H. 1927. *Pyhtään pitäjän historia.* Translated by J. Vasenius. Helsinki.

Johnson, M. 2007. *Ideas of landscape.* Blackwell, Oxford.

Kaukiainen, Y. 1970. *Virolahden historia,* Vol. I: *1850-luvulle.* The Municipality of Virolahti, Virolahti.

Kerkkonen, G. 1952. *Karis socken från forntiden till våra dagar,* Vol. III: *Medeltiden.* The Municipality and the Congregation of Karjaa, Karjaa.

Knaapinen, M. A. 1930. 'Historiallinen osa.' In Salonen-Salmo, H. & Kaapinen, M. A. *Perniön pitäjä.* Yhdistys 'Perniö tunnetuksi', Turku, pp. 71–478.

Korhonen, M. 1984. *Vehkalahden pitäjän historia,* Vol. II: *Yhteiskunnallisesta kehityksestä 1600-lubulla sekä maakirjakantatilojen synty.* The Municipality of Vehkalahti, Vehkalahti.

Liepe, A. 1986. 'Kyrka i gränsbygd. Tidigmedeltida kyrkobyggandet i Södra Värend.' In Andrén, A. (ed.) *Medeltiden och arkeologin. Festskrift till Erik Cinthio.* University of Lund, Lund, pp. 171–182.

Lindberg, J. 1930. Församlingen, kyrkan och prästerskapet. In Jansson, A. (ed.) *Kyrkslätt Förr och Nu. Till 600-årsfesten.* Kyrkslätts hembygdförening, Kirkkonummi, pp. 279–400.

Litzen, V. 1980. 'Perniön varhaisempi historia.' In Salmo, H. & Litzen, V. *Perniön historia.* The Municipality of Perniö, Perniö, pp. 111–311.

Louekari, L. 2006. *Metsän arkkitehtuuri.* University of Oulu, Oulu.

Lowenthal, D. 1998. *The Heritage Crusade and the Spoils of History.* Cambridge University Press, Cambridge.

Luoto, R. T. A. 2001. *Espoon aikakirjat. Espoolaiselämää kivikaudesta nykypäiviin.* Karisto, Hämeenlinna.

Maaranen, P. 1997. 'Perniön kulttuurimaisema esihistoriallisella ja keskiaikana.' In Niukkanen, M. (ed.) *Perniö. Kuninkaan ja kartanoiden pitäjä.* University of Helsinki, Helsinki, 1997, pp. 17–26.

Maaranen, P. 2004. 'Hengellisen ja maallisen vallan manifestoitumisesta keskiajan maisemassa.' *Ennen & Nyt,* Vol. 4 (4). URL: <http://www.ennenjanyt.net/4-04/maaranen.html>.

Maaranen, P. 2005. 'Seascape as Multicultural Space. Medieval Seafarers on the Shores of Western Uusimaa.' In Lehti, M. (ed.) *The Baltic Sea as a Multicultural World. Sea, Region and Peoples.* Berliner Wissenschafts-Verlag, Berlin, pp. 81–104.

Maaranen, P. 2007. 'Vanhaa ja uutta historiaa. Joitakin huomioita paikallishistorian julkaisujen käyttämisestä maisematutkimuksen lähdeaineistona.' *Muinaistutkija* 2007 (3), pp. 35–45.

Mann, M. 1997 (1984). 'The Autonomous Power of the State.' In Angnew, J. (ed.) *Political Geography. A Reader.* Arnold, London, pp. 58–80.

Masonen, J. 1999. 'Uudenmaan meritiet.' In Mauranen, T. (ed.) *Maata, jäätä, kulkijoita. Tiet, liikenne ja yhteiskunta ennen vuotta 1860.* Edita, Helsinki, pp. 103–106.

McMann, J. 2000 (1994). 'Forms of Power. Dimensions of an Irish Megalith Landscape.' In Stoddart, S. (ed.), *Landscapes from Antiquity,* Cambridge Antiquity Publications, Cambridge, pp. 335–356.

Mileson, S. A. 2007. 'The Sociology of Park Creation in Medieval England.' In Liddiard, R. (ed.) *The Medieval Park. New Perspectives.* Windgather Press, Oxford, pp. 11–26.

Nikula, O. 1938a. *Tenala och Bromarf Socknars historia*, Vol. I. Helsinki.

Nikula, O. 1938b. *Tenala och Bromarf Socknars historia*, Vol. II. Helsinki.

Nikula, S. 1944a (1982). 'Kyrkomalm och deras skrud.' In Nikander, G. (ed.) *Kimitöbygdens historia*, Vol. I. Faksimiltryck ur Kimitöbygdens historia, Vols. I–II. Sagalunds hembygdsmuseum & kommunalförbund, Tammisaari, pp. 259–317.

Nikula, S. 1944b (1982). 'Kyrkorna ur ett senare perpektiv. In Nikander, G. (ed.) *Kimitöbygdens historia*, Vol. I. Faksimiltryck ur Kimitöbygdens historia, Vols. I–II. Sagalunds hembygdsmuseum & kommunalförbund, Tammisaari, pp. 323–367.

Nyberg, L. 1991. *Vallar och murar*. Västnyländska kultursamfundet, Tammisaari.

Nyberg, P. 1931. *Sibbo sockens historia*, Vol. I: *Intill början av 1700-talet*. Freckell, Helsinki.

Porteus, D. J. 1990. *Landscapes of the Mind. Worlds of Sense and Metaphor*. University of Toronto Press, Toronto.

Raivo, P. J. 1996. *Maiseman kulttuurinen transformaatio. Ortodoksinen kirkko suomalaisessa kulttuurimaisemassa*. University of Oulu, Oulu.

Ramsay, A. 1984 (1924). *Espoo. Espoon pitäjä ja Espoon kartano 1500-luvulla*. The Town of Espoo, Espoo.

Rancken, A. W. 1936. 'Ingå moderkyrka.' In Brenner, A. et al. *Ingå Fagervik Deggerby. En västnyländsk bygdekrönika*, Vol. I. The Municipality of Inkoo, Inkoo, pp. 40–63.

Rantanen, A. & Kuvaja, C. 1994. *Sipoon pitäjän historia vuoteen 1868*, Vol. I. The Municipality of Sipoo, Sipoo.

Rask, H. 1991. *Snappertuna. En kustbygdens hävder*, Vol. I: *Forntid–1809*. Snappertuna sockenhistorie kommitté, Tammisaari.

Rein, G. 1944. *Lohjan historia*, Vol. I. The Congregation of Lohja, Lohja.

Riska, T. & Sinisalo, A. 1968. *Suomen kirkot*, Vol. 5.5.1: *Turun arkkihiippakunta*, 5: *Perniön rovastikunta*, 1. The Finnish Antiquarian Society, Helsinki.

Rosén, R. 1936. '*Suur-Vehkalahden* asutushistoria ruotsalaisen paikan- ja henkilönnimistön valossa.' In Rosén, R. *Vehkalahden pitäjän historia*, Vol. I: *Suur-Vehkalahden* asutus- ja aluehistoria n. vuoteen 1610. Vehkalahti, Vehkalahden kunta, pp. 37–64.

Rosén, R. 1960. 'Kymjjoen suuseudun asutushistoriaa. Kymenkartano.' In Ulvinen, A et al. *Kymin historia*, Vol. I. The Municipality and the Congregation of Kymi & The Municipality of Karhula, Kymi, pp. 86–284.

Selén, G. 1996. *Borgå socken genom tiderna*, Vol. I. The Municipality of Porvoo, Porvoo.

Soikkeli, K. 1929. *Vihti. Kuvauksia Vihdin kunnan luonnosta, historiasta ja kansan elämästä*. Puromiehen kirjapaino, Helsinki.

Strang, J. 2000. 'Suomen kartastot.' In Rantatupa, H. (ed.) *Kartta historian lähteenä*. The Student Union of the University of Jyväskylä, Jyväskylä, pp. 14–17.

Suistoranta, K. 1997. 'Kirkko ja seurakunta.' In Suistoranta, K. & Asplund, H. *Kemiön suurpitäjän historia*, Vol. I. Sagalundin museon kuntayhtymä, Tammisaari, pp. 179–209.

Taavitsainen, J.-P. 1990. *Ancient Hillforts of Finland. Problems of Analysis, Chronology and Interpretation with Special Reference to the Hillfort of Kuhmoinen*. The Finnish Antiquarian Society, Helsinki.

Väärä, S. 1998. 'Kiskon ja Suomusjärven historia historiallisen ajan alusta kunnallishallinnon uudistamiseen 1347–1865.' In Sarvas, A. & Väärä, S. *Kiskon ja Suomusjärven historia*, Vol. I. The Municipalities of Kisko and Suomusjärvi, Kisko & Suomusjärvi, pp. 105–629.

Vahtola, J. 1993. 'Finland.' In Pulsiano, P. (ed.) *Medieval Scandinavia. An Encyclopedia*, Garland, New York & London, pp. 188–194.

Viertola, J. 'Yleiset tiet Ruotsinvallan aikana.' In Fogelberg, P. & Viertola, J. *Suomen teiden historia*, Vol. I: *Pakanuuden ajalta Suomen itsenäistymiseen,* Tie- ja vesirakennushallitus, Helsinki, 1974, 1999, pp. 36–40.

Voionmaa, V. 1950. 'Helsingin seudun historiaa ennen kaupungin perustamista.' In Hornborg, E. et al. (eds.) *Helsingin kaupungin historia*, Vol. I: *Vuoteen 1721.* The Town of Helsinki, Helsinki, pp. 79–107.

Wessman, V. E. V. 1925. *Boken om Sibbo. Bidrag till Sibbo sockens geografi och historia.* Porvoo.

Ylikangas, H. 1973. 'Lohjalaisten historia ruotsin vallan vuosisatoina.' In Ylikangas, H. & Siiriäinen, A. *Lohjalaisten historia*, Vol. 1. The Municipality of Lohja, Lohja, pp. 51–574.

Appendix 1. Stone churches within the study area.

Parish (present commune)	Date of construction*	References
Espoo / Esbo	1485–1490	Ramsay 1924 (1984), pp. 35, 52; Luoto 2001, p. 73
Helsinki / Helsinge Parish (Vantaa / Vanda)	1450–1460	Voionmaa 1950, pp. 94–95
Inkoo / Ingå	1490–1530	Rancken 1936, p. 40
Karjaa / Karis (Raasepori / Raseborg)	1460–1480	af Hällström 1957, pp. 8, 10–14
Kemiö / Kimito (Kemiönsaari / Kimitoön)	1460–1500	Gardberg 1944b, p. 195; Nikula 1944b, pp. 323–325; Suistoranta 1997, p. 181
Kirkkonummi / Kyrkslätt	15th century	Lindberg 1930, p. 280; Backman & Ihrcke-Åberg 2003, p. 32
Kisko (Salo) (sacristy)	1500–1550	Väärä 1998, p. 413
Lohja / Lojo	1510–1520	Ylikangas 1973, p. 94; Rein 1944, p. 29
Pernaja / Pernå	1430–1445	Antell 1956, p. 40
Perniö / Bjärnå (Salo)	1460–1480	Knaapinen 1930, pp. 139–141; Riska & Sinisalo 1968, p. 10; Litzen 1980, pp. 145–147
Pohja / Pojo (Raasepori / Raseborg)	1460–1490	af Hällström 1964, p. 160
Porvoo / Borgå	1450–1460	Gardberg 1996, pp. 141–142, 179, 222, 235
Pyhtää / Pyttis	1455–1465	Hultin 1927, p. 37
Sipoo / Sibbo	1450–1455	Rantanen & Kuvaja 1994a, p. 189
Siuntio / Sjundeå	1480–1490	Favorin 1984, pp. 33–34
Tenhola / Tenala (Raasepori / Raseborg)	1460–1480	Nikula 1938a, p. 142
Vehkalahti / Veckelax (Hamina / Fredrikshamn)	1430–1470	Rosen, 1936, pp. 136–138; Korhonen 1981, p. 104
Vihti / Vichtis	1480–1500	Soikkeli 1929, pp. 173–176; Rein 1944, p. 28
Virolahti / Virolax (sacristy)	1500–1550	Kaukiainen 1970, p. 63, 66, 97

* Hiekkanen 1994, pp. 250–254.

Appendix 2. Other church sites and some local graveyards within the study area.

h ent commune)	Name of site	Reference
la	Kalmistomäki (local graveyard)	Database of ancient monuments in Finland 10.5.2009
ɔ / Esbo	Espoon kartano Kapellängen	Luoto 2001, p. 74
	Prästgård – Pappila (local graveyard?)	Database of ancient monuments in Finland 10.5.2009
	Suomenoja (Finnå) (local graveyard)	Database of ancient monuments in Finland 10.5.2009
nki / Helsinge ı (Vantaa / Vanda)	Håkansböle Kyrksveden	Voionmaa 1950, p. 101
	Malmi	Voionmaa 1950, pp. 97, 101
	Nordsjö Porslahti Kyrkmalm	Voionmaa 1950, p. 101
	Sotunkylä Kyrkioberget	Voionmaa 1950, p. 101
ɔ / Ingå	Rövarbacken	Brenner 1936a, p. 39; Brenner 1936b, p. 75
	Vesterkulla	Brenner 1936a, p. 39
a / Karis epori / Raseborg)	Busö Jussarö 2 (local graveyard)	Database of ancient monuments in Finland 10.5.2009
	Haveråkersberget	Database of ancient monuments in Finland 3.10.2008
	Kasaby (local graveyard)	Gardberg 1944a (1981), p. 47; Rask 1991, p. 63
	Läppträsket NE	Kerkkonen 1952, pp. 32, 98; af Hällström 1957, pp. 8–9; Forsén & Moisanen 1995, p. 39
	Raasepori chapel	Kerkkonen 1952, p. 153; Rask 1991, p. 164
	Snappertuna Kyrkby	Database of ancient monuments in Finland 3.10.2008
	Sutarkulla	af Hällström 1957, p. 8
	Visanbacka	Gardberg 1970, p. 47; Nyberg 1991, p.16; Forsén & Moisanen 1995, p. 29
ö / Kimito (Kemi-ri / Kimitoön)	Helgeboda	Nikula 1944a, pp. 289–290

Parish (present commune)	Name of site	Reference
ditto	Kappalskroken	Database of ancient monuments in Fi 3.10.2008
ditto	Kyrkön Kyrksundet	Gardberg 1944a, pp. 3–6; Suistoranta 19 190; Asplund 1997, pp. 262–266
ditto	Vik gård	Nikula 1944a, p. 290
ditto	Vänö Kappelsbacken	Nikula 1944a, p. 291
Kirkkonummi / Kyrkslätt	Kyrkogårdsjön	Fleege 1901, pp. 28–29
ditto	Munkkulla/Smedjebacken	Fleege 1901, pp. 29, 148
ditto	Måsaskär (local graveyard)	Fleege 1901, p. 28
ditto	Räfsö (local graveyard)	Fleege 1901, p. 29
ditto	Skorfven (Skorvan)	Fleege 1901, p. 29
ditto	Tullandet	Fleege 1901, p. 29
Kisko (Salo)	Kiskonjärvi Kirkkoniemi	Väärä 1998, p. 413
Lohja / Lojo	Kyrkstadt	Ylikangas 1973, pp. 92, 105
Pernaja / Pernå	Sarflax/Sarvilahti	von Born 1949, pp. 18–19; Antell 1956,
ditto	Tejtom Malmgård	Hedengren 1898, pp. 3–5; von Born 194 18–19; Antell 1956, p. 39
Perniö / Bjärnå (Salo)	Perniöjokisuu	Litzen 1980, pp. 150–152
ditto	Yliskylä	Knaapinen 1930, pp. 139–141; Riska & S 1968, p. 10; Litzen 1980, pp. 145–147
Porvoo / Borgå	Kappelinmäki	Hiekkanen 1981, p. 10, quoting Blom 196
ditto	Pellinge Hagnäsbote (Hagnäs Kyrkogård)	Allardt 1925, p. 58; Database of ancient i ments in Finland 26.1.2009
ditto	Pellinge Sandholmen (local graveyard)	Allardt 1925, p. 58; Database of ancient i ments in Finland 1.8.2009
ditto	Saksala Kappeli	Selén 1996, p. 48
ditto	Svartså	Allardt 1925, pp. 58–59

Name of site	Reference
ı **ent commune)**	
ä / Pyttis	Munapirtti Malms	Hultin 1927, pp. 45, 79
/ Sibbo	Box Kyrkmässa-backen	Wessman 1925, p. 192
	Hangelby Kappel-backen	Wessman 1925, p. 192
	Norrkulla Kyrk-backen	Wessman 1925, p. 185; Nyberg 1931, p. 249
/ Sibbo nki / Helsingfors)	Östersundom	Wessman 1925, p. 192; Nyberg 1931, pp. 251, 282
o / Sjundeå	Dansbacka	Favorin 1986, p. 25
	Kapellbacka	Brenner 1953, pp. 55, 142–143; Favorin 1986, p. 33
	Munkby/Muncks	Favorin 1986, p. 25
la / Tenala pori / Raseborg)	Bromarv Vanha kappeli	Nikula 1938b, p. 30, pp. 33–35
	Hangö Kapellhamnen	Nikula 1938b, pp. 31–32; Database of ancient monuments in Finland 26.1.2009.
	Ängholm	Database of ancient monuments in Finland 3.10.2008
lahti/ lax (Kotka)	Kirkkomaan saari Kappelkangas	Rosén 1936, p. 133
	Kymenkartano Kappelpelto	Rosén 1936, pp. 5, 133; Rosen 1960, pp. 116–138, 226
alahti / Veckelax ina / Fredrikshamn)	Korvenojan kangas	Rosén 1936, p. 134; Anttila 1936, p. 6
	Savilahti Kappelkangas	Rosén 1936, p. 49
/ Vichtis	Nummela Kirkkomäki	Soikkeli 1929, p. 176
	Tarttila Kirkkomäki	Soikkeli 1929, p. 176
	Vanjärvi Niemi	Soikkeli 1929, p. 176
hti / Virolax	Koivuniemi Sakastinnotko	Kaukiainen 1970, pp. 66, 68
	Vaalimaa	Kaukiainen 1970, p. 66

Appendix 3. Fortification sites in the study area.

Parish (present commune)	Name of the site	Type	References
Artjärvi	Linnamäki	hillfort	Antin 1997, p. 156; Database of anc monuments in Finland 10.5.2009
Artjärvi	Nuppilinna 1	hillfort?	Database of ancient monuments in Fin 10.5.2009
Helsinki / Helsingfors	Vartiokylän linnavuori	hillfort	Database of ancient monuments in Fin 10.5.2009
Inkoo / Ingå	Riddarkil	small castle?	Database of ancient monuments in Fin 10.5.2009
Karjaa / Karis (Raasepori / Raseborg)	Haveråkersberget	hillfort	Database of ancient monuments in Fin 10.5.2009
ditto	Junkarsborg	small castle	Database of ancient monuments in Fin 10.5.2009
ditto	Sutarkulla	hillfort	Database of ancient monuments in Fin 10.5.2009
Porvoo / Borgå	Husholmen	small castle	Database of ancient monuments in Fin 10.5.2009
ditto	Iso Linnamäki	small castle	Database of ancient monuments in Fin 10.5.2009
Sipoo / Sibbo	Sibbesborg	small castle	Database of ancient monuments in Fin 10.5.2009
Siuntio / Sjundeå	Skällberget	hillfort	Database of ancient monuments in Fin 10.5.2009
Tammisaari / Ekenäs (Raasepori / Raseborg)	Horsbäck Kastalet	watch tower	Database of ancient monuments in Fin 10.5.2009
Tammisaari / Ekenäs (Raasepori / Raseborg)	Raasepori	stone castle	Database of ancient monuments in Fin 10.5.2009
Vehkalahti/ Veckelax (Hamina/ Fredrikshamn)	Salmenkylä Linnamäki	hillfort?	Rosén 1936, p. 135, 274; Database of anc monuments in Finland 10.5.2009

Note: ? = Uncertain character of archaeological remains.

CHAPTER 10

Virtual Landscape Modelling

Kari Uotila and Isto Huvila

Introduction

Attitudes towards the prospects, promises and limitations of archaeological perceptions of landscapes and their visualizations have ranged from enthusiastic optimism to rather deep reservation.[1] Rapidly expanding pathways in the field of advanced computer graphics and growing interest in landscape archaeology studies over the last two decades have, together, laid the ground for this discussion. In spite of all efforts to advance theories and methods of visualization[2] and the increased understanding of the effects of archaeological perceptions of earlier landscapes[3], it is evident that we still only have suggestions rather than answers to essential questions about visualizations. How could visualizations contribute to our understanding of cultures of the past and, by extension, why should visualization be used at all?

Archaeological landscape models are a form of archaeological perception and interpretation that present many theoretical and practical challenges. Models and current ideas about landscapes of the past are necessarily always ideational constructs.[4] As well as being an issue related to archaeological theory, landscape rendering is also a relatively new combination of scholarly representation and communication, as are other forms of digital modes of mediating scholarly information.[5] Like scholarly databases, data archiving and other digital methods, landscape models are instruments of scholarship. They open up new avenues for research and help to address earlier research questions in new ways. However, at the same time, such models also profoundly change the nature of many aspects of scholarship. A model can be viewed simultaneously both as a device of external communication (to other researchers and the general public) and as an active participant in the scholarly work.[6] A model explicates that which has been done and that which is known, but it is also an instrument that constructs new knowledge. This chapter discusses the evolution of archaeological landscape modelling and the dual role of models in archaeological scholarship.

The development of landscape rendering

Computer-aided rendering of the temporal development of a landscape is based on drawings and paintings. As well as being aesthetically pleasing, these artworks have also depicted nature and human activities over the decades and restored the scenery of the past with reference to known research data. The personal interpretation and skill of the artist defined the outcome. Some illustrators had backgrounds in archaeology,[7] but even in these cases the available methods limited the outcomes to educated impressions based on research data.

Since the beginning of the 1990s, the use of GIS – and later rendering software – has made it possible to create different re-enactments of historical landscapes. (Significantly, such advancements also meet the needs of graphic designers and the motion picture industry.) During the pioneer years the emphasis was primarily on the recreation of important historical objects and monuments, particularly the more significant objects of antiquity.[8] Little by little, other themes and objects – less well known but interesting from a research perspective – began to be explored.[9] Digital reconstructions made it possible to combine measurement data and interpretations in seamless renderings.

The two-dimensional GIS-analysis of a landscape and its many tools has been in use for more than twenty years. GIS-analysis is an effective research method and a way of visualizing archaeological landscape data. In addition to the traditional tools for diagrammatic visualizations, the present GIS-software packages also tend to have limited tools for quasi-realistic visualization. The emphasis of the GIS-based graphics is, however, on cartographic and diagrammatic presentation rather than qualitative visualization.[10]

The cartographic mode of presentation has many advantages in presenting and communicating both overviews and carefully chosen details and sub-sets of data. One could argue that the 'serious' mode of explicating the data might have also added to the perceived credibility of the material. The diagrammatic mode of presentation strikes a note of precision and high quality, whereas an aesthetic visualization is more likely to give an impression of approximation and imprecision.[11]

The visualization of large geographical areas through the use of three-dimensional rendering software has only been possible since the beginning of the twenty-first century. Before this time, the capacity of mainstream computer hardware limited the size and detail of models to relatively small or simple objects. Larger renderings were less detailed.[12] During the early 2000s, functions for the creation and presentation of landscape models were added to the major rendering software packages. At the same time, the ability to combine the GIS-based geographic information with three-dimensional modelling was introduced. To a contemporary viewer, the results were high-quality three-dimensional images, virtual models and animations, all of which will seem very crude and simplified in five or ten years. The aesthetic appeal of visualization has changed and will continue to evolve. Furthermore, the more fundamental qualities of what is perceived to be 'realistic' are equally transient.[13] In the 1990s, a plane surface was a natural and scientifically sound solution to represent the ground level in a rendering of a building. The idea of rendering the surroundings and their form in the same detail as the reconstruction of a building is fairly new in virtual archaeology (Picture 4 see colour plate section 2, p. 6).

The act of visualization inevitably simplifies data as part of the process.[14] This is partly a question of limited computing power and partly the deliberate effort to create an example, a representation of reality rather than the whole of reality. The simplification is often more difficult to discern, but could be compared to presenting a large forest by reducing it to a few hundred or thousand trees.[15] Landscapes used to be represented through painting an impression of a forest using, for instance, watercolours. A rendering is a kind of 'fact sheet' used by its compilers to explain various phenomena to its viewers. The challenge is that it often proves difficult, if not impossible, to interpret small, practically hidden, features (like presenting leafy trees) without a thorough written interpretation. An inherent problem of visual representations is that each individual will interpret them differently. Even though a text is also open to multiple interpretations, it is more strictly codified and thus leaves somewhat less room for such highly individualized readings.

Even though simplification and interpretation are rather apparent in landscape renderings, geographic information systems also simplify data and present qualitative readings of the past. The unit of analysis during the early 1990s, when earlier forms of software were in use, was typically rather large, around 25 m² even in small-scale projects. Large unit size might not be a problem when dealing with a proportionally large total area. If the analysed phenomena can be clearly represented, a 25 m² unit of analysis might be acceptable.[16] However, if one was attempting to examine a hamlet or the fields and pastures belonging to a single house, or to evaluate the suitability of various parts of a terrain for agricultural usage, a much more exact grid would be needed in order to obtain even remotely accurate results. It is practically impossible to find a one or two hectare optimal field area for early agriculture using a large background grid. The problem of large grid size became apparent in the early twenty-first century, when rendered field models began to be much more detailed than the corresponding grid data.

Challenges of landscape data

Accuracy of source material and accuracy of processing are the two central issues raised by source-critical scrutiny of renderings of past landscapes. Specific problems vary according to location and depend on the quality and precision of datasets and multiple other factors. In the following discussion, the diversity and complexity of data-related issues is highlighted using Finland and its local conditions as an example.

In Finland, almost all landscape renderings are based on contour data provided by the National Land Survey of Finland (NLSF) and supported by the more accurate local materials provided by municipal or communal organizations. Even more detailed contour data can be obtained using measurements from archaeological excavations, for example. The difference between the 2.5–5 m contour data provided by the NLSF and *in situ* measurements from a total station or GPS equipment is enormous, but as far as rendering is concerned the focus is of course on the objective and on what equipment is in use. When one interprets the rendering, it is vital to know what material it has been based upon.

The method chosen has a profound effect on how accurately the contours of the terrain are presented. In Finland the challenges of countrywide terrain models become apparent when we consider the long coastline and archipelago regions. In some places the lowest mapped contour is +5 m asl (above sea level) and in other places +25 m asl; the ±0 m contour is missing and replaced by the shoreline, which in some cases can represent the boundary of an area covered by reeds or rushes. The area of the lowest 2–3 m contours is significant in Finland, as many medieval layers and structures were situated quite near the medieval shoreline. (Interestingly the very same objects of historical conservation are the first to be threatened by rising sea levels caused by climate change, which exceed the rate of postglacial land uplift on the Finnish coastline.)

In conjunction with this, we should note that in some cases during the 1990s and the early 2000s it was customary to emphasize the size or height of the rendered model with level surfaces or wooded areas to add drama. The systematic elevation of the terrain does not, however, affect the form of an archipelago forest, which is often a quite straight line on the horizon, in contrast to the alignment of the terrain. Moreover, revision of the contours makes it impossible for non-experts unacquainted with such techniques to interpret the resultant images. It is clear that the method has its advantages in research, but when results are presented to a wider public audience the manipulation of contours presents a great risk (Picture 5 see colour plate section 2, p. 6).[17]

One factor that distorts or at least hampers interpretation of the results is the lack of data about lake depth in the rendering data. As result of postglacial land uplift, Finnish lakes continue to incline towards the southeast at varying velocities. In simple terms, this means that the present shorelines of the lakes and their contours have little or nothing to do with the form of ancient lakes. In spite of this, the lakes are often depicted in models in their modern forms. In a successful rendering of a terrain, the lakebeds – preferably the original shapes rather than the present sediments – should be analysed in addition to the existing contours. This is especially important when presenting interpretations of the oldest terrain forms that were exposed from the sea immediately after the last glaciation. This has not been yet been implemented in any extensive terrain presentation in Finland, but as research and computing advance (and access to the relevant technology increases) it will become possible and necessary to incorporate such analysis within models.[18]

It has recently become apparent that the effect of soft soil sediments deposited after the last glaciation (~10,000 BP in Finland) should also be taken into consideration. In a natural landscape this involves the natural layers; in archaeological or historical landscapes this also includes the anthropogenic layers, both *in situ* and as secondary deposits. There is awareness of this problem and some attempts have been made to address the lack of soft soils in the contours, but there is still a great deal of work to be done in this area. It, like other issues, is related to questions about the size of the studied terrain, the accuracy of the analysis and the objectives of the research.

The sedimentation of soft soils in estuaries and the subsequent land uplift in shallow areas is one of the most important issues in the history of the Finnish coastline and is also arguably of significant importance in other areas of Finland. Shallow shore meadows and eutrophic[19] estuaries have in all likelihood been important areas for livestock-based economies for the last few thousand years. In Finland, land uplift has caused these areas to shift over time. In many cases, the population is believed to have followed the uplift and repeatedly moved their settlements back to the coastline. Those who stayed in the area have been forced to find new sources of livelihood.

This is not only a question of the formation, flourishing and disappearance of reedy areas; when the sea recedes, a new kind of microclimate develops. Recently, various forms of geographic research have been conducted on past, present and future microclimates in the Turku archipelago, but this methodology has not yet been transferred to an entirely different geographical environment (the 3000 BP Bronze Age coast and its evolution, for example).[20]

Reasons to render

The applicability of virtual realities in an archaeological simulation and their potential usefulness in reviewing and evaluating scholarly propositions has been touched upon briefly in recent literature. Various researchers have proposed that a kind of 'grammar' should be developed in order to express the validity of the virtual reality arguments.[21] In spite of awareness and required technical skills, 'everyday archaeology' is still far from capable or prepared to exploit the potential of methods and techniques based on virtual reality.

In comparison to traditional forms of inquiry and reporting, visual representations of the cultural landscape offer a number of benefits. Through visualization, it is possible to get a visual glimpse of a representative landscape as it might have been. Visualization provides us with an opportunity to explore inconsistencies in the evidence, verify the coherence of sources that describe aspects of landscapes, bring historical and archaeological evidence together, and illustrate and test research findings. Naturally, visualization allows us to communicate research results in a considerably more tangible form than does a traditional textual description. The significance of the communication aspect has been particularly emphasized by younger generations accustomed to digital forms of visual aesthetics.[22]

Earlier studies in landscape archaeology and history have demonstrated that a comprehensive analysis of the relationship between humans and landscape requires a mass of heterogeneous sources. Various scientific and scholarly observations and data sources provide evidence to support contrastingly different aspects of a complex cultural and social sphere.[23]

Using a computer model to weld this material together, and thus create a landscape visualization that depicts an interpretation of the ancient maritime landscape, is hardly a shortcut to clearer understanding of the research subject. Such visualization could be considered another, complementary, tool of analysis, but hardly much more than that.

Isto Huvila interviewed twenty-five archaeology professionals from Finland and Sweden about the benefits of archaeological virtual reality visualizations.[24] According to his informants virtual reality visualizations enable archaeologists to 'enter' a site and can be used as a composite of thematic and temporal layers. Such visualizations might function as an instrument for visualizing and seeing contexts; they might also be used to allow remote availability of data and to provide a way to replay an investigation process.

John Counsell has outlined a list of possible roles for virtual realities in the stages of the conservation process:

1) The use of virtual reality in a preparatory or briefing role before visiting the real world site

2) Models may be used to immerse users in environments that no longer exist and to augment their present state of conservation with reconstructed information

3) Complete replicas may be used to allow remote 'visits' and inspections of the sites.[25]

Theoretically, a visualization might act as a device for telepresence, and could empower archaeologists to undertake remote consultation and investigation. This aspect of archaeological visualization has been discussed briefly in the literature,[26] although telepresence applications have been the focus of some public and analytical attention.[27] Comparable telepresence applications have been developed to allow surgeons to consult a paramedic or to operate remotely.[28] The omission of collaborative applications may be explained by the fact that within archaeological discourse, unlike museums and other areas of application, virtual realities have been considered primarily as objects rather than (participatory) environments.[29]

One of the central benefits of visualization is its capacity to address the practical research issue of making a past landscape a tangible object of study. The promise of landscape research lies in its attempt to adopt a quasi-holistic approach through which one can reach beyond the confines of one piece of evidence to present an interpretation in context rather than study historic phenomena in isolation.[30]

Even though the practical difficulties involved in environmental and landscape archaeology often lead to only a limited set of variables being studied, visualization could (at least in theory) still allow a comprehensive quantity and variety of available data to be processed within one conceptual space. Attempts to construct visualization pose both technical and conceptual challenges. Mostly tool-related and quantitative, the technical challenges are by no means easy to resolve; however, they are still considerably more straightforward to address than the conceptual issues raised by visualization. A particularly critical conceptual issue concerns the limits of computer visualization: what can such visualization communicate and what is inherently impossible?[31]

The essential questions regarding both computer and hand-drawn visualizations of the past do not, in the end, differ considerably in terms of the methodologies and practices involved in studying the past. The technical challenge of making a computer-generated representation of the past is new, but interpreting the past as something visual differs very little from how an archaeologist or historian reads the past from the records. Cultural historian Robert Darnton believes that much of the mental world of the past could be recovered through asking the right questions and understanding that the past may be just as foreign as a contemporary alien culture.[32] The same idea also applies to landscape visualizations. Rather than not pursuing the right questions (as can often happen with textual material), we may fail to pursue any real questions at all. Their seeming comprehensiveness may make us believe that landscape visualizations can to recover more of the past than is actually possible. A landscape could be visualized from the source material without any real thought being given to the concrete questions to which the resulting model or the visualization might provide answers (Map 32a–d see colour plate section 2, pp. 4–5).

Visualization is capable of restoring some elements of the past (in both the material and the mental worlds), but not necessarily those aspects that are seemingly visible to a spectator. A researcher should be capable within the scope of his or her own expertise to judge how or whether to visualize something explicit in the landscape. A further problematic issue is how to manage the implicit information that emerges from the relationships and mechanisms of depiction.[33] As Geoffrey Bowker argues, the way in which we record knowledge, for instance, in the form of landscape visualizations is bound to affect the ways in which we perceive past and present landscapes.[34] Such implicit meanings are particularly important because – in contrast to the well-established traditions of scholarly writing – scholarly visualization is in its infancy and has been undertaken by only a few researchers.

Reasons not to render:
the traps of realism and photorealism

Although illustration has a long tradition in archaeology, dating back well into the eighteenth century,[35] a major issue regarding archaeological illustration (with and or without the use of computer modelling) persists: how can we understand and communicate the actual possibilities and extent to which we can visualize the past? Visualizations allow improbabilities and impossibilities to be tested, but they can also easily lead to the creation of believable images that are based on non-existent information.

Visualization may be a representation of one plausible interpretation, a valuable tool of research or a graphic illustration of research results. But, in essence, it is nothing more than a construct created by a researcher and viewed through the scholarly lens of interpretation of the past. A visualization is certainly not a replica of the past landscape as it once was; more importantly, neither is it a visualization of anything other than what is actually visualized.

Myron Kruger's notion about avoiding the trap of realism – copying existing settings and workflows into computer-generated environment[36] – is also important from an archaeological point of view. Not being innovative in one's choice of research methods is not sensible, but neither, on the other hand, is falling into the trap of photorealism.[37] The most immanent interpretative dangers inherent in visualizations are the implicit communication of non-existent details, providing a false impression of completeness, the inability to communicate the levels of interpretation in the visualization and placing false emphasis upon the significance of visual perception in the past cultures.

No research approach (irrespective of scientific or scholarly discipline) can entirely eliminate the innate possibility that false conclusions might be drawn. Thus, results are always a compromise between getting it all and getting nothing at all. The accurate modelling of all features of the landscape (including physical, social and cultural elements) is the ideal but impossible goal of visualization. Because establishing an objective truth about the past is impossible, a practical goal has to be the representative modelling of relevant aspects of landscapes.

The meaning of relevance and essentialness is a separate question. If one does not intend to use the same computer model for both mathematical analysis and visual analysis of the landscape, the model does not have to be prepared for both purposes. If a qualitative approach is taken (as is always the case in final interpretations of past societies in archaeology and historical disciplines) the visualization has to be qualitatively accurate.

Of course, even then every decision to resort to approximations, add a detail or leave something out, for instance, has to be the result of proper motivation. Even if the tool (for example, the computer) leads us to think of certain measurable relevancies and accuracies, the final measure of the past is the measure of interpretation. Understanding the innate rationale of feasibility is about understanding the relevance of expectations about different constructs. A representation of cultural landscape features is hardly accurate enough for numerical analysis, but it would be also be implausible to expect that a physically accurate representation would be culturally representative.

Conclusion

The intricacies of landscape visualizations do not end at the philosophical discussion of their nature and their limited capacity to represent various aspects of reality or at the issues related to quality and limitations of available data. Landscape renderings also represent a new form of scholarly communication; the traps of representation are also traps of communication and of management of research data and results. Christine Borgman[38] and Geoffrey Bowker[39] have discussed how databases and digital information infrastructures have changed scholarly inquiry and the communication of scholarship. Landscape renderings represent a similarly challenging form of infrastructure. The data used to visualize the past contain implicit and explicit deficits (some known and some unknown by the archaeologist working with a visualization). These biases are reproduced in a visualization and add a further layer of interpretation. Renderings directly affect how scholarly considerations and results are mediated and re-mediated both within the community of researchers and outside to the general public. The question is not about what a visualization can represent or communicate *per se*, but how it communicates the intentions of the researcher and how much it communicates something unexpected and unwanted.

Notes

1 Frischer et al. 2002; Earl 2006; Reilly 1992.
2 Baltsavias 2006; Cameron & Kenderdine 2007.
3 See e.g. Johnston 1998; Wickstead 2009.

4 Knapp & Ashmore 1999.
5 Bowker 2005; Borgman 2007.
6 Uotila et al. 2006.
7 Adkins & Adkins 1989.
8 Renfrew 1997; Forte 2000.
9 Lock 2003; Valenti & Nardini 2004; Gabucci 2005.
10 Löwenborg 2010.
11 Roussou & Drettakis 2004.
12 Renfrew 1997; Uotila & Sartes 2000; Uotila et al. 2002.
13 Arnold & Geser 2008 86–90.
14 Pletinckx 2008.
15 See e.g. Sogliani et al. 2009.
16 Pukkila and Uotila 2005.
17 See e.g. Koivisto 2004, Uotila et al. 2002.
18 Tikkanen & Oksanen 2002, Virkki & Häkkinen 2007.
19 A body of water with an aquatic ecosystem with high primary productivity or fertility due to an increased amount of nutrients. Eutrophic waters are subject to algal blooms and tend to have poor water quality.
20 Kalliola & Suominen 2007.
21 See e.g. Ryan 1996; Frischer et al. 2002; Ryan 2001; Niccolucci & Cantone 2003; Vatanen 2003; Beex 2008.
22 Sanders 2008.
23 See e.g. Tilley 1994; Schama 1995.
24 Huvila 2006.
25 Counsell 2001.
26 See e.g. Boyle 2003.
27 See e.g. Frischer et al. 2002; Benko et al. 2004.
28 Moline 1997; Söderholm et al. 2007.
29 Brown et al. 2003.
30 Frischer et al. 2002.
31 Barceló 2001.
32 Darnton 1984; Pallares-Burke 2002.
33 Solomon 2002.
34 Bowker 2005.
35 Adkins & Adkins 1989.
36 Turner 2002.
37 Frischer et al. 2002.
38 Borgman 2007.
39 Bowker 2005.

Bibliography
Literature

Adkins, L., & Adkins, R. 1989. *Archaeological Illustration*. Cambridge University Press, Cambridge.
Arnold. D and Geser, G. 2008. *EPOCH Research Agenda for the Applications of ICT to Cultural Heritage*. EPOCH Project, Brighton and Salzburg.

Baltsavias, E. P. 2006. *Recording, Modeling and Visualization of Cultural Heritage.* Taylor & Francis, London.

Barceló, J. A. 2001. 'Virtual Reality for Archaeological Explanation. Beyond "Picturesque" Reconstruction.' *Archeologia e Calcolatori,* Vol. 12, pp. 221–244.

Beex, W. 2008. *Fact and Fiction on a Normal Daily Basis in Virtual Reality. Abstract of a Paper Presented in the 34th Annual Meeting and Conference of Computer Applications and Quantitative Methods in Archaeology CAA2006, Fargo, April 18–21, 2006.*

Benko, H., Ishak, E. W., & Feiner, S. 2004. 'Collaborative mixed reality visualization of an archaeological excavation.' In *ISMAR '04. Proceedings of the 3rd IEEE/ACM International Symposium on Mixed and Augmented Reality.* IEEE Computer Society, Washington, pp. 132–140.

Borgman, C. L. 2007. *Scholarship in the Digital Age. Information, Infrastructure, and the Internet.* MIT Press, Cambridge, Mass.

Bowker, G. C. 2005. *Memory Practices in the Sciences.* MIT Press, Cambridge, Mass.

Boyle, A. 2003. 'Explorer Plans a Digital Dig Beneath the Sea. Titanic Co-Discoverer Wants to Take Telepresence to New Scientific Depths.' *Science on MSNBC.* URL: http://www.msnbc.msn.com/id/3077232/.

Brown, B., MacColl, I., Chalmers, M., Galani, A., Randell, C., & Steed, A. 2003. 'Lessons from the Lighthouse. Collaboration in a Shared Mixed Reality System.' In *CHI '03. Proceedings of the SIGCHI Conference on Human Factors in Computing Systems.* ACM Press, New York, pp. 577–584.

Cameron, F., & Kenderdine, S. (eds.) 2007. *Theorizing Digital Cultural Heritage. A Critical Discourse.* MIT Press, London & Cambridge, Mass.

Counsell, J. 2001. 'An Evolutionary Approach to Digital Recording and Information about Heritage Sites.' In Arnold, David B., Chalmers, Alan, Fellner and Dieter W. (eds.) *VAST '01. Proceedings of the 2001 Conference on Virtual Reality, Archeology, and Cultural Heritage.* ACM Press, New York, pp. 33–42.

Darnton, R. 1984. *The Great Cat Massacre and Other Episodes in French Cultural History.* Allen Lane, London.

Earl, G. P. 2006. *Digital Archaeology. Bridging Method and Theory.* Routledge, London.

Forte, M. 2000. 'About Virtual Archaeology: Disorders, Cognitive Interactions and Virtuality.' In Barceló, J. A., Forte, M. & Sanders, D. H. (eds.) *Virtual Reality in Archaeology. Proceedings of the Computer Applications and Quantitative Methods in Archaeology (CAA) 1998, Barcelona.* Archaeopress, Oxford, pp. 247–259.

Frischer, B., Niccolucci, F., Ryan, N., & Barceló, J. (2002). 'From CVR to CVRO. The Past, Present, and Future of Cultural Virtual Reality.' In Niccolucci, F. (ed.) *Proceedings of VAST 2000. British Archaeological Reports,* Vol. 843, Archaeopress, Oxford, pp. 7–18.

Gabellone, F. & Sogliani, F. 2009 'The fortified medieval settlement of Rocca Montis Dragonis (Mondragone, Caserta, Italy) Virtually Alive.' In Boerner, W. (ed.) *Proceedings of the 14. International Congress 'Cultural Heritage and New Technologies'. Workshop 'Archäologie & Computer'. Wien 16.–18.2009.* Magistrat der Stadt Wien – Stadtarchäologie, Vienna.

Gabucci, A. 2005. *Informatica applicata all'archeologia.* Carocci, Rome.

Huvila, I. 2006. *The Ecology of Information Work. A Case Study of Bridging Archaeological Work and Virtual Reality Based Knowledge Organisation.* Åbo Akademi University Press, Turku.

Jerpåsen, G. B. 2009. 'Application of Visual Archaeological Landscape Analysis. Some Results.' *Norwegian Archaeological Review,* Vol. 42 (2), pp. 123–145.

Johnston, R. 1998. 'Approaches to the Perception of Landscape. Philosophy, Theory, Methodology.' *Archaeological Dialogues*, Vol. 5, pp. 54–68.

Kalliola, R. & Suominen, T. (eds.) 2007. *Spatial Modelling in Coastal Areas. Mapping of Exposure, Sea Surface Temperature and Shore Occupation.* UTULCC Publications, Vol. 13. University of Turku, Turku.

Knapp, A. B., & Ashmore, W. 1999. *Archaeologies of Landscape. Contemporary Perspectives*, Blackwell, Oxford.

Koivisto. M. 2004. *Jääkaudet.* WSOY, Helsinki.

Lock, G. 2003. *Using Computers in Archaeology. Towards Virtual Pasts.* Routledge, London.

Löwenborg, D. 2010. *Excavating the Digital Landsscape. GIS analyses of social relations in central Sweden in the 1ˢᵗ millennium AD.* AUN 42.

Moline, J. 1997. *Virtual Reality in Neuro-Psycho-Physiology.* Ios Press, Amsterdam.

Niccolucci, F., & Cantone, F. 2003. 'Legend and Virtual Reconstruction. Porsenna's Mausoleum in x3d.' In Doerr, M. & Sarris A. (eds.) *CAA 2002 The Digital Heritage of Archaeology. Computer Applications and Quantitative Methods in Archaeology. Proceedings of the 30th Conference, Heraklion, Crete, April 2002.* Archive of Monuments and Publications, Hellenic Ministry of Culture, Athens, pp. 57–62.

Pallares-Burke, M. L. G. 2002. *The New History. Confessions and Conversations.* Polity, Cambridge.

Pletinckx, D. 2008. 'Interpretation Management. How to Make Sustainable Visualisations of the Past.' The Interactive Institute, Stockholm.

Pukkila, J. & Uotila, K. 2005. 'From Ancient Monument to Virtual Model. GIS as a Content Production Tool in 3D Visualization.' In Mäntylä, S. (ed.) *Rituals and Relations. Studies on the History and Material Culture of the Baltic Finns.* The Finnish Academy of Science and Letters, Helsinki.

Reilly, Paul and Rahtz, Sebastian 1992. *Archaeology and the Information Age.* Routledge, London & New York.

Renfrew, C. 1997. Introduction. In Forte, Maurizio and Siliotti, Alberto (eds.) *Virtual Archaeology. Great Discoveries Brought to Life Through Virtual Reality.* Thames and Hudson, London.

Roussou, M., & Drettakis, G. 2004. 'Photorealism and Non-Photorealism in Virtual Heritage Representation.' In Arnold, D., Niccolucci, F. & Chalmers, A. (eds.) *VAST 2003. Proceedings of the 4th International Symposium on Virtual Reality, Archaeology and Intelligent Cultural Heritage.* Eurographics Association, Aire-la-Ville, pp. 51–60.

Ryan, N. 1996. 'Computer Based Visualisation of the Past. Technical "Realism" and Historical Credibility.' In Higgins, P. M. T. & Lang, J. (eds.) *Imaging the Past. Electronic Imagining and Computer Graphics in Museums and Archaeology.* The British Museum, London, pp. 95–108. URL: http://www.cs.kent.ac.uk/pubs/1996/315.

Ryan, N. 2001. 'Documenting and Validating Virtual Archaeology.' *Archeologia e Calcolatori*, Vol. 12, pp. 245–273. URL: http://www.cs.ukc.ac.uk/pubs/2001/1520.

Sanders, D. 2008. *Why do Virtual Heritage? Abstract of a Paper Presented in the 34th Annual Meeting and Conference of Computer Applications and Quantitative Methods in Archaeology CAA2006, Fargo, April 18–21, 2006.*

Schama, S. 1995. *Landscape and memory.* A.A. Knopf & Random House, New York.

Sogliani, F., Gabellone, F., Ferrari, I & Crimaco. L 2009. 'The Fortified Medieval Settlement of Söderholm, H. M. Sonnenwald, D. H. Cairns, B. Manning, J. E. Welch, G. F. and Fuchs, H. The potential impact of 3D telepresence technology on task performance in emergency trauma care. GROUP '07: Proceedings of the 2007 International ACM conference on Supporting group work, ACM, New York, pp. 79–88.

Solomon, P. 2002. 'Discovering Information in Context.' *The Annual Review of Information Science and Technology*, Vol. 36, pp. 229–264.

Tikkanen, M. & Oksanen, J. 2002. 'Late Weichselian and Holocene Shore Displacement History of the Baltic Sea in Finland.' *Fennia*, Vol. 180 (1–2), URL: http://www.helsinki.fi/maantiede/geofi/fennia/demo/pages/oksanen.htm.

Tilley, C. Y. 1994. *A Phenomenology of Landscape. Places, Paths, and Monuments.* Berg, Oxford & Providence, Rich.

Turner, J. 2002. 'Myron Krueger live.' *CTHEORY*, A104. URL: http://www.ctheory.net/text_file.asp?pick=328.

Uotila, K., & Sartes, M. 2000. 'Medieval Turku. The Lost City. A Project Trying to Reconstruct a Medieval Town in Finland.' In Barceló, J. A., Forte, M. & Sanders, D. H. (eds.) *Virtual Reality in Archaeology*, Vol. 843. Archaeopress, Oxford, pp. 219–223.

Uotila, K., Alho, P., Pukkila, J. & Tulkki, C. 2003. 'Modeling Natural and Human Landscape in Prehistoric and Medieval Southwest Finland from 500 BC to 1500 AD. Computer Based Visualization.' In Doerr, M. & Sarris, A. (eds.), *The Digital Heritage of Archaeology, CAA2002.* Archive of Monuments and Publications, Hellenic Ministry of Culture, Athens, pp. 191–194.

Uotila, K., Huvila, I., Vilkuna, A.-M., Lempiäinen, T., Grönlund, E. & Zetterberg, P., A 'Simulation of the Medieval Environment and its Change around Medieval Castles. Special Case in Finland.' In Campano, S. & Forte, M. (eds.) *From Space to Place. 2nd International Conference on Remote Sensing in Archaeology. Proceedings of the 2nd International Workshop, CNR, Rome Italy, December 4–7, 2006.* Archaeopress, Oxford, pp. 271–278.

Uotila, K., Vilkuna, A.-M., Huvila, I., Grönlund, E. & Simola, H. 2008. 'Bringing Together the Interdisciplinary Strategies for the Study of the Seats of Power in Medieval and Early Modern Finland in 3D-modelling.' In Lamberg, M., Keski-aho, J., Räsänen, E. & Timofeeva, O. (eds.) *Methods and the Medievalist. Current Approaches in Medieval Studies.* Cambridge Scholars Publishing, Newcastle-upon-Tyne, pp. 199–221.

Valenti, M., & Nardini, A. 2004. 'Modello dei dati e trattamento del dato sul gis di scavo.' *Archeologia e Calcolatori*, Vol. 15, pp. 341–358.

Vatanen [Huvila], I. 2003. 'Deconstructing the (Re)constructed. Issues on Annotation of the Archaeological Virtual Realities.' In Doerr, M., & Sarris, A. (eds.) *CAA2002 The Digital Heritage of Archaeology. Computer Applications and Quantitative Methods in Archaeology. Proceedings of the 30th Conference, Heraklion, Crete, April 2002.* Archive of Monuments and Publications, Hellenic Ministry of Culture, Athens, pp. 69–74.

Virkki, H. & Häkkinen, K. 2007. *Kanta-Hämeen muinaisrannat. Itämeren varhaisvaiheiden visualisointi.* Hämeen liitto, Hämeenlinna.

Wickstead, H. 2009. 'The Uber Archaeologist. Art, GIS and the Male Gaze Revisited.' *Journal of Social Archaeology*, Vol. 9 (2), pp. 249–271. URL: http://jsa.sagepub.com/cgi/content/abstract/9/2/249.

PART VI

FRAMEWORKS OF EVERYDAY LIFE

CHAPTER 11

A Rural Living Sphere

Marko Lamberg, Minna Mäkinen and Merja Uotila

Introduction

We all have a living sphere that is familiar to us and that includes places and customs we know. We also have an idea of where that sphere of familiarity ends and unfamiliar space begins – in other words, we know the boundaries of our living sphere. However, that idea or sense is not necessarily explicit or even something we are fully aware of, and usually it involves many partially overlapping layers. In this chapter, questions related to boundaries and spaces are addressed at the microspace level through the prism of a long-range study of a single village community and its environment. Our primary research task is to examine how the environment and natural circumstances have both restricted and guided human activities. First of all, we will examine how the interaction between people and their environment shaped the communality of early modern and 'modernizing' people. Our examination extends to the present day, thus providing a point of comparison for the circumstances of the past.

Boundaries and space interact with one another: a space is something that is separated from another or different type of space by a border. Nature shapes and generates boundaries that affect people. In practice this means that certain natural elements (such as water systems and land surface formations) are experienced as factors that restrict people's activities or define the spaces they govern. Single elements that stand out from an environment can also be perceived as boundaries, or at any rate border sites, through which people trace the limits of their existence and governance – in other words, those lines that separate 'us' from the 'others'.

But how clear were those boundaries? Which natural elements have attracted people's attention, and what does this reveal about human relationships with nature? To what extent have legal and administrative boundaries based partly on natural elements created a sense of affiliation within the community and distinguished it from other communities? How has communality produced through senses of locality manifested itself?

During the agrarian period in Finland, villages consisted of houses situated close to one another and were surrounded by fields and forests. Shared responsibilities and practices – such as the joint taxation of common land and shared agricultural activities (strip farming was predominant during the Middle Ages and the beginning of the modern era) – promoted the formation of networks of mutual assistance and thus a sense of community.[1] In the modern era, this traditional way of life and communality began to give way to a more family-centred and individualistic lifestyle. The change occurred at a different pace in different parts of Europe – in the peripheries it was visible only after the Second World War – but the causes and manifestations were similar everywhere: changes in agricultural production structure, increasing commercialization and use of technology, growing differences in income, urbanization and abandonment of the countryside (as well as the decrease of rural population resulting from these phenomena).[2]

In this chapter, we will largely concentrate on the village community during the 'good old' agrarian times. The village we have chosen, Toivola (literal meaning: 'a village of hope'[3]), is located in the parish of Hollola in the southern Finnish province of Häme (Sw. Tavastland).[4] Toivola belongs to the western Finnish cultural region, in which crop farming has been practised throughout the period studied. The landscape of Toivola is still characterized by undulating fields and a large ridge formation (Salpausselkä)[5] covered by forest, which in the south borders on the village. In size, Toivola is typical of a group village with the number of village farms increasing over time as the five original estates were divided into the twenty households or so that exist today. Toivola remained a tightly inhabited village situated on a single hill from medieval times up until the 1920s, when major agricultural and land ownership reforms resulted in the disintegration of the cohesive village hill and the farms becoming more widely dispersed.[6]

Within the Finnish context, Toivola was far from isolated and had long been close to travel routes. In the Middle Ages the early travel artery The Upper Vyborg Road (Fi. Ylinen Viipurintie), which connected Häme Castle (Sw. Tavastehus) and Vyborg Castle (Fi. Viipuri, Sw. Viborg), ran alongside the village.[7] The town of Hämeenlinna (Sw. Tavastehus) was 'only' 60 kilometres away (in others words, a journey of about two or three days), but being only a small inland town, its significance as a place of commerce was not as great as that of more distant coastal towns, such as

Turku (Sw. Åbo) or Porvoo (Sw. Borgå), and later Helsinki (Sw. Helsingfors), some 100 kilometres away at the end of the southern road. However, throughout the eighteenth and nineteenth centuries the closest market was held in the neighbouring parish of Asikkala.[8] Toivola has therefore enjoyed reasonably good and stable connections with the outside world, which must be taken into account when examining the community and its relationship to space (Map 33 see colour plate section 2, p. 7).

In this study, we explore in some depth the various forms of boundaries within the village of Toivola. We consider boundaries in terms of landscape, mental images and marriage fields. First, we examine how the geographical borders of the village were formed and how they have changed or remained static over the course of centuries. After considering the physical borders, we look at the more abstract aspect of boundaries, in other words, how boundaries have been involved in the construction of a sense of locality and regional conceptions of 'us' and 'others'. The section that follows is also concerned with the sphere of mental images, for it deals with the description and mapping of 'scary' places. We approach these themes primarily through oral tradition. Finally we consider boundaries through the geography of Toivola marriages: where did brides and bridegrooms from outside Toivola come from? By mapping the marriage fields, we are able to begin to assess the effects that physical and mental environment had on the movements of Toivola residents and how these environments also affected the villagers' interactions with their neighbours.

Intentions, sources, methods

Temporally, our study extends from medieval times to the present day. We have consulted various sources from a multidisciplinary position. Thus, we have taken diverse approaches to our subject matter, making use of archaeological inventory, historical cartography, placenames, mapping and statistical analysis, as well as analysis of oral tradition and interview material (an essential part of folkloristic and ethnological study).

First we look at how the 'natural', that is, geographical, borders of the village were formed. We have chosen to place the word 'natural' in quotation marks, since the 'naturalness' of borders is, after all, always more or less artificial and variable, determined by the movement, activities and interests of people. The geographical borders of the village, marked through border sites in the terrain, have nevertheless provided both local inhabitants and outside authorities with a particular mental image of a legal and administrative community located and functioning in a specific place.

Historical border sites can be traced by combining information contained in different kinds of sources: maps (both contemporary and present-day), placenames, written documents dealing with border demarcations and archaeological surveys. By means of archaeological prospecting terrain inventories it may be possible to find out whether and how the old border sites were distinguished on the ground and what kinds of factors influenced the selection of earlier border sites. The earliest available data about borders and border sites in Finland can be found in medieval court rolls, which in their records of border disputes include lists of border sites.[9] Border disputes sometimes continued for centuries, and in these cases court minutes often refer to earlier judgements. Since the beginning of the eighteenth century, the borders of Toivola village have also been mapped.[10] Part of the job of the land surveyors who drew up the maps was to also provide verbal descriptions of the border sites.[11] With the help of various written sources it is thus possible to map and compare the border sites of Toivola from the fifteenth century onwards. However, the variety of sources and the long-range nature of the study present interpretative challenges, particularly with regard to the process of synthesizing source data.

When we consider the more abstract aspects of boundaries, the most important issues relate to forms of neighbourhood and everyday interaction within the community, as well as villagers' conceptions of outsiders. As a phenomenon that sheds light on the formation of regional boundaries and a sense of locality, we examine mocking songs and names (Fi. *köllit*) that were used in Toivola. Through humour and jeering these songs and names provided descriptions of neighbouring villages and parishes from the perspective of Toivola residents. Largely a male tradition, mocking songs were often sung on the way to church, at markets and at lodging houses for boasting purposes.[12] The oldest Finnish mocking songs can be traced back to the seventeenth century, but the real golden age of the genre extended from the nineteenth century into the first decades of the twentieth century.[13] It is material (relating to Toivola and its neighbours) from this period that we examine here.

Oral tradition not only serves as a means in the mapping process, but also becomes an object of mapping when we examine the local tradition of beliefs from a geographical perspective. We direct our attention to early modern rural folk tradition and in particular to stories and beliefs about places that inspired fear among local residents. These beliefs were transmitted and maintained orally up until the beginning of the twentieth century, when collectors of Finnish popular culture visited Hollola Parish among many others and conducted interviews about local folk tales. It was at this time that oral culture was recorded in a written form: short and sometimes very laconic summaries – interviewers sought to distil what they perceived to be the essence of their informants' accounts – were placed in the Folklore Archives of the Finnish Literature Society in Helsinki.[14] The collections contain material relating to oral tradition, folk music and oral history (including mocking songs and stories about places that inspired fear) as well as ethnological descriptions and biographies.

Since the collection of oral tradition about Toivola (and more widely the parish of Hollola as a whole) has taken place only in modern times, its folklore data must be applied retrospectively to the study of earlier ways of life and thinking. However, we must remember that not all oral culture has been preserved: the collectors of folklore are unable to interview all members of a community, informants do not share all their knowledge (for a variety of reasons) and, likewise, the collectors do not record everything shared by their informants. The collections preserved in the Folklore Archives primarily consist of material sent by individual collectors. Moreover, oral traditions change and vary over time, and the written descriptions we are now able to read present only the latter-day layer of such traditions – as evident, for instance, from the references to bus stops in the collected material.[15] Thus, the mental landscape we are able to reconstruct is almost certainly not a complete reflection of that which was experienced by previous generations. But on the other hand, not all the residents of Toivola necessarily ever shared all the beliefs ascribed to the parish as a whole and its neighbouring areas: some tales may have been locally bound and maintained only in certain villages, and of course such individual factors as gender, age, occupation and educational background must also have played an important role in whether a person actually believed or transmitted a tale he or she had been told.

Most of the places referred to as suspicious in folk tales can be mapped. This makes it possible to compare the mental and physical landscapes. Reputedly dangerous, scary, mystical or unnatural elements in the vicinity of Toivola have been charted with reference to four military maps[16] produced at the end of the eighteenth century. (The maps depict the southern part of Finland some decades before the end of the Swedish rule.) Thanks to their richly detailed depiction of early modern local geography (inhabited areas, cultivations, woodlands, water systems, road networks etc.) and their temporal proximity to recorded local folklore (based on the well-founded assumption that at least some of the tales collected at the beginning of the twentieth century were of older origin), these charts serve as a suitable foundation for the mapping of somewhat earlier mental landscapes.

In addition to folklore material, our study has also used interviews with present-day residents of Toivola. These informants describe Toivola and their own experiences of living in the village. The interviews (conducted in 2007 and 2008) focused on changes in the appearance and landscape of Toivola over the last few decades, as well as the present state of the village and thoughts about its future. Questions relating to the establishment of the boundaries of the village and its coexistence with neighbouring villages were also addressed, as were questions relating to the village's internal borders and processes of localization.

As we attempt to form an idea about the abstract dimension of boundaries, we in fact encounter the multilayered nature of boundaries: we are simultaneously examining both a real physical space and mental landscapes based on this real space. If we direct our attention to the natural surroundings, we might ask how early modern people perceived the space surrounding them: was it experienced as a threat that restricted movement, or perhaps as the opposite? Earlier studies about early modern – particularly agrarian – communities have tended to foreground such communities' introversion and even their fear of the unknown.[17] A similar emphasis has been placed on the fear that characterized agrarian people's relationships with nature, which has been explained through reference to 'fantasies' either of Christian or earlier origin.[18] But space is neither only real nor only imaginary: it always involves human interpretation of the surrounding environment – an interpretation can be called mental landscape or mentality. Spaces are both real and imagined.[19]

To conclude, we focus on people's movement in space and border crossings by examining how geographical and mental boundaries were manifested in one of the most important forms of individual and communal interaction, namely the selection of a marriage partner. Through mapping the marriage fields between 1750 and 1850 we can begin to assess the ways in which physical and mental environment affected the movements of residents of Toivola and their interactions with their neighbours.

In Finland, as in other parts of the Swedish kingdom, the clergy kept records about their parishioners. From the seventeenth century onwards parish records included details about an individual's knowledge of Christianity, their participation in the Holy Communion and the most significant events of their lives (in other words christenings, marriages and burials). With the help of these 'church books', we are able to examine the demographic history of early modern Finland. The practice of record-keeping continued throughout the nineteenth century despite the fact that Finland was ceded to Russia in 1809. Undoubtedly, the level and quality of record-keeping varied from parish to parish, and most of the earliest registers have been destroyed. Nevertheless, church books dating back to the early or mid-eighteenth century are available, in one form or another, for most parishes. These books have served as the basis for a number of demographic research databases developed since the 1990s. The most important of these is the freely available internet database HiSKi ('History Books'), which contains church book data collected from all over Finland, including births, marriages and deaths in Toivola.[20] This source series contains chronologically recorded information on the births, marriages, movement and deaths of the members of a parish. Of course, not even these records are unproblematic sources: over the years there was considerable variation between individual priests with regard to the manner and accuracy of their record-keeping.

The border around the village

Generally, the ownership of land requires that the land in question is encircled by and marked with borders and border markers. Those areas that belong to a single village are also determined by certain border points that have been named and commonly agreed upon. Therefore, a border site presents a sign of power and ownership for both the inhabitants of a village and their neighbours.[21] Although specific demarcations of borders had not always been necessary (and uninhabited forest areas had once provided adequate living sphere boundaries), with increased density of settlement private owners of villages and wildernesses felt a greater need to define and indicate the borders of their lands more precisely.[22] Crossing a border or travelling through a forest owned by someone else was not always allowed. Instead, the borders of a village could only be crossed at certain predetermined sites, usually along public roads and paths. Trespassing rights could also be granted on the basis of an agreement, which would be recorded in the court minutes.[23]

The borders of a village lay at the outer edge of fields, meadows and forests owned by the village and were based on either natural sites or man-made markers. Prominent natural elements (such as large stones, rocks, hills and ridges) that stood out from their surroundings were often used as border markers (Picture 6 see colour plate section 2, p. 8). Bodies of water (including rivers, brooks, rapids, springs and lake sites) would frequently be used as borders. In addition, living and growing natural elements such as trees (and stumps) were also seen as suitable border markers. In cases where no suitable natural feature was available, human constructions (such as roads, bridges and fenced enclosures)[24] would be used as sites to indicate a border or border markers would be built out of stones.[25] The border points required around villages varied according to environment. It was particularly important to indicate the border with a specific site in those areas where the line of the border turned. Further border markers were sometimes added later in order to clarify the course of the border.

Since Toivola is located on the western fringe of Hollola Parish, it shares some of its twelve border sites with the neighbouring parish. The northern border of the village follows the aforementioned public road, which in practice forms almost the entire northern border of the village. The southern border of the village follows the top of the ridge formation, which separates the villages, and also parishes. To the west, the border partly runs along a ditch (Haisevanoja). Today the border still follows the old course of the ditch, even though the ditch itself was straightened and cleared a long time ago. The eastern border of the village runs through woodlands through various border sites. Unlike the other parts of the border, the eastern section is not determined by conspicuous natural elements or roads. Because of the considerable age of the border sites and the disputed nature of the borderline, we have chosen to focus our attention on this border between Toivola and the village of Sairakkala.

The eastern border of Toivola has been the cause of disputes between the two villages for centuries, and is discussed in a number of legal documents. It seems that a dispute over borders markers between Toivola and Sairakkala villages was first recorded in 1432, although border points were not referred to by name until the border dispute was mentioned for the second time, in 1486. At that time, five border points (Biörnin orcko, Tuli kiwi, Olkisilda, Aidanjatco and Licalammin silda[26]) seem to have formed a line running in a south–north direction. It appears that the medieval border ran from one border site to another without further demarcation.[27] The legal documents indicate that the border issue was next addressed in court during the sixteenth century. The issue is once again mentioned in a seventeenth-century court roll in connection with an argument over the ownership of an area of farmland bought from the northern part of Toivola.[28] A document from the late eighteenth century concerning land reform also indicates that there continued to be disputes over the course. As late as the mid-nineteenth century, the inhabitants of Toivola and Sairakkala had to summon a land surveyor to settle their border disputes.[29]

In total there are six named border points through which the eastern borderline runs. The border point to the southeast was, and still is, Pyörinorko (Biörnin orcko). It is situated alongside a road (or, more accurately, a bridle path) that leads southeast to the neighbouring village of Tennilä. This road travels over the top of the Salpausselkä ridge that dominates the landscape, through a narrow strip of land formed between two kettle formations. Today the border marker, built out of stones, is prominently situated at the lowest point of this isthmus, right next to the road. The border point's name also provides a good idea of the surroundings: the Finnish word *orko* refers to an isthmus located between two hollows or depressions in the land. In this case, considering the type of the terrain, the name could be thought to refer to a steep kettle.[30]

The next border site, Koivunotta (the original meaning may have been 'the brow of the birch', but we cannot be certain), is not mentioned in medieval court rolls, but was later established as a border point. It is probable that it was selected as a new border point at a time when it became necessary to define the border more accurately. The Koivunotta site is located at the bottom of a small but, nevertheless, distinctive sandy hill, by the side of the road to Tennilä. At this point, the road is joined by a path leading to the village of Sairakkala. This road configuration, along with the hill, allows the site to be easily identified.[31]

Viewed from the south, the third border point is Tulikivi. According to the first map depicting the village of Toivola and its borders, from 1705, the site consisted of two large stones lying on the ground, indicating a separate border marker (Map 34 see colour plate section 2, p. 9).[32] Today, only a man-made square pile of stones marks the site (most probably constructed at a later period).[33] The site is located on a hillside, a short distance from the Olkisuo swamp. Local tradition claims that burnt stones were found in the area, hence its name Tulikivi ('firestone') (Picture 7 see colour plate section 2, p. 8). Moreover, it is possible that people came to collect stones for sauna stoves from this area; at any rate this has been believed to be the source of the name.[34] This forest terrain was also traditionally used for slash-and-burn cultivation. Whatever the origins of the border site name, the area was clearly connected to fire in some way and is still called Tulikivenmaa ('firestone land'). The border site itself, however, is no longer easily identifiable, apart from the pile of stones.

It seems that the medieval site of Olkisilta ('straw bridge') was later replaced as the fourth border site by Rajamänty ('border pine'). (There is still a swamp called Olkisuo ('straw swamp') in the area today). The Rajamänty border site was located alongside Matkotie ('journey road'), a road that leads from Ylinen Viipurintie ('The Upper Vyborg Road') through Sairakkala and Toivola towards the southern coastal towns. Because of this the border site has also been known as Matkotienmänty ('journey road pine').[35] In 1705, a pine into which border marks, or blazes, were etched stood on the site.[36] By the end of the century, only a tree stump remained, which was in turn utilized as a border marker. Today there is no separate border marker remaining at the site.

Aidanjatko ('extension of the fence'), the fifth border point between Toivola and Sairakkala, is today marked by a number of stones at the side of a field. The site is situated between a hillock and a swampy hollow. There used to be a large swamp in the area, but this was drained for cultivation purposes. According to the notes from the 1705 map, this border site was determined by a fence that ran between the estates of Toivola and Sairakkala, as the name also suggests. However, at the end of the century, a stone border marker was erected on the site.[37] The site was such a short distance away from the Toivola village lands and the traditional fenced fields that it may have belonged to an area that had to be fenced according to the obligation to fence land. There was also a farming field nearby, now it has become overgrown with trees; the shallow ditches that are visible in the area today are reminders of its landscape during the earlier period.

The bridge at Likalammi or Likalemmi (perhaps a place for linen soaking)[38] – the final border point mentioned in medieval records – crosses a small ditch on the Upper Viborg Road. In seventeenth-century documents, this border site is referred to as Kivioja ('stone ditch') bridge.[39] Even today, at this site the old road crosses over a small ditch (which has now been cleared). However, there is no bridge left at the site, only the culvert remains. Although local people have referred to the site by various names, the bridge site –which at one time lay on one of the main arterial roads of Finland – is still used and retains its function as a border site.

It is not self-evident that the names of border sites have been preserved or that they can still be recognized and identified. The traditional names that have been preserved are those that have been in active use during different periods. Maintaining existing borders was most important when such borders marked the boundaries of people's farmlands, pastures and forest areas. The fact that the legal border of Toivola largely follows natural formations has made it easier for landowners to manage the borders and the areas within them. However, sometimes it has proved difficult to find natural elements to serve as border points, and thus it is no surprise that the eastern border of Toivola and the woodland sites that define it have been the subject of numerous disputes over the centuries. For this reason, natural formations have often later been replaced by constructed stone markers, whose purpose was to render the border fixed and indisputable.

Borders as sources of segregation

Borders may be border sites visible in the landscape as described above or geographical borderlines and points on maps. However, borders may also have more invisible, mental and ideal forms, which are created – demarcated – consciously or, quite often, unconsciously. One important aspect of borders is their changeability: borders move and resemble processes; borders are created, barriers brought down, but also reinforced. Borders are maintained: they are produced and reproduced for example through speech. Thus, borders have a verbal aspect, which is concretely displayed in our ways of talking, our expressions and the stories we tell about ourselves and others.[40] To mark and maintain borders therefore requires not only concrete border markers and sites and agreements over these, but also speech and activities that give meanings to borders.[41] The medieval and later border sites around the village of Toivola, particularly their names, present a good example of such meaning-giving activity. The names of border sites have been preserved as part of local tradition and history. There are still Toivola residents who are able to locate the old border sites (and even name some of them) and who are also interested in passing on this 'border tradition' to others.[42]

The creation or maintenance of borders is commonly related to power and economic ownership, but it is also an act of categorization and an attempt to distinguish oneself from others. In the case of borders that exist in a geographical place, this means senses of locality and communality that are attached to a place: the ways they are defined and manifest themselves.[43] Borders shape the identity of a place, in other words they define what makes a place recognizable and distinguishes it from other places or regions. Borders are an important part of collective symbolism (expressed in stories, documents and rituals), through which a place exists.[44]

In Finland, villages, congregations and parishes have traditionally been important, demarcated communities within and to which people have spontaneously situated and attached themselves. Numerous locally recorded stories, jokes, proverbs, mocking songs and names demonstrate the significance of communities and boundaries, as well as people's desire to maintain and reinforce them. The mocking songs that involved neighbouring villages or parishes highlight the practice of associating neighbours with a whole host of mocking names. These names were sometimes dismissive, sometimes even indiscreet. When such names referred to certain perceived negative characteristics, they simultaneously reinforced the idea that, of course, the name-callers themselves were not like that.[45] Performing mocking songs or using derisive names was seldom motivated by malice or a downright intention to insult. This kind of neighbour humour arose from an attempt to separate oneself (us) from the inhabitants of other parts of the village, other villages or parishes (others) under the guise of jokes. Even though people jeered at the silly behaviour or minor misfortunes of their neighbours, they were also curious about their neighbours' activities. The participants in a mocking relationship could not live with each other, but neither could they live without one another.[46]

People's use of humour related to otherness has been connected to the regulation of relationships between local communities in various ways. Jesting provided an outlet for communal conflicts that could not have been addressed otherwise – words sometimes proved mightier or at least less costly than the sword or court proceedings.[47] Nevertheless, disputes between neighbouring villages did sometimes have to be settled in court. For example in 1643, the village of Toivola as a whole was ordered to recompense a peasant from the neighbouring village of Kastari. Toivola's neglect of its responsibility to maintain part of the border fence had led to cattle getting loose and damaging fields in the neighbouring village. Twenty years later, Toivola inhabitants made a complaint about damage to their fields caused by horses from another neighbouring village, Tenhiälä. In this case, the court ordered both villages to participate in the erection of a fence.[48]

As well as mocking names related to villages and parishes, individuals were also often the object of jeering and name-calling in Finnish rural communities. Nicknames, pet names or mocking names could describe a single characteristic, certain events in an individual's life or their role within the community. The name-calling tradition served an important purpose as a kind of coding activity: a name operated as an instant reminder of the story associated with the individual and thus helped to preserve the story in communal memory. The practice of name-calling also revealed how the community perceived an individual; in other words, it was control exercised by the community. In a small community, people's lives intersected in various ways, and this made inhabitants all the more interested in each other's activities.[49]

Mocking songs and names are not as common today as they were for example in the rural villages of the late nineteenth and early twentieth centuries. However, neighbour humour has not completely disappeared from our culture and can appear in the form of jokes about different ethnicities, regions or celebrities. In addition, older people may still remember some of the more memorable mocking songs. Interviewees from Toivola, for example, recalled some of the mocking names that were used about people from their village or the neighbouring villages.

> Interviewer: What significance did the borders of the village have?
> Interviewee: They had significance, of course. You would see people being parochial. In these parts they sure used to call people from other villages names: they called people from Kastari 'crows', and Kastari people replied with 'cockroaches from Toivola'. You would see these kinds of things. (Interview conducted on July 26, 2007.)[50]

Another aspect of neighbour humour in the interview material are the informants' somewhat playful accounts that their own village has traditionally been viewed as in some way superior, for instance, more quiet and peaceful than neighbouring villages. The inhabitants of Toivola seem to have perceived themselves as perhaps more virtuous and even more abstinent than the residents of neighbouring villages.[51] Putting one's own community on a pedestal and appreciative and positive narratives associated with one's own village can be understood in part through the concept of territoriality. One important purpose of territoriality is the unification of the community and the reinforcement of local boundaries. In this way, the areas and people that make up the community become islands of safety and a certain kind of idealization for individuals; whereas areas belonging to others are perceived as strange and thus as something that arouses feelings of uncertainty.[52] Relating to the construction of spatiality, the dichotomy between familiar and strange regions – in other words between good and evil or at any rate between better and worse – is part of the basic territoriality of human life, territoriality that is always socially produced.[53] This idea of good against evil (or better against worse) that is constructed through distinction-laden speech thus marks an attempt to reinforce the necessity and significance of the boundaries of for example one's own village.[54]

When mapping the borders of the village, we should also consider the internal and sometimes invisible boundaries and sites that affect everyday relationships between the villagers. In Toivola, the structure of habitation changed radically as a result of the reorganization of the village farmlands that took place during the first decade of the twentieth century. Houses had previously been largely clustered on the village hill. With land reorganization, dwellings gradually became more widely dispersed. Even though distances within the village are no greater than a few kilometres, over the course of decades the spread of habitation has produced separate groups of houses within the village. Inhabitants tend to have a lot of interaction with their close neighbours, but they have less contact with residents from other parts of the village. Among women, in particular, outdoor walks or other types of daily interaction 'take place' more frequently within the immediate neighbourhood, where they are also usually able to find 'helping hands' when needed. Indeed, geographical distances and locations have an influence on how the village is perceived at a mental level, which is concretely manifested in the locations in which social everyday interaction takes place in the village, for instance.[55]

As a result of the reorganization of farmlands and the consequent disintegration of areas of habitation, Toivola lost its coherent village centre, which has since relocated more than once. (Map 35 see colour plate section 2, p. 10). As a village shop and post office had been operating from the same premises in the northern part of Toivola since the end of the nineteenth century, this area of the village seemed to be a natural place for the new village centre.[56] The villagers would meet each other on their visits to the shop and the post office, and nearly all the inhabitants would often have an errand of some sort to run in the direction of the shop. Once at the shop they would exchange personal news; it was also a place where young people would congregate.[57] After the shop and post office closed down at the beginning of the 1980s, the area around the village school and clubhouse began to be seen as the centre of the village. With the closure of the village school at the beginning of the 2000s, the location of the centre is once again in transition and has become all the more difficult to define.[58]

A 'landscape of fear'?

Thus far, we have approached Toivola largely as a community that occupies and controls part of the physical space and landscape surrounding it. We have also seen how this 'holding of a place' was reflected mentally.

We continue our survey of the inhabitants' mental landscape by looking further at the relationship between village dwellers and the nature around them.

Previous research has indicated that untamed nature, especially remote and uninhabited places and areas, could be regarded with fearful eyes in various parts of early modern Europe. Plenty of evidence suggests that woodlands, moors, marshes and mountains – that is, places outside human habitation and infrastructure – were seen not only as boundaries around human habitation areas, but also as portals and gateways to the supernatural.[59] In some cases, it was not the remoteness of the place but a strikingly different element in its physical landscape, such as a rock or a ravine, that evoked connotations of the supernatural.[60]

People believed that nature had also been created by God and that in the wilderness a person could sense the proximity of God or at least sense something sacred. But often works composed from learned Christian culture and ideas expressed within folk culture in local folklore, for example have tended to connect remote or uninhabited natural places with negative and even demonic elements, such as restless or evil spirits, unexplainable phenomena or inhuman creatures. Indeed, even the scarcely populated countryside *per se* could be regarded as an ungodly scene on account of its proximity to nature.[61] Thus, to borrow a phrase from cultural historian Vito Fumagalli, the pre-modern rural landscape was also a 'landscape of fear'.[62]

Local folklore from the parish of Hollola, recorded in the early twentieth century, 'knew' places that were experienced as dangerous or where ghosts or other supernatural phenomena had allegedly been encountered. This lore was expressed and preserved in the form of tales that characterized different parts of the early modern living sphere. Some of these tales also referred to specific houses or villages where individuals with supernatural abilities had lived. The tales of witches and healers can be contrasted with the aforementioned stereotypical constellations of perceptions between different communities: even in the context of supernatural phenomena (good or evil), other villages and their inhabitants were likely to be regarded as different.

In many cases, tales preserved local history, albeit probably in an altered form. It seems that some stories had apparently been composed as etymological explanations for local placenames: for instance, the name Haisevanoja (the ditch that constitutes the geographical and administrative boundary of Toivola to the west) can be literally translated as 'a smelly ditch'. So it is not very surprising that local inhabitants have explained the name by inventing a story of a dead man whose corpse was found in the very same ditch. Moreover, the place was rumoured to be haunted: it was supposedly impossible to cross the Haisevanoja Bridge by horse at night.[63] Similar processes and 'folk etymologies' may explain why certain other places, such as the Parinpelto field, were also connected with supernatural phenomena – in this case, the name evoked an association with the word *paarit*, 'bier' (once again leading one's thoughts to corpses and ghosts).[64] Of course, the degree of fear attached to different places seems to have varied a great deal: some places must have been more frightening than others. Analysis of the folk tales suggests that frightening places did not necessarily inspire fear during daylight hours. The same informant who in 1938 described the popular etymology of Haisevanoja and its haunted bridge also mentioned that she and her sister had seen 'a great number' of boys from Toivola going to swim in Haisevanoja.[65]

As we can see from Map 36 (see colour plate section 2, p. 11), within local folklore in Hollola, even Toivola village and Hollola Church were seen as sites of haunting and inexplicable happenings. However, overall only a minority of these mysterious tales involved man-made environments and buildings: certain houses and the 'old place' in Toivola, Hollola Church and the community hall in Uskila village were mentioned in the early 1900s. As indicated by the tales that mention bus stops, the modernization of agrarian society did not immediately put an end to perceptions that some places were dangerous. An individual travelling in a motorized vehicle could also experience fear when approaching desolate and shadowy locations.[66]

Usually unnatural elements were 'situated' in areas some distance from human habitation and infrastructure. This is not surprising considering what we already know of the relationship between people and nature in pre-modern Europe. But we should also note that frightening or mystical places were *not too remote*. Instead, they were located close to routes that people had to use almost daily: relatively near or very near roads, bridges, shores (waterways) or cultivated land or pastures. Indeed, the aspects of the physical landscape in the Hollola area labelled as frightening, threatening or mysterious could usually be seen from the road or the lake, or sometimes even from one's very own yard. Even when a place with such associations lay within in a forest, it would be relatively easy to reach rather than situated in a distant wilderness. Such sites might be located in forested areas where people would hunt, tend cattle or pick berries. This is, in fact, quite

Map 31. Map of Huittinen (Huittis), part of a military atlas drawn in the last decades of the eighteenth century. Kouvonoja Village is at the bottom of the map while Hannula is one of the villages by the river, which flows from east to west towards the heartland of Huittinen. In the forest between the river area and Kouvonoja there are large swamps ('Ilmiön-suo', 'Iså Hotsin Suo' and 'Iså Parpon Suo'), which made it difficult to travel from north to south and vice versa. The white area at the bottom left has not been mapped. Finska rekognosceringsverket, The Swedish Military Archives, Stockholm.

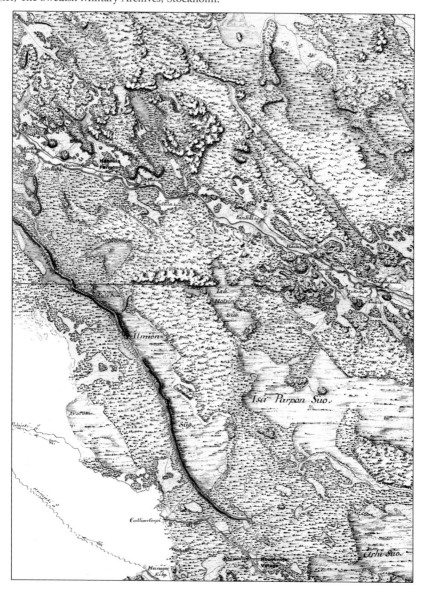

Picture 2. The church of Karjaa (Karis) lies on the hill near a shore of lake. The lake is part of a larger water route system from the inland to the sea. The church was built in the middle of the fifteenth century but the clock tower is younger, as in cases of other medieval stone churches too. Photograph by Päivi Maaranen.

Picture 3. The stone castle of Raasepori (Raseborg), now virtually in ruins, dominated the local milieu from the fourteenth to the sixteenth century. It was erected on a rock and it was surrounded by shallow water. Photograph by Päivi Maaranen.

Map 32a-d. The development of the Laitila diocese based on archaeological research material and GIS analysis in the period 1000–1500 AD.

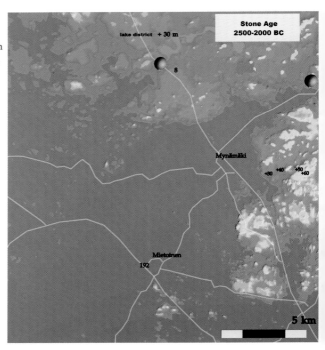

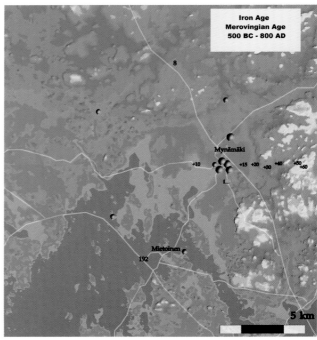

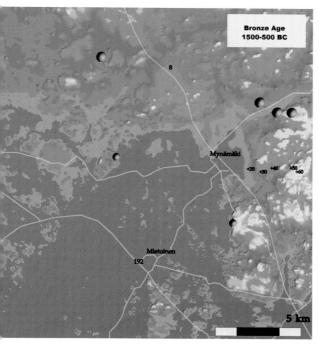

Bronze Age
1500-500 BC

8

Mynämäki

+20 +40 +50
+30 +60

Mietoinen

192

5 km

One wealthy settlement
in a shallow bay becomes
a hamlet with several
dwellings while the
environs change into a
lake and river. The area
develops gradually to an
extensive village centre, in
which the dwellings form
enclosured yards. The
changes in the environs
during the centuries are
interpreted by presenting
models of the fields,
pastures, meadows and
adjoining forests. The series of models is available
for viewing at the Laitila
library and it contains
a literary reference for
the public in which the
backgrounds regarding
the different chronologi-
cal levels are explained.
3d model by Kari Uotila,
GIS analysis by Jouko
Pukkila.

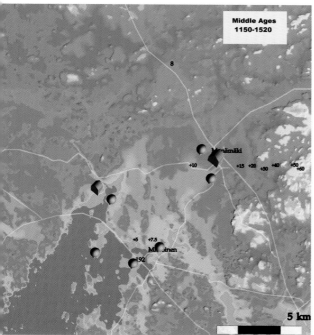

Middle Ages
1150-1520

8

Mynämäki

+10 +15 +20 +40 +50
+30 +60

+5 +7.5

Mietoinen

192

5 km

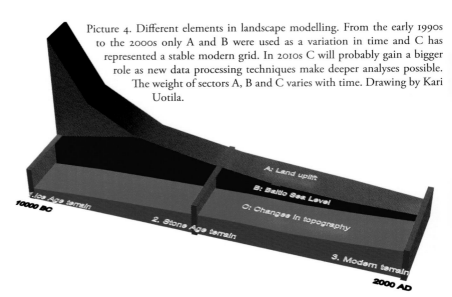

Picture 4. Different elements in landscape modelling. From the early 1990s to the 2000s only A and B were used as a variation in time and C has represented a stable modern grid. In 2010s C will probably gain a bigger role as new data processing techniques make deeper analyses possible. The weight of sectors A, B and C varies with time. Drawing by Kari Uotila.

A: Land uplift

B: Baltic Sea Level

C: Changes in topography

10000 BC

1. Ice Age terrain

2. Stone Age terrain

3. Modern terrain

2000 AD

Picture 5. Thematic model of a landscape in time. Phases A & B represent a rocky and sandy island growing as the Baltic Sea level is changing and land uplift is very fast. Timeline 10000–6000 BC.

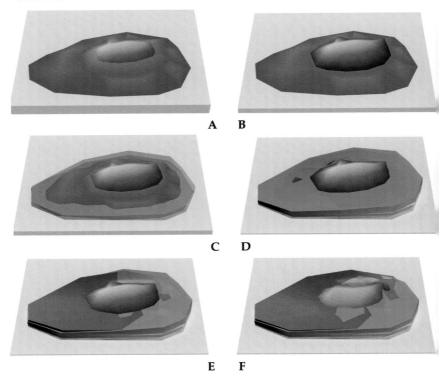

A   B

C   D

E   F

Picture 6. Although the fields and meadows are bigger today, making the landscape in modern Toivola more open than during earlier centuries, Salpausselkä ridge with its forested hills continues to form part of the visible and judicially defined boundary of the village. Photograph by Merja Uotila.

Picture 7. Today the Tulikivi border site – photographed here in 2008 – is indicated by a stone border marker, most likely dating back to the late nineteenth or early twentieth century. Photograph by Merja Uotila.

Map 33. Toivola Village with its nearest surroundings on a military map drawn in the last decades of the eighteenth century. The Upper Vyborg Road runs in an east–west direction approximately 700 metres north from the village centre. Finska rekognosceringsverket, The Swedish Military Archives, Stockholm.

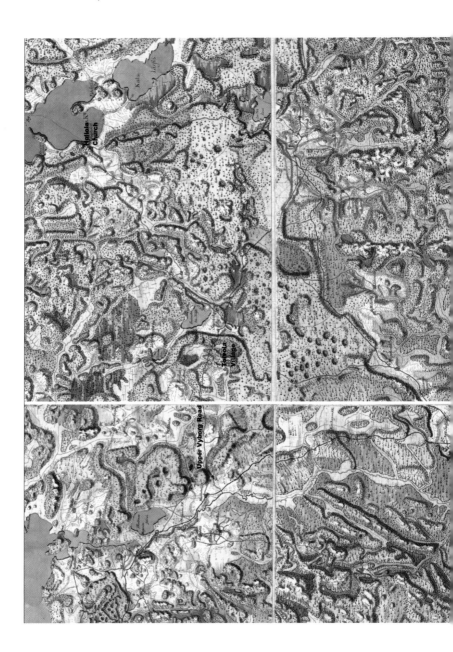

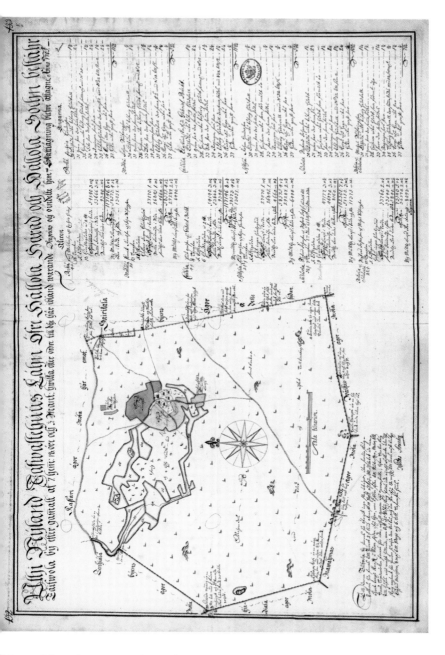

Map 34. The earliest preserved map depicting Toivola Village and its boundaries was drawn in 1705. Map H21 5/10–11, The maps of the National Land Survey (Maanmittaushallitus), The National Archives of Finland, Helsinki.

Map 35. The map below depicts the village of Toivola in the 1930s. There was only the Mäkelä estate remaining on the village hill, while for example the estates of Alitalo, Kerppilä and Mäki-Sylkkylä had been moved to the fringes of the village. The centre of the village moved from the old village hill first towards the Sulonen estate, to the surroundings of the village shop and post office, and later to the surroundings of the village school and club house. Map: National Land Survey of Finland, Pitäjänkartta 1947, page 676/256 Koski.

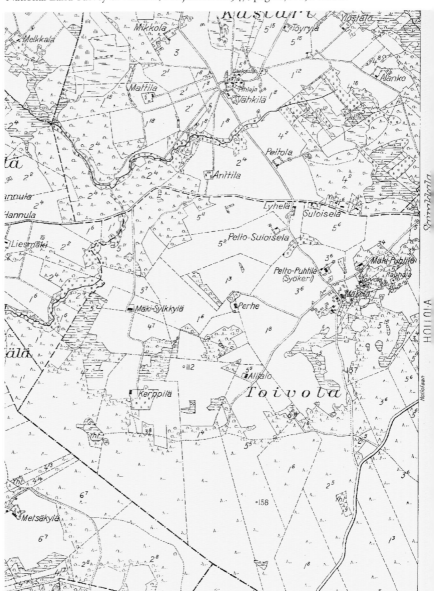

Map 36. The primary marriage fields of the inhabitants of Toivola (highlighted with red and yellow) between 1750 and 1850 contrasted to the local eighteenth-century road system (major roads are emphasized with violet) and the 'landscape of fear' (the allegedly scary or mysterious places are marked with black diamonds). The basis of the visualization is formed by late eighteenth-century military maps (Finska rekognoseringsverket, The Swedish Military Archives, Stockholm). © Marko Lamberg.

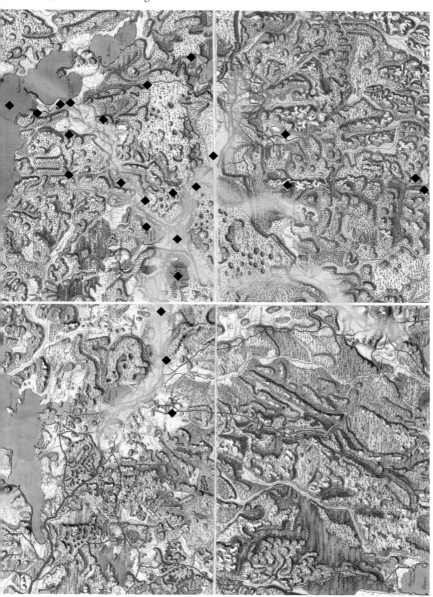

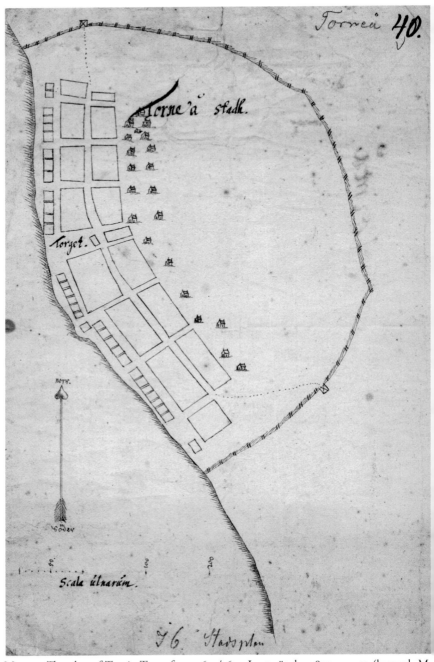

Map 37. The plan of Tornio Town from 1620/1621. Lantmät. lev 1892, no. 40 (kartavd. M. form.). The National Archives of Sweden, Sockholm.

Map 38. Tornio in 1697. The map is a copy made in 1758. The Provincial Museum of Tornio Valley, Tornio.

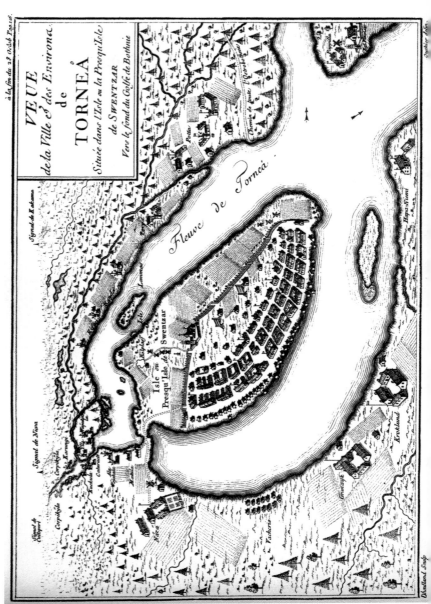

Map 39. Enclosed town space in Tornio in 1736/37. The Provincial Museum of Tornio Valley, Tornio.

Picture 8. Window without curtains in Turkansaari Open-Air Museum, Oulu. Photograph by Timo Ylimaunu.

Picture 9. Window with curtains in Turkansaari Open-Air Museum, Oulu. Photograph by Timo Ylimaunu.

understandable: we humans project our fears and expectations onto what we perceive around us. Thus, the landscape of fear, such as we have been able to reconstruct it, reflects knowledge rather than ignorance of the details of the physical landscape.

By means of recorded folklore, we at least get an impression of how earlier inhabitants of Toivola may have perceived their mental environment. However, it is also important to consider whether such beliefs had any significant influence upon inter-village encounters – whether, for instance, the exchange of marriage partners between villages decreased (or even ceased) if the two communities in question were connected by a road that led through a dense forest associated with ghostly apparitions.

To hold on to and cross borders

Just as legal, administrative and proprietary boundaries have not prevented people from transgressing boundaries, neither has fear. On the contrary, contact and interaction with the external environment on the part of the community or individual is a prerequisite of drawing physical or mental borders. Marriage was an important means by which a village community could have close relationships with other villages or alternatively isolate itself from other communities.

In early modern society – or at any rate in groups of society that owned land – marriages were not only agreements between individuals, but also involved those who were part of the individuals' social spheres, especially their families. Male guardians usually had the final power of decision over the marriages of the young women under their care.[67] Of course, the type of relationship between the two communities involved also played a part in the selection of a marriage partner. Individuals were unlikely to travel to a neighbouring parish or town (much less a different region) to find a marriage partner, daughter- or son-in-law, or sister- or brother-in-law, if they did not already have existing connections with the area and its inhabitants. The geographical dimension of marriages can therefore be utilized when examining interaction – or it its absence – between communities.

Certainly, marriages were only one manifestation of social interaction: other family relationships, networks of godparents, ties of friendships, economic engagements and feuds also shed light on the interaction between individuals or communities, as well as its boundaries. However, on account of their binding nature, marriages in early modern societies can be regarded as the most significant form of interaction between communities. Moreover, the question of the influence of the environment on inter-community marriages can be associated with the issue of early modern communities' alleged localness or even local xenophobia.[68]

A concept that has often been used in research on the history of communities is that of the marriage field. The area from which the marriage partners of the inhabitants of a community originated can be divided into 'fields' (measured in kilometres) according to the number of established marriages with respect to geographical distance. The concept of the marriage field combines the social and geographical aspects of marriages; however, marriage fields are not constants. As researchers who have studied early modern village communities suggest, the actual size of the marriage field varied according to (among other factors) the size of the community, the kinds of connections of communication and travel connections that were possible (given the community's environment and infrastructure) and the distances to the neighbouring communities.[69]

In early modern times, the Western European family model, characterized by nuclear families, also prevailed in Toivola, although families could also include grandparents, other relatives and servants.[70] Between 1750 and 1850 (which are covered for the most part by the earliest preserved marriage records from Hollola) there were 65 marriages in Hollola and the neighbouring parishes in which the bridegroom came from Toivola; brides came from Toivola in 84 marriages In 23 cases both the bride and groom were Toivola residents. Thus, according to church statistics, a total of 126 weddings were held in Toivola between 1750 and 1850.[71]

The primary marriage field of Toivola inhabitants would have corresponded to a circle whose circumference would have been about 20 kilometres from the centre of the village. The 23 marriages between residents of Toivola accounted for 18 per cent of marriages in the village. There were 101 marriages between residents of Toivola and other Hollola parishioners (80 per cent of all marriages). These results support the idea, also suggested by earlier studies, that communication with the outside world was geographically limited for early modern rural inhabitants. A distance of 20 kilometres was roughly equivalent to a day's journey (or at any rate the great part of a day), but this still meant that a traveller who was seeking a marriage partner would have to spend the night outside his or her home village.[72] Still, intra-village marriages were not very common. Marriages within the same household were even rarer – such marriages usually involved two servants or a servant and a widow or widower. It seems that, within the parish of Hollola, residents of Toivola were most strongly connected with the villages of Tennilä and Sairakkala. The size of the villages, their proximity to one another and the good travelling connections between them help to explain the strength of these connections.

At their broadest, the marriage fields of Toivola inhabitants extended more than a hundred kilometres to the southern coastal towns of Loviisa (Sw. Lovisa) and Viapori (Sw. Sveaborg). However, a marriage partner from such a distant place was a rare spectacle. When we compare the marriage fields of Toivola inhabitants with the contemporary geographical circumstances and infrastructure,[73] it is evident that they were connected to the local road network. Our survey also proves that that the inhabitants of Toivola tended to travel along roads and paths more than waterways (or frozen lakes and rivers in the winter).[74] It is apparent that Vesijärvi (a lake just over ten kilometres to the northeast of the village) presented mostly an obstacle that restricted interaction between Toivola residents and people living on the eastern shore of the lake. It seems that not even forests – frequently depicted as frightening or supernatural spaces in local folk tradition – could restrict the connections between the Toivola community and its immediate environment to the same extent as a fairly large lake (Map 36 see colour plate section 2, p. 11). The villages on the western shore of Vesijärvi were connected to Toivola through a network of roads that led to Hollola Church. This connection resulted in the exchange of marriage partners between the villages. A bridle path, leading southeast from Toivola, accounts for the marriages between inhabitants of Toivola and the southern villages. The road network also brought Toivola people into contact with the inhabitants of neighbouring parishes. The fact that Toivola is located on the western fringe of Hollola Parish explains the number of weddings held between Toivola residents and inhabitants of the relatively close parishes of Kärkölä and Hämeenkoski. Such marriages were, in fact, more numerous than intravillage unions. Towns do not appear to have played a significant role in the marriage fields of Toivola inhabitants; instead, they are located on the outer fringes of the primary marriage field.

Marriage fields and consequently the movement of people were gendered, as one might expect. However, the results of our study do not clearly or definitively suggest that the movement of women was more limited than that of men. In most cases, men from Toivola found their marriage partners closer to home than Toivola women, whose marriage partners arrived from more distant locations (and in isolated cases lived in Loviisa or Viapori or elsewhere on the southern coast).

The fact that Toivola men chose relatively local marriage partners probably suggests that close ties were valued. Close ties certainly had practical significance in rural communities, and enabled mutual activities, workforce, support and help. Geographical distance was one factor that determined when a rural wedding was held. For farm-owners or their children, taking part in preparations and organizing a wedding feast crucially required time and food reserves. The availability of both of these resources would fluctuate over the course of a year.[75] Additionally, the change of seasons had a significant influence on the rural rhythm of life in Northern Europe: opportunities and means of travel differed in summer and winter. During spring and autumn roads would often become almost impassable. These communication restrictions could also affect the timing of some weddings.

Late summer and early autumn were the busiest time of the year in rural communities, and thus this was not a popular season for weddings in Toivola. People preferred to marry either in October and November – after the stores had been filled (at least in good years) and when animals were also about to be slaughtered – or in early or late winter – usually the best time of the year to travel (thanks to skis and sleighs). During the nineteenth century, it became more common for Toivola weddings to be held in June. This enabled a more restful period before the beginning of the harvest and meant that the wedding feast could be combined with midsummer festivities.[76]

In cases where both the bride and groom came from Toivola, weddings took place fairly evenly throughout the year (with the exception of the late summer and early autumn work season). It appears that when inter-community marriages took place it was more important to ensure that there were sufficient food reserves to offer to guests or that the family of the bride or the bridegroom arriving from another village could make the journey. At weddings an effort was made to push boundary drawing and disputes as well as hostility towards otherness (hidden in mocking songs and names) into the background. A wedding was a space of encounters and crossing borders.

Conclusion

By mapping a single community from different approaches (and employing a variety of materials and methods), we have been able to examine the multilayered nature of the boundaries of a village community. The boundaries of Toivola and the 'unknown' spaces beyond them were not only diverse, but also elastic and sometimes ambiguous. Although boundaries had significance in a number of different contexts, it was also possible to cross or ignore boundaries under certain circumstances.

Official boundaries are characterized by their stability. They can only be altered through administrative processes. Because of their stability, official boundaries create a sense of security and are also readily defended – through both words and actions. With the help of boundaries, the inhabitants of a place form a mental image of themselves as part of their living environment. In other words, boundaries engender a sense of locality, which plays an important role in the wider process of identity formation. A good example of this is the tradition of mocking songs and names that was discussed above.

On the other hand, functions of boundaries (like boundaries themselves) can vary according to geographical and temporal location. Boundaries do not merely restrict or confine inhabitants; boundaries can also be transgressed. In the case of marriage partner selection, for example, village borders did not seem to restrict marriage fields. Even frightening places do not seem to have limited the formation of marriage fields. Although certain places might have inspired fear, this did not necessarily prevent people from encountering or travelling past them. Indeed, boundaries are always dependent on particular circumstances.

The living sphere that we have traced in this survey appears to be wide but nevertheless finite. It seems, on the basis of reconstructed marriage fields, that for most Toivola inhabitants the outer boundary of their living sphere was one day's journey from the village. It seems that people embarked on journeys with the intention of arriving at familiar lodgings at the end of the day. Venturing on a longer journey would have required resting at intermediary stopping points. This would only have been possible for those few inhabitants who had more extensive networks or could afford to pay for their lodgings. During agrarian times, Toivola residents largely remained in their immediate surroundings, but their living sphere comprised a wider area than only their own backyard or village landscape.

We have examined the living sphere of Toivola inhabitants from the point of view of the community. It must, however, be remembered that boundaries, both as a concept and as a cultural phenomenon, are diverse and complex and also involve personal experience. On an individual level, there may have been considerable variation between perceptions of boundaries. For example, adults and children – who have different opportunities to move between various places – encounter boundaries in different ways. Similar variations might also be expected between men and women, as well as between individuals belonging to different social groups.[77] Whether a person has remained in the same region their entire life or is a migrant (or has, at least, seen other places) would also seem to be significant. Of course, personal characteristics also have an effect on the way in which boundaries are experienced. Because of the personal and circumstantial nature of boundaries, the attempt to map mental boundaries is both particularly challenging and potentially rewarding.

Notes

1 Lindkvist 1991; Kirveennummi-Räsänen 2000, p. 8; Saarenheimo 2003, p. 361.

2 Holmila 2001, esp. pp. 33–48; 143–151; Junkala & Määttä (eds.) 2002; Helsti, Stark & Tuomaala (eds.) 2006.

3 The name may also be derived from a Finnish, male name Toivo.

4 This chapter forms part of the multidisciplinary research project 'Ihminen, aika, maisema' ('Human, Time and Landscape') based in the Department of History and Ethnology and Agora Virtual Environment Center at the University of Jyväskylä. The purpose of the project is to study and illustrate the changes that have taken place in the landscape of a Finnish village, Toivola, over more than half a millennium. At the same time, we examine the cultural heritage and cultural layers of Finnish village landscape through long-range historical and ethnological study and illustrate the observed changes in the landscape with the help of virtual technology. The webpage of the project can be found at http://research.jyu.fi/aikamaisema/.

5 The Salpausselkä ridge (a massive natural formation in the southern part of Finland) was formed during the glacial period.

6 These reforms (which in Finland began during Swedish rule in the eighteenth century) aimed to increase agricultural productivity and taxation. The purpose of land enclosure was to reorganize the landholdings (both forest land and fields) of farms in such a way as to form coherent geographical entities. The first wave of reorganization failed to sufficiently integrate farmlands, and thus further rearrangements were required. The rearrangement that took place in Toivola during the 1920s was, in fact, part of a third wave of land reorganizations.

7 The present-day highway number 12 largely follows the same route. Local inhabitants still use the old road.

8 Kuusi 1937, pp. 151, 166–168.

9 Some medieval court rolls (or fragments of them) from the province of Häme have been preserved. Such sources are rare in the Finnish context. Thanks to them, we can survey border disputes and related judgements from the mid-fifteenth century onwards. These documents have been published in the source publication BFH I.

10 The earliest map to depict Toivola village is a cadastral map from 1705, the next is from 1723. A map depicting the reorganization of farmlands dates from 1787: see the maps H21 5/10–11, H21 5/12–13, and H21 5/1–6 among the collections of Maanmittaushallituksen arkisto (MHA; i.e. The archives of the National Land Survey) in Kansallisarkisto (KA; i.e. The National Archives of Finland, Helsinki). A street-level visualization based on the map from 1705 makes it possible to pay a virtual visit to the early modern village of Toivola. URL: <http://virtuaalitoivola. jyu.fi/>.

11 Gustafsson 1933, pp. 17, 42; Huhtamies 2008, pp. 47–113. The code of conduct for land surveyors included the examination of different kinds of borders.

12 Mäkinen 2007, p. 47.

13 Mäkinen 2007, pp. 44–46.

14 These one hundred typewritten cards belong to the Topographica series of the Folklore Archives (SKRA) of the Finnish Literature Society in Helsinki (SKS): The Folklore Archives, the collection of manuscripts on folklore and oral tradition, Topographica series, Hollola. Most of the tales have also been published in a work entitled *Hollolan lahles ja Nastolan kappelis* (1978).

15 SKS KRA, The Folklore Archives, the collection of manuscripts on folklore and oral tradition, Topographica series, Hollola.

16 The Swedish Military Archives, Stockholm (SKA), Finska rekognosceringsverket (Finnish intelligence department). Map A XVII nos. 9 and 10; Map A XVIII nos. 9 and 10.

17 See, for example, Tak 1990; Holmila 2001, pp. 99–100; Snell 2003; Takahashi 2007; Mäkinen 2007.

18 See, for example, Virtanen, P. 1987, pp. 462–465; Fumagalli 1994, pp. 127, 147; Virtanen 1994.

19 See the introduction of this volume.

20 HisKi's webpages can be found at http://hiski.genealogia.fi/historia/. The database is maintained by the Genealogical Society of Finland (Suomen Sukututkimusseura). In rare cases, the earliest preserved church books of congregations and parishes date from the seventeenth century. However, in most Finnish parishes the preserved series begin in the early or mid-eighteenth century. This is also the case with the records from Hollola parish, which begin in 1756. Record keeping continues in present-day Finland, albeit in slightly different forms. The role of records kept by the secular authorities is far more important today. The HisKi database generally covers Finnish church books from the earliest preserved records to the mid- or late nineteenth century.

21 It must also be remembered that in Western Finland forests and the fields that were jointly farmed under the open-field system were commonly owned by the village between the fifteenth and eighteenth centuries. This practice came to an end with the efforts to improve the productivity of agriculture and the consequent redistributions of village lands at the end of the eighteenth and the beginning of the nineteenth centuries.

22 Melander 1933, 73; Julku 1987, pp. 15–16.

23 Lamberg 2005, p. 15.

24 According to the Swedish laws, border sites had an internal hierarchy of their own. For more on the subject, see Melander 1933, pp. 74–76; Lamberg 2005, pp. 15–16. For border sites used in the province of Häme, see for example Niitemaa 1955; Suvanto 1972.

25 These stone border markers were later used to replace natural border sites or to make them more distinct.

26 BFH I, pp. 77–78. Until the end of the nineteenth century, Swedish was generally used in official documents. Finland had been part of the Swedish kingdom until 1809 and the influence of Swedish culture continued for many decades. Placenames as well as the names of border markers were marked in Finnish, but at times the Swedish language scribes' unstable orthography as well as terms that have already disappeared from modern Finnish present problems of interpretation.

27 See Katajala 2006. By the end of the eighteenth century, borders determined by

border sites had become fixed. Debates about borders concerned concrete border-lines and pointer stones. Pointer stones were placed near border sites and indicate the direction of the borderline. In principle, borderlines had to be kept free of vegetation, but in practice they were only cleared in before an inspection of the border. See for example a map of Toivola depicting the general parcelling out of land, records concerning the parcelling and records detailing the border markers. KA MHA H21 5/1–6 (a map drawn by J. M. Bellman in 1800–1802).

28 For more detailed information about the border dispute, see for example Niitemaa 1955, pp. 218, 355; Kuusi 1935, p. 217.

29 Hämeenlinnan maakunta-arkisto (HMA; i.e. The Provincial Archives of Hämeen-linna/Tavastehus), MHAs (The map collection of the National Land Survey of Finland), Sairakkala 33:6, Isojakoasiakirjat (Records concerning the general par-celling out of land).

30 Kettles (round hollows of various sizes formed during the glacial period) are a very common natural phenomenon in this area.

31 This name became fixed in the late eighteenth century; in 1705 the site was still referred to by a different name. The local placenames were gathered by the Western Hollola village association in 2008 and they are analysed in Uotila & Helén 2009.

32 KA MHA, Map H 21 5/10–11 (Toivola 1705).

33 Borders were cleared of vegetation and stone border markers erected in con-nection with the general parcelling out of land in 1802 and the supplementary distribution of land in 1899. KA MHA, Map H 19 14/2–21 (Järventaka, Kastari, Pinnola, Isojakoasiakirjat 1802); HMA MHAs, Toivola 38:a, Isojakoasiakirjat 1787.

34 See also Suvanto 1972, pp. 136–143. 'Firestone' is a name rarely given to border stones.

35 The map of Toivola from 1723: KA MHA, H21 5/12–13. Pine trees were often used as border markers. Suvanto 1972, pp. 70–74.

36 For more about blazes, see Voionmaa 1947, p. 114 and note 2; Melander 1933, pp. 76–77; Suvanto 1972, pp. 162–164.

37 Trees or other border markers that were likely to disappear were sometimes later replaced by markers constructed out of stones. There were various instructions as to the number of stones that should be used for a border marker, but in practice the number varied (Melander 1933, p. 78). About border sites related to fences, see Suvanto 1972, pp. 164–165.

38 The spelling of the name varies in the Swedish documents, and thus it is difficult to specify the name and its meaning. The record of placenames gathered by the Western Hollola village association in 2008; Uotila & Helén 2009.

39 The disagreement over Lyhelänmaa in 1649. Kuusi 1935, p. 217.

40 Uusitalo 2003, 79.

41 Nenola 2005, p. 310.

42 The Western Hollola village association is presently conducting a project to map old placenames in an area of eight villages (including Toivola). The record of placenames gathered by the Western Hollola village association in 2008. See also Uotila & Helén 2009.

43 For example Relph 1976; Walmsley 1988; Massey 2008; Paasi 2008.

44 Paasi, 1998, pp. 175–176; Knuuttila 2006, p. 9.

45 For example, there used to be many horse owners and horse dealers in Hollola, which

is why inhabitants of Hollola have traditionally been ridiculed as horse whippers, horse thieves and whip lashers (among other names). They were said to have been born with 'a notch for the whip under their arm'. Mäkinen 2007, p. 175.

46 Knuuttila 2007, p. 12. Finnish studies of villages and mocking names – in which the immediate mental surroundings of a village community have appeared as in a more or less playfully antagonistic relationship to the wider local area – have many points of convergence with international studies of conflicts between villages and of local xenophobia. For example Tak 1990; Snell 2003.

47 On the other hand, village brawls (sometimes instigated through the use of mocking names or songs) can be seen as a part of young men's behaviour that maintained a sense of locality and established boundaries. About Finnish village brawls, see for example Haavio-Mannila 1958.

48 Kuusi 1935, p. 229.

49 Kotilainen 2008, pp. 284–291.

50 The entire mocking rhyme is: '*Hatsinas on harakat, Sairakkalas saivarit, Toivolan torakat, Tenhelän territ, Järventaustan jääkärit*' ('In Hatsina they are magpies, in Sairakkala nits, in Toivola cockroaches, in Tenhelä black grouses, and in Järventausta troopers.') It was deposited in the collection of the Folklore Archives (SKA) in 1947, having been told to Terttu Tupala by Tyne Rasila of Hatsina: SKS KRA Topographica series: Hollola.

51 Interviews conducted on 24 and 25 July 2007 and 29 July 2008.

52 Jukarainen & Kuusisto-Arponen 2003, pp. 58, 60.

53 Knuuttila & Paasi 1995, p. 55.

54 Nenola 2005, p. 303. About the mental aspect and social control related to borders, see for example Korpela 2006 and the chapter written by Jukka Korpela in this volume.

55 Interviews conducted on 28 and 29 July 2008.

56 Helén 2002a, p. 74; Helén 2002b, p. 163.

57 An interview conducted on 29 July 2008.

58 Interviews conducted on 28 and 29 July 2008.

59 Dinzelbacher 1981, p. 97; Barros 1998. See also note 18 above.

60 Anttonen 1994, pp. 27–28.

61 Le Goff 1982, pp. 87–97.

62 Fumagalli 1994, pp. 127, 147.

63 SKS, Hollola, Hilma Jokela 1938. PK 10:1811.

64 SKS, Hollola, Hilma Jokela 1938. PK 10:1852.

65 SKS, Hollola, Hilma Jokela 1938. PK 10:1811.

66 SKS, Hollola, Hilma Jokela 1938. PK 10:1830 and PK 10:1831.

67 Sarmela 1981, pp. 11–17; Gaunt 1983, pp. 48–51; Pylkkänen 1999, chapter III; Fauve-Chamoux 2001, pp. 222–223, 229–234.

68 See in particular Snell 2003.

69 Lehtonen 1968; Pirttimäki 1991; Pöllä 1993; Pöllä 1997; Stenqvist Millde 2007, pp. 203–216, 307–316; Piilahti 2007, pp. 204–236.

70 Gaunt 1981, p. 90–108; Sirén 1999; Waris 1999; Barbagli & Ketzer 2001, p. xv.

71 We used the HisKi database to examine the information contained in the church archives of Hollola and the neighbouring parishes.

72 Harrison 1998, pp. 198–199; Nenonen 1999, p. 274; Simonson 1999, chapter 9; Lamberg 2003, pp. 266–268; Snell 2003; Stenqvist Millde 2007, chapter 9.

73 Krigsarkivet (SKA; i.e. The Swedish Military Archives, Stockholm), Finska rekognosceringsverket (Finnish intelligence department). Maps A XVII nos. 9 and 10;
Maps A XVIII nos. 9 and 10.

74 However, one particular ice road may have been important. According to the military
maps from the late eighteenth century, this ice road connected the aforementioned
Kutajoki village to the western side of Lake Vesijärvi: it led to the parish village
of Hollola, which was in turn was connected to Sairakkala and further west to
Toivola by a road. This offers one explanation as to why Kutajoki was included in
the Toivola marriage fields more often than the other eastern lake shore villages.

75 For descriptions of rural weddings in Hollola, see Kuusi 1937, pp. 337–348.

76 According to Kustaa Vilkuna, late autumn was the most popular time for weddings in agrarian Finland. However, Boxing Day, for instance, was also a popular
day on which to get married in the nineteenth century; see Vilkuna 1968, p. 300.
For an attempt to analyse the 'seasonality' of early modern marriages in a more
general European context, see Fauve-Chamoux 2001, pp. 227–231. Cf. Lamberg
2003, p. 268 (regarding the medieval period).

77 The socially determined relationship with space in early modern culture is also
discussed in Lahtinen 2008, pp. 82–83.

Bibliography
Archival sources

The National Archives of Finland (Kansallisarkisto), Helsinki (KA)
The Archives of the National Land Survey (MHA)

The Swedish Military Archives (SKA), Stockholm
Finska rekognosceringsverket

The Folklore Archives of the Finnish Literature Society (SKS KRA), Helsinki
Topographica series: Hollola.
The HISKI database, URL: < http://hiski.genealogia.fi/historia/>
    Births, baptisms and marriages in Hollola and neighbouring parishes 1750–1850
Hämeenlinnan maakunta-arkisto (HMA; The Provincial Archives of Hämeen linna)
The Archives of the National Land Survey (MHA)

Source editions

Bidrag till Finlands Historia (BFH). Edited by R. Hausen. The National Archives of
    Finland, Helsinki, 1881.
Hollolan lahles ja Nastolan kappelis. Hollolan ja Nastolan kertomusperinnettä. Edited by
    M. Jauhiainen. Lahden Museo- ja taidelautakunta & The Finnish Literature Society,
    Lahti & Helsinki, 1978.

Official publications

Arvokkaat maisema-alueet. Maisema-aluetyöryhmän mietintö II. Mietintö 66/1992.
    Ministry of Environment, Helsinki, 1993.

Interviews

Interviews with several local people conducted by Minna Mäkinen in Toivola 24–26 July 2007 and 28–29 July 2008.

Literature

Ahvenainen, J. 1996. 'Man and the Forest in Northern Europe from the Middle Ages to the 19th Century.' *Vierteljahrschrift für Sozial- und Witschaftsgeschichte*, Vol. 83 (2), pp. 1–24.

Allen, R. L. 1999. 'The Socio-Spatial Making and Marking of "Us". Toward a Critical Postmodern Spatial Theory of Difference and Community.' *Social Identities*, Vol. 5 (3), pp. 249–277.

Anttonen, V. 1994. 'Erä- ja metsäluonnon pyhyys.' In Laaksonen, P. & Mettomäki, S.-L. (eds.) *Metsä ja metsänviljaa*. The Finnish Literature Society, Helsinki, pp. 24–35.

Barbagli, M. & Ketzer, D. I. 2001. 'Introduction.' In Kertzer, D. I. & Barbagli, B. (eds.) *The History of the European Family*, Vol. I: *Family Life in Early Modern Times 1500–1789*. Yale University Press, New Haven & London, pp. ix–xxxii.

Barros, C. 1998. 'Die "Vermenschlichung" der Natur im Mittelalter.' In Spindler, K. (ed.) *Mensch und Natur im mittelalterlichen Europa. Archäologische, historische und naturwissenschaftliche Befunde*. Wieser, Klagenfurt, pp. 281–310.

Dinzelbacher, P. 1981. *Vision und Visionliteratur im Mittelalter*. Stuttgart 1981

Ekman, J. 2008. *Skogen i vårt inre. Utmark och frihetsdröm*. Carlsson, Stockholm.

Fauve-Chamoux, A. 2001. 'Marriage, Widowhood, and Divorce.' In Kertzer, D. I. & Barbagli, B. (eds.) *The History of the European Family*, Vol. I: *Family Life in Early Modern Times 1500–1789*. Yale University Press, New Haven & London, pp. 221–256.

Fryer, P. 1999. 'Heaven, Hell, or… Something in Between? Contrasting Russian Images of Siberia.' In Smith, J. (ed.) *Beyond the Limits. The Concept of Space in Russian History and Culture*. The Finnish Historical Society, Helsinki, pp. 95–106.

Fumagalli, V. 1994. *The Landscapes of Fear. Perceptions of Nature and the City in the Middle Ages*. Polity Press, Cambridge.

Gaunt, D. 1983. *Familjeliv i Norden*. Gidlund, Stockholm.

Gustafsson, A. 1933. 'Maanmittarikunta ja mittaustyöt Ruotsinvallan aikana.' Teoksessa Haataja, K. et al. (eds.) *Suomen maanmittauksen historia*, Vol. I: *Ruotsin vallan aika*. WSOY, Porvoo & Helsinki, pp. 1–176.

Haavio-Mannila, E. 1958. *Kylätappelut. Sosiologinen tutkimus suomalaisesta kylätappeluinstituutiosta*. WSOY, Porvoo & Helsinki.

Hall, S. 1999. *Identiteetti*. Translated by M. Lehtonen & J. Herkman. Vastapaino, Tampere.

Harrison, D. 1995. *Medieval Space. The Extent of Microspatial Knowledge in Western Europe during the Middle Ages*. Lund University Press, Lund.

Harrison, D. 1998. *Skapelsens geografi. Föreställningar om rymd och rum i medeltidens Europa*. Ordfront, Stockholm.

Helén, P. 2002a. 'Toivolan kylä.' In Helén, P. et al. (ed.) *Länsi-Hollolan kyläkirja*. The Western Hollola Village Association, Hollola, pp. 63–76.

Helén, P. 2002b. 'Kauppoja ja kauppiaita Länsi-Hollolassa.' In Helén, P. et al. (ed.) *Länsi-Hollolan kyläkirja*. The Western Hollola Village Association, Hollola, pp. 158–176.

Helsti, H., Stark, L. & Tuomaala, S. (toim.) 2006. *Modernisaatio ja kansan kokemus Suomessa 1860–1960*. The Finnish Literature Society, Helsinki.

Holmila, M. 2001. *Kylä kaupungistuvassa yhteiskunnassa. Yhteisöelämän muutos ja jatkuvuus*. The Finnish Literature Society, Helsinki.

Huhtamies, M. 2008. *Maan mitta. Maanmittauksen historia Suomessa 1633–2008*. Edita, Helsinki.

Jansson, J. 2007. 'Roads, tracks and communication areas. Human movement in the old parish of Sysmä, Eastern Häme (Tavastia) from the Late Iron Age to the Middle Ages.' In Immonen, V., Lempiäinen, M. & Rosendahl, U. (eds.) *Hortus Novus. Fresh Approaches to Medieval Archaeology in Finland*. The Society for Medieval Archaeology in Finland, pp. 131–139.

Jukarainen, P. & Kuusisto-Arponen A.-K. 2003. 'Konfliktin paikka? Paikallista arjen identiteettipolitiikkaa Pohjois-Irlannissa.' In Linjakumpu, A., Villa, S. & Jukarainen, P. (eds.) *Sodan ja rauhan identiteetit*. Rauhan- ja konfliktintutkimuskeskus, Tampere, pp. 45–69.

Julku, K. 1987. *Suomen itärajan synty*. Pohjois-Suomen historiallinen yhdistys, Rovaniemi.

Junkala, P. ja Määttä, J. (eds.) 2002. *Paikallisuuden juuret ja versot. Jatkuvuuksia Judinsalon maalaismaisemassa*. Jyväskylä, Atena.

Katajala, K. 2006. 'The Origin of the Border.' In Gustafsson, H. & Sanders, H. (eds.) *Vid gränsen. Integration och identitet i det förnationella Norden*. Centrum för Danmarksstudier & Makadam förlag, Göteborg & Stockholm, pp. 86–106.

Kirveennummi, A. & Räsänen, Riitta 2000. *Suomalainen kylä kuvattuna ja muisteltuna*. The Finnish Literature Society, Helsinki.

Knuuttila, S et al. 1996. *Kyläläiset, kansalaiset. Tulkintoja Sivakasta ja Rasimäestä*. Joensuun yliopiston Karjalan tutkimuslaitos, Joensuu.

Knuuttila, S. 2006. 'Paikan moneus.' In Knuuttila, S., Laaksonen, P. ja Piela, U. (eds.) *Paikka. Eletty, kuviteltu, kerrottu*. The Finnish Literature Society, Helsinki, pp. 7–11.

Knuuttila, S. 2007. 'Naapurihuumori. Iloa, uteliaisuutta ja epäluuloa.' In Mäkinen, K. *Lollot ja kollot. Suomalaista naapurihuumoria*. Otava, Helsinki, pp. 10–19.

Knuuttila, S. & Paasi, A. 1995. 'Tila, kulttuuri ja mentaliteetti. Maantieteen ja antropologian yhteyksiä etsimässä.' In Katajala, K. (ed.) *Manaajista maalaisaateliin. Tulkintoja toisesta historian, antropologian ja maantieteen välimaastossa*. The Finnish Literature Society, Helsinki, pp. 28–94.

Korpela, J. 2006. 'Pähkinäsaaren rauhan raja.' *Historiallinen aikakauskirja*, Vol. 104 (4) 2006, pp. 454–469.

Koskinen S. et al. 2007. *Suomen väestö*. Gaudeamus, Helsinki.

Kotilainen, S. 2008. *Suvun nimissä. Nimenannon käytännöt Sisä-Suomessa 1700-luvun alusta 1950-luvulle. The Finnish Literature Society*, Helsinki.

Kulonen, U. et. al. 2000. *Suomen sanojen alkuperä. Etymologinen sanakirja*, Vol. 3: R–Ö. The Finnish Literature Society & The Research Institute for the Languages of Finland, Helsinki.

Kuusi, S. 1935. *Hollolan historia*, Vol. I: *Hollolan pitäjän historia muinaisuuden hämärästä kunnallisen elämän alkuun 1860-luvulle*. The Municipality of Hollola, Hollola.

Kuusi, S. 1937. *Hollolan historia*, Vol. II: *Hollolan pitäjän historia muinaisuuden hämärästä kunnallisen elämän alkuun 1860-luvulle*. The Municipality of Hollola, Hollola.

Lähde, H. K. 2007. *Isojako ja Lieson uudisasutus. Tutkimus asutuksen muotoutumisesta ja sidonnaisuudesta maakirjataloihin laajassa talonpoikaiskylässä*. Heikki Lähde, Lahti. URL: <http://lib.tkk.fi/Diss/2007/isbn9789512287949/isbn9789512287949.pdf>.

Lahtinen, A. 2008. 'Presence, Absence and Distance. Physical and Mental Local Landscape in Pre-Modern Finland.' In François, P., Syrjämaa T. & Terho, H. (eds.) *Power and Culture. New Perspectives on Spatiality in European History*. Pisa University Press, Pisa, pp. 73–87.

Lamberg, M. 2003. '1300-luvun suomalaisten tietoympäristöt.' In Ahonen, K. et al. (eds.) *Toivon historia. Toivo Nygårdille omistettu juhlakirja*. Department of History and Ethnology, Jyväskylä, pp. 261–271.

Lamberg, M. 2005 'Metsän ja metsäluonnon hahmottaminen ja haltuunotto keskiajan yhteiskunnassa.' In Roiko-Jokela, H. (ed.) *Metsien pääomat. Metsä taloudellisena, poliittisena, kulttuurisena ja mediailmiönä keskiajalta EU-aikaan*. Minerva, Jyväskylä, pp. 11–28.

Le Goff, J. 1982. *Time, Work and Culture in the Middle Ages*. University of Chicago Press, Chicago.

Lehtonen, J. U. E. 1968. *Suomenlahden suomalaisten saarikylien avioliittokenttiä*. The Finnish Literature Society, Helsinki.

Lindkvist, T. 1991. 'Kollektiv eller territoriell indelning. Socken som profan gemenskapsform i Sveriges medeltidslagar.' In Ferm, O. (ed.) *Kyrka och socken i medeltidens Sverige. En samling uppsatser*. Riksantikvarieämbetet, Stockholm, pp. 505–519.

Mäkinen, K. 2007. *Lollot ja kollot. Suomalaista naapurihuumoria*. Otava, Helsinki.

Melander K. R. 1933. 'Vanhimmat maanjaot.' In Haataja, K. et al. (eds.) *Suomen maanmittauksen historia*, Vol. I: *Ruotsin vallan aika*. WSOY, Porvoo, pp. 1–84.

Masonen, J. 1999. 'Kirkon, kruunun ja kansan tiet keskiajalla.' In Mauranen, T. (ed.) *Maata, jäätä, kulkijoita. Tiet, liikenne ja yhteiskunta ennen vuotta 1860*. Edita, Helsinki, pp. 57–138.

Massey, D. 2008. *Samanaikainen tila*. Lehtonen, m. et al. (eds.). Vastapaino, Tampere.

Nenola, A. 2005. 'Raja suojaa, uhkaa houkuttaa.' In Hirsiaho, A., Korpela, M. & Rantalaiho, L. (eds.) *Kohtaamisia rajoilla*. The Finnish Literature Society, Helsinki, pp. 301–310.

Nenonen, M. 1999. 'Kulkijan taival.' In Mauranen, Tapani (ed.) *Maata, jäätä, kulkijoita. Tiet, liikenne ja yhteiskunta ennen vuotta 1860*. Edita, Helsinki, pp. 274–334.

Niitemaa, V. 1955. 'Hämeen keskiaika.' In *Hämeen historia*, Vol. I: *Esihistoria ja keskiaika*. Hämeen heimoliitto, Hämeenlinna, pp. 191–484.

Paasi, A. 1998. 'Alueiden renessanssi ja identiteettipuhe.' In Hänninen, Sakari (ed.) *Missä on tässä*. University of Jyväskylä, Jyväskylä, pp. 170–190.

Paasi, A. 2008. 'Finnish Landscape as Social Practice. Mapping Identity and Scale.' In Jones, M. & Olwig, K. (eds.) *Nordic Landscapes. Region and Belonging on the Northern Edge of Europe*. Center of American Places, Chicago, pp. 511–539.

Pentikäinen, J. 1994. 'Metsä suomalaisten maailmankuvassa.' In Laaksonen, P. & Mettomäki, S.-L. (eds.) *Metsä ja metsänviljaa*. The Finnish Literature Society, Helsinki, pp. 7–23.

Piilahti, K.-M. 2007. *Aineellista ja aineetonta turvaa. ruokakunnat, ekologis-taloudelliset resurssit ja kontaktinmuodostus Valkealassa 1630–1750*. The Finnish Literature Society, Helsinki.

Pirttimäki, T. 1991. 'Etninen raja – elinkeinoraja-avioliittoraja. Enontekiön talollisten avioliittokenttä 1776–1805.' In Laaksonen, P. & Mettomäki, S.-L. (eds.) *Kolme on kovaa sanaa. Kirjoituksia kansanperinteestä*. The Finnish Literature Society, Helsinki, pp. 157–167.

Pöllä, M. 1993. 'Vuokkiniemen avioliittokenttä ja perheiden koko 1760-luvulla.' *Karjalan heimo*, Vol. 11–12, pp. 168–169.

Pöllä, M. 1997. 'Itävienalaisen Voijärven pitäjän avioliittokenttä 1779–1810.' In Julku, K. (ed.) *Rajamailla*, Vol. IV. Pohjois-Suomen Historiallinen Yhdistys, Rovaniemi, pp. 75–110.

Pylkkänen, A. 1999. *Puoli vuodetta, lukot ja avaimet. Nainen ja maalaistalous oikeuskäytännön valossa 1660–1710.* Lakimiesliiton kustannus, Helsinki.

Relph, E. 1976. *Place and Placeness.* Pion Limited, London.

Saarenheimo, J. 2003. 'Isojako.' In Rasila, V., Jutikkala, E. & Alitalo, A.-M. *Suomen maatalouden historia*, Vol. I: *Perinteisen maatalouden aika. Esihistoriasta vuoteen 1870.* The Finnish Literature Society, Helsinki, pp. 349–364.

SAOB. *Svenska Akademiens Ordbok.* URL: <http://g3.spraakdata.gu.se/saob/>.

Sarmela, M. 1981. 'Suomalaiset häät.' In Sarmela, M. (ed.) *Pohjolan häät.* The Finnish Literature Society, Helsinki, pp. 9–55

Schmidt Sabo, K. 2000. *Vem behöver en by? Kyrkheddinge, struktur och strategi under tusen år.* Riksantikvarieämbetet, Stockholm.

Simonson, Ö. 1999. *Den lokala scenen. Torstuna härad som lokalsamhälle under 1600-talet.* Uppsala University.

Sirén, K. 1999. *Suuresta suvusta pieneen perheeseen. Itäsuomalainen perhe 1700-luvulla.* The Finnish Literature Society, Helsinki.

Snell, K. D. M. 2003. 'The Culture of Local Xenophobia.' *Social History*, Vol. 28 (1), pp. 1–30.

Stenqvist Millde, Y. 2007. *Vägar inom räckhåll. Spåren efter resande i det förindustriella bondesamhället.* University of Stockholm, Stockholm.

Stenqvist Millde, Y. 2008. 'Traces of Roads and Travel in Pre-Industrial Agrarian Society.' In Lamberg, M., Keskiaho, J., Räsänen, E., Timofeeva O. & Virtanen, L. *Methods and the Medievalist. Current Approaches in Medieval Studies.* Cambridge Scholars Publishing, Newcastle-upon-Tyne, pp. 177–198.

Suvanto, S. 1972. *Satakunnan ja Hämeen keskiaikainen rajalaitos.* University of Tampere, Tampere.

Tak, H. 1990. 'Longing for Local Identity. Intervillage Relations in an Italian Mountain Area.' *Anthropological Quarterly*, Vol. 63 (2), pp. 90–100.

Takahashi, M. 2007. 'Family Continuity in England and Japan.' *Continuity and Change*, Vol. 22 (2), pp. 193–214.

Uotila, M. & Helén, P. 2009. *Sulenko, Uikura ja Ävinä. Länsi-Hollolan paikannimistö.* Länsi-Hollolan kyläyhdistys, Hollola.

Uusitalo, Eeva 2003. 'Traditional Knowledge as a Living Strategy. The Case of an Unemployed Woman.' In Korhonen, T., Ruotsala, H. & Uusitalo, E. (eds.) *Making and Breaking of Borders. Ethnological Interpretations, Presentations, Representations.* The Finnish Literature Society, Helsinki, pp. 79–86.

Vilkuna, K. 1968. *Vuotuinen ajantieto.* Otava, Helsinki.

Virtanen, P. 1987. 'Kansanperinteen metsäkuvia.' *Silva Fennica*, Vol. 21 (4), s. 462–465.

Virtanen L. 1994. 'Suomen kansa on aina vihannut metsiään.' In Laaksonen, P. & Mettomäki, S.-L. (eds.) *Metsä ja metsänviljaa.* The Finnish Literature Society, Helsinki, pp. 134–140.

Voionmaa, V. 1947. *Hämäläinen eräkausi.* WSOY, Porvoo & Helsinki.

Walmsley, D. J. 1988. *Urban Living. The Individual in the City.* Longman Scientific & Technical, Essex.

Waris, E. 1999. *Yksissä leivissä. Ruokolahtelainen perhelaitos ja yhteisöllinen toiminta 1750–1850.* The Finnish Literature Society, Helsinki.

CHAPTER 12

Urban Boundaries

*Vesa-Pekka Herva, Timo Ylimaunu, Titta Kallio-Seppä,
Tiina Kuokkanen and Risto Nurmi*

Introduction

This chapter discusses how people in a small early modern town perceived
the urban landscape and how material culture – from maps to the built
environment – mediated their perception and understanding of the world.
The chapter focuses on the creation and reproduction of boundaries in the
urban and lived environment, and is primarily based on the consideration
of historical documents (especially maps) within a framework derived from
material culture studies. From this perspective, historical maps are social
products that do not merely describe past landscapes: they also convey
information about the cultural ordering, perception and understanding
of space. Furthermore, maps, as such, mediated relationships between
humans and the environment. Probate inventories, in turn, can provide
information about domestic material culture, which both created and
expressed social boundaries on a smaller scale. Probate inventories can
thus be used to explore the boundaries between (and the nature of) public
and private space in early modern urban contexts.

Humans have identified and drawn all kinds of physical, symbolic and
social boundaries from the deep past, but the metaphysical and social
divisions that are taken for granted today are not necessarily universally
valid. Therefore, the projection of modern categories and boundaries
onto the past – even a fairly recent past, such as the early modern period
– can misrepresent how people organized and understood the world
around them.[1] This chapter considers the formation and meaning of
some physical, social and symbolic boundaries in a northern periphery
of early modern Sweden: the small town of Tornio (Sw. Torneå). Our
aim is not to provide a thorough case study of the subject matter but
rather to chart the way in which a broadly 'boundary-oriented' perspec-

tive can enhance our understanding of early modern (urban) landscapes and mindscapes.

Although the approach adopted in this chapter draws primarily from material culture studies, historical documents (especially maps and probate inventories) provide the data for this study. The material-culture perspective focuses on the interface and interaction between people and all kinds of material 'things' from portable artefacts to buildings and elements of the landscape. Human life unfolds in relation to the things that surround people, which also means that artefacts and other material things play a more important and active role in shaping human lives than is readily obvious from historical documents or conventional historical narratives.[2] The reasons for the relative neglect of things need not be discussed here; it merely suffices to note that the material-culture perspective seeks to unravel and understand the dynamics between people and things rather than reconstruct fine-grained sequences of events in the past or pin down causal relationships in any straightforward sense. This shift in perspective is potentially useful for various reasons, not least because it can help to elucidate the dynamics and mechanisms of changes – that is, how things happened in history, especially on a local scale.

Both maps and probate inventories were, for all practical purposes, new types of documents in the early modern world, and we aim to briefly discuss the implications of the appearance and development of (urban) maps to the making of boundaries in Sweden, and more generally to the perception and understanding of the world. Maps and probate inventories are also used as sources that can shed light on the spatial organization and boundaries in urban space, with special reference to the small town of Tornio in early modern northern Sweden. While revolving around Tornio, the themes raised by this study also have more general relevance. The first two sections of this chapter provide the necessary background to the key issues. Our discussion proper begins with the making of abstract or metaphysical boundaries (as related to the reorganization of the world in the early modern period) and proceeds to a discussion of how social boundaries were created.

Maps and probate inventories

Maps were fairly rare in the medieval world. The origins of 'proper' cartography date back to the Renaissance. It has been estimated that only some thousands of maps were in circulation in Europe in the fifteenth century; this figure had risen to millions in the sixteenth century.[3] At least some of these early maps had functions that are commonly assigned to maps (and that readily make sense) today, but Renaissance maps also had a variety of non-cartographic functions and meanings. They could be collectible items, devices for spiritual reflection and mnemonic tools; some might even have had broadly magical associations.[4]

Relatively few maps had been made in Sweden prior to the 1620s. The systematization of map-making began in 1628 with the founding of the Swedish land survey. By the late seventeenth century this had resulted in a collection of maps that was in many ways unparalleled in Europe.[5] Early modern Swedish maps can be roughly divided into large-scale geometric (cadastral) maps and small-scale geographic (topographic) maps. Urban maps are geometric maps according to this classification, but it might be more useful to view them as a distinct group, which in turn includes three subtypes of maps: fortification maps, urban surveys and urban plans.[6]

Early modern Swedish maps presumably served several purposes. Cadastral mapping, for instance, can be understood as a continuum and improvement of the fifteenth-century Land Books (Sw. *jordeböcker*) (in which land holdings were registered).[7] The making of topographic and fortification maps was perhaps motivated by military needs. Urban maps, in turn, were arguably created because the Crown wanted to collect information about towns for the purposes of urban planning and development.[8] This would seem to make sense when one considers that towns were centres of trade and therefore economically important.

Although various kinds of maps were at least sometimes designed to serve (or were put to) practical uses, the launching of the large-scale map-making campaign in Sweden may not be reducible to purely rational reasons and the practical usefulness of maps.[9] In other words, the functions of seventeenth-century Swedish maps have seemed more or less obvious to us primarily because they have been considered in almost purely modernist terms; however, there are good reasons to believe that the broadly symbolic aspects of maps were rather more central to early map-making in Sweden than has previously been recognized.[10] In our study we have explored these symbolic functions of maps – or, more specifically, the role of maps as mediators of human relationships with the world – with a particular emphasis on boundaries.

Like maps, probate inventories were a new kind of document in the early modern world. Probate inventories recorded the estates of the deceased and are, as a class of documents, reflective of the Crown administration's increased interest in and control over the property of its subjects.[11] The earliest probate inventories from southern Sweden and Finland date from the sixteenth century and the inventories from northern towns, such as Tornio, from the mid-seventeenth century.[12] The first Swedish legislation relating to the recording of estates was passed in 1734. This law probably aimed to regularize established practice.[13]

Valuable as they are, the use of probate inventories for the purposes of historical research presents certain problems. First, inventories were not made of all estates; the poor are particularly under-represented.[14] (It seems that the estates of only about half of the deceased were inventoried in Tornio during the eighteenth century.)[15] Second, not all artefacts were systematically recorded.[16] Nonetheless, probate inventories provide information about household material culture and supplement archaeological data, which often does not include the sort of things recorded in probate inventories. Thus, notwithstanding their problems, probate inventories can be valuable to the study of the introduction and spread of new artefact types. These data, in turn, can cast light on broader changes in society,[17] as will be illustrated in our brief discussion of curtains and their relationship to the creation of social and spatial boundaries.

Towns in early modern Sweden

Although medieval and sixteenth-century urban centres of Sweden, including those in Finland, were largely concentrated in the southern parts of the kingdom (that is, south of the Ulvila (Sw. Ulfsby) – Gävle line), there were several important harbours and market places in the northern regions of the Gulf of Bothnia in the Middle Ages. When Sweden established itself as a northern European great power in the early seventeenth century, the kingdom had relatively few urban centres. It was for this reason that King Gustav II Adolf set about building a series of new towns to encourage and control trade. Tornio, for instance, was founded at the same time as several other towns (1620–1621).

The Crown had sought to control town planning and building since the Middle Ages, but in practice its instructions were rather unspecific and supervision of construction was poor, which tended to result in more or less uncontrolled urban development.[18] At the time Tornio was founded, a surveyor laid out the general plan of towns in chosen locations.[19] In 1641 an order was given which dictated that new towns were to be built according to a designed urban plan; the reorganization of existing towns into a regular grid plan began at roughly the same time.[20] In the discussion that follows we explore the relationship and interconnections between the development of (urban) cartography and urban space, focusing particularly on the meaning of certain observed phenomena in both maps and urban space. The case of Tornio serves as an illustration of this discussion.

The town of Tornio was founded on the small island of Suensaari in the delta of Tornio River (Tornionjoki) in 1621, but there had long been a church and an important market place on the site. (Olaus Magnus provided a lively description of the fairs in Tornio during the 1510s.)[21] Like most small towns in Sweden, seventeenth-century Tornio was village-like and agrarian in character.[22] Despite only having a few hundred residents in the early modern period, Tornio controlled trade over a huge area in northernmost Fennoscandia and began to prosper towards the end of the seventeenth century. The town was completely destroyed in the 1710s during the Great Northern War, but after hostilities ended it was rebuilt according to the original plan (albeit in a somewhat modernized form) and the town flourished again in the eighteenth century.[23]

Maps and boundaries

The early urban maps of Swedish towns provided only limited information. The earliest map of Tornio has conventionally been dated to the early 1640s,[24] but it may actually date from around 1620 (Map 37 see colour plate section 2, p. 12). This would mean that the map represents the (staked-off) plan of the town and that it is roughly contemporaneous with the earliest urban maps made in Sweden.[25] The next map of Tornio, from 1647, is at least partially based on a survey of the actual urban space inside the toll fence.[26] These two maps (like similar maps of other towns) document only the general town plan, essentially the streets and blocks. Blocks appear as blank spaces and the only built structures represented on the maps are the toll fence, town hall, church, warehouses and a few other buildings. (The small perspective drawings of buildings outside the planned area in the first Tornio map are probably not intended to document actual buildings but merely to suggest that there were (expected to be) some buildings outside the planned area.)[27] The next Tornio map (from 1697/8) is rather more detailed: it shows the division of blocks into plots and depicts the fields within the toll fence (Map 38 see colour plate section 2, p. 13). This map also contains more written information – plots are now connected to their tenants. The 1750 map is largely similar to its predecessor, but in addition it includes details of the tenants' occupations. Residential buildings began to be recorded on such maps during the second half of the eighteenth century and were depicted in the 1782 map of Tornio.

The development of Swedish urban cartography, as illustrated by the Tornio maps, has conventionally been understood as a process of 'natural' evolution: that is, better techniques, instruments and instructions supposedly resulted in more detailed and 'objective' or 'better' maps as the modern age unfolded.[28] However, in order to appreciate why and how things changed, it is necessary to relate the observed changes in urban cartography to broader developments in society and attitudes to the environment. Maps were drawn for a purpose – which, however, may not be self-evident – and this purpose partially dictated what information was eventually included in maps and what was left out. Surveyors were officials of the Crown, and whatever was documented on maps perhaps reveals more about the Crown's interest than about an 'objective' reality. For example, the depiction of warehouses but not actual household buildings in seventeenth-century maps seems to reflect the Crown's preoccupation with trade. By the same token, the toll fence is marked on maps because it marks the outer boundary of towns and separates urban space from the administratively separate countryside. Yet it is not at all clear that the toll fences marked on urban maps represented actual real-world constructions.[29]

Maps were an important tool for boundary-making in the early modern world. In today's vernacular thought, maps are taken to represent the world 'as it is', but map-making actually shapes the world and how people understand it. This aspect may have been rather more important to early modern cartography, both in urban and in extra-urban contexts, than has been acknowledged in conventional narratives of the development of Swedish cartography. Systematic map-making began at a time when the kingdom was expanding around the Baltic region; Sweden, during its era as a great power, comprised a culturally and administratively heterogeneous group of provinces which were linked to 'Sweden proper' in different ways.[30] This association supports the view that maps and map-making can be understood as a means by which 'porous', heterogeneous and geographically loosely defined composite monarchies of Europe were transformed into absolutely demarcated and internally homogenized states.[31]

Maps and map-making, then, could be used to unify and internally homogenize territories, but they also served to split land into smaller and more manageable pieces.[32] The cartographic material relating to Tornio illustrates the general tendency towards increased detail and information in urban maps over the course of the seventeenth and eighteenth centuries. Information was, of course, needed for the purposes of the bureaucratic state, but this change in urban and other cartography can also be linked to deeper and broader changes in the contemporary understanding of the world. A particularly interesting development was the increasing use of boundaries – that is, lines – in maps, which led to the identification and definition of smaller and smaller spatial units. Just as clocks divide the flow of time into neat units,[33] lines on maps divide land into distinct, separate elements. This, in turn, implies that the real world is also composed of separate physical entities whose outer boundaries can be identified in a relatively straightforward manner.[34]

There are obviously lines and boundaries of all kinds in the real world, but lines in the real world are actually permeable and dynamic, and they do not mark such absolute divisions between things as seems to be the case with lines on maps. Maps mediated, intentionally or unintentionally, a particular understanding of the world – a world where things 'are sealed by an outer boundary or shell that protects their inner constitution from the traffic of interactions with their surroundings'.[35] In other words, because of the mode of representation they appropriated, maps contributed to the formation of the modernist image of a clockwork universe populated by independent and bounded physical entities with certain fixed properties. Maps arguably mediated the emergence of a subject–object dualism by conjuring up an illusion of a world detached from those who inhabited it.[36] The issue of lines and boundaries is best understood as a part of this broader development. These abstract ideas also assumed more concrete expressions, as the following discussion of the development of urban space shows.

Enclosing urban space

A desire to regularize and enclose urban space characterized official Swedish urban planning from the 1640s onwards. Towns founded before this time generally followed a more or less 'organic' plan; the streets of Tornio, for instance, reflect the curvilinear shape of the western shore of Suensaari. The 'classical' form of regular wooden towns is believed to have emerged by around 1650 and was characterized by unified street facades and plots enclosed by buildings.[37] However, there was more to regularization and enclosure than simply a new style of town planning and new aesthetic ideals, and one should also remember that enclosure was by no means something limited to Swedish urban planning. Rather, as Matthew Johnson has argued, enclosure of space is a broad and multi-faceted phenomenon associated with the definition and redefinition of boundaries in the world, the origins of which can (at least in Britain) be traced back to the late medieval period.[38] The organization and building of the environment, in turn, influences not only how people move around their world, but also how they think about and understand it.[39]

There is little documentary information from the seventeenth century relating to the spatial organization of Tornio. However, archaeological data indicate that, while buildings were not randomly placed and aligned, the organization of urban space in seventeenth-century Tornio was open and 'village-like' and did not constitute an enclosed 'classical' wooden-town landscape. Some reordering of the urban space took place in the 1670s and a new grid plan was designed after the end of the Great Northern War in the late 1710s. Although the townsfolk ultimately rebuilt the town according to the original plan, it was, however, partly regularized.[40]

The enclosing of plots began in Tornio after the Great Northern War at the latest, as is evident from both the perspective drawing and the map drawn by French explorers of the town in the late 1730s (Map 39 see colour plate section 2, p. 14). However, the enclosure process was by means complete. Plots along the first and second street were more or less completely enclosed, but the situation was somewhat different along the third street. Given that 'the most able traders' are reported to have lived on the first street, 'common people' on the second and 'the poorest' on the third,[41] there appears to be an association between enclosure – that is, the definition and manifestation of the boundaries of households – and social or economic status. Material culture also expressed and reproduced social boundaries in other ways. For instance, the wealthier town residents started to paint their (larger) houses in the eighteenth century; whereas those who were poorer lived in smaller, unpainted houses. Even in death social status was reflected through the location of graves underneath church floors, with the wealthiest being laid to rest closest to the altar. [42]

With the exception of Tornio, during the seventeenth century all wooden towns on the Gulf of Bothnia were fairly rapidly regularized to a grid plan, despite the objections of the townsfolk. The adoption of the orthogonal grid plan and the gradual enclosure of urban space in mid-seventeenth-century Sweden – and the regulation and 'geometrization' of urban space more generally – has conventionally been understood in art-historical terms and attributed to the adoption of Renaissance ideals of town planning.[43] As with maps, however, these changes in the urban space environment can also be considered as part of the broader 'disciplining' of space and definition of boundaries between different types of spaces. This development relates to the forming of the conceptual boundaries between nature and culture or the private and the public, for example, and ultimately reflects the early modern preoccupation with controlling people and the environment.[44]

Straightness, or a tendency towards rectilinearity, characterized Swedish urban planning from the mid-seventeenth century onwards. 'The straight line', according to Ingold, is 'an index of the triumph of rational purposeful design over the vicissitudes of the natural world'.[45] The regular grid plan underlined the cultural character of the urban environment and promoted 'rectilinear behaviour'; culture was separated from nature conceptually and materially, and the latter was subjected to human control. The somewhat utopian regularization plan for Raahe (Sw. Brahestad) is an illustrative example of this attitude. The plan simply disregarded the fact that its execution would have required a massive earth-moving operation to fill in a small bay.[46] Geometric plans, furthermore, also altered the relationship between the Crown and the people by bringing the everyday lived environment of townsfolk under the control of central administration, thus concretely bringing the Crown closer to the people.[47] Finally, it seems likely – given the symbiotic relationship between people and spatial organization – that the enclosure of plots also mediated a new understanding of public and private space: the lining of plots with buildings would have created a tangible boundary between a plot and the world beyond it. This notion can be illustrated further by considering a particular class of domestic material culture.

Demarcating domestic space

The case of curtains exemplifies boundary-making through material culture on a smaller scale. Curtains are first mentioned in the Tornio probate records in 1730[48] and almost half of the probate inventories include curtains after 1750 (Table 9). Although in the second half of the eighteenth century almost all of the wealthiest residents owned curtains, according to probate inventories they were used by only 10 per cent of the poorest townsfolk.[49] By way of comparison, probate inventories from Lautiosaari (a hamlet close to Tornio) indicate that, during the seventeenth and eighteenth centuries, curtain ownership was only prevalent among the local gentry and Crown and ecclesiastical officials.[50] In a wider perspective, curtains began to appear in urban contexts of the Baltic Sea around the mid-eighteenth century and become more common in the nineteenth century.[51] In England, too, curtains were uncommon before the mid-eighteenth century, although they were used in the households of wealthy tradesmen in London before this time.[52] The residents of Tornio, then, began to own curtains at roughly the same time as the townsfolk elsewhere in the Baltic region but slightly later than was the case in the centre of the early modern world, London.

Table 9. Number of probate records of Tornio residents and number of probates that included curtains (1723–1776).

	Number of probate inventories	Number of inventories that included curtains
1723–1749	20	5 (25%)
1750–1776	89	39 (44%)
Total	109	44 (40%)

Sources: OMA, Finland, The Archives of the town of Tornio, Probate inventories 1723–1776.

The early modern town is likely to have caused stress among the residents due to a relative scarcity of space in narrow plots and the location of houses in rows close to each other and to the street. In such circumstances, curtains not only represented a kind of soft furnishing, but 'could be regarded as giving greater privacy to households living close to one another'.[53] Curtains, in other words, served as screens between the domestic sphere and the outside world. They also symbolically elaborated the boundary between private and public spaces. Furthermore, because they were first adopted by those in higher socioeconomic classes, the ownership and display of curtains expressed and reproduced social boundaries in the urban landscape in a similar way to enclosed plots and painted houses. It is instructive that curtains were still rare among working-class households in Tampere (Sw. Tammerfors) around 1900: in this social environment those families that hung curtains in their windows were ridiculed by their neighbours (Pictures 8–9 see colour plate section 2, pp. 15 and 16).[54]

Material culture, as the case of curtain ownership and use implies, is integral to the formation and manifestation of social identities. Clothes, personal adornments, houses and other material things associated with particular people, along with patterns of movement and behaviour, contribute to the development of personal identities and the definition of boundaries between different groups of people.[55] The adoption of curtains in Tornio, and elsewhere, was perhaps associated with the emergence of a middle class, or at least a wealthy merchant identity. Those who self-identified with this 'class' shared similar values and used material culture in certain ways to visually express their identity, or at least some aspect of their identity. An increasing desire for privacy, expressed in and achieved through material culture, was one defining aspect of the emerging middle class or merchant identity. Merchants were better able to purchase curtain cloth for themselves, but thus far there has been little consideration given to whether the curtain cloth was imported or woven by the town residents.

In addition to distinguishing the wealthy from the poor, curtains were also expressive of a cultural difference between urban and rural people. Although during the eighteenth century curtains had become fairly common in the urban environment, curtains were generally not found in the countryside at the time. In a very broad sense, then, curtains played a similar symbolic function to, for example, the toll fence. This may appear a self-evident – if not downright banal – point, but there is more to this issue than a superficial association between seemingly different kinds of things. Various cultural and material phenomena in early modern Sweden, and indeed the world, were related to each other on various levels and in different ways, even when they initially appear to have had little or nothing in common or were associated with mutually different domains of thought and action.[56] In order to understand these constellations of things and ideas – and ultimately the dynamics of historical processes – it is necessary and useful to view things and their relationships from various perspectives, of which boundary making is but one perspective, albeit an important one.

Conclusion

In this chapter we have discussed the making of different kinds of boundaries – from metaphysical to social and material – in early modern Sweden, focusing specifically on urban environments and by drawing from the specific example of Tornio. We have argued that a variety of artefacts from maps to buildings and domestic material culture were expressive of and contributed to boundary-making in the past. Maps, for example, were not only a means of recording information: they also rendered real those divisions of land that could not necessarily be seen in the landscape. Changes in the urban landscape, specifically the enclosing of plots, can similarly be connected to this desire to define the boundaries of things.

The reordering of urban space according to a rectilinear plan, in turn, mediated other changes. These included the emergence of the division between the public and the private, which was elaborated through household material culture, such as curtains. The study of material culture, then, can provide access to – or enhance our understanding of – how people in the past understood and related to the world around them.

Notes

1 See further, e.g. Brück 1999; Henry 2008; Herva and Ylimaunu 2009.
2 E.g. Johnson 1996; Clark 1997; Tarlow and West 1999; DeMarrais et al. 2005.
3 Woodward 2007.
4 Tolias 2007; Herva 2010.
5 Baigent 1990, pp. 156–157.
6 Kostet 2000, p. 38; Mökkönen 2006, p. 56.
7 Rystedt 2006.
8 Kostet 1995, pp. 29, 33.
9 See also Baigent 1990, pp. 64–67.
10 Herva & Ylimaunu 2010.
11 E.g. Johnson 1996, pp. 109–111.
12 Markkanen 1988; Nordberg 1996; Majantie & Uotila 2000, p. 61; Rosén 2004, pp. 95–96; Herva & Ylimaunu 2006.
13 Markkanen 1980; Markkanen 1988.
14 Markkanen 1980; Markkanen 1988.
15 Nordberg 1996; Herva & Ylimaunu 2006.
16 E.g. Markkanen 1988; Herva & Ylimaunu 2006.
17 E.g. Leone & Shackel 1987.
18 Jutikkala 1968; Ranta 1981, pp. 109–110; Lilius 1985, pp. 16–17.
19 Kostet 1995, p. 37.
20 Kirjakka 1982, p. 78; Kostet 1995, pp. 170–172.
21 Olaus Magnus 1973 [1555], Book XX.
22 Mäntylä 1971; Lilja 1995; Ylimaunu 2007.
23 Mäntylä 1971; Ylimaunu 2007.
24 E.g. Kostet 1995, pp. 54–55.
25 Ylimaunu 2007, pp. 70–71, 103; Herva and Ylimaunu 2010; on early urban maps, see Kostet 1995, pp. 35–37.
26 Kostet 1995, p. 56; Ylimaunu 2007, pp. 79–82.
27 Mäntylä 1971, p. 29; Ylimaunu 2006, pp. 34, 37.
28 E.g. Kostet 1995; Mökkönen 2006, pp. 16–19.
29 See Nurmi 2009; Herva & Ylimaunu 2010.
30 See Gustafsson 1998, pp. 198, 201, 203–206.
31 Biggs 1999.
32 See e.g. Given 2002.
33 Lucas 2006.
34 Cf. Ingold 2006.
35 Ingold 2006, p. 11.

36 E.g. Cosgrove 1985; Turnbull 1993.
37 Lilius 1985, p. 15.
38 Johnson 1996; cf. Ailio 1902.
39 E.g. Akkerman 2001.
40 Mäntylä 1971.
41 Brunnius 1965 [1731], pp. 24–25.
42 Ylimaunu 2007.
43 E.g. Lilius 1985.
44 See further e.g. Mrozowski 1999; Ingold 2000; Henry 2008; Herva & Ylimaunu 2009.
45 Ingold 2007, p. 153.
46 Kostet 1995, pp. 120 (Map 80).
47 Matthews et al. 2002; Ahlberg 2005, p. 78.
48 PK 2 June 1730/TKA/OMA.
49 Ylimaunu et al. 2009.
50 Helistö 1992, pp. 337, 362.
51 Nordmann 1978, pp. 292–293; Rosén 2004; Pullat 2007.
52 Weatherill 1996, pp. 6–8.
53 Weatherill 1996, pp. 81–83.
54 Jäntti 1997, p. 70.
55 Johnson 1999; Ylimaunu 2005; Mrozowski 2006, 2, pp. 57–59; Ylimaunu 2007; White and Beaudry 2009.
56 See also Deetz 1977; Johnson 1996.

Bibliography

Archival sources

Provincial Archive of Oulu (Sw. Uleåborg), Finland (OMA)
The Archives of the town of Tornio (Sw. Torneå)
Probate inventories (PK)

The National Archives of Sweden (Riksarkivet), Stockholm (SRA)
Lantmät.lev 1892, no 40 (kartavd. M. form.)

The Provincial Museum of Tornio (Sw. Torneå) Valley Maps

Literature

Ahlberg, N. 2005. *Stadsgrundningar och planförändringar. Svensk stadsplanering 1521–1721*. Uppsala University, Uppsala.
Ailio, J. 1902. *Lopen asunnot eri kehitysasteissaan*. The Finnish Literature Society, Helsinki.
Akkerman, A. 2001. 'Urban Planning in the Founding of Cartesian Thought.' *Philosophy and Geography*, Vol. 4 (2), pp. 141–167.
Baigent, E. 1990. 'Swedish Cadastral Mapping 1628–1700. A Neglected Legacy.' *Geographical Journal* 156 (1), pp. 62–69.
Biggs, M. 1999. 'Putting the State on the Map. Cartography, Territory, and European State Formation.' *Comparative Studies in Society and History*, Vol. 41 (2), pp. 374–405.

Brück, J. 1999. 'Ritual and Rationality. Some Problems of Interpretation in European Archaeology.' *Journal of European Archaeology*, Vol. 2 (3), pp. 313–344.

Brunnius, E. 1965 (1731). *Tornion kaupungista ja sen lähipitäjistä* (Latin original *De Urbe Torna eiqe adjacentibus paroeciis*. Translated by T. Itkonen). Lion's Club, Tornio.

Clark, A. 1997. *Being There. Putting Brain, Body and World Together Again*. MIT Press, Cambridge Mass.

Cosgrove, D. 1985. 'Prospect, Perspective and the Evolution of the Landscape Idea.' *Transactions of the Institute of British Geographers*, NS 10, pp. 45–62.

Deetz, J. 1977. *In Small Things Forgotten. The Archaeology of Early American Life*. Anchor Press, New York.

DeMarrais, E., Gosden, C. and Renfrew, C. (eds.) 2005. *Rethinking Materiality. The Engagement of the Mind with the Material World*. McDonald Institute for Archaeological Research, Cambridge.

Given, M. 2002. 'Maps, Fields, and Boundary Claims. Demarcation and Resistance in Colonial Cyprus.' *International Journal of Historical Archaeology*, Vol. 6, pp. 1–22.

Gustafsson, H. 1998. 'The Conglomerate. A Perspective on State Formation in Early Modern Europe.' *Scandinavian Journal of History*, Vol. 23, pp. 189–213.

Helistö, M. 1992. 'Lautiosaaren kylän pesäluetteloja 1697–1810.' *Jatuli*, Vol. 22, pp. 328–385.

Henry, J. 2008. 'The Fragmentation of Renaissance Occultism and the Decline of Magic.' *History of Science*, Vol. 46 (1), pp. 1–48.

Herva, V.-P., 2010. 'Maps and Magic in Renaissance Europe.' *Journal of Material Culture*, Vol. 15 (3), pp. 323–343.

Herva, V.-P. & Ylimaunu, T. 2006. 'Posliiniastiat, varallisuus ja kuluttajakäyttäytyminen 1700-luvun Torniossa.' *Suomen Museo*, Vol. 118, pp. 79–89.

Herva, V.-P. & Ylimaunu, T. 2009. 'Folk Beliefs, Special Deposits, and Engagement with the Environment in Early Modern Northern Finland.' *Journal of Anthropological Archaeology*, Vol. 28 (2), pp. 234–243.

Herva, V.-P. & Ylimaunu, T. 2010. 'What's on the Map? Reassessing the First Urban Map of Torneå and Early Map-Making in Sweden.' *Scandinavian Journal of History*, Vol. 35 (1), pp. 86–107.

Ingold, T. 2000. *The Perception of the Environment. Essays in Livelihood, Dwelling and Skill*. London, Routledge.

Ingold, T. 2006. 'Rethinking the Animate, Re-animating Thought.' *Ethnos*, Vol. 71 (1), pp. 9–20.

Ingold, T. 2007. *Lines. A Brief History*. London, Routledge.

Jäntti, L. 1997. *Isoäitiemme aika kuvien kertomana*, 3rd edition. WSOY, Helsinki.

Johnson, M. 1996. *An Archaeology of Capitalism*. Blackwell, Oxford.

Johnson, M. 1999. 'Reconstructing Castles and Refashioning Identities in Renaissance England.' In Tarlow, S. & West, S (eds.) *The Familiar Past? Archaeologies of Later Britain*. Routledge, London, pp. 69–86.

Jutikkala, E. 1968. 'Town Planning in Sweden and Finland until the Middle of the Nineteenth Century.' *Scandinavian Economic History Review*, Vol. 16, pp. 19–46.

Kirjakka, M. 1982. *Kaupunkirakentaminen Suomessa vuoteen 1875. Asemakaavoituksen sekä rakentamista ohjanneiden määräysten ja päätösten vaikutus kaupunkirakenteeseen*. Teknillinen korkeakoulu, Espoo.

Kostet, J. 1995. *Cartographia urbium Finnicarum. Suomen kaupunkien kaupunkikar-*

tografia 1600-luvulla ja 1700-luvun alussa. Pohjois-Suomen Historiallinen Yhdistys, Rovaniemi.

Kostet, J. 2000. '1600-luvun kaupunkikartat.' In Rantatupa, H. (ed.) *Kartta historian lähteenä.* Kampus kustannus, Jyväskylä, pp. 29–49.

Leone, M. P. & Shackel, P. A. 1987. 'Forks, Clocks and Power.' In Ingersoll Jr., D. W. &c. Bronitsky, G. (eds.) *Mirror and Metaphor. Material and Social Constructions of Reality.* University Press of America, Lanham, pp. 45–61.

Lilius, H. 1985. *Suomalainen puukaupunki.* Anders Nyborg, Rungsted Kyst.

Lilja, S. 1995. 'Small Towns in the Periphery. Population and Economy of Small Towns in Sweden during the Early Modern Period.' In Clark, P. (ed.) *Small Towns in Early Modern Europe.* Cambridge University Press, Cambridge, pp. 50–76.

Lucas, G. 2006. 'Historical Archaeology and Time.' In Hicks, D. & Beaudry, M. (eds.) *The Cambridge Companion to Historical Archaeology.* Cambridge University Press, Cambridge, pp. 34–47.

Majantie, K. & Uotila, K. 2000. 'Laukon löydöt.' In Uotila, K. (ed.) *Vesilahden Laukko. linna, kartano, koti.* The Society for Medieval Archaeology in Finland, Turku, pp. 60–72.

Mäntylä, I. 1971. *Tornion kaupungin historia,* Vol. 1: *1621–1809.* The Town of Tornio, Tornio.

Markkanen, E. 1980. 'Das finnische Erbschaftsinventarmaterial.' In van der Woude, A. & Schuurman, A. (eds.) *Probate Inventories. A New Source for the Historical Study of Wealth, Material Culture and Agricultural Development.* HES, Wageningen, pp. 97–114.

Markkanen, E. 1988. *Perukirja tutkimuslähteenä.* University of Jyväskylä, Jyväskylä.

Matthews, C. N., Leone, M. P. & Jordan, K. A. 2002. 'The political economy of archaeological cultures.' *Journal of Social Archaeology* Vol. 2 (1), pp. 109–134.

Mökkönen, T. 2006. *Historiallinen paikkatieto. Paikkatiedon tuottaminen historiallisista kartoista.* Ministry of the Environment, Helsinki.

Mökkönen, T. 2007. 'From the Present to the Past. Archaeological Surveys in Postmedieval Towns in Finland and the Use of Urban Cartography.' In Immonen, V., Lempiäinen, M. & Rosendahl, U. (eds.) *Hortus Novus. Fresh Approaches to Medieval Archaeology in Finland.* The Society for Medieval Archaeology in Finland, Turku, pp. 52–64.

Mrozowski, S. 1999. 'The Commodification of Nature.' *International Journal of Historical Archaeology,* Vol. 3 (3), pp. 153–166.

Mrozowski, S. 2006. *The Archaeology of Class in Urban America.* Cambridge University Press, Cambridge.

Nordberg, H. 1996. 'Pesäluetteloiden kirjamaininnat 1700-luvun Torniossa.' *Tornionlaakson vuosikirja 1996,* pp. 149–167.

Nodermann, M. 1976. 'Heminredning.' In Bringéus, N.-A. (ed.) *Arbete och redskap. Materiell folkkultur på svensk landsbygd före industrialismen.* Liber Läromedel, Lund, pp. 263–296.

Nurmi, R. 2009. '(The) Memory Remains. The Immaterial Remnants of the Toll Fence in Tornio Town.' *Interarchaeologia.,* Vol. 3. University of Tartu, University of Latvia & University of Vilnius, Tartu, Riga & Vilnius, pp. 121–134.

Olaus Magnus Gothus 1973 [1555]. *Pohjoisten kansojen historia. Suomea koskevat kuvaukset.* Translated by K. Hirvonen, comments by K. Vilkuna). Otava, Helsinki.

Pullat, R. 2007. *Die Nachlassverzeichnisse der literaten in Tallinn 1710–1805.* Estopol, Tallinn.

Ranta, R. 1981. 'Suurvalta-ajan kaupunkilaitos.' In P. Tommila (ed.) *Suomen kaupunkilaitoksen historia,* Vol. 1. Suomen kaupunkiliitto, Helsinki.

Rosén, C. 2004. *Stadsbor och bönder. Materiell kultur och social status i Halland från medeltid till 1700-tal.* Riksantikvarieämbetet, Stockholm.

Rystedt, B. 2006. 'The Cadastral Cartographic Heritage of Sweden.' *e-Perimetron,* Vol. 1 (2), pp. 155–163. URL: < http://www.e-perimetron.org/Vol_1_2/Vol1_2.htm>.

Tarlow, S. & West, S. (eds.) 1999. *The Familiar Past? Archaeologies of Later Historical Britain.* Routledge, London.

Tolias, G. 2007. 'Maps in Renaissance Libraries and Collections.' In Woodward, D. (ed.) *The History of Cartography,* Vol. 3: *Cartography in the European Renaissance.* University of Chicago Press, Chicago, pp. 637–660.

Turnbull, D. 1993. *Maps Are Territories. Science Is an Atlas.* University of Chicago Press, Chicago.

Weatherill, L. 1996. *Consumer Behaviour and Material Culture in Britain 1660–1760.* Routledge, London.

White, C. L. & Beaudry, M. C. 2009. 'Artifacts and Personal Identity.' In Majewski, T. & Gaimster, D. (eds.) *International Handbook of Historical Archaeology.* Springer, New York, pp. 209–225.

Woodward, D. 2007. 'Cartography and the Renaissance. Continuity and Change.' In Woodward, D. (ed.) *The History of Cartography,* Vol. 3: *Cartography in the European Renaissance.* University of Chicago Press, Chicago, pp. 3–24.

Ylimaunu, T. 2005. 'Postimerkit ja identiteetti. Kuva suomalaisesta yhteiskunnasta 1930-luvulla.' In Karhu, J. & Pärssinen, H. *Tabellarius.* Postimuseon ystävät & Postimuseo, Helsinki, pp. 84–101.

Ylimaunu, T. 2006. 'Ranta-aitat ja kirkko Tornion 17. vuosisadan ensimmäisen puoliskon kaupunkikartoissa.' In Alenius, K., Jalagin, S., Mäkivuoti, M. & Wunsch, S. (eds, *Mielikuvien maanosat. Olavi K. Fältin juhlakirja.* University of Oulu, Oulu, pp. 29–37.

Ylimaunu, T. 2007. *Aittakylästä kaupungiksi. Arkeologinen tutkimus Tornion kaupungistumisesta 18. vuosisadan loppuun mennessä.* Pohjois-Suomen Historiallinen Yhdistys, Rovaniemi.

Ylimaunu, T., Kallio-Seppä, T., Kuokkanen, T. and Nurmi, R. 2009. 'Pöytäliinat, servietit ja ikkunaverhot: rajapintoja Torniossa 1700-luvulla.' In Ikäheimo, J. & Lipponen, S. (eds.) *Ei kiveäkään kääntämättä. Juhlakirja Pentti Koivuselle.* University of Oulu, Oulu, pp. 285–292.

CHAPTER 13

Regional Inequality

Ilkka Nummela

Introduction

In medieval times Finland – then part of the Kingdom of Sweden – was on the outer periphery of Europe. Permanent settlement of the territory had begun ten thousand years earlier, after the last Ice Age, and Finland remained sparsely populated for several millennia. The Finnish economy was largely based on self-sufficient hunting and gathering and had very few direct connections to world markets. The total number of inhabitants in the area is estimated to have been 20,000–30,000 in the twelfth century. As a result of subsequent estimated population growth of 0.5% per annum, the number of inhabitants reached 250,000–300,000 by the late sixteenth century. However, the population growth rate was practically reduced to 0.0% per annum at the end of the sixteenth and beginning of the seventeenth centuries.

Although sixteenth-century Finland could only boast six small towns (compared with forty in Sweden proper), economic expansion was underway by the late Middle Ages: Finland (like the rest of the Kingdom of Sweden) had become more closely incorporated into the market system dominated by the Hansa league in north-western Europe.[1] The ascension of Gustav Vasa to the throne in 1 5 2 3 can be seen as the dawn of the modern era in Sweden-Finland. Under his reign, the hold of central government tightened. The new king managed his realm like a large private enterprise, and the modern Swedish state, which included efficient administration and taxation, was his creation. At this time the economy was run on proto-mercantilist lines, and Gustav ruthlessly violated people's rights when they ran counter to the interests of the Crown. After the Reformation, a large part of the property belonging to the church was confiscated and declared the property of the Swedish state.[2]

What were the consequences of this new era for standard of living and economic inequality in various parts of Finland? The nutritional

335

status of the population is the one of the key indices often employed in discussions about the consequences of economic changes. Thanks to the excellent research undertaken by Janken Myrdal and Johan Söderberg on Sweden proper in the sixteenth century, development in Finland can also be placed in a larger European frame of reference. Myrdal and Söderberg speak of a hidden agrarian revolution in sixteenth-century Sweden, which they argue offered the Swedish people increased prosperity. The conditions in Finland at that time were, in many respects, similar to those in Sweden itself. There is evidence of substantial economic growth: we know that the total area of cultivated land increased in all Finnish counties during the early modern period[3] and that real wages also grew in some parts of rural Finland during the sixteenth and seventeenth centuries.[4]

Many historians imply that economic equality was common in Finland at the beginning of the early modern period – in other words they assume that there were not substantial differences in material wellbeing between the inhabitants of different Finnish regions. However, others, like Seppo Suvanto and Eli F. Heckscher, explicitly argue that such inequalities also pervaded medieval society and that wealth was not evenly distributed among medieval Finns. Within a broader European framework, the prominent Dutch economic historian Jan L. van Zanden maintains that levels of economic inequality were, in fact, relatively high in western European cities of the late medieval period.[5]

In economic analysis two main types of income distribution are usually considered: functional distribution (the way in which each factor of production – land, labour or capital – receives compensation for its contribution to the gross domestic product) and size distribution of personal income (the way in which financial resources received from economic production are distributed among individuals, families or households). Within Finnish historiography changes in economic inequality are usually analysed only in a descriptive manner: through comparison of the mean values of different social groups, rather than analysis of the differences between individuals or regions.

In this chapter, I will examine variations both in levels of wealth and in concentration of wealth in different parts of rural Finland in the late sixteenth century. Distribution of wealth refers to the comparison of the wealth of various individuals or groups within a society. It differs from distribution of income in that it is concerned with the distribution of ownership of assets within a society, rather than the current income of members of that society. Historians who concentrate on the early modern period have to focus on wealth rather than income due to the relative scarcity of source material about incomes.

This chapter is part of my broader investigation of regional differences in economic inequality in Finland from the late medieval era to the Second World War.[6] As such, its attempt to understand and explain the past from both contemporary and modern perspectives is grounded in empirical and theoretical knowledge from economics, history and the social sciences. I am not the first to venture into this field of inquiry. The renowned early twentieth-century Finnish historian E. G. Palmén took this path before me. The economic-statistical research on the economic conditions in different parts of Finland during the early modern period undertaken by Palmén and his research team was ahead of its time.[7] Although their research was based on the same archival material as this project (land registers and evaluations, various types of tax registers and poll lists),[8] Palmén and his team lacked the possibilities offered by modern statistical analysis.

Economic growth and economic inequality

Simon Kuznets's presidential address to the Sixty-Seventh Annual Meeting of the American Economic Association in December 1954 has been widely viewed as a pioneering moment in research into the relationship between economic growth and economic inequality. In his pivotal speech (published in 1955) Kuznets discussed 'the character and courses of long-term changes in the personal distribution of income', posed the question 'Does inequality in the distribution of income increase or decrease in the course of a country's economic growth?', and finally asked 'What factors determine the secular trends of income inequalities?' According to Kuznets, economic inequality grew during the first phase of modern economic growth in the nineteenth century but later levelled in the twentieth century. The graphical representation of Kuznets's discovery is known as the Kuznets curve. The inverted U-shaped Kuznets curve has been widely used as a theoretical framework in economic history to describe the trends of economic inequality over the past two centuries.[9]

Growth history (largely concerned with the industrial revolution of the eighteenth and nineteenth centuries) has generally accepted the Kuznets curve as a model to explain development in economic inequality. The primary sector was also the subject of increasing attention among researchers in the 1980s and 1990s. S. Robinson (1976) further developed Kuznets's idea by focusing on the movements of people

337

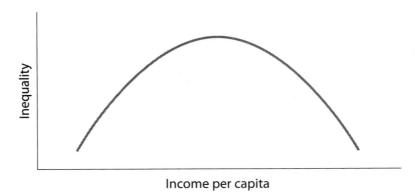

Diagram 1. The Kuznets curve.

from agriculture to manufacturing. This modified model can be used to explain the increase in economic inequality during the first stage of industrialization.[10] On the other hand, the application of the Kuznets curve to the early modern era (from the sixteenth century to the French revolution of the late eighteenth century) has not been uncontroversial. The beginning of the early modern period has been the subject of much dispute in recent economic history research. The exploration and explanation of the sixteenth century within most European school curricula is dominated by an overriding emphasis on change. The conquest of America, the flow of silver to the Old Continent, and inventions, along with, of course, the Reformation, the birth of a new type of state and the development of armies, have all been seen as contributions to this development. However, the documented progress in agriculture was ongoing and underwent a number of minor innovations, which often remain outside this narrative of change.[11]

Inequality can be seen primarily as an economic problem and secondarily as a political or social problem. There have been (and still are) various reasons for economic inequality within different societies and time periods. The term 'economic inequality' usually refers to disparities in the distribution of economic assets or income, and it is closely connected with questions about the conditions of existence and the material conditions of life (e.g. incomes, wealth), the most fundamental issue in economic history. Research suggests that the causes of economic inequality in the past have been (and will continue to be) interrelated, non-linear, and complex. Much research in the field has, therefore, very often sought to establish why some countries or individuals are rich and others not. School curricula usually say very little or nothing about levels of economic inequality in the sixteenth and seventeenth centuries. The limits of what is possible have always varied for different people and the fruits of development have never been evenly distributed among nations, social groups or individuals. Economic inequality has existed throughout the history of mankind, and the early modern period in Finland (and elsewhere) was no exception. In general terms, economic inequality refers to equality of outcome and is related to the idea of equality of opportunity both in the early modern period and later.

Was economic inequality only an economic matter? What role did the state play in the change, and was it an active agent of change? It is also worth considering the significance of changes in technology and whether progress in peripheral Finland created opportunities for entrepreneurship. The sixteenth century has been a subject of increased attention and dispute among those interested in growth history (traditionally concerned with the industrial revolution and the eighteenth century, as mentioned above) and the primary sector. Researchers have paid particular attention to agriculture, the principal industry of the early modern period. Within this research, two main trends can be discerned: one pessimistic and the other optimistic.[12]

The pessimistic school can be traced back two centuries to Thomas Malthus and David Ricardo. Their work is underpinned by the notion that the production of food is inelastic in comparison with the increase in population. Most typically, this is illustrated by the familiar axiom that the population increases in a geometric progression, while the food supply increases in an arithmetic progression. In this way Man was truly at the mercy of nature and only the fittest could survive in the competition for food. This school of thought can be characterized as pessimist in its supposition that agricultural production is inelastic. The more positive viewpoint, on the other hand, can be traced back to Adam Smith. The essential point in this context is Smith's emphasis on economic growth (although his main concern was, in fact, trade and its freedom). The optimism of his position lies in his assertion that resources are substitutable.[13]

The uneven distribution of income and wealth were fundamental to Karl Marx's view of the economic history of the world. In the late nineteenth century, Eduard Bernstein, through the use of statistical data, demonstrated that Marxian prognoses of widening economic inequality were not consistent with historical development in the nineteenth century. Bernstein's analysis was followed by several other studies on economic inequality (including Heikki Renvall of Finland). Although these studies were largely descriptive, they shifted the focal point of research towards the size distribution of income.[14]

The main concern of this chapter is economic inequality, which usually refers to disparities in the distribution of economic assets or income. The social structure of households and the classification of different kinds of household during various sub-periods are also considered to some extent. Economic historians have tended to use mean values (whether of countries, communities or groups) as the basis of their research on early modern economic inequality. Such accounts largely seek to highlight the social stratification of the population in a specific place or to demonstrate the differences in the mean wealth of different groups within the studied population. It has been less common to focus on the size distribution of wealth or income among the population: that is, differences between individuals or in the personal distribution of economic assets. Although several monographs and articles address early modern wealth distributions within different towns and rural regions, in only a few have economic inequalities been considered within a wider perspective. Therefore, the connection between early modern economic growth and the development of economic inequality (of income and wealth) in Europe still requires further investigation. This need for more research has been stressed by van Zanden, who himself has demonstrated the upward development of economic inequality in the Netherlands 1561–1800 during its time of so-called 'greatness'.[15]

Here the term economic inequality is used to refer to inequality among individuals: in the vocabulary of economics, the personal distribution of wealth. This is measured by the Gini coefficient (G), the most prominently used measure of income or wealth inequality. It is a measure of statistical dispersion developed in 1912 by the Italian statistician Corrado Gini. The Gini coefficient is a widely used indicator of inequality, in which the extent of the dispersion of income is described using one numerical value. The higher the value of the Gini coefficient, the more unequally is income distributed. The greatest possible value of the Gini coefficient is 1. This would indicate that the highest earning income recipient, in fact, receives all the income. The smallest Gini coefficient value is 0, which would indicate that the income of all income recipients is equal. In the case of wealth distribution, given a sufficient number of observations, the Gini coefficient can be used to indicate (although not quite exactly) how much of the total wealth would need to be redistributed from the

$$G = \frac{1}{2\mu n}\frac{1}{(n-1)} \sum_{i=1}^{n} \sum_{j=1}^{n} |xi - xj|$$

more wealthy to the less wealthy in order to ensure, in absolute terms, even distribution of total wealth.[16]

The Gini coefficient can be defined mathematically based on the Lorenz curve. It can be thought of as the ratio of the area that lies between the line of equality and the Lorenz curve over the total area under the line of equality. The Lorenz curve is a graphical representation of the cumulative distribution function of the empirical probability distribution of wealth or income. The American economist Max O. Lorenz published the Lorenz curve in 1905, in which the cumulative percentage of households is plotted on the x-axis and the cumulative percentage of total income on the y-axis. The Lorenz curve is commonly used to demonstrate economic inequality (originally wealth distribution). Economies with similar incomes and Gini coefficients can still have very different income distribution patterns. This is because Lorenz curves can have different shapes and yet still yield the same Gini coefficient.[17]

Method and sources

The starting point of this work has been the estimation of the total personal wealth of each taxpayer. The analysis of regional wealth and differences in mean wealth will be carried out in every parish and town (not reported here) and every province (Fi. *maakunta*, Sw. *landskap*). Early modern contemporary assessments of different kinds of wealth are available in the historical documents. Wealth values will also be recalculated on the basis of historical documents and price information. Wealth will be measured in contemprorary Swedish monetary units, i.e. in marks and *thalers*. From the sixteenth century, Sweden had two silver currencies with a floating exchange rate between them. The main currency was the mark, equal to 8 ore or 192 *penningar* (pennies). The secondary currency was the silver daler (*thaler*, dollar). The silver daler was an international coin and was first minted in Sweden in 1534. During the following centuries additional currencies, based on silver, copper and gold, came into use in the Swedish realm. They can also be converted into silver equivalents (e.g. grams of silver) in order to make international comparison easier.[18] Finland in this context and throughout is understood as the territory of

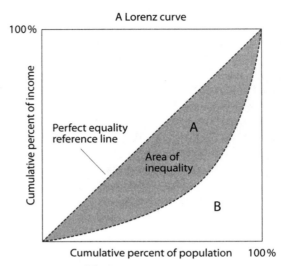

Diagram 2. The Lorenz curve.

the Finnish state in the 1930s. (In other words, some areas lost as the result of the Second World War will also be examined in this research). The geographical units used here are based on the administrative divisions of the state at the beginning of the sixteenth century and not those of the church. However, both the administrative and church geographical divisions had their roots in older forms of organization that had their origins in pagan times.[19]

Three different sources (or groups of sources) can be used to examine economic inequality and levels of wealth in late sixteenth-century Finland and Sweden. The most significant of these is the so-called silver tax of 1571 (Sw. *Älvsborgs lösen*). It is possible to identify this property tax (which was generally levied at the rate of 10%) and the property on which it was based for almost all of Finland, with the exception of part of Karelia and part of Ostrobothnia (Fi. Pohjanmaa, Sw. Österbotten). This tax was non-recurrent and, importantly, sufficiently severe for even minor variations among taxpayers to be revealed.[20] In 1600 a corresponding tax was levied at the rate of 2%. The current price level was 51% higher than had been the case three decades earlier. Significantly, in 1600 cultivated land was recorded in the assessments of tax liability (this had not been included in the 1571 assessments). The ownership of land, or more precisely of the right to the use of land, was of great importance in defining how the total product was distributed in preindustrial societies. However, the tax rolls of 1600 have unfortunately not been preserved to nearly the same extent as the rolls of 1571.[21]

In addition to these rolls, there is also available data on the distribution of tax units from the early modern times. However, the use of tax units as an indicator of the distribution of wealth is problematic. Many historians have pointed out that the distribution of land property displayed in the old tax units refers to the earlier distribution of land (i.e. assessment was not made on the basis of contemporary land distribution). In the case of Finland there is some debate about whether the tax units take into account other factors besides agricultural land. Most prominent authors agree that other elements of wealth were also taken into account in calculation of taxation. As these are not necessarily as dependable as the former, they will now be cast aside.[22]

Mean wealth as a spatial variable: the case of Finland in 1571

There is some evidence of economic growth in Finland at the beginning of the early modern period. The conditions in Finland were, in many respects, similar to those in Sweden – which enjoyed economic growth in the sixteenth century. As discussed above, Myrdal and Söderberg's research allows the development of Finland to be placed within a broader European frame of reference.[23] Nevertheless, very negative assumptions about economic growth underpin much research in the field of sixteenth-century Finnish local history (and that of elsewhere). Based on the crude measure of the estimated number of farms in Finland, the last decades of the sixteenth and the first decades of the seventeenth centuries saw a Finnish growth rate of practically 0.0% per annum. However, on the basis of available information about yield-to-seed ratios from the late 1500s, it seems that productivity in grain cultivation actually decreased at this time in both Finland and Sweden. It seems that we can speak of a hidden agrarian revolution in sixteenth-century Finland, just as Myrdal and Söderberg have argued was the case in Sweden. Development in the eastern part of the Swedish realm offered increased prosperity for the Finnish people. Although it is not my intention to reproduce Myrdal and Söderberg's more general frame of reference slavishly, I support their assertion that arguments about the sixteenth century are often poorly grounded, as is revealed by close analysis of the source materials.[24]

The central research concepts applied here are local community

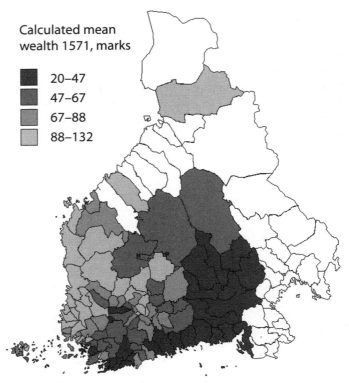

Map 40. Mean wealth in 1571, marks.

and the household both in itself and in the context of economic well-being or standard of living. Measures of wealth and concentration of wealth will yield different results when applied to individuals rather than households. In the early modern period the head of the household represented the entire household in the tax rolls. To ensure meaningful comparisons, consistent definitions have been applied to all the populations studied. The first research objective of this study is to estimate the total personal wealth of every person documented in the tax rolls in different parts of Finland in selected years during the sixteenth and seventeenth centuries. There were significant geographical variations in mean wealth during the research period: the differences between eastern and western parts of Finland in terms of economic and social structures seem to stem from variations in density and duration of settlement.

344

Map 40 depicts the mean wealth of different Finnish parishes in 1571. Of course, there may be systematic and random errors in the basic archival data as, indeed, there can be in any statistical data. It is worth noting, however, that the tax roll information was collected in a uniform manner across the country, which makes data comparison between different areas more straightforward than is often the case. According to the data presented in the appendix there was a significant difference between levels of wealth in the eastern and western parts of Finland:

Table 10. Wealth per taxpayer (marks) in different provinces of Finland in 1571.

Satakunta (Sw. Satakunda)	95
Ostrobothnia (Fi. Pohjanmaa, Sw. Österbotten)	83
Finland Proper (Fi. Varsinais-Suomi, Sw. Egentliga Finland)	73
Åland (Fi. Ahvenanmaa, Sw. Åland)	71
Häme (Sw. Tavastland)	70
Uusimaa (Sw. Nyland)	41
Savo (Sw. Savolax)	41
Swedish part of Karelia (Fi. Karjala, Sw. Karelen)	33

Sources: Silver taxation rolls from 1571.
Note: 10 marks = 1 cow.

In the west, settlement was of a more permanent nature and open field agriculture predominated. Whereas in the east, slash-and-burn agriculture was more prominent and settlement was in some senses more mobile than was the case in western Finland.

Some documents are missing from the original tax rolls of 1571. I have attempted to correct these deficiencies by using of other taxation rolls from the same time. The resultant estimated wealth values can be seen in Map 41.

Research into economic inequality should also focus on personal wealth within certain social groups, including early modern tradesmen, artisans and clergymen. For example, according to the tax rolls of 1571, many vicars in Finland were very wealthy. On the other hand the level of wealth inequality among the clergy in Finland Proper was roughly the same as that among all taxpayers in Finland. According to Armas Luukko, in early modern Finland most of the very rich outside

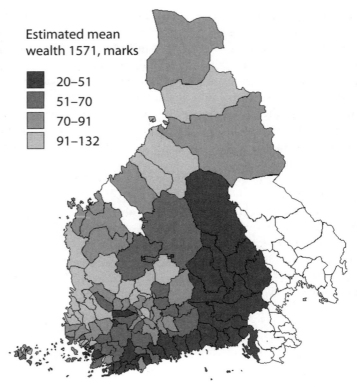

Map 41. Estimated mean wealth in 1571.

the clergy were rural tradesmen. Among the wealthiest taxpayers in 1571 were also several individuals from the peasantry who had been elected as local sheriffs.[25]

The role of landowners in the economy

During the medieval and early modern periods, landowning farmers had a central role the economic structure of Finland and Sweden. Landowning farmers made greater contributions than other members of society both to the 'Gross Domestic Product' and to the running of the 'machinery of society' through the taxes that they paid. At the end of the fifteenth century the number of freehold estates was still very small. In contrast to the situation of their continental European counterparts, farmers in Sweden and Finland were free men with some political influence. In relative terms, farmers paid the majority of the taxes, which were largely based on landownership.[26]

At the end of the sixteenth century the price of grain in Europe increased considerably (before levelling out during the second half of the following century). The increased price of grain also fuelled the expansion of agriculture within the Nordic countries. At the same time, real wages in continental European cities decreased as a result of the rise in bread prices. This development can also be seen as having provided the Scandinavian countries with an opportunity for economic growth, as has been discussed by the Danish-American historian John P. Maarbjerg.[27] The *huuhta* technique (burn-beating of trees, usually large, old spruces) originated in eastern Finland and was an innovation that resulted in greater yields than those produced using ordinary agricultural techniques[28]

It is worth asking whether progress in the periphery of Finland created an opportunity for entrepreneurship. It would also be appropriate to apply the Kuznets and Robinson models to slash-and-burn agriculture specifically, because the new *huuhta* technique adopted in slash-and-burn agriculture provided the opportunity for an enormous short-term increase in the productivity level of agriculture. Slash-and-burn agriculture provided an excellent opportunity for entrepreneurship: by buying seed grain and hiring seasonal labour, one could make a sizeable fortune. Several 'axe men' are listed in the tax rolls from province of Savo. In the mid-sixteenth century they formed a particular class of rural 'paupers'. The tax rolls of 1571 mentioned several individuals whose wealth was less than a single mark.[29] Slash-and-burn agriculture also seemed to encourage the organization of temporary companies. Such companies, which were relatively common, were very often inaccessible to the tax authorities since taxation was based on place of permanent residence. As was the case for field cultivation, a tithe had to be paid by slash-and-burn agriculturists. Court material from seventeenth-century Satakunta indicates that, for fiscal reasons, the government favoured the involvement of ordinary peasants in slash-and-burn agriculture.[30] Slash-and-burn methods were very much in the forefront of agriculture until the 1560s.[31]

The expansion occurred at a time when labour was relatively inexpensive. In the early 1570s, real wages in the countryside rose as a result of a considerable expansion in the size of the armed forces.[32] The end of the sixteenth century in Sweden and Finland was characterized by many years of war. Prolonged war both destroyed commercial relations and led to an expansion of public demand for commodities. This in turn initiated, at least to some extent, proto-industrial activity both in towns and in the countryside (e.g. the growth of shipyards).[33] We can even state that war, rather than peace, was the norm in early modern Scandinavia. Between 1561 and 1721 Sweden and Finland enjoyed less than fifty years of peace.[34] The Nordic Seven Years War (1563–1570) had a significant impact on foreign trade in the Baltic territories. The war against Russia (1570–1595) and 'The War of Clubs' (a civil war which also had the character of a peasant uprising; 1596–1597) were central to the economic and social development of Finland in the early modern period. At this time the costs of warfare were, for the most part, financed by peasant society (through money, economic assets in kind and manpower in the form of soldiers). The Thirty Years' War (1618–1648) likewise contributed to economic and social development in seventeenth-century Finland. The military was thus a key element in the building of modern Sweden in the sixteenth and seventeenth centuries. The many incentives for those in the army and navy also had consequences for wealth distribution.[35]

It is worth examining real wages in rural areas alongside the simultaneous increase in *Wüstung* or desertation (which could be real as well as simply fiscal). Although statistics of GDP and real wages are often criticized on the grounds that they do not represent changes for the whole population, they are usually strongly correlated with standard of living. Thus, at least two questions can be formulated: did the economic structure of Finland change as the number of farms decreased, and what did *Wüstung* or desertation really signify? *Wüstung* is usually interpreted as an indicator of poverty.[36] However, this is only partly true in the context of late sixteenth-century Finland. As the number of deserted settlements grew in one part of a province, the number of settlements may have increased in another part of the same province. In fact, the overall average farm size and total area of arable land grew.[37] This means that the question of *Wüstung* in Finland at the end of the sixteenth century should also be understood within the context of structural change in the economy. Compared to its significance in other Scandinavian countries, *Wüstung* played a relatively minor role in Finland. The discussion of *Wüstung* also needs to incorporate the possibility of an 'active' alternative. In other words, many peasants may have given up their livelihoods because there was a better alternative. The traditional model of passive adaptation in the spirit of Malthus cannot suffice.[38]

In 1530, 93% of the farms in Finland belonged to the ordinary

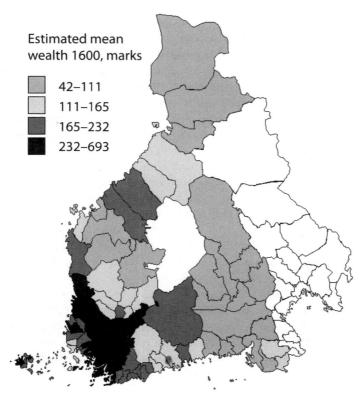

Estimated mean
wealth 1600, marks

42–111
111–165
165–232
232–693

Map 42. Estimated mean wealth in 1600.

peasantry; by 1600, this figure had fallen slightly to 90%. Landowning patterns in Finland Proper diverged from those in the eastern and northern parts of the country. With the growth of the nobility at the end of the sixteenth century, many farms and farmers in south-western Finland disappear from the sources. This can be seen in a wider perspective as a seventeenth-century phenomenon as well as related more specifically to feudal thinking about landownership in Finland (Maps 42 and 43).[39]

Prices, harvests and the role of the state

Across the time-series, the important relationship between the prices of butter and grain and the productivity of grain harvesting was generally marked by large variations in annual prices and by differences in the

349

linear and exponential trends. During the sixteenth century the prices of cereals rose more than those of animal products; this is indicative of certain problems in grain production in Finland. This can also be observed from the time-series of yield-to-seed ratios drawn from the accounts of different Crown manors and from tithe data. The late sixteenth century saw a reduction in total tithes. In other words, Finnish agriculture was simultaneously faced, on the one hand, with incentives to expand grain production and, on the other, with problems that arose from decreasing productivity.[40]

Compared to present-day levels, there were sizable variations in the yields of early modern harvests. Known large-scale crop failures in Finland can be estimated as follows: 10 occurrences in the fifteenth century, 16 in the sixteenth century, 33 in the seventeenth century, 30 in the eighteenth century and 15 in the nineteenth century.[41] On the basis of Finnish and Swedish material, it seems that productivity of grain cultivation decreased as a result of the yield-to-seed ratios during the last decades of the sixteenth century. This can be confirmed by consulting the accounts of different Crown manors and tithes. As noted above, tithes decreased during the late sixteenth century.[42] There is further evidence from Ostrobothia of a decline in productivity in the late sixteenth century: a downward oriented linear trend can be calculated from the data on yield-to-seed ratios in Korsholma (Sw. Korsholm). This trend was also evident in the production of butter per cow at the same manor.[43]

Naturally, climatic factors have also played an important role both in harvests and in agrarian settlement patterns. Historians have long talked of the so-called 'Little Ice Age'. A period of higher temperatures in the mid-sixteenth century, advantageous for agricultural activity in the north, was followed by less advantageous weather conditions towards the end of the century. However, even the temperatures until 1600 were over the mean temperature for several centuries. The really cold period can be dated to the seventeenth century.[44]

It is certainly worth considering the role of the state in the ongoing societal change: did the state simply adapt in response to changes in society, or was it an active agent in this process? It seems clear that the Crown was an active agent of change. Gustav Vasa was eager to colonize sparsely populated areas of his country. Areas of wilderness (which had earlier belonged to individual farms) were cleared and new settlements were established in the interior. Gustav's successors continued his project. Alongside its colonization activities, the state also provided new opportunities for employment, particularly within the army. An indi-

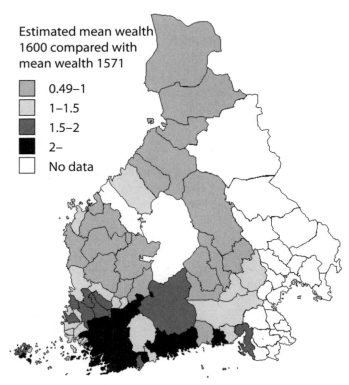

Map 43. Levels of relative wealth, 1571 and 1600.

rect result of the state's activities was the homogenization and increased 'peasantization' of what had been a more heterogeneous peasant class (as is evident from the tax rolls).[45]

Growth also occurred in southern Finland, along the supply routes of the army, where peasant navigation existed. The shipping distances from Finland to Sweden Proper and Estonia are relatively small. Therefore, peasant vessels and burgher ships were able to transport exports and imports. The Crown tried to restrict peasant navigation in favour of municipal transport with some success before the seventeenth century. After the 1570s exports of tar enjoyed a period of growth, as did shipping. Such phenomena may well have had some influence on economic inequality.[46]

Regional differences in development trends

In many of the old provinces, including Uusimaa, Finland Proper and Häme, the level of wealth increased in clay soil areas during the late sixteenth century. What was the significance of changes in technology in this case? It can be assumed that the technological development of the plough improved farming conditions, particularly in areas with heavy clay soil. There has been general research into the impact of soil and climatic factors upon farming and settlement. Particular attention has been paid to the 'supra-aquatic' areas in the eastern part of the country, which had not been covered with ice during the Ice Age. However, local history researchers have tended to neglect the role played by soil fertility in agrarian settlement patterns. A notable exception is Eino Jutikkala's article published in *Suomen kulttuurihistoria* in 1933.[47] The favourable economic development in heavy clay soil areas in the latter half of the sixteenth century can be traced to the use of a new type of plough. Given this context, the wealth of blacksmiths in these areas hardly seems surprising.[48]

The general impression of economic conditions in late sixteenth-century Finland Proper is one of recession. Between 1571 and 1600 livestock numbers grew in the district of Halikko (Sw. Haliko) and in the district of Masku (Sw. Masko). However, the districts of Piikkiö (Sw. Pikis) and Vehmaa (Sw. Vemo) saw a decline in livestock numbers. In eight of the province's fourteen parishes, there were fewer taxpayers in 1600 than there had been in 1571. Furthermore, levels of taxable mean wealth in 1600 had shrunk (from 1571 levels) in every second parish (see appendices).[49]

The archipelago province of Åland remains a special case. Although there were 8% fewer taxpayers in 1600 than there had been in 1571, during the same period total estimated wealth in the area grew by 154% (68% in real terms). Mean wealth increased in every parish of the province, although most markedly in the central area of Åland.[50]

Most areas in Häme remained unchanged between 1571 and 1600; whereas in Satakunta, one can find distinct areas of growth and decline. Because grain production had not been mentioned in 1571 but was reported in 1600, parishes such as Ulvila (Sw. Ulfsby) and Karkku (also known as Sastamala) where the growth was less than 10%, are considered growth areas. As noted above, heavy clay soil areas, like the parish of Loimaa (Sw. Loimijoki), had favourable economic development thanks to the introduction of the new plough, and blacksmiths in the clay soil areas of the old south-western provinces flourished.[51] Total wealth increased in all parishes in Uusimaa between 1571 and 1600, and mean wealth per capita enjoyed nearly threefold growth.[52] In contrast, the counties of Savo and Ostrobothia saw generally negative development during the same period.[53]

What general conclusions can we reach about changes in differences of wealth in Finland? The examination of wealth and prosperity province by province and parish by parish indicates that the overall picture is in no way uniform. Great differences clearly existed both between and within individual provinces. The sharp variations between provinces are perhaps unsurprising given the great differences in economic and social structures in eastern and western parts Finland (which themselves stemmed from variation in density and duration of settlement).[54]

Regional differences in levels of economic inequality

The second objective, after calculating the mean values of the personal wealth in different areas and time periods, is to estimate the corresponding rates of economic inequality in every parish and town, and in every province. Here, the term economic inequality refers to the concentration of wealth in households (the commonly used unit of taxation). As discussed above, the Gini coefficient (G) will be used to measure level of wealth concentration (Maps 44–46). It should be noted that the Gini coefficient measures concentration of income, wealth etc. by means of ratio analysis and not by per capita incomes or wealth.

It is generally accepted that the Gini coefficient as a measure of inequality can be used to compare wealth distributions across different areas or subpopulations. If the Gini coefficient rises alongside total wealth, levels of poverty may not necessarily change. In 1571, the Gini coefficient for wealth concentration achieved the value of 0.32 in Åland, 0.33 in Satakunta, 0.38 in Häme, 0.39 in Ostrobothnia, 0.40 in Finland Proper, 0.42 in Savo, 0.45 in Uusimaa and 0.51 in the Swedish part of Karelia.[55]

In 1571 parishes on the Åland islands showed relatively strong negative correlation between mean wealth and wealth concentration. On the other hand, the rates of wealth concentration in the province showed high positive correlation.[56] On the basis of parish-level data from Finland Proper there were no statistically significant correlations between wealth concentration and mean wealth level in the province.[57]

The level of wealth inequality in 1571 was appreciably higher in the east than it was in western rural Finland. The research material from

Ostrobothnia points to increased economic inequality in the sixteenth century.[58] There is some evidence of growth in standard of living in Ostrobothnia during the sixteenth century up until the 1580s. The number of Ostrobothian vessels that visited Stockholm harbour grew during the end of the sixteenth century (with the exception of the 1570s). Economic development from the 1580s onwards can be at least partly explained by the expansion of the tar trade during this period.[59] The beginning of the seventeenth century saw a reversal of this trend, especially in the north. In most of Savo the decreased levels of wealth were accompanied by increased economic equality.[60] In Karelia, the late sixteenth century was characterized by its recovery from the long war between Sweden and Russia. There were substantial differences in wealth in the province of Käkisalmi (Sw. Kexholm) on the Russian side of the border.

The question of change in social inequality remains largely unanswered: the more significant changes seem to have been part of the development that took place in the seventeenth century. In this regard, this chapter's time span is somewhat too narrow. The simple explanation of increasing rural polarization in the sixteenth century is not generally supported by the results presented here or by my earlier studies. Measurements from the seventeenth century are also expected to be controversial, particularly with regard to the role of landless people. The Gini coefficient is used here to measure inequality of wealth, but we should bear in mind that it does not measure inequality of opportunity. For example, the Gini coefficients presented here do not reflect the barriers to upward mobility in Finland that resulted from privileges awarded to the growing ranks of nobles in the early modern period.

The Gini coefficients are usually larger for a whole country than for its sub-regions, particularly in the case of an economically diverse country. Decomposing Gini coefficients is not a simple task. The Gini coefficient of different sets of people cannot be averaged to obtain the Gini coefficient of all the people within these sets.

According to the growth theories of the American economist Robert J. Barro, economic development involves, in part, a shift of individuals and resources from the primary sector (agriculture) to the secondary sector (industry); we can also characterize this as a shift from the rural to the urban side of the economy. This two-sector model of the economy assumes that those who move from the primary sector to the secondary sector also receive a higher income per capita.[61] There are several examples that the Gini coefficient for urban areas and that of rural areas were rather different. For example, the 1571 Gini coefficient for wealth con-

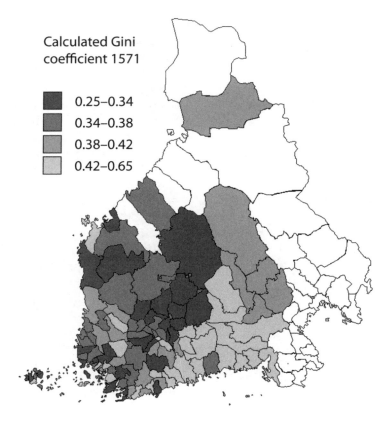

Map 44. Gini coefficient in 1571.

centration reached a level of 0.66 in the town of Pori (Sw. Björneborg) and 0.69 in the city of Rauma (Sw. Raumo), both located on the Gulf of Bothnia; these figures were higher than the Gini coefficients from the contemporary countryside.[62] There is no doubt that the model proposed by Barro in its modified form is a suitable tool for analysing the move in Finland from the 'primitive' slash-and-burn agriculture to the more 'developed' open field agriculture during the early modern period. Technological change was clearly a significant contributing factor to sixteenth- and seventeenth-century social change.[63]

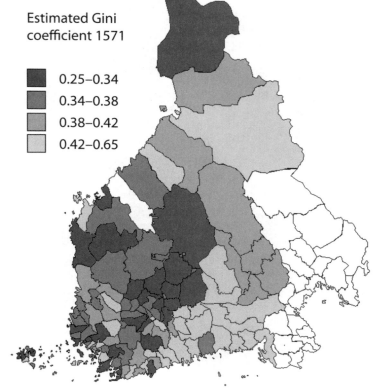

Map 45. Estimated Gini coefficients in 1571.

Inequality mapped

The Gini coefficient is sufficiently simple that it can be easily interpreted and used for comparative purposes (across parishes, counties etc.). It can also be used to indicate how the distribution of income has changed within different areas over a particular period of time. Thus, it is possible to see whether inequality has increased or decreased. When the Gini coefficients from 1571 and 1600 are compared, we can see that development in the level of economic inequality has not been uniform across all the counties of Finland (Map 47). In Åland the level of wealth concentration in 1600 had shrunk from its 1571 level; in Finland Proper no larger changes occurred; and in Satakunta areas nearer the coast

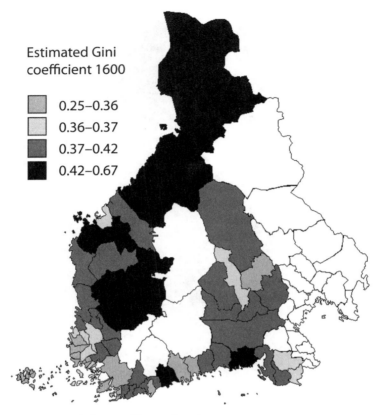

Map 46. Estimated Gini coefficients in 1600.

remained almost unchanged, but inland areas saw increased economic inequality. Personal wealth in the southern part of Ostrobothnia was much more unevenly distributed in 1600 than had been the case three decades earlier. This seems to offer support for the widely-held supposition that skewing of wealth distribution was one of the main factors that led to the outbreak of the War of Clubs in the 1590s. More detailed studies on wealth distribution within the province of Ostrobothia, however, have indicated that increases in wealth inequality in the area took place after, rather than before, the war. Wealth also became more unequally distributed in Kainuu, where hostilities between Finns and Russians had been commonplace in the late sixteenth century.[64]

The need for a nuanced overall explanation is quite understandable,

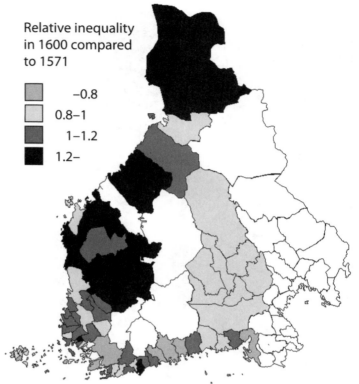

Map 47. Levels of relative inequality, 1571 and 1600.

given the number of upheavals society endured during the period studied. All across Europe, people were subjected to a century of price revolution. At the same time new kinds of states, with more complex administrative machinery and expanded standing armies, began to emerge. The period was also marked by technological development, which, in the view of this study, had great significance as an agent of change in economic relations both in the countryside and in the towns of Finland. As mentioned earlier, the level of economic inequality has often been higher in urban areas than has been the case in rural areas.

Because the main research interest of this chapter lies in personal wealth distribution, the reliability of the sources consulted must be tested against other available data (e.g. forms of distributions). One objective is to examine whether the economic structure of Finland changed as the number of farms decreased. The first step in this process is to estimate the number of people or households that were not included in the tax registers. In 1695, there were approximately fourteen inhabitants per farm in Finland – a very high figure when compared with a normal peasant farm of the period. If we assume that there were, in fact, only seven inhabitants per farm on average (as has been the usual practice in local histories), approximately half of all inhabitants must have lived outside the farm households. There is no doubt that the relative number of landless poor (those without any wealth) grew in Finland during the seventeenth century. The number of peasant farms grew by 15% between the 1630s and the 1690s, while the estimated size of the population grew by twice as much during the same time period. This disparity increased the values of Gini coefficients on wealth. Society generally became more specialized, and markets for hired labour emerged as a source of employment for those from the lower level of Finnish society. On the basis of this preliminary research it is evident that during the research period the economic and social structure of Finland changed.

Conclusions

The Gini coefficient is a suitable tool for analysing economic inequality in rural Finland in the early modern period. As a measure of concentration, it satisfies four important principles: anonymity, scale independence, population independence and transferability. By using Gini coefficients it does not matter who the poor and the wealthy are, and the Gini coefficient does not consider the size of the population or economy, or whether it is on average a rich or poor group or area. The transfer principle means that a transfer from a wealthier than average person to a person with less than average wealth makes the resulting distribution more equal and reduces the corresponding Gini coefficient.

The overall picture of the sixteenth century is by no means uniform. There is certainly scope for further research here (particularly with regard to the later part of the seventeenth century, which has not been discussed in this chapter). On the basis of this study's preliminary mapping, we can see sharp variations between and within individual provinces and regions, as well as differences between sixteenth- and seventeenth-century trends. The relationship between economic and social inequality remains partially unexplored: it seems that the most changes were in fact part of seventeenth-century development.

The Crown (in the person of Gustav Vasa and his successors) was clearly active in the Swedish realm in the sixteenth and seventeenth centuries. As well as its colonization of the interior, the state both provided new employment opportunities (most notably in the army) and indirectly contributed to the increased 'peasantization' of the peasant class. However, the passive Malthusian interpretation of *Wüstung* needs to be tempered by the recognition that an active alternative was possible: many peasants gave up their livelihood because there was a better alternative. The relationship between technological changes and social change was also significant, as exemplified by the development of a new plough and the impact of its use in areas with heavy clay soil. The role of entrepreneurship in sixteenth-century rural Finland emerges as being more central than we have generally been led to believe. This is reflected, above all, in navigation and in slash-and-burn agriculture. The adoption of the *huuhta* technique, for example, provided an opportunity for an enormous increase in the productivity level of agriculture. It seems clear that the population did not merely passively adapt: there is clear evidence of some active agency.

The modification of the Kuznets-Robinson model presented here is a new innovation within Finnish historiography. The main hypothesis is that the modified Kuznets curve is well suited to explain the development of economic inequality and economic growth after the aforementioned questions are taken into consideration. The model proposed by Barro can be used to analyse the development of the Kuznets curve during and after the industrial revolution. Furthermore, it is also possible to apply this model to the early modern period. In the case of sixteenth- and seventeenth-century Finland, two more 'shifts' should be taken into consideration: a) the move from 'primitive' slash-and-burn agriculture to more 'developed' open field agriculture and b) the move from the primary sector to the tertiary sector (services).

One objective of this chapter has been to explain the observed development in relation to other changes in the society and economy of Finland. Questions connected to regional economic inequality have been approached through the use of traditional historical methods in conjunction with concepts, models and theoretical frameworks drawn from neighbouring academic fields (economics and social sciences). The subject of wealth and its distribution has not yet been exhausted. A more nuanced and complex picture of the sixteenth century has emerged than that afforded by the simplistic explanation of increasing polarization in the countryside. E. G. Palmén and his students were ahead of their time with their economic-statistical research.[65] There seems ample reason to continue it.

In conclusion, what, if any, general remarks can we make about the changes in differences in wealth in Finland? It is abundantly clear that the fruits of development were not evenly distributed among nations, social groups or individuals and that economic inequality was present in sixteenth-century Finland. It also seems reasonable to expect that some of the results will challenge the traditional picture of the Finnish early modern economy. Essentially, what matters is not just inequality in any particular year, but the composition of distribution over time. Although the Gini coefficients presented here are point-estimates of equality at a certain time, it is feasible to conclude that the economic structure in Finland underwent changes and that early modern rural society became more specialized.

Notes

1 Jutikkala & Pirinen 1979, pp. 26, 53; Kaukiainen 1993, p. 10; Pitkänen 1994, pp. 26–48. At the moment there is no general reference book published in English, French or German on the economic history of Finland during earlier centuries. For a general history of Finland see e.g. Jutikkala & Pirinen 1979.
2 Jutikkala & Pirinen 1979, chap. 4.
3 Nummela 2003; Nummela 2007.
4 Karonen & Nummela 1993a; Nummela & Karonen 1993b.
5 Cf. Nummela 1993a.
6 Some of the preliminary and very descriptive results about sixteenth-century development can be found in Nummela 1993a. I previously published some regional results from the counties of Häme (Sw. Tavastland), Satakunta and Savo (Sw. Savolax); see Nummela 1988, 1989 and 1990. Some of the results have also been published in *Suomen historian kartasto* ('The Historical Atlas of Finland'). The results of those reports focus on sixteenth- and early seventeenth-century development.
7 SKA, The Collections of The Finnish Historical Society, Taloushistoriallisia ainek-sia, Palmén, E. G.: Huittinen, Suomen taloudellisista oloista. Yleiskatsaus Suomen taloudellis-tilastollisiin aineksiin Vaasakuninkaiden ajoilta; Harmaja 1921; Melander 1922; Rommi 1965.
8 The bulk of the data used here was collected in the late 1980s thanks to grants from Liikesivistysrahasto (Foundation for Economic Education) and during the year that I spent as a junior research fellow in the Academy of Finland in the early 1990s. There are still some gaps in the collected data and control material from the cadastral records.
9 Kuznets 1995.
10 Robinson 1976
11 Myrdal 1985; Myrdal & Söderberg 1991, p. 259; Alfani 2010.

12 Abel 1978a; Abel 1978b; Abel 1978c; Beckett 1990; Braudel 1989 & 1990 & 1990; Houtte 1977; Jutikkala 1987; Komlos 1989; Le Roy Ladurie 1987; Maddison 1991; Myrdal & Söderberg, 1991; Nummela 1993b; Tsoulouhas, 1992; Wrigley 1981; Wrigley 1988.

13 Myrdal & Söderberg 1991, p. 27.

14 Bernstein 1902, pp. 46ff; Renvall 1900.

15 Zanden van 1995.

16 Pizetti & Salvemini (eds.) 1955.

17 The French-Italian economist and sociologist Vilfredo Pareto provided an account of the distribution of wealth. He maintained that his law of income distribution (Pareto distribution) was universal and thus should be valid in every human society, in every time period and in every country. For Pareto the distribution of income and wealth is always highly skewed, with a few holding most of the wealth. He argued that all observed societies follow a regular logarithmic pattern (log N = log A + m log x, where N is the number of people with income or wealth higher than x, and A and m are constants). Pareto 1896 & 1897; Lorenz 1905, pp. 209–219. For measures of (economic) inequality see, e.g., Nygård & Sandström 1981.

18 In Sweden (and hence in Finland) the *mark* was basic unit of currency from the Middle Ages until the last quarter of the eighteenth century. There was a difference between the silver mark (a weight measure) and the mark in pennies (a currency unit). In the Middle Ages, the mark penningar was a unit of account only. In the sixteenth century the Swedish state began to mint coins with the value of one mark penningar (Edvinsson, Franzén, & Söderberg 2008; Edvinsson 2010).

19 Jutikkala & Pirinen 1979, chap. II.

20 Myrdal & Söderberg 1991, pp. 58–69; The silver taxation rolls from 1571.

21 Melander 1897; Hedar 1937; Nummela 1993a.

22 For Satakunta: Jokipii 1974, pp. 49–50; Rosenborg 1860, pp. 52–54; Suvanto 1973, pp. 163–164. – For Åland: Voionmaa 1912, pp. 108ff. – For Uusimaa: Mäkelä-Alitalo 1979, pp. 61–62; Allardt 1898, pp. 22–25. – For Ostrobothnia: Luukko 1945, p. 376. – For Savo: Saloheimo 1990, pp. 37–44. – For Karelia: Kuujo 1959, pp. 7–8, 15, 47–49; Novgorodin vatjalaisen viidenneksen henki- ja verokirja v. 1500; Toikka 1916, p. 26, 41–44; Ranta 1985, p. 145; Saloheimo, p. 98.

23 Myrdal & Söderberg 1991.

24 Cf. for the Finnish discussion Ylikangas 1977 and Mäkelä-Alitalo 1982.

25 Luukko 1952; Juva 1955, pp. 96–98, 116; Blomstedt 1958; Nummela 1993, pp. 54–55, 112–113.

26 Jutikkala & Pirinen 1979, pp. 53–54.

27 Braudel 1982.

28 Soininen, pp. 65–72, 450–451; Myrdal & Söderberg 1991, pp. 356–378.

29 Pirinen 1982, pp. 93–100, 358; Voionmaa 1915.

30 Cederlöf 1934, pp. 259ff.

31 See Nummela & Karonen 1993.

32 Fagerlund 1987; Nummela & Karonen 1993.

33 Nikula 1987; Jokipii 1974, pp. 456–462; Jokipii 1972; Rinne 1963.

34 Jutikkala 1987, p. 68.

35 See Maarbjerg 1992, pp. 1–24; Ylikangas 1990, pp. 13–82.

36 See e.g. Lehtinen 1961; Orrman 1986; Renvall 1979.

37 Jokipii 1974, pp. 49–63.
38 Gissel et al. 1981.
39 Jutikkala 1958, pp. 140–142; Orrman & Jutikkala 1974, Föredrag och mötesförhandlingar 1976; Orrman 1984.
40 For prices see: Nummela & Karonen 1993; Karonen & Nummela 1993; Orrman 1982; Palm 1991; Ruuth 1916; Söderberg 1987; Söderberg & Jansson 1988; Jansson & Söderberg 1991.
41 Keränen 1989, p. 221; Melander & Melander 1924.
42 Cederlöf 1934; Tornberg 1989; Myrdal & Söderberg 1991, pp. 273–292. For the local practice in collecting tithes see Pirinen 1962.
43 Ström 1932, pp. 55–57.
44 Orrman 1991, p. 3; Keränen 1989, pp. 219–227. Tornberg 1989; Jutikkala 1987, pp. 61–68.
45 Jutikkala & Pirinen 1979, chap. 4.
46 Kaukiainen 1993, chap. 1–2; Jokipii 1974, pp.456ff; Rinne 1963, pp. 82–88.
47 Orrman 1991, p. 3; Jutikkala 1933; Solantie 1988. – For the supra-aquatic regions see e.g. Soininen 1961, pp. 146–148; Keränen 1984, pp. 201–218.
48 Myrdal & Söderberg 1991, pp. 381–401; Suvanto 1987, pp. 165–168.
49 Säihke 1963, pp. 57–60.
50 Nummela 1993a, p. 42.
51 Nummela 1988; Nummela 1989, pp. 203–217.
52 Nummela 1993a, pp. 100–103.
53 Nummela 1993a, p. 162.
54 Kaukiainen 1980, pp. 66–73; Soininen 1961; Pirinen 1982; Jutikkala 1958; Orrman 1984, pp. 61–62.
55 See Appendix and Nummela 1993a.
56 Nummela 1993a, pp.41–44.
57 Nummela 1993a, p. 50.
58 Nummela 1993a, chap. 7; Vennola 1900.
59 Maarbjerg 1995, p. 187.
60 Nummela 1990.
61 Barro 2000, pp. 87–120.
62 Nummela 1993a, 67.
63 See Barro 2000.
64 See Nummela 1996.
65 See note 7.

Bibliography
Archival sources
The National Archives of Finland (SKA), Helsinki
The Collections of The Finnish Historical Society
Taloushistoriallisia aineksia
Palmén, E. G.: Huittinen
Palmén, E. G.: Tutkimuksia Suomen taloudellisista oloista. Yleiskatsaus Suomen taloudellis-tilastollisiin aineksiin Vaasakuninkaiden ajoilta.

Source editions

Todistuskappaleita Suomen historiaan, Vol. VI: *Novgorodin vatjalaisen viidenneksen henki- ja verokirja v. 1500*, ed. by J. V. Ronimus. The Finnish Historical Society, Helsinki 1906.

The Finnish Silver Tax Lists from the Year 1571 (*Finlands sölfskattsregister af år 1571/ Suomen hopeaveroluettelot 1571 (Suomen historian lähteitä V:1–7)*, Vol. I: *Egentliga Finlands sölfskattregister*, ed. by A. G. Fontell. Helsinki 1892; Vol. II: *Uudenmaan hopeavero ja hopeaveroluettelo v. 1571*, ed. by K. Soikkeli. Helsinki 1912; Vol. III: *Häme*, ed. by J. E. Roos. Helsinki 1944; Vol. IV: *Satakunta*, ed. by M. Jokipii. Helsinki 1953; Vol. V: Ahvenanmaa, ed. by G. Kerkkonen. Helsinki 1965; Vol. VI: *Pohjanmaa*, ed. by M. Walta. Helsinki 1985; Vol. VII: *Karjala*, ed. by M. Walta. Helsinki 1987.

Literature

Abel, W. 1978a. 'Landwirtschaft 1350–1500.' In Aubin. H. & Zorn, W. (eds.) *Handbuch der deutsche Wirtschafts- und Sozialgeschichte*, Vol. 1. Weinsberg, Stuttgart, pp. 300–333.

Abel, W. 1978b. 'Landwirtschaft 1500–1648.' In Aubin. H. & Zorn, W. (eds.) *Handbuch der deutsche Wirtschafts- und Sozialgeschichte*, Vol. 1. Weinsberg, Stuttgart, pp. 386–413.

Abel, W. 1978c. 'Landwirtschaft 1648–1800.' In Aubin. H. & Zorn, W. (eds.) *Handbuch der deutsche Wirtschafts- und Sozialgeschichte*, Vol. 1. Weinsberg, Stuttgart, pp. 495–530.

Alfani, G. 2010. 'Wealth Inequalities and Population Dynamics in Early Modern Northern Italy.' *Journal of Interdisciplinary History*, Vol. 40 (4), pp. 513–549.

Alfani, G. 2010. 'Wealth Inequalities and Population Dynamics in Early Modern Northern Italy.' *Journal of Interdisciplinary History*, Vol. 40 (4), pp. 513–549.

Allardt, A. 1898. *Borgå läns sociala och ekonomiska förhållanden åren 1539–1571*. Helsinki.

Barro, R. J. 2000. 'Inequality and Growth in a Panel of Countries.' *Journal of Economic Growth*, Vol. 5, pp. 8–120.

Beckett, J. V. 1990. *The Agricultural Revolution*. Basil Blackwell, Oxford.

Bernstein, E. 1902. *Die Voraussetzungen des Sozialismus und die Aufgaben der Sozialdemokratie*. J. H. W. Dietz, Stuttgart.

Blomstedt, Y. 1958. 'Hämeen "mahtitalonpojat". Erään yhteiskuntaryhmän kehityksen hahmottelua 1500-luvulta 1600-luvulle.' *Historiallinen Aikakauskirja*, pp. 289–300.

Braudel, F. 1989. *Civilisationer och kapitalism 1400–1800*. Vol. I: *Vardagslivets strukturer. Det möjligas gränser*. Gidlunds, Stockholm.

Braudel, F. 1990a. *Civilisationer och kapitalism 1400–1800*. Vol. II: *Marknadens spel*. Gidlunds, Stockholm.

Braudel, F. 1990b. *Civilisationer och kapitalism 1400–1800*. Vol. III: *Världens tid*. Gidlunds, Stockholm.

Cederlöf, J. 1934. *Det finländska prästerskapets ekonomiska ställning intill sjuttonde seklet*. Svenska Litteratursällskapet i Finland, Helsinki.

Corrado, G. 1955. 'Variabilità e mutabilità.' In Pizetti, E. & Salvemini, T. (eds.) *Memorie di metodologica statistica*. Libreria Eredi Virgilio Veschi, Rome.

Edvinsson, R., Franzén, B. & Söderberg, J. 2010. 'Swedish Payment Systems 995–1534.'

In Edvinsson, Rodney, Jacobson, T. & Waldenström, D. (eds.) *Historical Monetary and Financial Statistics for Sweden. Exchange Rates, Prices, and Wages, 1277–2008*, pp. 67–132. <http://www.riksbank.se/templates/Page.aspx?id=45003>.

Edvinsson, R. 2010. 'The Multiple Currencies of Sweden-Finland 1534–1803.' In Edvinsson, Rodney, Jacobson, T. & Waldenström, D. (eds.) *Historical Monetary and Financial Statistics for Sweden. Exchange Rates, Prices, and Wages, 1277–2008*, pp. 133–237. <http://www.riksbank.se/templates/Page.aspx?id=45003>.

Fagerlund, R. 1987. '"Då bönderna inte räckte till." Kring borglägerstungan i sydvästra Finland under äldre vasatid.' In Villstrand, N.-E. (ed.) *Kustbygd och centralmakt 1560–1721. Studier i centrum-periferi under svensk stormaktstid*. Svenska Litteratursällskapet i Finland, Helsinki, pp. 37–56.

Gissel, S. et al. 1981. *Desertion and Land Colonization in the Nordic Countries c. 1300–1600. Comparative Report from the Scandinavian Research Project on Deserted Farms and Villages*. Almqvist & Wiksell International, Uppsala.

Harmaja, L. 1921. 'E. G. Palmén kansantaloudellisena kirjailijana ja talouspoliitikkona.' *Valvoja*.

Hedar, S. 1937. 'Karl IX:s förmögenhetsbeskattningar. En undanglömd källa till vår inre historia.' *Historisk Tidskrift*.

van Houtte, J. A. 1977. *An Economic History of the Low Countries 800–1800*. St. Martin's Press, New York.

Jansson, A. & Söderberg, J. 1991. 'Priser och löner i Stockholm 1600–1719.' In Jansson, A., Palm, L. A. & Söderberg, J. (eds.) *Dagligt bröd i onda tider, Priser och löner i Stockholm och Västsverige 1500–1770*. University of Göteborg, Göteborg.

Jokipii, M. 1972. 'Satakunnan laivanrakennuksesta ja maalaispurjehduksesta 1500- ja 1600-luvuilla.' In Jokipii, M. (ed.) *Historica*, Vol. III. University of Jyväskylä, Jyväskylä.

Jokipii, M. 1974. *Satakunnan historia*, Vol. IV: *Satakunnan talouselämä uuden ajan alusta isoonvihaan*. Satakunnan maakuntaliitto, Pori.

Jutikkala, E. 1933. 'Asutuksen leviäminen 1600-luvun alkuun mennessä.' In Jutikkala, E. & Suolahti, G., *Suomen kulttuurihistoria*, Vol. I. Gummerus, Jyväskylä, pp. 51–103.

Jutikkala, E. 1958. *Suomen talonpojan historia*. Second edition. The Finnish Literature Society, Helsinki.

Jutikkala, E. 1987. *Kuolemalla on aina syynsä. Maailman väestöhistorian ääriviivoja*. WSOY, Helsinki.

Jutikkala, E. & Pirinen, K. 1979. *A History of Finland*. Revised edition. Weilin+Göös, Helsinki.

Juva, E. W. 1955. 'Kirkko- ja seurakuntaelämää sekä henkisen elämän piirteitä uskonpuhdistuksen vuosisadalla.' In Juwa, E. W. et al. (eds.) *Varsinais-Suomen historia*, Vol. V:4. Varsinais-Suomen historiantutkimusyhdistys, Turku.

Karonen, P. & Nummela, I. 1993a. 'Reaalipalkka Pohjanmaalla 1541–1617.' University of Jyväskylä, Department of History (Unpublished manuscript).

Karonen, P. & Nummela, I. 1993b. *Hinnat ja palkat Hämeessä 1541–1617*. University of Jyväskylä, Jyväskylä.

Kaukiainen, Y. 1980. 'Suomen asuttaminen.' In Jutikkala, E., Kaukiainen Y. & Åström, S.-E. (eds.) *Suomen taloushistoria*, Vol. I. Tammi, Helsinki, pp. 11–145.

Kaukiainen, Y. 1993. *A History of Finnish Shipping*. Routledge, London.

Keränen, J. 1984. *Kainuun asuttaminen*. University of Jyväskylä, Jyväskylä.

Keränen, J. 1989. 'Hyviä ja huonoja vuosia, Ilmastovaihtelut historiallisten ilmiöiden selittäjinä.' In Markkanen, E. & et al. (eds.): *Pysy lujana omalla maalla! Erkki*

Lehtiselle omistettu juhlakirja. Studia Historica Jyväskyläensia, Vol. 40. University of Jyväskylä, Jyväskylä.

Komlos, J. 1989. *Nutrition and Economic Development in the Eighteenth-Century Habsburg Monarchy. An Anthropometric History.* Princeton University Press, Princeton.

Kuujo, E. 1959. *Taka-Karjalan verotus v:een 1710.* The Finnish Historical Society, Helsinki.

Kuznets, S. 1955. 'Economic Growth and Income Inequality.' *American Economic Review,* Vol. 45, pp. 1–28.

Lehtinen, E. 1961. 'Autoitumisesta Ala-Satakunnassa 16. ja 17. vuosisadan vaihteessa.' In Jokipii, M. et al. (eds.), *Juhlakirja Jalmari Jaakkolan 75-vuotispäiväksi 1.1.1960. (Satakunta,* Vol. *17),* Satakuntalainen osakunta, Helsinki, pp. 115–137.

Le Roy Ladurie, E. 1987. *The French Peasantry 1450–1660.* Scolar Press, Aldershot.

Lorenz, M. O. 1905. 'Methods of Measuring the Concentration of Wealth.' *Publications of the American Statistical Association,* Vol. 9, pp. 209–219.

Luukko, A. 1945. *Etelä-Pohjanmaan historia,* Vol. III: *Nuijasodasta isoonvihaan.* Etelä-Pohjanmaan historiatoimikunta, Vaasa.

Luukko, A. 1952. 'Kustaa Vaasan "rikkaat pirkkalaiset".' *Historiallinen Aikakauskirja,* pp. 106–116.

Maarbjerg, J. P. 1992. 'The Economic Background to "the War of Clubs".' *Scandinavian Journal of History,* Vol. 17 (1), pp. 1–24.

Maddison, A. 1991. *Dynamic Forces in Capitalist Development. A Long-Run Comparative View.* Oxford University Press, Oxford.

Mäkelä[-Alitalo], A. 1979. *Hattulan kihlakunnan ja Porvoon läänin autioituminen myöhäiskeskiajalla ja uuden ajan alussa.* The Finnish Historical Society, Helsinki.

Mäkelä[-Alitalo], A. 1982. 'Linnaleiri kameraalisena tutkimusongelmana.' *Turun historiallinen arkisto,* Vol. 37, pp. 65–79.

Melander, K. R. 1897. 'Muutama tieto apu- eli viidennenkymmenennen rahan verosta Suomessa.' *Historiallinen arkisto,* Vol. 15 (1), pp. 204–213.

Melander, K. R. 1922. 'Ernst Gustaf Palmén historiantutkijana.' *Historiallinen Arkisto,* Vol. 30:2.

Melander, K. R. & Melander, G. 1924. 'Katovuosista Suomessa.' In *Oma Maa,* Porvoo, pp. 350–359.

Myrdal, J. 1985. *Medeltidens åkerbruk. Agrarteknik i Sverige ca 1000 till 1520.* Nordiska museet, Stockholm.

Myrdal, J. & Söderberg, J. 1991. *Kontinuitetens dynamik. Agrar ekonomi i 1500-talets Sverige.* University of Stockholm, Stockholm.

Nikula, O. 1987. 'Finland i de äldre vasakungarnas försvarssystem. Åbo som en centralort för Finlands försvar.' In Villstrand, N.-E. (ed.) *Kustbygd och centralmakt 1560–1721. Studier i centrum-periferi under svensk stormaktstid.* Svenska Litteratursällskapet i Finland, Helsinki, pp. 93–113.

Nummela, I. 1988. 'Varallisuuserot Hämeessä ja Satakunnassa vuonna 1571.' *Sukuviesti* (1), pp. 26–27.

Nummela, I. 1989. 'Taloudellinen eriarvoistuminen Satakunnassa 1500-luvun lopulla.' In Markkanen, E. et al. (eds.) *Pysy lujana omalla maalla! Erkki Lehtiselle omistettu juhlakirja.* University of Jyväskylä, Jyväskylä, pp. 203–217.

Nummela, I. 1990. *Savolaisten varallisuuserot historian valossa. Vuoden 1571 hopeaveroluettelosta tämän vuosisadan alkuun.* Snellman-instituutti, Kuopio.

Nummela, I. 1993a. *Alueelliset varallisuuserot Suomessa uuden ajan alussa* (= Regional differences in Wealth inequality in the early modern Finland). Unpublished manuscript, University of Jyväskylä, Department of History.

Nummela, I. 1993b. 'Maatalouden vihreä vallankumous. Uuden ajan alun keskeinen kysymys?' In Vilkuna, Kustaa H. J. (ed.) *Artikkeleita tekniikan ja teknologian historiasta.* University of Jyväskylä, Jyväskylä.

Nummela, I. 1996. 'Nuijasota ja Pohjanmaan taloudellinen tilanne.' In Roiko-Jokela, H. (ed.) *Siperiasta siirtoväkeen. Murrosaikoja ja käännekohtia Suomen historiassa.* Kopijyvä, Jyväskylä, pp. 94–110.

Nummela, I. 2003. 'Asutus, pelto ja karja.' In Rasila, V., Jutikkala, E. & Mäkelä-Alitalo, A. (eds.) *Suomen maatalouden historia,* Vol. 1: *Perinteisen maatalouden aika esihistoriasta 1870-luvulle.* The Finnish Literature Society, Helsinki, pp. 133–158.

Nummela, I. 2007. 'Maanviljelys, viljelystavat ja sadot.' In Haapala, P. & Toivo, R. M. (eds.) *Suomen historian kartasto.* Karttakeskus, Helsinki, pp.102–103.

Nygård, F. & Sandström, A. 1981. *Measuring Inequality.* University of Stockholm, Stockholm.

Orrman, E. 1982. 'Bidrag till Finlands prishistoria. Priserna på råg, smör, tjära och salt i egentliga Finland 1541–1610.' *Historisk Tidskrift för Finland,* pp. 361–384.

Orrman, E. 1984. 'Maanomistuksen kehitys 1400- ja 1500-luvuilla Suomessa.' *Historiallinen Arkisto,* Vol. 84, pp 61–89.

Orrman, E. 1986. *Bebyggelsen i Pargas, S:t Mårtens och Vemo Socknar i Egentliga Finland under senmedeltiden och på 1500-talet.* The Finnish Historical Society, Helsinki.

Orrman, E. 1991. 'Geographical Factors in the Spread of Permanent Settlement in Parts of Finland and Sweden from the End of the Iron Age to the Beginning of Modern Times.' *Fennoscandia Archaeologia Fennica,* Vol. 7, pp. 3–21.

Orrman, E. & Jutikkala, E. 1976. *Adlig godsdrift i Finland under 1600-talet. Från medeltid till välfärdssamhälle.* Nordiska historikermötet i Uppsala 1974, Föredrag och mötesförhandlingar, Uppsala 1976.

Palm, L. A. 1991. 'Priser i Västsverige.' In Jansson, A., Palm, L. A. & Söderberg, J. (eds.) *Dagligt bröd i onda tider. Priser och löner i Stockholm och Västsverige 1500–1770.* University of Göteborg, Göteborg.

Pareto, V. 1896–1897. *Cours d'économie politique.* F. Rouge, Lausanne.

Pirinen, K. 1962. *Kymmenysverotus Suomessa ennen kirkkoreduktiota.* The Finnish Historical Society, Helsinki.

Pirinen, K. 1982. *Savon historia,* Vol. II:1: *Rajamaakunta asutusliikkeen aikakautena 1534–1617.* Kustannuskiila, Kuopio.

Pitkänen, K. 1994. 'Suomen väestön historialliset kehityslinjat.' In Koskinen, S. et al. (eds.) *Suomen väestö.* Gaudeamus, Helsinki, pp. 26–48.

Ranta, R. 1985. 'Verotus Viipurin komendanttikunnassa revisioon 1728 asti. *Turun historiallinen arkisto,* Vol. 39, pp. 142–171.

Renvall, P. 1949. 'Valtiolliset vaiheet ja hallinnollis-oikeudellinen kehitys. In Juva, Einar W. et al. (eds.) *Varsinais-Suomen historia,* Vol. V:1. Varsinais-Suomen historiantutkimusyhdistys, Turku.

Rinne, T. 1963. 'Varsinais-Suomen talonpoikaiskauppa, kalastus ja teolliset elinkeinot 1500-luvulla.' In Juva, Einar W. et al. (eds.) *Varsinais-Suomen historia,* Vol. V:6, Varsinais-Suomen historiantutkimusyhdistys, Turku.

Robinson, S. (1976). 'A Note on the U-hypothesis Relating Income Inequality and Economic Development.' *American Economic Review,* Vol. 66 (3), pp. 437–440.

Rommi, P. 1965. 'Ernst Gustaf Palmén.' In Papunen, P. (ed.) *Suomalaisia historian-tutkijoita. Historiallisen Yhdistyksen juhlakirja 1890–1965.* The Finnish Historical Society, Helsinki.

Rosenborg, J. W. 1860. *Jordbeskattningens historia i Finland under medlet af sextonde seklet.* Helsinki.

Ruuth, J. W. 1915. 'Työväen päiväpalkoista Suomessa 1500-luvulla.' In Komppa, G. (ed.) *Suomalainen Tiedeakatemia. Esitelmät ja pöytäkirjat 1915.* Suomalainen Tiedeakatemia, Helsinki.

Säihke, I. 1963. 'Varsinais-Suomen maanviljelys ja karjanhoito 1500-luvulla.' In Juva, Einar W. et al. (eds.) *Varsinais-Suomen historia,* Vol. V:5. Varsinais-Suomen historiantutkimusyhdistys, Turku.

Saloheimo, V. 1976. *Pohjois-Karjalan historia,* Vol. II: *1617–1721.* Karjalaisen kulttuurin edistämissäätiö, Joensuu.

Saloheimo, V. 1990: *Savon historia,* Vol. II:2: *Savo suurvallan valjaissa 1617–1721.* Savon säätiö, Mikkeli.

Söderberg, J. 1987. 'Hade Heckscher rätt? Priser och reallöner i 1500-talets Stockholm.' *Historisk tidskrift,* Vol. 107, pp. 341–356.

Söderberg, J. & Jansson, A. 1988. 'Corn-Price Rises and Equalisation. Real Wages in Stockholm 1650–1719.' *Scandinavian Economic History Review,* Vol. 36 (2), pp. 42–67.

Soininen, A. M. 1975. *Vanha maataloutemme, Maatalous ja maatalousväestö Suomessa perinnäisen maatalouden loppukaudella 1720-luvulta 1870-luvulle.* The Finnish Historical Society, Helsinki.

Solantie, R. 1988. 'Climatic Conditions for the Cultivation of Rye with Reference to the History of Settlement in Finland.' *Fennoscandia Archaeologia Fennica,* Vol. 5, pp. 3–20.

Ström, H. 1932. 'Korsholms kungsgård åren 1556–1622. *Historiallinen Arkisto,* Vol. 39:3, pp. 1–57.

Suvanto, S. 1973. *Satakunnan historia,* Vol. III: *Keskiaika.* Satakunnan maakuntaliitto, Pori.

Suvanto, S. 1987. *Knaapista populiin, Tutkimuksia erilaistumisesta Satakunnan talonpojistossa vuosina 1390–1571.* The Finnish Historical Society, Helsinki.

Toikka, P. 1916. 'Muutamia oikaisuja ja lisiä Vatjan viidenneksen verokirjan suomennokseen.' *Historiallinen Arkisto,* Vol. 26, pp. 1–19,

Tornberg, M. 1989. 'Ilmaston- ja sadonvaihtelut Lounais-Suomessa 1550-luvulta 1860-luvulle.' In Kuparinen, E. (ed.) *Työ tekijäänsä kiittää. Pentti Virrankoski 60 vuotta 20.6.1989. Turun Historiallinen Arkisto,* Vol. 44. The Historical Society of Turku, Turku, pp. 58–87.

Tsoulouhas, T. C. 1992. 'A New Look at Demographic and Technological Changes: England. 1550 to 1839. *Explorations in Economic History,* Vol. 29 (2), pp. 169–203.

Vennola, J. H. 1900. *Pohjois-Suomen maalaisvarallisuus 16:lla ja 17:llä vuosisadalla. Ylipainos teoksesta Tutkimuksia Suomen taloudellisesta historiasta.* Helsinki.

Voionmaa, V. 1912. *Suomalaisia keskiajan tutkimuksia.* WSOY, Porvoo.

Voionmaa, V. 1915. *Suomen karjalaisen heimon historia.* Kansanvalistusseura, Helsinki.

Wrigley, E. A. 1988. *Continuity, Chance and Change. The Character of the Industrial Revolution in England.* Cambridge University Press, Cambridge.

Wrigley, E. A. & Schofield, R. S. 1981. *The Population History of England. A Reconstruction.* Arnold, London.

Ylikangas, H. 1977. *Nuijasota.* Otava, Helsinki.

Ylikangas, H. 1990. *Mennyt meissä. Suomalaisen kansanvallan historiallinen analyysi.* WSOY, Helsinki.

van Zanden, J. L. 1995. 'Tracing the Beginning of the Kuznets Curve. Western Europe during the Early Modern Period.' *Economic History Review*, Vol. 48, pp. 643–664.

Appendix 1. Wealth inequality in Finland 1571

Parish	n	Mean	Gini coefficient
Korppoo / Korpo	258	83	0.47
Rymättylä / Rimito	158	85	0.33
Maaria / S:t Marie	96	86	0.41
Raisio / Reso	115	118	0.42
Rusko	65	122	0.28
Masku	170	101	0.34
Lemu / Lemo	132	104	0.28
Mynämäki / Virmo	399	90	0.36
Pöytyä / Pöytis	216	79	0.32
Nousiainen / Nousis	186	68	0.28
District of Masku	*1795*	*90*	*0.37*
Lieto / Lundo	180	110	0.43
Kaarina / S:t Karins	150	61	0.38
Piikkiö / Pikis	184	47	0.44
Sauvo / Sagu	410	42	0.42
Parainen / Pargas	363	39	0.35
Nauvo / Nagu	222	55	0.39
District of Piikkiö	*1509*	*54*	*0.44*
Kemiö / Kimito	453	52	0.32
Hiittinen / Hittis	96	48	0.37
Perniö / Bjärnå	241	70	0.34
Muurla and Uskela	350	58	0.34
Halikko / Haliko	345	51	0.33
Paimio / Pemar	247	56	0.36
Marttila / S:t Mårtens	305	55	0.41
District of Halikko	*2037*	*56*	*0.36*
Laitila / Letala	301	103	0.34
Kalanti / Kaland	585	90	0.33
Vehmaa / Vemo	393	88	0.37
Taivassalo / Tövsala	316	68	0.33
Lappi	296	118	0.35
District of Vehmaa	*1891*	*93*	*0.36*
FINLAND PROPER	7232	73	0.40
Finnström	148	79	0.35
Föglö	161	36	0.44
Hammarland	150	72	0.25
Jomala	160	55	0.42
Kumlinge	99	65	0.40
Lemland	100	57	0.37
Saltvik	107	89	0.33
Sund	128	122	0.30
ÅLAND / AHVENANMAA	1053	71	0.40
Hattula	46	92	0.45
Janakkala	116	71	0.39

Lehijärvi	111	83	0.32
Loppi / Loppis	170	60	0.30
Mäskälä	109	83	0.42
Renko	85	59	0.41
District of Hattula	*637*	*73*	*0.38*
Kalvola	129	64	0.29
Kulsiala	161	76	0.36
Porras	397	60	0.35
Pälkäne	186	76	0.34
Rautalampi	219	62	0.30
Saarioinen	293	47	0.37
Sääksmäki	155	61	0.36
District of Sääksmäki	*1540*	*62*	*0.35*
Asikkala	409	52	0.42
Hollola	208	77	0.45
Tennilä	136	71	0.37
Uusikylä	164	60	0.42
District of Hollola	*917*	*62*	*0.43*
Hauho	133	104	0.36
Jämsä	103	101	0.30
Lammi	158	83	0.33
Padasjoki	171	63	0.28
Sysmä	215	88	0.33
Tuulos	179	88	0.32
District of Hauho	*959*	*89*	*0.33*
HÄME / TAVASTLAND	4053	70	0.38
Loimaa / Loimijoki	314	82	0.43
Huittinen / Huittis	318	111	0.40
Kokemäki / Kumo	287	101	0.35
Köyliö /Kjulo	136	102	0.39
Eura	158	100	0.38
Eurajoki / Euraåminne	157	93	0.36
Ulvila / Ulvsby	264	110	0.39
Närpiö / Närpes	329	132	0.30
(Lappi)			0.35
District of Ala-Satakunta	*1963*	*105*	*0.38*
Tyrvää / Tyrvis	332	54	0.47
Karkku	391	78	0.41
Kyrö / Kyro	422	99	0.34
Pirkkala / Birkala	425	97	0.30
Kangasala	275	111	0.32
Orivesi	160	108	0.31
Lempäälä / Lembois	231	86	0.34
Vesilahti / Vesilax	222	75	0.37
Ruovesi	147	63	0.35
District of Ylä-Satakunta	*2605*	*86*	*0.38*
SATAKUNTA / SATAKUNDA	4568	95	0.38

Pernaja / Pernå	507	29	0.45
Porvoo / Borgå (parish)	710	30	0.49
Pyhtää / Pyttis	576	34	0.37
Pohja / Pojo	208	34	0.40
Siuntio / Sjundeå	201	34	0.43
Lohja / Lojo	433	37	0.38
Karjalohja / Karislojo	127	37	0.34
Sipoo / Sibbo	290	40	0.60
Tenhola / Tenala	303	43	0.31
Karjaa / Karis	316	43	0.42
Kisko	49	44	0.41
Vehkalahti / Veckelax	471	46	0.44
Inkoo / Ingå	284	46	0.38
Espoo / Esbo	288	47	0.38
Vihti / Vichtis	184	57	0.62
Helsinki / Helsingfors (parish)	324	67	0.43
Kirkkonummi / Kyrkslätt	190	76	0.27
UUSIMAA / NYLAND	5461	41	0.45
Mustasaari / Korsholm	577	90	0.51
Kyrö / Kyro	595	70	0.34
Vöyri / Vörå	347	79	0.27
Ilmajoki / Ilmola	148	90	0.32
Kaarlela / Karleby	482	90	0.35
Ii / Ijo	193	93	0.38
POHJANMAA / ÖSTERBOTTEN	2342	83	0.39
Pellosniemi	699	34	0.46
VesIlahti / Vesilax	663	43	0.43
Juva / Jockas	569	46	0.41
Sääminki / Säminge	774	39	0.40
Rantasalmi	567	44	0.39
Tavinsalmi	367	47	0.41
SAVO	3644	41	0.42
Virolahti / Vederlax	254	20	0.53
Viipuri / Viborg (parish)	664	26	0.65
Säkkijärvi	292	33	0.47
Lappee	744	36	0.46
Taipalsaari	757	40	0.44
KARJALA / KARELEN	2711	33	0.51

Source: Nummela 1993a.

Appendix 2. Wealth inequality in Finland 1600.

Parish	n	Mean wealth	Gini coefficient
Föglö	128	81	0.30
Kumlinge	125	125	0.32
Jomala	163	201	0.27
Finnström	142	220	0.28
Lemland	97	221	0.32
Sund	117	224	0.26
Saltvik	94	232	0.28
Hammarland	147	237	0.24
ÅLAND / AHVENANMAA	967	196	0.32
Korppoo / Korpo	199	130	0.36
Masku	161	190	0.34
Kalanti / Kaland	437	221	0.34
Lappi	221	234	0.36
Vehmaa / Vemo	345	157	0.31
Rymättylä / Rimito	132	150	0.36
Pöytyä / Pöytis	311	309	0.37
Nousiainen / Nousis	233	233	0.34
Maaria / S:t Marie	98	201	0.34
Rusko	35	340	0.31
Raisio / Reso	114	255	0.36
Lemu / Lemo	129	187	0.31
Mynämäki / Virmo	408	211	0.36
Taivassalo / Tövsala	260	141	0.35
Loimaa / Loimijoki	345	305	0.40
Huittinen / Huittis	277	315	0.41
Kokemäki / Kumo	248	279	0.40
Köyliö / Kjulo	128	257	0.42
Eura	119	285	0.36
Eurajoki / Euraåminne	124	243	0.38
Ulvila / Ulvsby	207	232	0.37
Lappi	228	231	0.36
District of Ala-Satakunta	*1676*	*274*	..
Tyrvää / Tyrvis	309	152	0.54
Karkku	325	153	0.52
Kyrö / Kyro	321	132	0.56
Pirkkala / Birkala	382	139	0.49
Kangasala	413	161	0.46
Lempäälä / Lembois	217	153	0.52
Vesilahti / Vesilax	209	165	0.50
Ruovesi	221	75	0.67
District of Ylä-Satakunta	*2397*	*143*	*0.53*
Espoo / Esbo	210	201	0.38
Inkoo / Ingå	..	..	..

Karjaa / Karis	..	..	..
Karjalohja / Karislojo	127	215	0.34
Kirkkonummi / Kyrkslätt	148	204	0.35
Kisko	34	233	0.36
Lohja / Lojo	283	187	0.38
Pohja / Pojo	143	192	0.37
Siuntio / Sjundeå	152	182	0.40
Tenhola / Tenala	201	277	0.31
Province of Raasepori /	*1298*	*201*	*0.38*
Raseborg			
Helsinki / Helsingfors (parish)	351	121	0.45
Pernaja / Pernå	445	171	0.33
Porvoo / Borgå (parish)	551	115	0.31
Sipoo / Sibbo	344	162	0.45
Province of Porvoo	*1 691*	*141*	*0.39*
UUSIMAA / NYLAND	2 989	167	0.40
Pellosniemi	635	57	0.38
Vesilahti / Vesilax	649	59	0.37
Juva / Jockas	597	56	0.36
District of Suur-Savo	*1881*	*58*	*0.37*
Sääminki / Säminge	804	89	0.38
Tavinsalmi	431	63	0.38
Rantasalmi	538	71	0.35
District of Pien-Savo	*1773*	*77*	*0.38*
SAVO	3654	67	0.38
Säkkijärvi	340	80	0.47
Viipuri / Viborg	579	69	0.41
+ Koivisto / Björkö			
Lappee + Taipalsaari	1180	78	0.38
Jääski / Jäskis	..	..	..
District of Jääski	..	..	..
Muolaa / Mola	361	113	0.36
Kivennapa / Kivinebb	167	111	0.36
Uusikirkko / Nykyrka	193	101	0.41
District of Äyräpää	*721*	*110*	*0.38*
Elimäki / Elimä	260	88	0.45
Pyhtää / Pyttis	266	135	0.40
Vehkalahti / Veckelax	464	73	0.41
Virolahti / Vederlax	176	68	0.44
Province of Kymenkartano	*1166*	*90*	*0.45*

Source: Nummela 1993a

Afterword
Beyond Space?

Marko Lamberg and Marko Hakanen

A map, a picture, a photograph, a letter, a diary, a record in official registers, a placename, a folk tale, a building, archaeological remains, even nature and the physical space *per se* – there is indeed a plentitude of different sources available when a researcher seeks to comprehend the use and the role of space in past times. Of course, the more sources a researcher is able to utilize and combine, the more holistic will be his or her interpretation. This book has offered us more than a dozen different angles towards how spatiality can be approached in the field of history and adjacent arts and sciences, like archaeology, art history, ethnology and sociology. The point of departure in all the chapters has been to explore how mapping can be used as a methodological tool when researchers track people's movements, networks, information flows, everyday living spheres and changes in mental and physical landscapes.

At the same time, the variety of the available research methods – the multiple ways of mapping – has been clarified: it is possible to be influenced by the spatial turn and lean on traditional written sources and traditional ways of presentation and opting freely for a qualitative or a quantitative mode, but a historian can also apply a more interdisciplinary point of view and adapt even modern IT applications, if necessary and if possible. Mapping as a tool has several adaptation possibilities and it serves well both as a research method and as a method of visualization and concretization of the results.

For the reader it should have by now become evident how significant space was for medieval and early modern European communities and societies. Although the emphasis of this book lies on Finland and Sweden, we argue that the results can be applied to the study of general European circumstances and development trends. After all, medieval and early modern Sweden was not the only conglomerate state in Europe –

several other realms, too, occupied relatively wide areas or consisted at least of both more central and more peripheral areas.

Space is unavoidable in current physical order of things, but as we have seen, for medieval and early modern men it was an obstacle more than anything. In the form of physical distance space made travel, communication and exchange of goods slow and difficult. Simultaneously it alienated local communities from each other and also complicated the interaction between the central power and its subjects. Moreover, in the form of physical nature space limited people's possibilities to control and utilize their environment. The space outside man-made environment could even appear strange and frightening.

Indeed, the slow conquest of the physical space challenges the historians' traditional interpretation, according to which there occurred a shift from scattered medieval realms to more strictly controlled early modern states during the sixteenth century (or at least in the course of the 'long sixteenth century').[1] Such a shift has happened, but it has taken centuries rather than just one century. We have already seen how those processes started already in the Middle Ages when interregional hegemonies like expanding kingdoms or the similarly expanding Catholic Church attempted to mark areas as their own by establishing new land roads or by erecting churches and fortresses in local and sometimes also peripheral spaces. To establish a new supreme power meant that areas had to be conquered and controlled, in one way or another. New elements in the physical landscape must have functioned also as visualizations of the power. Centuries later, the Reformation Era strengthened the idea of the superiority of human societies over nature as cartography gradually was distanced from religious symbolism and state borders become commonplace on maps. The potential of the maps as tools in the state- and nation-building processes was early noticed. Rulers used maps and mapmaking as a tool of power and propaganda, but also a way to build a mental picture of their states. Benedict Anderson has described nations as imagined communities where nationalism has created an image of the nation inside certain space which is marked with borders.[2] In geographically expanded societies, macro spaces, the communality is a creation of imagination rather than reality, because people cannot know all the members of the society personally anymore.

But when we consider the state- and nation-building processes, we must remember, also on the basis of the contents of this book, that there continued to exist considerable cultural and economic differences between different regions within one and same realm, sometimes even in one and same community, still at the beginning of the twentieth century. Such variation is not uncommon in modern societies, either. The rulers and governments and all other representatives of the central power imagined the communality of the realm most likely in a partly different way than their subjects did. Pre-industrial societies were in many ways pronouncedly diversified and heterogeneous entities, at least at the micro level. Local communities were not entirely isolated from each other, but also due to physical distances, the interaction between them was not as vivid as it is today. The pre-industrial space consisted of territories.

Besides the cultural diversity, the vague grip of the central power over local communities offered opportunities to common people and lower officials to act independently – to gain space of their own. In some places also the grip of the local authorities over the lives of the common people seems to have been very weak or the explanation lies simply in the lack of interest. At the local level the servants of the Crown did not necessarily share the same values and ideas as the officials at the higher levels. In any case, offenders were not necessarily punished for their crimes, nor did they always have to flee abroad or far away from their homes in order to continue living their lives in peace. However, in other places unscrupulous officials were more ambitious and utilized the limited possibilities of the central power to control their actions and created mini-realms, for instance by means of family networks, and thus interfered successfully – that is, from their point of view – in the relationship between the ruler and his subjects.

We usually label medieval and early modern cultural and societal forms as 'collective' and 'corporative', but we should not be too much taken by their official ideologies, although they stressed unity and harmony. The sixteenth-century town-plans were more 'planned', that is more straight-lined and more rectangular, which made the local space more open and public and easier controllable than had been the case in their medieval predecessors, but as we have seen on the basis of early probate inventories, even in small peripheral communities there were inhabitants who needed segregation and privacy and who also could afford them by acquiring curtains for their windows. The curtain example was a small but culturally and mentally significant response to the changes in the physical space.

Rulers and their representatives as well as other parties with power aspirations had no chance to control all space personally, nor did they have time to visit all places and regions. Consequently, they were extremely dependent on two important things: trust and letters. They needed to trust that their subjects and their officials as well as their trustees and allies would keep themselves loyal to them and act accordingly. Written communication in the form of letters was the only effective way to deliver messages from centres to peripheries and vice versa. Correspondence kept realms and networks in function, but virtually it, too, was based on trust.[3] Thus it can be argued that early modern society as well as political culture was heavily influenced by space – by attempts to overcome the obstacles it posed.

Nevertheless, space also created homogeneity in pre-industrial societies: both local communities and realms defined their borders towards 'others' and by doing so they strengthened the idea of who and what 'we' are or at least should be. At the grassroots level the isolative character of the medieval and early modern culture created spaces which were invisible for the contemporaries but which modern scholars are able to trace by means of church registers: marriage fields where spouses were most often chosen among the nearest neighbours, usually those ones living in the same village. Due to the economic and societal aspects and functions of the marriage, such marriages must reflect geographically limited interaction patterns. However, there were always exceptions: individuals who moved more or made longer journeys or kept in some other way in touch with more distant areas.

In recent years, spatial studies and gender studies have joined their forces and their questions. Especially the question of boundaries between male and female spaces has attracted researchers' interest.[4] Naturally, as a cultural product and setting of everyday life, space is and has been gendered. Even though the surface and the core of the pre-industrial societies were dominated by men, it is possible to trace women's actions as well. Also in this book we have seen how women could have important roles when networks were created and maintained. Some women were able to move independently and it was possible even to a relatively low-class woman to find a gap, a retreat, within the 'controlled patriarchal space'. And when we consider early curtains, it is probable that they were acquired on the initiative of women or at least under their supervision – after all, the curtains covered and sheltered the home which traditionally has been regarded as the natural sphere of women.

Finally, we have to ask what comes next. Is it already possible to see beyond space, to predict the next 'turn'? Perhaps there is no immediate need to hurry further because we can probably still learn a lot from spatiality as a scholarly issue. When it comes to the central themes of this book and its temporal setting, this book has mainly dealt with the micro level – local communities and individuals. One possible way to continue further, at least regarding early modern state-making, could consist of a holistic analysis of how and why the central power in Sweden concretely mapped its realm and how much or little the mappings affected its policy towards different parts of the realm. We do know that the Swedish government launched a massive operation in the 1630s and during the following decades and centuries thousands of villages and their environments in all parts of the realm, Finland included, were depicted in detailed maps, so-called *geometriska kartor* eller *maakirjakartat*. These maps, which were also furnished with some written information on the physical environment and how it was or could be used, have served as excellent sources for local historical studies as well as more generalizing syntheses in economic and agrarian history. But we know little about the reason why this concrete mapping project actually was started,[5] and there has been no comparative research dealing with how the central power actually utilized the information it received by means of these maps and if this information changed its relationship with the local communities – after all, not all villages were mapped, or the first cartographer appeared and drew his map only several decades after the mapping project had begun elsewhere. In principle, the ruler and his or her assistants knew certain places and spaces far better than other places and spaces. This could and should have some significance, for example considering the interaction between them and the differently mapped parts of the realm.

This concrete research theme is of course only one possibility among a multitude of other topics. The fruitfulness of mapping lies in its adaptivity. The reader is now free to adapt and explore.

Acknowledgements

The editors thank Professor Laura Stark for her editing of this afterword.

Notes

1 See, for example, Baumgartner 1995 and Goodare, J. & MacDonald, A. A. (eds.) 2008.
2 Andersson 2007, pp. 39–41.
3 Cf. Hosking 2006.
4 Romano 1989; Stark 1998; Raguin & Stanbury (eds.) 2005; Flather 2007.
5 Tollin 2007, p. 52. 68.

Bibliography

Anderson, B. 2007. *Imagined Communities.*

Baumgartner, F. J. 1995. *France in the Sixteenth Century.* Palgrave Macmillan, Basingstoke.

Flather, A. 2007. *Gender and Space in Early Modern England.* Boydell Press, Woodbridge.

Goodare, J. & MacDonald, A. A. (eds.) 2008. *Sixteenth-Century Scotland. Essays in Honour of Michael Lynch.* Brill, Leiden & Boston.

Hosking, G. 2006. 'Trust and Distrust. A Suitable Theme for Historians?' *Transactions of the Royal Historical Society*, Sixth Series (16), pp. 95–115.

Raguin, V. C. & Stanbury, S. (eds.) 2005. *Women's Space. Patronage, Place, and Gender in the Medieval Church.* State University of New York Press, New York.

Romano, D. 1989. 'Gender and the Urban Geography of Renaissance Venice.' *Journal of Social History*, Vol. 23 (2), pp. 339–353.

Stark[-Arola], Laura 1998. *Magic, Body and Social Order. The Construction of Gender Through Women's Private Rituals in Traditional Finland.* Finnish Literature Society, Helsinki.

Contributors

Piia Einonen, PhD, researcher, University of Jyväskylä. Her speciality is urban history and her dissertation (2005) dealt with the burgher community of Stockholm in the sixteenth and seventeenth centuries. Recently she has studied language, ethnicity and religion in Vyborg in the early nineteenth century.

Janne Haikari, PhD, researcher, University of Jyväskylä, Finland. He completed his doctoral thesis (2009) on local exercise of power in rural parts of the kingdom of Sweden. Currently he is approaching the seventeenth-century Swedish nobility from a biographical perspective.

Marko Hakanen, PhD, researcher, University of Jyväskylä, Finland. His main research topics include social networks, state-building and the material culture of the nobility in early modern Sweden.

Vesa-Pekka Herva, researcher, gained a PhD in archaeology from the University of Oulu, Finland. He has studied various aspects of material culture and human-environment relations in post-medieval Europe, with a focus on the Northern Baltic Sea region.

Isto Huvila, PhD, senior lecturer, Department of Archive, Library and Information, Museum and Cultural Heritage Studies, Uppsala University, Sweden. His main research interests are management, organization and use of information in different contexts ranging from social media to cultural heritage and archaeological information.

Titta Kallio-Seppä, MA, MSc (econ), is a PhD student in archaeology at the University of Oulu, Finland. Her doctoral research concerns early modernization of Oulu. Her research interests include historical and urban archaeology and dendrochronology.

Kimmo Katajala, PhD, Professor of History at the University of Eastern Finland. Main topics of research have been medieval and early modern peasant revolts, the history of Karelia and Eastern Finland and the history of borders.

Jukka Korpela, PhD, Professor of General History at the University of Eastern Finland and Head of the Department of Geographical and Historical Studies. He has studied medieval state formation in eastern and northern Europe and cults of medieval saints of the orthodox church.

Ulla Koskinen, MA, is a researcher at the University of Tampere, Finland. She has concentrated on early modern social life, especially concerning the nobility, in Sweden and Finland. Currently she is finishing her doctoral thesis on the correspondence and the networks of the sixteenth-century nobility.

Tiina Kuokkanen, MA, is a PhD student in archaeology at the University of Oulu, Finland. She studies early modern clothing from the perspective of gender archaeology, focusing on the questions of how people created, maintained and expressed their identity by means of clothing.

Christian Kühner holds a bi-national PhD from the Ecole des hautes études en sciences sociales (EHESS) and the University of Freiburg im Breisgau. His research interests include the history of friendship and patronage, the Counter-Reformation, and more generally the application of social and cultural theory to early modern European history.

Marko Lamberg, PhD, senior lecturer, Universities of Tampere and Jyväskylä, Finland. He has studied Nordic social and cultural history with special emphasis on the late medieval period and communities of different kinds.

Päivi Maaranen works as a senior researcher in the National Board of Antiquities, Finland, and she is a post-graduate student of the University of Helsinki. She is a trained archeologist with studies of geography and geology. Her research work concerns past landscapes as well as interaction between man and nature.

Minna Mäkinen, Lic. Phil., University of Jyväskylä, Finland. Her ethnological research interests concerns relations between humans and places. She is currently finishing her dissertation on the consequences of changes in borders between local government areas in modern society.

Ilkka Nummela, PhD, Professor of Economic History at the University of Jyväskylä, Finland. He has dealt with a variety of topics including early modern price building and long-term development of standard of living.

Risto Nurmi has recently gained a PhD in archaeology from the University of Oulu, Finland. His research interests focus on artefact studies and social development in Northern Europe during the medieval and early modern period.

Ismo Puhakka is a doctoral student at the University of Jyväskylä, Finland, and at the European University Institute in Florence, Italy. He is writing his thesis on Sebastian Münster's *Cosmography* in the context of the protestantizing debate on God, knowledge and nature in the sixteenth century.

Kari Uotila, PhD, is senior lecturer at the University of Turku, Finland, and Director of the Muuritutkimus company. He has specialized in medieval archaeology especially regarding built environments such as castles, manors and towns.

Merja Uotila is a doctoral student at the Department of History and Ethnology, University of Jyväskylä, Finland. In her dissertation project she studies rural artisans in the early nineteenth century. Her other research interests include historical archaeology and place-name research.

Timo Ylimaunu has a PhD in archaeology from the University of Oulu, Finland. His recent research has focused on the modernization of the early modern towns of Tornio and Oulu in Northern Finland. His interests cover space, power, memory and identity in historical and urban archaeology.

Index of personal names

384

Index of placenames

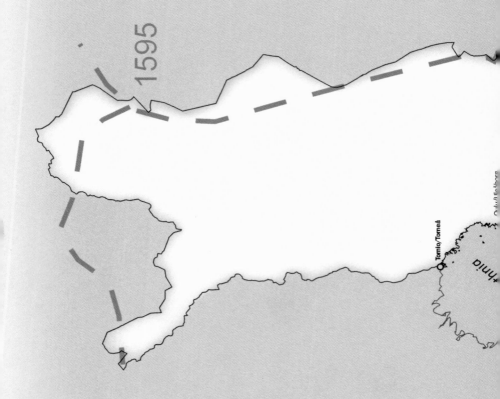

1595

Tornio/Torneå

Oulu/Uleåborg

Finla

Map 2. A map representing the Finnish part of the early modern kingdom of Sweden. The map shows the boundary of 1595, the locations of the most important Finnish and Russian places mentioned in the current volume as well as the most important Finnish roads in the sixteenth century. For road systems of the seventeenth and eighteenth centuries, see Maps 27 and 28). Drawing by Jari Järvinen.